More praise for *Hillary's Choice*

"*Hillary's Choice* fascinated me. Sheehy has amassed some wondrous details and sheds light on some heretofore dim events. . . . Much of this book reads like the transcript of a group of women having coffee at a kitchen table and talking about the intimate details of relationships."

—*St. Louis Post-Dispatch*

"Sheehy also explores Hillary's character—her toughness, her ambition, her willingness to blame her husband's problems on others—without suggesting these qualities are less appealing in a woman than in a man."

—*People*

"A complex picture of a woman with a keen intellect, fiery ambition, passion—and a need for the competitive high-stakes thrill that only politics provides."

—*The Seattle Times*

"Sheehy is a tenacious reporter. . . . She elicits new, fascinating testimony."

—*Rocky Mountain News*

ALSO BY GAIL SHEEHY

Lovesounds

Speed Is of the Essence

Panthermania

Hustling

Passages

Pathfinders

Spirit of Survival

Character: America's Search for Leadership

Gorbachev: The Man Who Changed the World

The Silent Passage

New Passages

Understanding Men's Passages

Hillary's Choice

Every one of us has a choice. . . . I think that in everyday ways, how you treat your own disappointments and whether you're able to forgive the pain that others cause you and, frankly, to acknowledge the pain you cause to others, it's one of the big challenges we face as we move into this next century. And it's something that I certainly have faced. But I look into the eyes of people all over my country and the world, and I know it's something all of us face.[1]

—HILLARY RODHAM CLINTON, 1999

GAIL SHEEHY

Hillary's Choice

BALLANTINE BOOKS

NEW YORK

For Clay

ACKNOWLEDGMENTS

To write a biography of a subject very much alive and running her own race is rather like a marathon. I did, however, have a seven-year head start, having accompanied Hillary Rodham Clinton in 1992 on her first presidential campaign. From our first encounter I was conscious that here was an extraordinary person, unique on the political stage. Since then, I have had many conversations with her, followed her on travels at home and abroad, and worked with her on the Women's Health Days she introduced. Most biographers, unless they have a pipeline to the grave, never have the opportunity to talk to their subjects. My challenge was different: to delve behind the masks of a public woman notoriously obsessive about guarding her own privacy and that of those close to her. Hundreds of people possessed pieces of the puzzle. As those people were found and interviewed, in thousands of hours of taped discussions, the thrill was to discover the unknown Hillary Rodham who existed before Bill, and the interlocking between Hillary and Bill Clinton over the course of their turbulent history.

In this marathon I have been coached and supported by two great institutions. *Vanity Fair*, my journalistic home since 1984, gave me the opportunity for extensive travel and research and published at unusual length two of my articles on Hillary Clinton. Random House, my publisher, paced me as I began, in January 1999, to do the deeper research and the revisiting of origins of character required by a book.

I was lucky to be able to assemble a fine research team, all of whom remained dedicated through many nights and weekends, computer crashes, and the tedium of fact-checking. Led by Bruce Littlefield, my editorial assistant, who gave so much of himself, they were Jason Haber, fact checker; Jan Cottingham in Little Rock; DeDe Lahman; Ann Wozencraft and Heather Kalish in New York; Heather Baukney and Joseph Werzinski in California. My *Vanity Fair* colleagues Elise O'Shaunnessey and George Hodgman offered valuable editorial comment, and my computer guru, Josh Skaller, always came to the rescue.

Of all those who provided original material, I would particularly like to thank Dorothy Rodham, Hillary's mother, who was the first to share with me her insights and favorite photographs. I was fortunate to locate Professor John Peavoy, a high school classmate of Hillary's, who showed me the thirty letters that Hillary had written to him during her college years, a period when she was mutating both socially and politically. Don Jones, the Methodist minister who has been an intellectual touchstone for Hillary over the years, was equally generous in helping to place letters from Hillary in the context of various stages of her life. Dr. Arthur Curtis was a resourceful guide to the subculture of Park Ridge. David Rupert, Nancy Pietrefesa, and John Danner were helpful in filling in the postgraduate period. For their assistance in tracking the Arkansas years, I am grateful to Mary Lee and Paul Fray, Claudia Riley, Susan McDougal, Carolyn Yeldell Staley, Bobby Roberts, and Joe Purvis. Fellow journalists in Little Rock—Gene Lyons, Max Brantley, and John Brummett—offered not only facts, but a healthy dose of skepticism and hearty laughs. Thanks, too, to Judy Lange, librarian at Main South High School.

I am indebted to Betsey Wright for her trust and candor. The Reverend Ed Matthews was a revelation. Dick Morris provided a through-line of real politik from his seventeen years of experience as a Clinton strategist, together with his wife, Eileen McGann. Dee Dee Myers, now a colleague at *Vanity Fair,* was extremely helpful, as were former White House attorneys Bernard Nussbaum and Jane Sherburne. Melanne Verveer, Dr. Susan Blumenthal, Ann Lewis and Mandy Grunwald cooperated to the degree they could without incurring the First Lady's wrath. I would also like to thank Don Baer, Robert Boorstin, Bill Curry, Lanny Davis, Rose Styron, Senator Chistopher Dodd, Senator Joseph Lieberman, Congresswoman Nita Lowey, Congressman Charlie Rangel, and Judith Hope.

Words are inadequate to express my esteem for my editor, Robert Loomis, who was always there as a touchstone of clarity and paragon of patience throughout the extended marathon. Many members of the Random House family, including editor in chief Ann Godoff, legal adviser Lesley Oelsner, art director Robbin Schiff, interior designer Barbara Bachman, picture researcher Sarah Longacre, production editor Sybil Pincus, copy editor Lynn Anderson, editorial assistant Barbé Hammer, and production manager Richard Elman spared no effort even as they sprinted the book into print. My agent, Lynn Nesbit, was as always an enthusiastic champion.

My heartfelt thanks to Ella Council for sustaining us all and, finally, to my husband and resident editor, Clay Felker, for his gift of constant belief and surrender of so much of my attention.

CONTENTS

Hillary's Choice

CHAPTER ONE

Into the Flames

These two people are intertwined on every level,
as a man and woman, as friends, as lovers,
as parents, as politicians. This is a love story.

—LINDA BLOODWORTH-THOMASON

When under siege she rises early, dresses quickly, and cauterizes her emotions. The bubble of anger rising from her gut will remain level. Head must be separated from heart. Of necessity, given her station in life, she will summon her apolitical Washington hairstylist, Isabel, to blow, wax and spray her expensively blonded hair into an unflappable helmet. She does not read the newspapers. Or watch TV. She does not want to know any more about her husband's scandalous behavior than she absolutely has to know.

This morning, Tuesday, January 27, 1998, scarcely a week into the firestorm of accusations about a President and a dark-haired intern in an unforgettable beret, she does not worry about makeup. The *Today* show's makeup artists are able to make a tense First Lady look serene (or, a year later, a vampy intern look like a proper author). It is five in the morning and Hillary Rodham Clinton paces around her suite in the Waldorf-Astoria, priming herself for yet another crucial television appearance that will either pull Bill Clinton out of a nosedive or help ensure a crack-up. Dark smudges beneath her eyes belie her apparent equipoise. She joins her chief of staff, Melanne Verveer, and rides stoically across Fifth Avenue, arriving at NBC's Rockefeller Center studio.[1] Anchor Matt Lauer, who was called back from vacation when the story broke, has the outlines of a scandal that already sounds like the finale of the Clinton Show.

At 6:55 A.M., between promos and airtime, Lauer dashes up to the makeup room to greet the First Lady. She is warm, though some tension is detectable in her demeanor. That's hardly surprising. In the six days since the sex-and-lies scandal broke, the face of Monica Lewinsky and a few squirmy denials by the President have occupied the first half hour of all the morning TV shows and carpeted the cable shows wall to wall. Is there anyone in America who has not heard accusations that the President enjoyed sex sessions in the White House with an intern barely older than his daughter and then told her to lie about it?

This twisted fairy tale has already captured the imagination of the public. Characters outrageous and grotesque are emerging. The plotters appear to be two older unmarried women, dead ringers for Cinderella's ugly stepsisters: Linda Tripp, an older coworker of Monica's, who coached the intern to narrate the whole sordid affair, and Lucianne Goldberg, a politically zealous literary agent who urged Tripp to tape her chats with Lewinsky in hopes of getting a hot book out of it. There are twenty hours of audiotapes.

And there are other shades of Nixon's Watergate beyond tapes, including a faithful secretary who is said to have provided cover for the President's frequent sexcapades. There are tortured definitions: Lewinsky claims Clinton wanted oral sex because he didn't count that as adultery. There is name-calling: Monica refers to the President as "the Big Creep," Lewinsky's lawyer calls the President a "misogynist." *The New York Times* reports that Monica is prepared to testify that she *did* have a sexual relationship with the President, provided she is granted immunity. Late-night talk shows are already lampooning the new souvenir of an Oval Office visit: a semen-stained dress.

With this flood tide of titillating and damning detail washing over Washington in only the first week, Bill Clinton's official stance is to be "outraged" by the allegations; White House insiders describe him as "freaking out." "I don't think there was a person in the White House who gave him a snowball's chance in hell, except Hillary," a former official later told *Time*. And congressional Democrats are not rushing to stand by their man.

Hillary Clinton stands alone, prepared to fight.

The First Lady tries to paint a very different scene, one in which she and Bill Clinton appear the homiest of characters. Up in the second-floor bedroom of their residence, the husband had awakened his wife the previous Wednesday morning, January 21, and said there was something he had to tell her.

"You're not going to believe this, but . . ." he said, bewildered.

"What is this?" she asked sleepily.

". . . but I want to tell you what's in the newspapers."

That is how Hillary describes on the *Today* show learning from her husband that their enemies were trying to bring them down with yet another preposterous scandal.[2] She makes the dialogue sound so innocuous, it evokes images of that widely loved comic-book couple, Dagwood, the greatest victim of circumstance the world has ever known, and Blondie, who always comes to his rescue, rather than what it was—the President's first mention to his wife of explosive sex allegations that he knew were about to break in that morning's *Washington Post.* When Hillary labors to make the First Couple sound like just plain folks, there is almost always more to read between the lines.

In fact, the *Post*'s meticulously reported story reads like a compilation of the greatest-hit scandals of the Clintons' six years in office: reckless sex, a suicide, easy lies, cover-up, betrayal of the President's friends and aides, and a looming shoot-out at the OK Corral with his nemesis Kenneth Starr. The special prosecutor named in 1994 to investigate the collected allegations known as Whitewater, Starr was suspected of being in cahoots with lawyers for Clinton's other accuser, Paula Jones. For the past week Starr had been raining subpoenas on Clinton's people. In sum, there was enough ammunition to blow sky-high everything that these two bright stars of their generation had struggled to achieve since they had first met at Yale Law School twenty-eight years before.

On *Today,* Lauer astutely points out that the President has described to the American people only what this relationship was *not.* Has he described to his wife what it *was?*

Mrs. Clinton stammers a bit: "Yes. And we'll—and we'll find that out as time goes by, Matt. But I think the important thing now is to stand as firmly as I can and say that, you know, that the President has denied these allegations on all counts, unequivocally, and we'll—we'll see how this plays out."

During these onslaughts, the Clintons—united professionally—can hide for days behind their public faces. Even from each other. "Being in the White House when a crisis blows is like nothing else," recalls the President's former press secretary Dee Dee Myers.[3] "This type of siege is like

World War One to the Clintons," elaborates Dick Morris, the strategist who, upon Hillary's command, engineered Clinton's greatest comebacks. "They're in the foxhole. Shells are bursting all around. The two of them against the world. If your buddy does something stupid . . . you allow yourself maybe a moment of 'Schmuck, what did you do that for?' But there just isn't a whole lot of time to allow yourself the luxury of reacting to things personally."[4]

For this crucial interview Hillary has chosen the battle camouflage of a dark brown suit lightened at the neckline with a twist of seed pearls. A large presidential eagle brooch is pinned to her chest like a general's medal. Her lips are precisely outlined, as are her thoughts. "Everybody says to me, 'How can you be so calm?' or 'How can you just, you know, look like you're not upset?' " she says. "And I guess I've just been through it so many times. . . ."

Has she become numb to this kind of scandal?

Mrs. Clinton says, "It's not being numb so much as just being very experienced."

But a couple of minutes into the interview her anger begins to simmer beneath the surface. She is asked about the gifts her husband allegedly gave Monica. She refuses to comment on "specific allegations." Her voice turns brittle. She tries to change the subject to "the intense political agenda at work here." Lauer promises to let her talk about Kenneth Starr in a moment. But first, has she ever met Monica Lewinsky? Mrs. Clinton vaguely demurs. Well, then, did her watchdogs at the White House ever come to her and say, "We may have a problem with one of the interns at the White House," and mention Monica Lewinsky?

"No," she says.

In fact, the First Lady herself had recommended the young woman for an internship as a favor to a heavyweight contributor, Walter Kaye, who was also a friend of Monica's mother.[5] But Hillary was no fool. She had installed in the White House a handpicked Warden of the Body, the President's deputy chief of staff, Evelyn Lieberman. This short, stern, fiftyish woman, known as the "Mother Superior of the West Wing," went back with Hillary to their working days at the Children's Defense Fund. Lieberman took her role as chief enforcer very seriously. And out of the whole class of four hundred interns, she had spotted Monica early on. This one was trouble. Classic Bill bait. Fleshy with big hair and hydraulic lips swabbed with lipstick over the lines—a shoulder-baring, switch-hipped exhibitionist who came on just like Gennifer Flowers, just like Virginia Kelley, his mother, the template for most of Bill Clinton's temptresses.[6] The Mother

Superior caught Monica hanging out in the hallways near the Oval Office and reprimanded her: *Get back to your post.* But Monica was what staffers call a "clutch." She had pushed up front in every Rose Garden event and tried to cling to the President to get in the picture; and with his ready cooperation, she had. Lieberman had reassigned Monica out of the White House. But had it been soon enough to prevent an "improper relationship" with the President?

Lauer poses a hypothetical question: "Let—let me take you and your husband out of this for a second. . . . If an American president had an adulterous liaison in the White House and lied to cover it up, should the American people ask for his resignation?"

The question takes Hillary by surprise. She slides away from it: "Well, they should certainly be concerned about it."

Lauer goes after it again: "Should they ask for his resignation?"

"Well, I think—if all that were proven true, I think that would be a very serious offense." Suddenly she is transformed from Blondie into the chief attack dog for Bill Clinton: "That is *not* going to be proven true."

Lauer later told me, "I felt this was a woman who knew there had been trouble in the past and who was believing, and hoping against hope, *not again.*"[7]

The story of the Clinton presidency has always been the story of the Clinton marriage. Would Bill Clinton have become President without Hillary? Would Hillary Rodham have become one of the most remarkable women of our century without Bill? Although they have been on the public stage for a quarter century, there is so much we don't know about either of them. That is the complex and contradictory love story this book seeks to unravel, and beneath it, to find the cords that have created the unique political texture and tensions of our times.

The saga of Bill and Hillary, with its echoes of Eleanor and Franklin, or Tracy and Hepburn with undertones of Bonnie and Clyde, is animated by melodrama, high passion, narrow escapes, and knock-down-drag-outs. Never more united than when they are battling adversaries and displaying their ferocious tenacity, the pair cannot resist a spitting match or all-out political war. His recklessness and her eagerness to step in and save the day have created a dynamic of crisis (his) and management (hers). They have always seemed to thrive on it.

Every time he goes down, she rears up and turns into a lioness, tearing into the political veldt to rip the flesh off their enemies. Bill Clinton, whom a former presidential adviser describes as having "the passivity of a Buddha" during a crisis, characteristically sits in a huddle of legal experts and flak catchers as Hillary lays down the battle plan. "He's like the little kid who's been told to go to his room," says a former Democratic political appointee who knows the Clintons. "Mom will handle everything. Knowing that the little kid will probably screw up again, even if she hides the cookie jar."[8]

The costs of sustaining this volatile political partnership have been high, but the benefits over the past thirty years have also been high. Hillary's disowning of her private circumstances allows her to be First Lady, where she wields tremendous political power without electoral accountability. She is in a position to open up all kinds of private and nongovernmental avenues to do the good things she believes in for children, parents, the poor, the protection of women against violence—the list goes on and on. To Hillary Rodham Clinton, these are the most important things.

And one more thing. She gets to keep Bill.

"I think she's in love with this guy" is the nearly ubiquitous refrain of their friends and advisers, although most admit that they are mystified by the dynamics of the Clintons' relationship. Until this grand episode, their friends had idealized their marriage. "Most of us have thrown in the towel," says the movie actress Mary Steenburgen, a friend of the Clintons. "These people didn't. It's exciting to be around them and to see how it can be to be a married couple."[9] Another member of the "Arkansas Diaspora" in Los Angeles, television producer Linda Bloodworth-Thomason, is one of Hillary's most loyal intimates. "These two people are intertwined on every level, as a man and woman, as friends, as lovers, as parents, as politicians," she says. "This is a love story."[10]

How emotionally dependent is Hillary on Bill Clinton? I asked her former mentor, attorney Bernard Nussbaum, in the Year of Monica. "I think she needs him desperately," he replied. "And I know he needs her desperately."[11] In 1998, however, Hillary paid more than she could ever have anticipated for choosing to stay with Bill Clinton.

Now Hillary leans into the *Today* show cameras, her head bobbing for emphasis as she cleverly shifts the story line: "I do believe that this is a battle. . . . The great story here, for anybody willing to find it and write about it and explain it, is this vast right-wing conspiracy that has been conspiring against my husband since the day he announced for president." She fires off a threat: "When all of this is put into context . . . some folks are going to have a lot to answer for."

Lauer brings up painful history: "The last time we visited a subject like this involving your family was 1992, and the name Gennifer Flowers was in the news . . ."

> *HILLARY: Mm-hmm.*
> *LAUER: . . . and you said at the time of the interview, a very famous quote, "I'm not some Tammy Wynette standing by my man."*
> *HILLARY: Mm-hmm.*
> *LAUER: In the same interview, your husband had admitted that he had, quote, "caused pain in your marriage."*
> *HILLARY: Mm-hmm.*
> *LAUER: Six years later you are still standing by this man, your husband . . .*
> *HILLARY: Mm-hmm.*
> *LAUER: If he were to be asked today, Mrs. Clinton, do you think he would admit that he again has caused pain in this marriage?*
> *HILLARY: No. Absolutely not, and he shouldn't. You know, we've been married for twenty-two years, Matt.*

And then, with an utter certainty that few married men or women could muster, Hillary Clinton declares that she and her husband "know everything there is to know about each other."[12]

But this time, she didn't know everything.

CLEANING OUT CLOSETS

Ten days before her *Today* show appearance, Hillary's husband, the President of the United States, denied under oath having had sexual relations with Jane Doe No. 6 (Monica Lewinsky). That was the weekend when lawyers for Paula Jones, a low-level state employee who was suing the President for sexual harassment in an incident at an Arkansas hotel seven years earlier, at last had their chance to confront him. Paula herself would be there.

In a highly unusual courtesy, Susan Webber Wright, the federal judge from Little Rock who was presiding over this tortured case, had flown in to Washington to act as a mediator. Like just about everyone else in a high position in Arkansas, Judge Wright had a connection to Bill Clinton, having been a student in his admiralty law class at the University of Arkansas Law School back in 1974. His laxity had already come up against her astringency. Clinton had been an absentee professor, more interested in his own campaign for Congress than in monitoring his students. When he lost their final exam papers, he offered to give them all a grade of B. Susan Webber refused; she preferred to take another exam to uphold her A average.

Throughout the six-hour deposition on Saturday, January 17, the President sat eyeball to eyeball with his former student, now a stout, scholarly Republican judge with a proper southern demeanor. As described by a Little Rock public defender, "She'll tell you, in a very ladylike way, she's going to throw you in the slammer forever."

The Jones lawyers began questioning the President at 10:30 in the morning, but for almost two hours they never mentioned Paula Jones. They wanted to know about a slew of other women, starting with Kathleen Willey, a volunteer who claimed the President had groped her outside his office. Not long into the deposition, the Jones lawyers gave Clinton what friends call his "Oh, shit" moment.

One or two questions about another woman, a twenty-four-year-old White House intern from Beverly Hills, dragged out into fifty questions on an exam for which he was totally unprepared. For once words failed him. His voice grew inaudible. How did they know about the phone calls and the gifts, even the Walt Whitman poetry book and the Black Dog T-shirt, for God's sake? Had Monica talked? He thought her testimony denying their affair was a done deal, but one of the questions during his deposition left him with grave doubts:

"If she told someone that she had a sexual affair with you beginning in November of 1995, would that be a lie?"

"It's certainly not the truth," said the President. "It would not be the truth."

And then they went after him about Gennifer Flowers. Now he knew he would have to go home and tell Hillary, tell her something, before he telephoned his good-ol'-boy friend Vernon Jordan and arranged to meet his loyal secretary in the office to rehearse their story.

On the Saturday evening of the President's marathon six-hour deposition, the First Couple had planned to take Erskine Bowles and his wife out for a celebratory dinner. It was to be a thank-you to the President's chief of staff for his two stints in the White House and, more important, a wooing of Bowles to stay on through the year, despite his aide's wish to escape the Beltway. The dinner was also apparently meant to counteract any impression that the President's forced deposition had shaken up their lives.

The Clintons never made it. Except for a visit to church on Sunday, they remained in seclusion until Monday. The wind had been knocked out of Bill Clinton. He is a man who hates confrontation and who is uncomfortable in any situation he doesn't control. Monica had not been granted immunity, that he knew, but what the devil had she told Starr and his henchmen in her now-sealed deposition? It was Hillary who almost immediately went into full battle mode. She granted several radio interviews that Monday in the map room at the White House. Although garbed in a bold plaid suit, she was pale, her voice was nasal, and her eyes seldom met those of the interviewer.

"Can I ask you, uh, how difficult a day Saturday was for you and your family?" inquired reporter Peter Mayer.

It "wasn't difficult for me," the First Lady said. On Saturday "I just kind of hunkered down and went through my household tasks. Then my husband came home and we watched a movie and we had a"—she pauses and shrugs while searching for the appropriately innocuous phrase—"a good time that evening."

"And Sunday?"

"Oh, we just stayed home and cleaned closets."[13]

Another folksy image: Hillary as the dutiful homemaker whose husband comes home on a Saturday night wanting nothing more than a good video. In fact, that was the Saturday night Hillary Clinton cleaned *his closets*.

The Dress Rehearsal

She is angry. Not all of the time. But most of the time.

Those were the notes I made after I first met Hillary Clinton. It was an earlier January morning, in 1992, the day after her famous "I'm no Tammy Wynette" appearance on *60 Minutes* to defend her husband, then the Democratic presidential front-runner, after his first national sex scandal had exploded. We met at Little Rock National Airport. Hillary was glowing. Her mother, Dorothy Rodham, had vetted me, and I was granted rare access. For several days I flew knee to knee with Hillary in her six-seat chartered plane, observing as she fashioned the strategy (as Bill Clinton later acknowledged) to bring him "back from the dead."[14]

I watched the Hillary iconography emerge. Voters seemed to accept her take-charge confidence. But there was a shadow. Many Americans I talked to even then seemed to feel she had sacrificed something, some human part of herself, in order to persuade us to vote for her husband. There was, and there remains to this day, a nagging suspicion about Hillary's motives and her marriage. We didn't know then that she was a woman with a secret, a wife experienced at drawing the draperies around her husband's demons.

During downtime in a motel in Pierre, South Dakota, I watched as Hillary flipped on the lobby TV and was suddenly faced with Gennifer Flowers playing tapes of her steamy calls to Governor Clinton. Hillary's eyes took this in with the glittering blink of a lizard. Not a tremor of emotion crossed her face. Nothing personal.[15]

"Let's get Bill on the phone," I heard Hillary order her teary-eyed male campaign manager. But Clinton, according to Hillary, said he wasn't concerned. Throughout the scandal Clinton behaved as if this problem were all about somebody else, not Bill. "Who is going to believe this woman?" he told his wife. "Everybody knows you can be paid to do anything." (*The Star*, a supermarket tabloid, had paid Flowers for her story.)

"Everybody *doesn't* know that," Hillary snapped. "Bill, people who don't know you are going to say, 'Why were you even talking to this person?' "[16]

Those who encounter the Clintons are always struck by how tough Hillary is on Bill. "But the more you see them," observes a former adviser, "the more you get why she withholds the approval that he seems to need, at times desperately." Hillary, adds the source, "has never held Bill accountable" for the transgressions that have rocked their lives. "She is in a perpetual state of suspended anger because of all that she has absorbed."

An hour after giving Bill his slap on the wrist, Hillary—soft and feminine—entered the Pork Producers Rib Feed in Pierre. She was all smiles until her campaign manager whispered, "All three nets led with Flowers." That's when I first saw the battle mouth. Hillary's lower lip juts out while the top one pulls tight. It is the look of a prizefighter with his mouthpiece stuffed in. In the plane I listened as Hillary rehearsed a retaliation: "In 1980, the Republicans started the negative advertising. In 1992, we have paid political character assassination. What Bill doesn't understand is, you've gotta do the same thing: pound the Republican attack machine and run against the press."

We had scarcely bumped down through the black hole of the Dakota night before Hillary, coatless, was clicking across the field toward a shack with a sign that said "Rapid City." She demanded a phone for a conference call: "Get Washington and Little Rock on the line." George Stephanopoulos and the other baby-faced boys were about to be "inspired" by the candidate's wife: "Who's getting information on *The Star*? Who's tracking down all the research on Gennifer?"

In an earlier aside she had seethed to me, "If we'd been in front of a jury . . . I would crucify her."[17]

Her. Not him. Never him.

THE NEED TO KNOW AND THE FEAR OF KNOWING

So into the flames Hillary strode just as always. It was Hillary who made the first call, on the morning the *Post* story broke, to establish the line the White House would use. Her chosen interlocutor with the President was Sidney Blumenthal, a wily former journalist who had ingratiated himself with the Clintons during the 1992 campaign by writing puff pieces for *Vanity Fair* and *The New Yorker*. After the election he had "gone inside" to become a presidential adviser. Blumenthal liked to think of himself as the most trusted messenger across the often choppy channel between the President and his wife.[18]

The First Lady told Blumenthal she was distressed that the President was being attacked, in her view, for political motives—for his ministry to a "troubled person." She said that the President ministers to troubled people all the time. She made it even more specific, saying that he had done this same thing dozens, if not hundreds, of times with troubled people (an interesting, perhaps Freudian, slip, since Clinton told Lewinsky he had had hundreds of women in the past). He was a compassionate person, Hillary emphasized. And he helped people also out of his religious conviction. "It was just part of his nature."[19]

Those who defend Hillary believe she was given an account similar to the one her husband gave Blumenthal later that day: The intern was going through a tough time. It got out of hand. She came on to him, but he told her he couldn't have sex. "I've gone down that road before," he said. "I've caused pain for a lot of people, and I'm not going to do that again." Monica had threatened to say they'd had an affair. She told him, he said, that she was known as a stalker.[20]

The story Bill Clinton carries around inside his head is that of the victim. He feels like the character in the classic Arthur Koestler novel *Darkness at Noon*, he told Blumenthal, "like somebody surrounded by an oppressive environment that was creating a lie about him." That novel depicts the far more nightmarish politics of Stalin's purge trials in Moscow. Its hero is an aging revolutionary, a disillusioned Communist having an affair with his secretary; he is imprisoned and tortured and pressured to confess to preposterous crimes. He is a victim of larger political forces. And Clinton can probably make himself believe that that is he.

Hillary's friends say she believed Clinton had done something inappropriate with Lewinsky and that she would hold him accountable for it—later—but the enormity of it, the sordidness, the fact that this was a *relationship*, hadn't entered her realm of thinking at all. The most painful revelation would not come for months: Her husband had sent her out into the world to lie for him, to risk her own reputation. Not only had he betrayed her, he had used her.

One reason Hillary Clinton is able to maintain her momentum is that she imposes a PG rating on the news digests her staff prepares for her: no sex, no late-night-talk-show gibes, no facts about scandal that might distress or distract her. Hillary is not a news junkie like her husband. She would rather review reports on HMOs than wallow in tabloid or television accounts of her problems. Clinton's veteran chief of staff Betsey Wright later said jokingly to me, "Hillary Clinton is probably the only person in America you could tell a cigar joke to and she wouldn't get it."[21]

Hillary carefully censors what she says about Bill—even with her own mother, Dorothy Rodham, who lives in a condo in Little Rock co-owned by Hillary and often listens to right-wing talk radio. She is not permitted to give interviews. I was able to engage her in a conversation in the fall of 1998.

"I don't talk to Hillary about anything deeply personal concerning her marriage," Dorothy Rodham told me. "We don't sit down and have those mother-daughter discussions about how she relates to her husband, her daughter, or anything else as far as her personal life is concerned. We don't talk about deeply personal things."[22]

Exposed only to her own censored views, Hillary was able to convince herself that Monica Lewinsky's story was a flat-out lie. Mandy Grunwald, who had served both Clintons well during the 1992 campaign, talked to Hillary's staff before the *Today* show appearance to warn them, "Here's what's out there, for those of you who don't read newspapers." Grunwald told me her friend was "completely unfazed by it all—*at that time.* In her mind, there was no difference between Filegate, Travelgate, Paula Jones, and Monica; they were all just more of the same political charges that the Clintons have to deal with."[23]

Why worry about this Monica Lewinsky anyway? She was obviously just another Bill-struck "rodeo queen"; that's what Hillary and Betsey Wright called all those Arkansas bimbos who came at him with the same matted hair and the same starstruck eyes when Bill so much as squeezed their arms. But given all that Bill depended upon Hillary for, they knew that no other woman could measure up.

LET THE WAR BEGIN

The official declaration was left to Democratic pit bull James Carville to snarl on Sunday, January 25, on *Meet the Press:* "There's going to be a war"—a war between "the friends of the President and the independent counsel . . . between these scuzzy, slimy tactics of wiring people up, of getting them in hotel bars and threatening to arrest their parents." Carville was referring to Kenneth Starr's co-opting of the Paula Jones sex hunt into Clinton's private life; the fact that Starr had used Linda Tripp to lure Lewinsky into a meeting at the Ritz-Carlton, where the perfidious friend had taped their incriminating conversation; and the fact that he had threatened to force Monica's mother to testify against her own child. But in defending the President, Carville could only repeat the President's rote denials: "He has denied it to his staff, has denied it to the news media, has denied it to the American people, and denied it to his Cabinet and denied it to his friends."[24]

Hillary was the one person who saw a larger story, a grand narrative in which her husband, the softhearted victim, was being persecuted by a modern-day Inspector Javert from *Les Misérables* who would pursue his miscreant into the sewer. Hillary's reasonable fury at Clinton for having jeopardized their life's work and, even worse, having handed their nemesis a silver bullet, was transmuted virtually overnight into venom-tipped arrows aimed at that mutual enemy, Ken Starr. He had been chasing the Clintons since the summer of 1994—almost four years now. This was the Alamo. She was up against the prissy prosecutor who had challenged her integrity, had found her fingerprints on every alleged Clinton misdeed, had forced her to face a "clusterfuck" of cameras staked out to record the first appearance of a First Lady before a grand jury. However bilious the shame she had to swallow, it was nothing compared to the specter of being beaten and driven out of the White House by her personalized enemy.

She demonized Starr (with his help), transforming him into a gruesome re-creation of J. Edgar Hoover by reminding people how disgusted they had been to learn, years after the fact, that Hoover had wiretapped Martin Luther King, Jr., and spread stories about his sex life. How could the country sit by and allow a right-wing political zealot to perform a sting operation on a sitting President and to hunt down every friend and relation of his from Washington to Arkansas?

Strangely enough, it seems it was something of a release for Hillary in those first weeks to have the accusations against her husband as ammunition to strike back at the man who had made her life miserable.

It was Hillary who brought back the old gang, lawyers Mickey Kantor, Harold Ickes, and Susan Thomases, who had been key figures in several campaigns; Hillary who shook up the defense team, advancing her law school classmate David Kendall over Bob Bennett; Hillary who summoned Harry Thomason (the husband of her best friend, television writer-producer Linda Bloodworth-Thomason): "Harry, you've got to get to Washington right away—everybody around here is crying and helpless." She wanted Harry to help coach the President on how to be more convincing in his denials; he had sounded too wimpy in his first interview, with Jim Lehrer on *The NewsHour.* When Clinton looked into national TV cameras on January 26 to give his famously defiant, finger-wagging performance—"I did not have sexual relations with *that* woman . . . Monica Lewinsky"—Hillary stood beside her husband, sunny in yellow, and nodded her head.

It was Hillary's idea to set up an information control operation out of the Democratic National Committee. The effort, paid for with Party dollars, would send their friends and political acquaintants "distilled information" to counter the confessions of "shock," "disappointment," "disgust," and "dismay" being offered in TV interviews by some of their closest former lieutenants, including George Stephanopoulos, who dared to use the "I" word. On Hillary's side of the White House the word "impeachment" was struck from the vocabulary. Instead, by February 1, she was saluting new polls that showed the President's popularity reaching new heights. Her surrogates warned darkly of a "day of reckoning" for foes of the President and for news outlets that ran unconfirmed reports about his private conduct.

THE FAMILY THAT DENIES TOGETHER . . .

A major soft spot in their defense remained. It was personal. It was Chelsea. Their beloved daughter, their best thing.

Little had been allowed to take precedence over Chelsea for either Clinton. When Hillary was making frequent trips between Little Rock and

Washington to carry on her public service career, baby Chelsea was the girl who would wait up for the Governor. The Governor took the time to practice the piano with her. The Clintons rarely went out together alone as a married couple. And they almost never took a vacation without their daughter. They had a spectacularly healthy, happy, attractive, and to all appearances well-adjusted teenager to show for it. Chelsea already had her first serious boyfriend, Matthew Pierce, a champion swimmer and upperclassman at Stanford University.

Chelsea was summoned home from Stanford on Friday, January 30, only two weeks after having spent Christmas with her parents. Who was going to tell her, and what? Hillary wanted to help prepare the nineteen-year-old girl for the rough days ahead. God knows, she had done it before.

Hillary's pastor, Ed Matthews, the now-retired minister of First United Methodist Church of Little Rock, agonized for Chelsea each time he read about another of the scandals produced by her father. Reverend Matthews had first became alarmed in 1990, shortly after Hillary had sought him out as her pastor. He came out of church one Sunday to find under his windshield a vulgar drawing of Bill Clinton's private parts. The flyer, which also implied that Clinton had sired children with black women, was affixed to all the cars outside the church. Matthews was appalled. He had Chelsea Clinton in his confirmation class. The more he thought of the governor's vulnerable twelve-year-old daughter and those vulgar drawings, the more puzzled he was: *How on earth do these parents explain all this? Chelsea will be going to school tomorrow.* So that night Matthews called Hillary and posed the question: "How do you help Chelsea deal with this?"

He remembers Hillary telling him how the Clintons had handled it in the past, starting when Chelsea was barely six. "The two of us sat Chelsea down and let her know that there were people who don't know the full truth of things, and they make things up and they gossip. But we know the truth of this story."

Reverend Matthews was not fully reassured. A reflective man who, at sixty-four, is involved in voluntary ministries building houses for low-income families, he confessed in a conversation with me in 1998 that he was mystified by how the Clintons handle all the public and private aspects of these scandals: "I've marveled at it long before all this current ugliness came to be. There is something almost superficial or synthetic that seems to be what ultimately binds this family together. It's hard for me to imagine what's bubbling underneath all that."[25]

This time Hillary would force her husband to take some responsibility for his actions. In effect, she told the President there was no room in their

White House for cowards: *You* take your daughter to Camp David for the weekend, and *you* explain it to her yourself. *I'm* going to Davos.

It was after the Monica story broke that Hillary decided to accept a last-minute invitation to address what an aide calls "the crème de la crème of the world" at the World Economic Forum in Davos, Switzerland. Davos gave her something else to think about. There, in the Swiss Alps, she would look out on an audience of two thousand global power brokers: presidents, prime ministers, CEOs of multinational corporations, Nobel Prize winners, academics, and media moguls. She was accustomed to looking powerful men straight in the eye.

While the President struggled at Camp David to find the words to keep his daughter's trust, the First Lady reminded the world of her own commanding voice. With her presidential eagle brooch clamped at her neck on a collar of pearls, Hillary Rodham Clinton delivered her vision of priorities for improving the state of the world in the twenty-first century. She challenged the leaders to invest in education and opportunities for women and to share their wealth and power. Her twenty-minute address, delivered without notes, was, according to Jim Hoge, editor of *Foreign Affairs,* "beautifully phrased" and "her manner was that of someone at the top of her game."[26] After a standing ovation, a top Democratic Party leader from Hillary's home state of Illinois was moved to political lust. "That's our winning candidate for the Senate," he said.

Somebody else said, "Are you serious?"

The official didn't hold back: "If we could get rid of the kid [Bill Clinton], I'd run her in a minute. Nobody could beat her."

The official had the wrong state but the right instinct. A personal scandal that would have silenced most spouses in shame or self-loathing seemed only to empower and energize the President's wife. Professionally, Hillary was on top.

There was no need to tell Hillary Rodham what Hillary Rodham already knew about Bill Clinton—that her husband had a long history of reckless infidelities. But there was a great deal more that Hillary did not know at this point, that she might never have had to face if not for special prosecutors or the triumvirate of Hear Evil (Linda Tripp), See Evil (Lucianne Goldberg), and Speak Evil (Matt Drudge). The dark side of her husband's soul was not a territory she cared to explore any more closely than was absolutely necessary for their political survival.

And so, just as countless times in the past, *Hillary's choice* was not to know what she knew.

CHAPTER TWO

Sleeping Through the Revolution

You have brains in your head. You have feet in your shoes.
You can steer yourself any direction you choose.

—Dr. Seuss

Anyone who has known Hillary Clinton, née Rodham, since her budding days remarks on her iron willpower, her desperate ambition to get the best grades, take on the boys, win the competition whatever it may be. What is the source of this inner core of steel?

Hillary was born an adult, according to her mother, Dorothy Rodham.[1] While that is surely an exaggeration, Dorothy's daughter never seemed to lack discipline or drive. Once she settled on a track, she stuck to it like the wheels of an express train. Her favorite lines from the Dr. Seuss books, she has said, read like an internalized motto: "You have brains in your head. You have feet in your shoes. You can steer yourself any direction you choose."[2]

It was the best of times, 1950, in the best of countries, America victorious, when two offspring of Welsh immigrants moved their little family out of the city of Chicago to the suburb where the white people lived, Park Ridge. It was the right place to bring up their daughter, their pride, their Hillary. She was three years old, and the first of her two brothers was on the way. Hugh Rodham, her driven father, wanted the finest house he could afford, although he was too scarred by the Depression to take out a mortgage. Even if he had to work fourteen hours a day—and he did—he was determined to live on Elm Street in a fine two-story stone house and keep a Cadillac parked conspicuously in his driveway. His daughter would have her own bedroom with a sundeck.

Hillary did not want to grow up.

In her shoes, who would? Her world was as rarefied and protective as the elm trees that canopied the streets of her neighborhood. It was nice to look out in spring at those good gray guardians: solid, old stock, rising straight up before spreading their fanlike leaves. By summer, a million of those little green fans lapped at the warm air up and down streets of staid English Tudor–style homes. Only gentle shafts of sunlight were admitted to dapple the grass.

Hillary would spend hours dancing and spinning in the sun. She saw herself as the only person in the whole world and imagined that if she whirled around, everyone else would vanish. But the best part was pretending that the sunlight was intended for her, beamed down by God, and that there were "heavenly movie cameras watching my every move."[3]

She always saw herself as a star.

The Rodhams' world was a suburban incubator of upward mobility, flush with GI Bill checks that bought up the land and paid the taxes for first-class public schools. The original buildings of this English-style village were 150 years old, and some still stood proudly, their white stucco fronts top-hatted with stiffly pointed gables. This quaint base was carefully overlaid by the neat, conformist homes of a middle-class community that would serve as a bedroom for workadaddies who commuted the forty-five minutes to Chicago.

"Back then, moms stayed home" is the wistful recollection of Hillary's old history teacher Paul Carlson, who was born and bred and remains insulated in Park Ridge. "Dads could make enough money to support the family. Mothers did what mothers are supposed to do, provide a gentle climate for the children and the husbands."[4] The mothers shopped and gave coffee klatches and had lunch ready when their kids biked home from school and waited for the crunch of gravel to signal the homecoming of the head of household. The mothers of Park Ridge were always waiting for life to happen.

It was a dry town, literally as well as symbolically: no liquor and no dissenting views to heat things up. All white, almost all white Anglo-Saxon

Protestant, its mostly English and German population belonged to the New Class of postwar Americans who invented the suburban dream. Republicanism was as solidly planted in Park Ridge as the American elms. When someone wanted to vote Democrat, there would be a flurry of activity trying to find a ballot for the oddball.

Hillary's early childhood is described as an idyllic collective experience: dozens of kids, "all growing up at the same time, all running in and out of one another's backyards, selling lemonade, spraining their ankles on Slip 'n' Slides, playing Parcheesi and checkers while they mended."[5] They went in groups to the Pickwick Theater for a twenty-five-cent movie and then for Cokes at Ted & Pearl's Happy House. The only time young Hillary went back to the city of her birth was in the rear seat of her father's Cadillac. The purpose of those "field trips" was to show her and her brothers the miserable bums on Chicago's skid row, "to see what became of people who, as he saw it, lacked the self-discipline and motivation to keep their lives on track," as Hillary later described her father's philosophy in her book *It Takes a Village.*[6]

On one or two special Sundays a year, her parents or grandparents would treat the children to a trip to Kiddieland for pony rides and the roller coaster. All dressed in their church best, her brothers in clip-on ties, they would stop at the Robin Hood restaurant for "red hots" (Chicagospeak for hot dogs). But Hillary, the budding academic, preferred outings to the Field Museum, where she could press her nose against the cases of dinosaur skeletons and study baby mummies.

The Arcadian portrait of her girlhood invariably offered by Hillary and her designated friends glosses over important social realities. In status-conscious Park Ridge, most of the fathers wore business suits and were considered professionals. Hugh Rodham commuted to Chicago, the same as his neighbors, and drove home at dusk, the same as his neighbors, but he was not a professional. None of Hillary's playmates or classmates knew exactly what Mr. Rodham did for a living. "I just assumed he was a professional," most will tell you. In fact, Mr. Rodham was a tradesman. His wife had barely finished high school. Their desperate ambition to better themselves was injected repeatedly into their children. It had been ever thus with the Rodhams, a scrappy clan of Welshmen and their long-suffering wives.

Hugh's grandmother Isabella, alone with her eight children, had endured the horrors of a steerage-class crossing from Wales in 1882, to begin life anew in Scranton, Pennsylvania, joining a husband who worked in the blackened pits of the "anthracite capital of the world." The immigrant coal miner had told his sons, "It doesn't always have to be like this. You can be whatever you want to be."[7] Their son Hugh went to work in a Scranton lace mill at the age of thirteen and stayed for the next half century, becoming a pillar of Republican respectability and the father of three sons. His namesake, Hillary's father, Hugh Ellsworth Rodham, managed to go through Penn State University on a football scholarship, studying physical education. But he graduated in the Depression and went to work in the mines, later joining his father at the Scranton Lace Company.[8] Big and burly and bursting with ambition, Hugh Jr. escaped the dreary mining town and literally rode the rails, jumping on and off passing freight trains until he got himself to Chicago and found a better job selling curtains at the Columbia Lace Company.

Hillary tellingly describes her father as "a self-sufficient, tough-minded, small businessman."[9] Indeed, he did eventually become his own boss and the sole employee of a little business. He made draperies for hotels and banks and offices. He took the orders, bought the material, cut and stenciled and sewed the curtains, delivered and hung them. Hugh Rodham was a one-man band. (Except when he put his sons to work helping him on a Saturday.)

The Rodhams emphasized self-reliance: no hands, no help, except perhaps from God or Goldwater. Pop-Pop, as the children called the authoritarian drillmaster at the head of the family, neither offered nor asked for nurturing. Matters of the heart were a fickle distraction in the Rodham household. Life was seen as combat. Hillary's father prided himself on having trained young recruits for combat during World War II. Mr. Rodham did serve as a chief petty officer in the navy, although he himself never saw combat or left the States. Notwithstanding, he gave a good imitation of General Patton in raising his children.

"Well, Hillary," he would demand, "how are you going to dig yourself out of this one?"

In her first book Hillary depicts a deeply religious family: "We talked with God, walked with God, ate, studied and argued with God. Each night we knelt by our beds to pray." Her father did come from a long line of Methodists, but he let his wife and daughter do most of the churchgoing to the First United Methodist Church of Park Ridge. The patrician manners and mores of the New Class were not something to which Hugh Rodham aspired. He swore. He chewed tobacco. He was gruff and intolerant and also famously tightfisted: he shut off the heat in the house every night and turned a deaf ear to his children's complaints that they woke up freezing in the morning. *Toughen up* was the message. In the Rodham code any emotional display signaled weakness.

"Maybe that's why she's such an accepting person," Dorothy has said of her daughter. "She had to put up with him."[10]

KEEPING THE BUBBLE IN THE CENTER

Where was Hillary's mother in this picture?

Dorothy Howell Rodham secretly harbored certain more liberal tendencies and, later, even some interest in—dare we say?—*Democrats*. But she would be loath to offer a dissenting view at a dinner table commanded by Pop-Pop Rodham. Thus did Dorothy Rodham echo his preachments on hard work and discourage time wasted in introspection, sentimentalism, or moodiness.

"I wanted my children to be able to keep their equilibrium," Dorothy told me, explaining how she had used a carpenter's level as a visual tool for instruction. She showed it to Hillary and her brothers with the bubble dead center. "Imagine having this carpenter's level inside you," she told them. "You try to keep that bubble in the center. Sometimes it will go way up here," she said, tipping the instrument to show how the bubble could drift, "and you have to bring it back."[11]

It was a lesson that Dorothy Howell had had to learn to survive her own emotionally starved childhood. Born in Alhambra, California, to a mother of fifteen, Dorothy was abandoned by her parents, who split up when she was only eight years old. Family chaos followed. She told a searing story of being dispatched at that age on a three-day train journey from Chicago to Los Angeles as the frightened caretaker of her three-year-old sister.

Dorothy must have inculcated in her daughter the horror of divorce that has shaped so many of Hillary's life choices. On hearing her mother's tale, Hillary did not cry; she got angry. "I was incredulous," she has written, "furious that any child, even in the safer 1920s, would be treated like that."[12] Young Dorothy's mother disappeared from her life for a decade. She was raised by a demeaning grandmother in California until the age of fourteen, when she was hired out to strangers to work for her room and board. Young Dorothy never had the opportunity to go to college. In Hillary's mind, her mother's experience became a parable of divorce and the pain of broken families. In her book she wrote, "Children without fathers, or whose parents float in and out of their lives after divorce, are precarious little boats in the most turbulent seas."[13]

It was while applying for a job as a secretary at the Columbia Lace Company in Chicago that Dorothy met Hugh Rodham. During the war they corresponded, and in 1942, when Dorothy was twenty-three years old, they married. When their daughter was born five years later, Mrs. Rodham chose for her what she considered a man's name because she thought it sounded "exotic"—the antithesis of her own limited life.

Clearly, Mrs. Rodham was a frustrated handmaiden to a husband who claimed the full prerogatives of men of his generation. "Hers was not the life I wanted" is the most common refrain of Hillary's classmates at Wellesley College, as collected in the book *Rebels in White Gloves* by Miriam Horn.[14] Most of their mothers lacked a college degree and the skills to support themselves and felt they had no license to speak with their own voices. Isolated by the geography of suburbia and the chores of young motherhood, they were even disconnected from one another by the need to "keep up appearances." Hillary's college classmates describe in the book homes with distant fathers, "drawn curtains, bottles of Valium, and cold silences. 'The smell of home,' one says, 'was the smell of gin and tonic.' "[15]

Behind drawn curtains Hillary's father and mother often yelled at each other. Their voices were so grating, Hillary later confided to a classmate, she would feel as if she were losing the top of her head. When the term "communication gap" later came into social discourse to describe the gulf between traditional Depression-sobered parents and their increasingly affluent, authority-flouting children, Hillary related to it. But between herself and her parents, she said, it was more like a "communication chasm."[16]

The secret behind Hillary's boldness goes back to the torch passed from a silent generation of mothers whose daughters started the feminist movement. "I was determined that no daughter of mine was going to have to go through the agony of being afraid to say what she had on her mind," Dorothy Rodham told me. Even then, in 1992, when I spent an afternoon with Hillary's mother going over family scrapbooks and memories, she kept her voice low. Hillary's father grunted an acknowledgment of my visit from the next room but did not get up from his recliner. His mere presence felt like a silent reproach.

Mrs. Rodham told me the defining story of her daughter's childhood. When the family moved to Park Ridge, four-year-old Hillary had to make her way in the cruel social hierarchy of preschoolers. The new neighborhood was dominated by a family with a daughter named Suzy who regularly decked both boys and girls, including the beribboned little Hillary. Suzy would watch in triumph as little Hillary ran home sobbing.

"There's no room in this house for cowards," Mrs. Rodham declared, an edict Hillary would later pass on to her husband. "You're going to have to stand up to her. The next time she hits you, I want you to hit her back."

Out trudged the trembling four-year-old. A circle of scowling boys and the pugilistic girl closed around her. Suddenly Hillary threw out her fist, knocking Suzy off her pins. The boys' mouths dropped open. Flushed with victory, Hillary ran home and exclaimed to her proud mother: "I can play with the boys now!"

"Boys responded well to Hillary," clucked her mother, when telling me the story. "She just took charge, and they let her." Mrs. Rodham obviously took subversive pleasure in shaping a daughter to compensate for her own submission to patriarchy. And the lesson sank in deep.[17]

FINDING WAYS TO BE NOTICED

She tried hard to excel at sports to please her father, but she was physically clumsy.[18] One spring he took her to Hinckley Park and every Sunday put her through grueling training sessions until she learned how to hit a decent softball. Decent, but not great.

If she couldn't be a star athlete, she would become a walking statistician. "She really has an amazing gift for any fact or statistic," says Rick Ricketts, a Park Ridge man who has known her since the age of five. She knew all the best pitchers and players. "She'd ask these fairly obscure questions, like what was the 1927 Yankee batting order?" he says. "If I didn't know the answers, she'd get exasperated and say, 'I can't believe you don't know that!'" Hillary made a game out of arguing. Ricketts was a grinning happy-go-lucky kid who lived down the street, and she loved to spar with him because she could usually show him up. If he said he was a Yankees fan, she'd say she was rooting for the Bums. Ricketts mocked her. Didn't she know that "bums" were guys with red bandanas on sticks who go from town to town because they don't have a job?

"No, dummy," Hillary would sneer, "that's a nickname for the Brooklyn Dodgers."[19]

The parents of Park Ridge placed great emphasis on their children's achievements. "I would say it was a highly overachieving group and very competitive," remembers Ricketts.[20] Being a baseball or football player was the top ticket to an enviable identity for the sons of Park Ridge. For daughters it was a different story. There wasn't all that much that girls could do to distinguish themselves. They couldn't be in Little League, of course, and in those days there were no intramural girls' sports teams. A keen though terminally mediocre athlete, Hillary later appreciated having learned the lesson few girls did in those days.

"You win one day, you lose the next day, you don't take it personally," she told me.[21] "You get up every day, and you go on." It became the pattern of her life.

As a good Girl Scout, Hillary loaded up her sash with merit badges and gold pins. Even as a child she thought in terms of mobilizing constituents for her causes, organizing neighborhood carnivals or clothing drives for migrant workers. "She would think things through to see what would be appealing to the group," recalls her brother Hughie.[22] "We would just follow along as little brothers." She liked running things.

But the social reality in Park Ridge was a Fifties reality. Girls were not stars. At best, females were moonlike creatures; they reflected the resplendence of males. In some ways young Hillary might be likened to the thinking heroine of George Eliot's great Victorian novel *Middlemarch,* Dorothea Brooke.[23] But unlike Dorothea, Hillary did not suffer greatly from the indefiniteness that hung like a summer haze over the desire of so many women to make their lives effective. Hillary always knew she would be effective. Someday.

"We were the two biggest overachievers in the class," says Art Curtis, her most serious classmate, the one who became a doctor. "Hillary was very competitive at everything. Even pugnacious. She was very ambitious." With some lingering chagrin Curtis admits, "Even I found it impossible to upstage her."

The first time Curtis met Hillary, in eighth grade, they stood in the sunlight on the corner of her home at Wisner and Elm and talked about Barry Goldwater. She was reading Goldwater's exigesis *The Conscience of a Conservative.* "I was immediately taken with her," says Curtis. Most girls in Park Ridge talked about boys or about nothing or just worried about straightening their teeth and padding their bras. "Hillary was absolutely political," he says. "She was very, very interested in politics early, and politics wasn't cool then."

Richard Nixon was running for president that year, 1960, against a young patrician senator with a powerful father, Joseph P. Kennedy. Illinois was a key battlefield. The Kennedys were close to the Daleys of Chicago, and "Boss," as Mayor Daley was known, ran a very tight Democratic political machine. Hillary and her father watched the Republican convention on television, but when that upstart John Kennedy turned on the charm at the Democratic convention, Hugh Rodham pulled the plug on the family TV.

The WASPs of Park Ridge had a strong sense of self-righteousness, according to Curtis.[24] And Hugh Ellsworth Rodham was an absolutist.

Like father, like daughter. Hillary, too, thought in absolutes: Republican or Democrat. Black or White. Right or Wrong. And it was clearly Wrong that John F. Kennedy beat Richard Nixon that fall. Hugh Rodham's outrage was transmitted to his thirteen-year-old daughter. A right-wing Republican group ran a bold ad in the *Chicago Tribune* accusing Mayor Daley and the Kennedy people of stealing the election and demanded a recount. Her father plugged Hillary into the group Operation Eagle Eye, which was soliciting volunteers to go to downtown Chicago and help ferret out proof of Democratic vote fraud. Hillary and a thirteen-year-old girlfriend caught a train and went to the city alone. Republican activists gave them questionnaires and dropped them at the edge of a Hispanic neighborhood on Chicago's notoriously rough South Side. The two little girls went from door to door, ringing doorbells and asking, "Did you vote?" and "Would you mind telling me who you voted for?" "They couldn't understand me, and I couldn't understand them," Hillary later said, laughing but horrified that Republicans were so culturally numb that they would send two little white girls to do a political investigation in an alien environment.[25]

At the time, of course, she wanted to impress her father. Her two brothers were jocks and as apolitical as they come. Hugh Jr., the elder, played baseball and varsity football all through high school, filling in for the team's injured quarterback in his senior year and pulling the squad through for an undefeated season. He earned a law degree from the University of Arkansas in 1980 and went on to become an assistant public defender in Dade County, Florida, though interestingly he did not bother to register to vote until 1991, at the age of forty-one. Tony Rodham, born in 1954, aped his older brother, playing football, wrestling, and weight lifting, but was undistinguished in almost every other way. The family is close-mouthed about where, or if, he went to college or what he has done for a living, beyond saying he was formerly a "private investigator" in Florida. In 1992, he was given a comfortable slot with the Democratic National Committee in Los Angeles, but no longer works for the DNC.

Even as a girl, Hillary lived mostly up in her head. If one could not be tough by the congenital virtue of brawn, then one had to be tough by using one's brains. And Hillary used just about all the brains in her head.

She once told Art Curtis, "I'm smarter than you." It wasn't said in an obnoxious way, simply as a matter of fact. Curtis never forgot it. That was one of the odd things about Hillary Rodham. "The major value in Park Ridge was to be *nice*," says John Peavoy, one of Hillary's classmates. Manners were important. Almost everyone spoke well, dressed well, and had at least a veneer of Victorian-style manners. But Hillary was blunt. She would just say what she thought.

One day she and Curtis were walking home from school together after their extracurricular activities when Laurie Johansen caught up with them. Art whispered, "Here comes your friend." Appropriately humble before two of the class brains, Laurie said, "I really feel dumb walking with you two guys."

Hillary replied, "Yes, you should, Laurie."[26]

"We all knew each other's grade point averages," said Bob Stenson, who became an accountant in Marin County. He still remembers his position out of the thousand students in their graduating class of 1965. He was seventh and Hillary was around fifteenth. Still, he admits, she was a formidable competitor: "I always felt a little funny around her. I was always hoping she'd stumble a little bit."[27] But she rarely did. She almost never got into trouble. She was a classic teacher's pet. Whatever the teacher asked for, she always gave more. Hillary was one of fifteen National Merit Scholarship finalists. But nothing she could do was ever enough.

"When I brought home straight A's from junior high," Hillary wrote, "my father's only comment was, 'Well, Hillary, that must be an easy school you go to.' " No matter how well his children did, her father was always "raising the bar." Hillary acknowledges that her father's "motivational ploy could have had the opposite effect on a child of a different temperament than mine."[28]

Her brothers were gentler in temperament but received the same treatment. When Hillary's hefty brother Hughie played quarterback in the final game of his team's championship season, his father sat beyond the bleachers in a lawn chair by himself. Hughie completed nine passes but missed the tenth. After he got home, all his father could talk about was his one incomplete pass.

Naturally, Hillary paid a price for being known as a brain. "I remember her as a girl about whom you would say with the other guys, 'For one of the smart ones, she's not bad-looking.' " That is the clearest recollection of John Peavoy, who was Hillary's peer in their senior English honors class. He thought Hillary was pretty in high school; others said she wasn't. "If anything," he says, "the reason she didn't date much is that she was formidable."[29]

Makeup and clothes were not Hillary's métier; perfect grades and good works were far more important. She did have naturally good looks—straight blond hair falling in a pageboy style and sloe blue eyes set in a moon-shaped face. By the age of sixteen she had a fully developed hourglass figure. In a photograph taken on a summer church retreat in Wisconsin, Hillary in her conservative one-piece bathing suit shows a nicely plumped bosom, rounded shoulders, and long, dimpled arms. A girlish waist spreads to womanly hips and thighs. She is much more soft-fleshed than muscular. "It's a Victorian body," says the fashion director of *Vogue*, Paul Cavaco. "The smaller shoulder and tinier waist, which accentuates the hips."[30] Cavaco later dressed Hillary for the famous *Vogue* cover photo shoot of 1998.

But until she was fifty years old Hillary didn't give a fig about how she looked to others. "She was totally unconcerned about how she appeared to people, and she was loved for that," remembers Jeannie Snodgrass Almo, a high school classmate who now runs a day care center in D.C.[31] In grammar school the Rodham girl wore sailor dresses and saddle shoes. In ninth grade she would come to class in her Girl Scout uniform. (Not coincidentally, it was the First Lady who later promoted school uniforms.) By high school she graduated to tightish sweaters and plaid skirts.

"She never wore makeup, but a lot of us didn't," says Patsy Henderson Bowles, the class homecoming queen. "She did have poor eyesight and wore really thick glasses. She may have been self-conscious about that." Hillary always wore her glasses in class, but when she was running for any political office she took them off, and one of her friends would walk with her through the halls and tell her who was who. Later, she turned her glasses into a statement of uniqueness. From his one date with Hillary, Dr. Jeff Phillips remembers her oversized red glasses frames.[32]

"None of my kids dated much until they were older," says Dorothy Rodham. "And Hillary always valued herself very highly. I liked that about her."[33] In most of the authorized accounts of Hillary's girlhood, Rick Ricketts claims to have been her first boyfriend. In fact, they had only one date. It was a Sadie Hawkins dance in their freshman year to which Hillary asked Rick to escort her. She made him a joke corsage of ribbons around a bunch of carrots. He wore a suit and tie, she a plain party dress, and her father drove them to the dance and afterward to De Leo's restaurant in Chicago. Their relationship was safely platonic.

Hillary was a prude then and is a prude to this day, according to her youth minister Don Jones: "She's a straitlaced Methodist. In all things, Hillary is circumspect and prudent."[34]

Park Ridge fostered prudishness. "Premarital sex was a no-no," remembers Art Curtis. "Abortion was never mentioned. There were greasers, but they weren't from Park Ridge."

Hillary liked "big beefy guys with charisma," an observation she later confirmed in a note to Art Curtis. "But she never dated one of the top twelve good-looking guys," remembers Curtis.[35] Except once. When it came time for the junior prom, a showcase occasion in any high school, Hillary secured herself a date with a showcase jock. Jim Van Schoyck was a big, extroverted football type like her father. Hillary was able to take him to the prom because she was in charge of it.

"My parents, because I'm a class officer, are going to be chaperones," she wrote in a letter to Don Jones. That helped influence her tightfisted dad to give her the money for a new dress, she explained. It was a simple white floor-length affair, and Hillary felt that for once she could compete with the pretty and popular girls. "Next to it," she wrote, "I think everyone else will feel overdressed."[36]

Boys her age did not hold much mystery for Hillary. She appears to have been at least five years ahead of most of her peers in cognitive development and certainly precocious in her aspirations. The people she related to were older and mostly intellectuals. Indeed, the two men who were truly important in her girlhood were both a decade older than she—and they fought over her.

BETTER DEAD THAN RED IN PARK RIDGE

In the fall of 1961, Hillary entered Maine East high school at the age of thirteen and came under the influence of her first history teacher, Paul Carlson. The teacher still holds forth at Maine East in a classroom whose walls and ceilings are a collage of military memorabilia: Viking helmets and model warplanes from the Great War through the Gulf War. Today Carlson looks like a character out of Dickens, a tall burly man with milky blue pop-out eyes resting on deep pouches and white muttonchop sideburns crawling across his full jowls. His manner is courtly and jovial. He is every bit the fiery defender of Joseph McCarthy's muscular anticommunism that he was decades ago when he taught Hillary in the ninth grade.

Old soldiers never die, they just go on teaching the love of fighting on the side of the Right, to paraphrase Carlson's most revered military hero, General Douglas MacArthur. A huge hand-tinted blowup of the general's likeness hangs at the head of the classroom. In 1960, Mr. Carlson described to Hillary and her thirteen-year-old classmates, who had known only peacetime, how this legendary warrior had led the Allied forces across the South Pacific and taken one bloody beachhead after another. After accepting the Japanese surrender, he told them, MacArthur had fought on when the Republic of Korea was invaded, seeing the Korean War as a global Communist threat and demanding a full naval and economic blockade of Red China. At this point, Mr. Carlson would redden with anger. He drilled into Hillary and her ninth-grade classmates that President Truman had made a historic error in removing MacArthur as supreme commander of the Allied forces in Japan and commander of the UN forces in South Korea. (MacArthur had refused to obey his president's orders.) But the unbowed general had returned to make a trip across the United States worthy of a triumphant Roman general. Carlson could not wait to play for his class General MacArthur's unrepentant farewell speech before both houses of Congress:

"The Communist threat is a global one."

He played the speech again a second day:

"In war there is no substitute for victory."

And again, a third day:

"I am closing my fifty-two years of military service. . . . The world has turned over many times since I took the oath on the plain at West Point . . . but I still remember the refrain of one of the most popular barracks ballads of that day . . . Old soldiers never die. They just fade away."

Having prepared the children with a hefty injection of patriotism, Mr. Carlson then delivered the coup de grâce. He told the class, "Better to be dead than Red."

Rick Ricketts, seated alphabetically right in front of Hillary Rodham, said to her in a stage whisper, "Well, I'd rather be alive!"

It struck Hillary as funny, and she snickered. Rick laughed.

Carlson purpled and sputtered, "Quiet! This is serious business!" The two could not contain themselves. They were thrown out of class—the one and only time Hillary Rodham suffered a reprimand in high school.

But Carlson was less angry than hurt. He had always thought of Hillary as a perfect lady. From Hillary's perspective, Carlson was a comfortable surrogate for her father. And she knew exactly how to play him. When he assigned a term paper, expecting fifteen or twenty pages, she turned in a seventy-five-page paper accompanied by 150 five-by-seven-inch note cards and fifty bibliography cards. She was his model student. "Nowadays, you can't get that out of kids," he grouses.

More than that, he believed, "She was a firm supporter basically of ideas I embraced and still embrace twenty-eight years later. I'm a Fifties person, madam," he told me, "and my generation fully supported any attempt to rout out Communists." Including the House Un-American Activities Committee? he was asked. "Yes, HUAC." He proudly recalls that in his "History of Civilization" course, Miss Rodham supported General Chiang Kai-shek, China's Nationalist ruler before the Communist revolution in 1948:

"Hillary was a hawk."[37]

In the same year that Hillary was being coached to be a hawk, unbeknownst to her, a very different, domestic issue of vital importance was starting to fire up her contemporaries. Thousands of black college students vowed to challenge the hundred-year hangover from slavery that went by the name segregation—even if it meant risking their lives. Which it did.

This was not a subject discussed in the classrooms or at the dinner tables of Hillary's hermetically sealed northern suburb.

Sheriff Bull Connor had met the young black college students in Birmingham, Alabama, with cattle prods and jailed many of them, but after arm-twisting by President Kennedy's people the demonstrators were released. Singing freedom songs, ten Freedom Riders headed on a bus toward Montgomery, Alabama, on a fateful morning in May 1961, eager to try out the techniques of Christian nonviolence to challenge segregation. But the local police, in cahoots with the Ku Klux Klan, sat on their nightsticks while men and women armed with baseball bats and cattle prods set upon reporters and photographers and then turned their lead pipes and bats murderously upon the skulls of the young Freedom Riders. President Kennedy ordered his man on civil rights, Harris Wofford—the man who would later interest First Lady Hillary Clinton in health care reform—to "Tell them to call it off! Stop them!"[38] That night, the Freedom Riders were knighted by the first broad national TV coverage as the cause of the day.

A revolution was taking place. But not in Park Ridge.

A HARD RAIN'S A-GONNA FALL

Another important older man entered Hillary's life that same year, when she was hovering between thirteen and fourteen on the cusp of adolescence. He was a tall, blond blue-eyed man who wore a crew cut and white bucks and tooled around town in a bright red Impala convertible. He was young, and all the girls thought he was so good-looking. But Don Jones was also a true intellectual—Hillary's type. Twenty-six and fresh from divinity school at Drew University across the Hudson River from New York City, he succeeded three youth ministers who had been safe and traditional. Jones represented a radical change for the sleepy First Methodist Church of Park Ridge.

"New ideas were frowned upon in our community," says Patsy Henderson Bowles. "We hadn't been exposed to diversity. Don wanted us to think about where other kinds of people were coming from and to understand their problems."[39]

Jones was the only alternative reality in town. On Sunday evenings, starting in September 1961, he would offer Hillary's church youth his version of the "University of Life" program. He had been outside the sterile world of suburbia and could offer a window onto the more exotic worlds of abstract art, Beat poetry, existentialism, and the rumblings of radical political thought and counterculture politics that were eventually to explode under the smug slumber of even the good gray burghers of Park Ridge.

Theologically, Jones was no liberal. His era in the seminary had seen a backlash against liberal theology fueled by Paul Tillich and his articulation of the "crisis of meaning," by the Swiss theologian Karl Barth's writings on sin and grace, by Reinhold Niebuhr and Søren Kierkegaard, even by Calvinism. And his Calvinist tinge appealed to Hillary's absolutist core. But Don Jones wasn't as fired by theology as he was by the cultural revolution he could sense was on the way. He asked one of Hillary's classmates, Bob Berg, to play for the youth group Bob Dylan's prophetic song "A Hard Rain's A-Gonna Fall."[40] The song spoke of guns and sharp swords in the hands of young children and people whispering and nobody listening.

"It was anticipating the turbulence all those kids were going to experience in the Sixties," says Jones. Then the young minister would pass out poetry sheets and get the kids talking about, for instance, how D. H. Lawrence had refuted Plato's separation of mind, body, and soul. Jones made connections for them. He told them that the most important question they would have to wrestle with was "Is God working in the world? And if so, how can we discern that presence?" The real was in the earthly; that was Don Jones's personal theology.[41]

Even as a precocious thirteen-year-old, Hillary was not ready to separate her worldview from her father's, but she listened intently to Jones. And when he invited his youth group to go into Chicago to meet with their counterparts belonging to inner-city gangs, she was excited.

At a community center on Chicago's South Side, Jones gathered the diverse group of young teenagers around a print of Picasso's *Guernica*. He had been inspired by Paul Tillich's claim that Picasso's terrifying mural of war and destruction was the most Protestant piece of art in the twentieth century. Why? Because it broke open the human condition in all its alienation and violence. Jones quoted Karl Barth: "Hidden deep down in the no is a yes"—meaning that even in the midst of life's tragedies there is hope. Employing a Socratic style, the minister opened a dialogue between the ghetto kids and his own coddled charges.

"What strikes you about this?" he began. "Any imagery?"

Then he asked, "If you had to title this painting with a current piece of music, what would it be?"

The inner-city kids were the ones who responded. One paraphrased the Stones: "It ain't got no satisfaction." Eventually, Jones got down to the more subjective level: "Have you ever experienced anything like this?" One young black girl asked angrily, "Why did my uncle have to get shot because he parked in the wrong parking place?"[42]

Hillary and her Park Ridge friends were stunned. They didn't say much.

"I think he [Don Jones] was wrong in taking kids to South Side Chicago and coming back and saying the white middle class was responsible for the condition of inner-city blacks," complains Paul Carlson to this day. "He hung these kids with a guilt trip: 'Look at these slums and look how you live!' "[43]

"It's not only a bad rap, it's not correct," counters Jones. "I had no notion of hanging a guilt trip. My purpose was not so much political and moral as it was educational—achieving that goal of searching for God in culture. We didn't talk about racism or discrimination—what we did was look at Picasso's *Guernica*."[44]

The exposure gave Hillary a great deal to think about during her summer job at the local park. As she watched privileged children splash around the public wading pool, she remembered the faces of the poor, oppressed youngsters she had seen in the slums of Chicago and Boston. That was "reality."[45]

"Don Jones and I were at each other's throats," recalls Carlson. The reactionary teacher saw the new minister of his church as a threat to impressionable minds like Hillary's. "Jones was a freethinker who leaned toward more involvement of government in people's lives. He only lasted two years before he was nudged out."[46] Minister Jones saw Carlson as "to the right of the John Birchers." He remembers those two critical years in Hillary's development as a thrilling challenge:

"We were fighting for her soul and her mind."[47]

WAKING UP

Hillary played both sides. She bounced between Carlson's reactionary chauvinism in the classroom and Don Jones's culturally hip "University of Life" on weekends. Unbeknownst to Jones, she joined Carlson's secret anti-Communist club called "Maine-ites in Motion." He had started it outside school "to make these middle-class students realize what they had in Park Ridge and what they'd lose if our philosophy of life was destroyed."[48] Twice a month, Hillary attended teacher Carlson's cult in the public library to hear rock-hard conservative or military speakers. The emphasis was on patriotism and free enterprise. But Carlson went further: he circulated literature in Hillary's place of worship, leaving on the pews of the First Methodist Church of Park Ridge an incendiary flyer warning that we would soon be living under communism. It created a big hullaballoo that divided the church into two camps. Carlson defended himself by accusing Jones of brainwashing the kids.

"Paul," Jones confronted Carlson in a meeting, "who do you think you are, Jesus Christ?" The teacher was fired at the end of that year but later reinstated.

Unbeknownst to her history teacher, in January 1963, Hillary went with her youth minister into Chicago to hear a southern black minister who was seen as a dangerous "rabble-rouser" by the middle-class white society of Park Ridge: Martin Luther King, Jr.

Hillary was fifteen. Jones did not ask permission from the parents of the twenty children he shepherded, and Hillary probably did not dare ask her father, who surely would have seen such a trip as going over the wall. "I wanted them to become aware of the social revolution that was taking place," says Jones. "Here was the major leader of that movement, a Protestant preacher, coming to town. It was an opportunity for them to meet a great person."

Orchestra Hall was unusually full for that evening's meeting of the Chicago Sunday Evening Club. A thousand members of the nondenominational club turned out to hear Martin Luther King, Jr., urge America's Negroes to fight for "first-class citizenship." His message was entitled "Remaining Awake Through a Great Revolution." (It was one of the earliest versions of the speech by the same name delivered by Dr. King at the National Cathedral in Washington four days before his assassination on April 4, 1968.)

That night in Chicago, Dr. King began his spellbinding speech by reminding his audience of the Rip Van Winkle story. When Rip first went into the mountains, the preacher said, the sign on the pub in his little town on the Hudson River had a picture of King George III of England; twenty years later, when Rip awoke from his deep slumber and came down the mountain, the sign had a picture of George Washington. He had slumbered through a revolution that was changing the course of history. He was completely lost.

Hillary perked up and obviously took in the next phrase: "Our world is a neighborhood."

Like any great preacher, Dr. King made Hillary feel as if he were talking directly to her. He challenged the kind of rote churchgoing she and her family practiced, saying that the most segregated hour of the week was the 11 A.M. Sunday worship service. He told his listeners that the guilt over racial injustice must be shared by all. His basso profundo voice building, Dr. King challenged his audience to work together to get rid of segregation, which he called a new word for slavery. (Freedom Rides had been going on in the South for several years, but Congress would not pass the Civil Rights Act for another two years.) The preacher told his audience that the time for action was now and the choice was no longer between violence and nonviolence, it was between nonviolence and nonexistence.

He drew a stark distinction between the kind of poll-driven politics that would eventually overtake the country, and the politics of conscience: "Vanity asks the question: Is it popular? Conscience asks the question: Is it right?"

He went on to talk about the poor, about how we don't see the poor because our expressways carry us away from the ghetto. As if preaching to the delegation from Park Ridge, he recounted Jesus' parable about a man doomed to Hell because he did not notice those in need.

Hadn't Hugh Rodham taken Hillary to look upon the poor of Chicago's skid row? But her father had seen them only with scorn.

Building on the story of Lazarus, Dr. King warned that one day we will all stand before God to have our accomplishments counted. He said ominously, "I can hear the God of history saying, 'That was not enough!' " His voice now a mighty tremble, he left his listeners with an inspirational guideline that must have been seared into the soul of Hillary Rodham:

"The end of life is not to be happy, but to do the will of God come what may."

As if Hillary in her teenage innocence were not sufficiently awed by the speech, Jones had arranged to take his charges onstage to meet the great man. One by one, they placed their small white hands in his warm palm. Then they filed back through the aisles, feeling the exuberance of soul brothers and sisters, and returned to their sequestered existence.

"Park Ridge was sleeping through the biggest social revolution this country has ever had," says Don Jones. Hillary did not grasp the relevance at the time, but in retrospect it had clearly shaken her rigid Republicanism. Twenty years later, when she invited Jones to the Arkansas governor's mansion for tea, Hillary told him, "I'll never forget when you introduced me to Martin Luther King, Jr."[49]

THE BUDDING POLITICIAN

Coming to political consciousness in the early 1960s, Hillary saw those years as "years dominated by men with dreams, men in the civil-rights movement and Peace Corps, the space program." Her use of the noun "men" was not accidental. The shock of sexism had first caught up with her in the same year that Carlson and Jones were fighting for her mind and soul. The ambitious fourteen-year-old wrote to NASA asking what it took to be an astronaut. She was told that girls need not apply. It made her furious.

"Growing up in the Fifties," she told me, "a lot of us sensed that we could redefine what women do." Her mother hoped that Hillary would be the first woman on the Supreme Court. But as she later joked, "Sandra Day O'Connor beat her to it."[50]

After hearing Dr. King, Hillary Rodham was eager to try out her own oratorical and political skills. In her junior year, without any noticeable stage fright, she addressed an all-school assembly—five thousand students, all staring up at the blond girl on the stage. "She gave a wonderful speech," says Patsy Bowles, her friend and the homecoming queen. "It was the first time I realized she had such poise, eloquence, and confidence in a speaking situation. Her ideas and her manner were way beyond her years. It knocked me over."[51]

By the age of sixteen, Hillary Rodham was ready to run for high office: "The Presidency," as she later referred to it in a letter to John Peavoy.[52] She was already vice president of her junior class and full of ideas about how to make things better, how to get things done. But in the competition for senior class president she was knocked out in the first ballot—"unceremoniously defeated," as she saw it, by dirty campaigning by her two male opponents. The other side was "slinging mud at us," she later lamented in a letter to Jones. "We did not retaliate. We took the high road and talked about motherhood and apple pie."[53]

It was her first exposure to what would later be called "negative campaigning." She learned the lesson well; she would not make that mistake again. Whatever it took, the next time she would not allow herself to lose.

Hillary dealt with this early, stinging defeat the way she would for the rest of her life—by throwing herself into projects such as "cleaning out closets." That spring she was an ambassador to the junior high schools being merged into Maine South for their senior year. She appeared on Chicago TV to talk about teenage values. She ran the junior prom and represented her class on the student council. And in the fall of 1964 she threw herself into campaigning as a "Goldwater Girl." It was Hillary who came up with the idea of holding a mock political convention in the school gym, complete with posters, caucuses in the aisles, and nominating speeches.

Hillary always *knew* what was right. Not until her senior year in high school did a teacher question her absolutism. "Can you have an absolute moral system?" asked her English teacher, Marlan Davis.[54]

"Yes, you can," stated Hillary, unwavering. She believed she should right the wrongs of the world. "The idea was you should be out there jousting with windmills," says Art Curtis.[55]

Yet, for all her ambition, the young daughter of suburbia did not want to involve herself in anything that would require her to surrender even part of her world. Each birthday brought a year filled with new discoveries. She wanted the presents, the cake, the party, but she didn't want to grow up. There came a time, she admitted in a letter to Peavoy, when birthdays symbolized steps toward sophistication: a driver's license, a drink in New York. She wanted the discoveries to keep coming. But she had to admit her ambivalence:

"I don't want to lose the little girl in the sunlight."[56]

CHAPTER THREE

"I Wonder Who Is Me?"

I wonder who is me. I wonder if I'll ever meet her.
If I did, I think we'd get along famously.

—HILLARY RODHAM

In 1965, when Hillary and her classmates graduated from Maine South, they were as neat and well groomed as the lawns in Park Ridge. "Four years later," says her fellow student council leader Myrna Pederson, "the lawns in Park Ridge were neat and well groomed and we weren't."[1]

To go east in 1965 to Wellesley College was a big stretch for a young woman from a sheltered midwestern suburb. Wellesley was "all very rich and fancy and very intimidating to my way of thinking," Hillary told me.[2] She entered college a good little Goldwater Girl but had been forewarned by her high school government teacher, Gerald Baker, "You're going to go to Wellesley, and you're going to become a liberal and a Democrat." Hillary had stiffened and said, "I'm smart. I know where I stand on the issues. And that's not going to change."[3]

WHAT IS HAPPINESS?

Although Maine South was one of the top public high schools in the country, most of Hillary's peers were going on to the University of Illinois or local schools. Very few kids went east. And at that time the Ivy League colleges—Yale, Dartmouth, Princeton, and the others—did not accept women. Janet Altman Spragens, a 1964 graduate of Wellesley who was a student teacher at Maine South, told Hillary that for a woman, the Seven Sisters schools, as they were called, were about as good as one could do.[4]

Her choice was partly vanity. She admitted to an intellectual soul mate that she wanted the solid gold–plated status that came with being able to say, "I went to Vassar or Wellesley or Radcliffe."[5] But no sooner had she achieved her goal of acceptance to all three schools than the first doubts about choosing such an elitist path began to shake the scaffold of certainties she had erected beneath her life choices. What was the point of going to college, anyway? Even more so, why Wellesley?[6]

Simple: besides being one of the most distinguished colleges in the country, it was a thousand miles away from Park Ridge and her father's iron control.

Perhaps as a parental substitute, she initiated a voluminous correspondence with a young man she had scarcely given a look in high school. John Peavoy was a fellow intellectual, something of a misfit at Maine South, but he had gotten himself into Princeton and she envied that. They commiserated over the shock of competition. They were no longer at the top of a class that ranged from bottom to top. At Wellesley and Princeton, *everyone* is creamed off the top. It was not going to be easy to be a star.

Her feelings in the first confusing month of the transition to college were a mixture of depression, anxiety, and ecstasy. She defined her mental state as "suppressive happiness," meaning being happy but unable to put one's finger on exactly why.[7] To Hillary the moral Methodist, happiness is something that one works at and analyzes and never quite trusts. "Happiness is temporal."[8]

What is reality? Should I worry about the state of the world and forget myself? Will I have the courage to be the person I really am? Who am I, anyway? These are the sorts of questions that any bright college student might ponder at this stage. Hillary wrestled strenuously with all of them and then some.

Constantly thinking through her own state of mind, Hillary adopted the role of den mother. Right from the start, she began counseling Peavoy on how to cope. Like most college freshmen, he felt waves of homesickness. Not Hillary. In the thirty letters she wrote to Peavoy over the next four years, she mentioned her mother only once. The few times she referred to her father, it was in the context of developing strategies to elude his oppressive control.

Members of her class were initiated into this hundred-year-old bastion of achieving women with a recitation of the Wellesley motto: *Non ministrari sed ministrare.* They were not to sit back passively and be ministered unto, they were *to minister.* They were also assured that they had been selected as "the crème de la crème." Yet within her first month at Wellesley, Hillary expressed impatience at the temerity of a college whose purpose seemed to be to turn out "well-rounded housewives" who were trained for gracious living and tame civic-mindedness.[9] A survey done by *McCall's* magazine singled out Wellesley girls as "making good wives."[10] Hillary was insulted. But the imprint of her eighteen years in a patriarchal community was not so easily erased. Now tucked away in the sylvan glades of Wellesley's beautiful rolling campus with a view of placid Lake Waban, she and her peers in the high school class of 1965 were suspended between their upbringing in the conformist Fifties and the hyperindividualistic spirit of the Sixties. They observed with ladylike detachment the feverish radical movements that began tearing apart many other campuses and communities.

Sizing up the competition in the freshman dorm where she lived alone, Hillary was suddenly conscious of being surrounded by a bevy of beautiful girls. Two were debutantes—a Carnegie and a Shell Oil, as she dubbed them—with jet set written all over them. These girls led lives she had only read about, sliding effortlessly from exclusive prep schools to dating Ivy League men with foreign cars. She covered whatever envy she might have felt in a blanket critique: they might have the most pricey wardrobes, but it didn't show. Their rooms were eyesores. They never acted, only reacted. Their vocabulary was moronically monosyllabic—everything was "fun." She was even more censorious about "the swinger," a lovely lanky blonde who majored in the study of boys. The swinger would be lucky to stay in college, Hillary sneered.[11]

For a young woman who had to win, contesting such girls on the level of beauty and clothes was not Hillary's game. She simply withdrew from trying to compete with traditional feminine wiles. Coincidentally, the anti-fashion of hippiedom was becoming cool at the same time. Hillary hid herself in shapeless denim dresses or sweater-vests over awning-striped bell-bottoms. Her long blond hair was dimming into a mousy brown but she paid no attention, pulling it back with a rubber band or twisting it up into a careless bun. Her dark-rimmed Coke-bottle glasses completed the donnish facade of a serious student who was not all that confident in herself as a woman.

Head dominated heart for Hillary. "Unthinking emotion is . . . pitiful to me," she wrote to Peavoy.[12] She preferred to have a long-distance, hands-off relationship with Peavoy, a witty philosophical egghead from high school, rather than to flirt with the flesh-and-blood frat boys in her backyard. Since Peavoy was working to put himself through Princeton, she admired him as a "self-made man." And self-made men like her father, she opined, were a vanishing breed. Her diagnosis of the "boys" she had met around Cambridge was that they knew a lot about "self" but were ignorant about being "men."[13]

Hillary diagnosed herself as neither a swinger nor a jet-setter nor a problem. She told Peavoy she saw herself as "normal." She complained to him that it was her luck to live near the "problem" student of the dorm. But after analyzing the causes of the girl's confusion, Hillary took it upon herself to minister to her as well as to other broken wings. Even then, Hillary maintained what she would later famously call a "zone of privacy" around herself. Some of her classmates saw her as quite a loner with a tendency to be self-righteous to a fault. She wrote a paper for English on "The Need for Intolerance." Her professor was not impressed.[14]

Hillary's only real interest was political science—that and getting A's and figuring out how to run things. Six weeks into college, she was already planning how she would revamp the Republican state organization, step by step, so that things would be running her way by her senior year. "So I'm going to stick to it," she vowed.[15]

True to her goal, by her junior year Hillary would be holding forth at a rally like a seasoned politician. Pitched forward intently in her navy pea jacket and severe ponytail, her hands outstretched toward an audience of professors and students who stood spellbound in the snow, she looked like an updated suffragette. She could even make them laugh.

Eleanor Dean Acheson remembers being astonished. Reflecting her own bias as the granddaughter of former Secretary of State Dean Acheson and member of a clan of extremely active Democrats, Eldie, as she was known, could not fathom Hillary: How could somebody that intelligent and "with it" be a *Republican?*

FIGHTING THE INNER DICTATOR

Clutched, panicked, overwhelmed, exhausted, trying to catch up but feeling forever behind—these were the dominant emotions that Hillary mentioned in her letters. She was desperate to do well academically. Over the next four years, her letters to Peavoy and Don Jones never mentioned a boyfriend. Her mind was focused almost exclusively on her work. Hillary was constantly worried that she might do poorly on a French test or write a less-than-perfect paper. Her greatest fear was disappointing her professors.[16]

She had brought with her to college the most severe of inner custodians.[17] This is the internalized parent, who may be experienced primarily as the guardian of one's safety or, more prohibitively, as the dictator of shoulds and should-nots. Hillary's drillmaster father was now more of an inner dictator. His demand for perfection and his readiness to demean his daughter were specters she saw in the faces of any authority figure. A Freudian might say that Hillary had an overactive superego. Whatever might explain Hillary's drive toward perfection, her severe self-discipline and overwhelming need for control were evident long before she ran up against the typical college exam clutch.

I once heard someone ask Hillary the question "What was the funniest thing that happened to you while you were in school?"

Her answer was anything but funny: "I had a third-grade teacher who was the most tyrannical human being I have ever met," Hillary said. "She would actually rap your knuckles with a ruler. I was in such a state of terror in my third-grade year—always worried that my penmanship was miserable." Her main goal that year had been to draw enough circles and lines to make her penmanship legible and avoid being rapped on the knuckles by the tyrannical teacher. But while she feared the tyrant, she also identified with the tyrant—her father. Thus the second part of the story is even more interesting.

Hillary thought she had successfully navigated the entire year when one of the boys in her class fired a spitball and hit her right between the eyes. "I do believe in the Golden Rule, but in third grade I thought what it meant was *Do unto others exactly what they did to you*," she explained. "So I waited until my teacher had left the room and took out my own ruler and whacked this kid on the shoulder."

Just then, the tyrannical teacher walked back in. The recess bell rang.

Hillary ran out to the playground and agonized over what she saw as a terrible dilemma: "There I was, torn between the kind of situations I seem to end up in all the time: Should I go back to class and face my teacher, who would tell me how much I had disappointed her, and take my rap on the knuckles? Or should I run away from home, never to return again?" It was only when one of her eight-year-old friends gave her the whispered wisdom of a child-adult—*This is not the worst thing that will ever happen to you*—that Hillary gathered the courage to return to class. To her surprise and relief, her teacher had forgotten the whole episode. Hillary, ever dutiful, "felt that I had fulfilled my responsibility to return."

Her correspondent relationship with Peavoy was also felt as a responsibility. The literary Princeton man wrote her amusing, mildly existential letters that she often reread to relieve the drudgery of listening to rote lectures in required freshman classes. For her own letters she routinely apologized. She never replied soon enough (though was seldom delayed more than a month). She also warned him that her letter writing would never be memorable. This articulate public speaker told her correspondent that her "epistles" would follow the incoherence of her speech.[18] In fact, she was almost always able to collect her thoughts into an elevated discourse, even as she quoted from writers, philosophers, and social scientists who were exciting ferment in her mind. Her letters were almost Victorian in their formality, though seldom poetic and sometimes cliché-ridden. She questioned her spelling (which was invariably correct). She asked a friend to choose stationery for her that would be "subtly dramatic," which turned out to be ivory with a deckled edge.[19] To break out of these self-imposed restraints, she sometimes tried a daring color of ink. Such as pink.

Hillary's parents kept her on a very short leash. Wellesley collaborated in the archaic practice of giving parents control over the movements of their freshman and sophomore charges. Only a blanket permission signed by parents could open the gates. Thus Hillary could not travel even as far as Boston to stay overnight with a girlfriend. Her father demanded that she produce a perfect set of A's before he would even consider allowing her such autonomy. But her parents couldn't stop her from going "back to womb and away from the world."[20] Sleep, alternating with feverish work, became her chosen form of escape.

She was pulling up roots intellectually, but she could not pull up roots socially. In addition to being prohibited from wandering too far out of her prescribed world, she probably felt inhibited about straying too far socially without violating the parental rules that she had internalized.

THE WONK GROUP

A critical leap from the purely cerebral to a romantically coated cerebral relationship occurred in Hillary's freshman year, when she met a Harvard junior named Geoffrey Shields. While students at more adventuresome colleges were jumping onto whatever ideological or romantic bus was passing by, Hillary chose her path slowly and deliberately. Her first boyfriend came from a Chicago suburb only a couple of bus stops away from the Rodham home in conservative Park Ridge.

Shields describes their less-than-passionate romance: "I thought she was attractive, interesting to talk to, and she was a good dancer. We spent a lot of time with small groups of friends, primarily my friends at Harvard, talking about political issues."[21]

This was a kind of "wonk group," recalls classmate Betsy Griffith: "This wasn't gossip about boys, it was how to solve the problems of the world."[22] Griffith later became an unabashed feminist and is now headmistress of the Madeira School outside Washington, D.C.

Hillary's Harvard boyfriend fell in love with her earnestness. "The thing that I remember most were the conversations," Shields told me.[23] Their dates would often start with a party at Shields's residence, Winthrop House, where they would dance to Elvis Presley and the amazing new rock-'n'-roll group from England, the Beatles. "But Hillary would rather sit around and talk about current events or politics or ideas than go to any party or football game."[24] She really lit up when a heated debate got started, especially if it concerned issues that had a practical impact on the world: racial issues, the Vietnam War, civil rights. One of Shields's roommates was a black man who was very active in racial politics. The wonk group spent a fair amount of time discussing integration.

"For both Hillary and me, it was a time of awakening," remembers Shields. But Hillary remained the absolutist. Shields, who today is a lawyer with an old-line Chicago firm, did recall an interesting debate with Hillary about whether there was an absolute or only a relative morality: "She was very much into debating the basis for moral decisions."

And she believed fervently in Acting. Peavoy wrote to tell her that he had selected the role of "observer." She challenged him: How could anyone prefer *reacting* to acting? It bored her intolerably to just sit and watch. (That's why she took a book whenever she was dragged to a football game.)

She used an analogy to advance her argument: the show would go on whether or not he took part, she argued, so he might as well be there. She quoted from *Dr. Zhivago:* "Man is born to live, not to prepare for life."[25]

When the tryouts for the Wellesley production of Edward Albee's play *Who's Afraid of Virginia Woolf?* were opened, Hillary showed up. To her surprise, when the callbacks were announced she made the cut. Just trying out for a play was exciting. The girls she was competing with were nervous wrecks. Hillary sat in the darkened theater writing a letter to Peavoy and admitted feeling a smidgeon of guilt, knowing how others would kill for the role of Martha when she couldn't have cared less. But she couldn't help herself. If there was a game, she had to compete.

And there was one other potential bonus: imagine what Hugh Rodham would think of his daughter playing the ballsy, foul-mouthed Martha. Delicious! He would probably deny she was even his daughter. She daydreamed about her gruff father turning up for Sophomore Father's Day and wrote, "Oh, what an experience awaits those girls who cross his path."[26] But for all her daydreams, she didn't get the part.

She and Peavoy made tentative plans to meet in New York City over the winter break. But the Park Ridge parents situation, as she called it, was not improving. New York! Too dangerous, too expensive, too tiring—their daughter running wild in the streets of Sin City?—they wouldn't hear of it. Not even when she offered to pay for the trip herself.

"So, I'm stuck." It was a rare admission for Hillary Rodham.[27]

A year later, unbeknownst to Rodham's parents, their daughter left the confines of Wellesley and went off for a party weekend at Dartmouth, where she met a boy and stayed overnight in Hanover. She was so proud of this filial misdemeanor that she reported it to Peavoy. And that Monday morning she simply couldn't drag herself out of bed to go to Bible class.[28] Despite her protestations to the contrary, Hillary was beginning to change.

CHOOSING AN IDENTITY

Although her friends emphasize that she has a good sense of humor and can laugh at herself, probably nobody in her class was more consistently serious about her aspirations than Hillary. Her first order of business was to choose an identity. That's right, choose. Over Christmas vacation in her sophomore year, by her own count, she went through no fewer than "three-and-a-half metamorphoses." Hillary Rodham was fully conscious of selecting her preferred personality from a "smorgasbord" spread before her:

"educational and social reformer, alienated academic, involved pseudo-hippie," political leader, or "compassionate misanthrope."[29] Looking at herself quite clinically in her letters to Peavoy, she considered them one by one:

Educational and social reformer. Students were already looking to her to set the tone and give the marching orders for their class, as well as to help them focus in the fog of conflicted feelings that enveloped most freshmen.

By sophomore year Hillary's charisma was strong enough to attract a half-dozen girls to move into the Gothic dorm Stone Davis to be near her. She lived with four roommates and a glorious view of Lake Waban. The inhabitants of Stone Davis all ate together in a stone-and-glass gazebo. Fresh-cut flowers adorned the tables. This cloistered setting was ideal for getting to know fellow dormmates and developing what would later come to be known as "sisterhood." Jan Piercey, one of Hillary's acolytes in the dorm, says of their all-female environment, "You were surrounded by role models. We came away just assuming that everyone had serious aspirations."[30]

Hillary took it as her responsibility to learn more about "Negroes." Before the end of her first month at school, she went out of her way to invite a black student to go with her to Sunday church services. Even in a place as self-righteously egalitarian as the Boston area in the 1960s, it was an act of some daring. Coming out of the church service, she telephoned a few people close to her back in Park Ridge and told them what she had done. They chided her for what they construed as a political act. Don Jones recalls a letter in which Hillary described the scolding: "They thought she did this not out of goodwill but as a symbolic gesture to a lily-white church."[31]

Possibly she remembered the charge made by Dr. King when he had spoken in Chicago: that the 11 A.M. Sunday worship service was the most segregated hour of the week. She acknowledged that, a year before, if she had seen someone doing what she had done, her reaction would have been "Look how liberal that girl is trying to be, going to church with a Negro." But her real motive in taking her Negro friend to church, she said, was to test herself as much as she was testing the church. Of the more than four hundred students in her class at Wellesley, who were predominantly upper-middle-class WASPs, only six were black. There were no black faculty members. Hillary would eventually become a political ally of the black students on campus, but initially, says schoolmate Karen Williamson, "she was just a friend. All the black students in our class felt we had a very close friend in Hillary."[32]

Yet she still seemed strangely removed from the momentous events of her generation. In January 1965, two years after Hillary had met one of the greatest black leaders of her century, Martin Luther King and his non-violent armies had stepped up their offensive against segregation in the South. Preacher-leaders from Dr. King's organization and "sit-in kids" from SNCC (Student Non-Violent Coordinating Committee) went to Selma, Alabama, and took turns leading mostly elderly and poor black women to the courthouse to register to vote. The sheriff, brandishing a cattle prod, smashed the head of a student leader. The incident was featured that night on national television—a shocking new sort of image.

Rodham wrote from college to Don Jones, voicing her support for civil rights but objecting to the "extremism" of SNCC. She worked at learning about blacks and urban issues in her customary fashion: taking it all in cerebrally rather than experientially. She would be one of the first Wellesley students to enroll in a new urban sociology class in the fall of 1967. The instructor, Steve London, remembers her as one of a fairly small number of students "who consistently and continuously demonstrated a very real concern with the nature of race relations."[33]

"Alienated academic." This was another identity she considered. She was a grind, no question about that. In a letter to Don Jones she talked about being the "good student" who spent her days and nights in the library. She dismissed the role of socialite and partygoer. She said she was having fun but then added a significant qualification: "as outrageous as a moral Methodist can get."[34]

Her heroes were scholars. And she often felt alienated or depressed by the imperfections of mankind. Hillary spent much of the summer of her sophomore year in an isolated little cottage on the shore of Lake Michigan, where she worked as a researcher and editor for political science professor Anthony D'Amato. He had been asked to leave Wellesley for being a dissident. She worshiped him. As she enumerated at length, the scholar had a law degree from Harvard and would soon earn his Ph.D. from Columbia, plus he had his own law firm and a new corporation. She also claimed, hyperbolically, that Professor D'Amato had published more than any man in the world of his age.[35]

D'Amato was "obsessed" with the cutting-edge behavioral research then going on at the University of Michigan, Ann Arbor. He turned Hillary on to books such as *In the Human Grain*, published that year by Jesuit polymath Walter J. Ong, who was both a student of and an influence on the media guru of the Sixties, Marshall McLuhan.[36] Both Ong and McLuhan were revolutionary theorists as well as Catholics. Ong's book argued that our consciousness was being reshaped by television, stereos, and computers. Before McLuhan had published *Understanding Media* or his celebrated *The Medium Is the Message,* Ong was pointing out that electronic channels of expression and transmission were restructuring our psyches and the whole mental universe. He wrote about the creation of the "global village" of instant telecommunication and how it would undermine the artificial security of print and make it possible to stage the kind of "electronic town meeting" that Bill Clinton would later use to such potent political effect. Hillary thought Ong's book was one of the most important she had ever read.

Professor D'Amato also had Hillary read *The Behavioral Persuasion in Politics,* by Heinz Eulau, which challenged the leftist assertion that "all teaching is political" as a platitudinous slogan: "Despite all human weaknesses and failings, the world of scholarship and teaching is not identical with the world of politics and its partisans and propagandists."[37] D'Amato indoctrinated his protégée in the belief that facts are the only tools for reaching the truth; subjective judgments must be ruled out. It was the classic male scientific rationalist's way of perceiving the world and must have felt familiarly like the boot-camp model of life inculcated by Hillary's father. This would have further alienated her from the intuitive feelings and insights that her mother and father discouraged. That kind of intelligence would be affirmed only five years later by the research and writing of Harvard professor Carol Gilligan as "a woman's way of knowing" and still later by Daniel Goleman as "emotional intelligence."

Enveloping herself in bookish pursuits and the contemplative atmosphere of long, wet, windy walks along the lake, Hillary enjoyed an Emily Brontë–ish summer. She was often alone but never complained of being lonely.

"Involved pseudohippie." This was another of the identities Hillary tried on. She dressed the part, but not because she was wedded to anything as weakminded as the flower-child philosophy. It just made it easier for her to be utterly unconcerned about her appearance.

The first evidence of her awareness of the psychedelic culture exploding in the mid-Sixties came with her breathless anticipation of attending the offbeat wedding of an artist friend in June 1967. The bride intended to screen-print her own gown and also to paint a tie for her beloved, who planned to wrap his hair in a wreath of flowers. The couple wanted to be married on the bride's family beach at Cape Cod, but there the parents drew the line—a wedding had to take place in a church. But afterward, Hillary and her Harvard boyfriend and the gaggle of guests had a ball parading from the church to the beach behind Harvard's Marching Schneider's Band. "Fantastic," Hillary exclaimed.

Back home in Park Ridge, the gossipy mother of a classmate started a rumor that Hillary was engaged. When Peavoy opened her next letter, written a day after the wedding, he laughed. It was so out of character for Hillary, he wondered what she was smoking:

> John:
> No—I am not engaged. I am married. Seriously, though, I'm only living in "sin" for the Summer.[38]

She went on to say that the "groovy truth" was that she had dropped out of college and was on the road to Haight-Ashbury with a bunch of hippie friends and their love children. She and her commune planned to show up in Park Ridge in a few weeks to stage a love-in on a Sunday afternoon. She told Peavoy to tell everyone or, better yet, post her letter on the church bulletin board.

It was a spoof letter meant to shock. In reality, "hippie" was the antithesis of Hillary Rodham. Always conscious of the rules, she never colored outside the lines. Even her letters were graphic evidence of her strict containment. She always filled the page from side to side, top to bottom, with perfect margins. If the writing paper had even a faint design, she always wrote around it. And her third-grade penmanship teacher would have been proud. The letters rolled like perfect little boats upon the waves. Her "love-in" letter was different. Printed. The *a*'s were formed like a typewritten *a*, as if by a correspondent making the most extreme effort to keep control. Even on a summer idyll it was not easy for Hillary to let go.

Political leader. She had already decided there were only three things worth doing at Wellesley: being appointed a Vil Junior (an honorary post), being elected to the student senate, and being elected student government president.[39] She had made Vil Junior, but no sooner had she been endorsed by the school paper for the student senate than she questioned herself: Why? She enjoyed winning elections as tangible proof of respect. But did she really want to expose herself to the life of the public personality?[40]

Wellesley not only offered Hillary an opportunity to effect change, it also offered her a chance to become an important figure on campus. "Recognition was important to her," recalls Geoff Shields.[41] The sting of her electoral defeat for senior class president in high school was still raw. And so deliberately, step by step, she laid the political groundwork to be ensured of winning the highest post at Wellesley: president of the student government.

No campus issue was too large or too small for Hillary. First, she worked to banish mandatory prayer in the dining hall. She pushed for a pass-fail grading option. She gently squeezed the administration to relax rigid course requirements that she believed stifled creative thinking. She campaigned to increase the number of black students and faculty members. She challenged parietal rules that decreed girls had to be home from dates by eleven on weeknights and that stopped male visitors at the door for a virginal kiss good night. And before she left Wellesley, she was successful in almost all of her efforts.

"She was very organized and articulate and goal-oriented," says Alan Schecter, her political science professor, who also oversaw the student government. "She knew what she wanted to accomplish and how to go about doing it. She was smart enough, in terms of organizing, and had no reluctance about asking 'How do I get X done?' "[42]

One of her cohorts was Ann Sherwood Sentilles. As managing editor of the *Wellesley News*, Ann often tackled issues from a different point of view than Hillary and other student government types did. Hillary would take Ann with her to talk to the university president, prepping her before the meeting and working her over afterward. "When it was all said and done, you'd look back on it and say, 'Oh. Hillary used me to get this done,' " says Sentilles. "And yet she had a wonderful way of doing that. She didn't use you and leave you in shreds, like many other people I've worked with. She did not make you feel like a pawn. It was an empowering process." Thinking back on each such encounter, Ann would say to herself, "Wow. Wasn't she smart? She's quite good at what she does."[43]

But not good enough for Hillary. In the middle of her sophomore year she told Peavoy, "I have not yet reconciled myself to the state of not being the star."[44]

"Hillary had a particular charisma," says classmate Nancy Gist. "Her ability to focus and her maturity made her stand out even in a place full of very, very talented women." Only rarely at Wellesley did Hillary herself talk about the possibility of running for public office. "Other people around her talked about it on her behalf," says Jan Piercey. Karen Williamson remembers that a lot of her classmates thought that if ever in their lifetime a woman became president, they knew who it would be. It would be Hillary Rodham.[45]

Misanthrope or Catcher in the Rye? Another identity she considered was one devoted to "withdrawn simplicity." The childhood fantasy of being the little girl in the sunshine, the only person in the universe, hung on. Her fantasy of the simple life took the form of retreating to a mountaintop with a basket full of books to lie in a field of flowers reading in the sunshine.[46]

When she was a sophomore in high school, Don Jones had given her what he thought was the perfect book, *The Catcher in the Rye.* He thought J. D. Salinger captured the sense of alienation abroad in our culture, and he saw Holden Caulfield as a kind of secular saint. Jones loved the novel.

Hillary hated it.[47]

She made that confession only after rereading the book at the end of her freshman year of college. It was her first—and last—boring summer back in Park Ridge, where she was stuck at the South Park Recreation Center, again guarding the kiddies at the wading pool. "I was probably not ready for it" on the first reading, she told her former youth minister. "But now I think I know why you gave it to me." She added that Holden reminded her very much of her brother Hughie. Both had a reverence for humanity and a sensitivity toward others.

"I do think that's a side of Dorothy that was passed on to Hugh and to Hillary—this concern for the disadvantaged and for helping others," says Jones. As Holden tells his sister in the novel, "You know what I'd like to be? I mean if I had my goddam choice?" Old Phoebe recalls for him the Robert Burns poem that begins "If a body meet a body coming through the rye." Holden pictures himself standing on the edge of a cliff while thousands of little kids run around in a field of rye, not looking where they are going. It is up to him to catch them before they go over the cliff. "That's all I'd do all day. I'd just be the catcher in the rye and all."[48]

Jones heard Hillary say more than once, "We're all here to help someone else." Noting her earliest intellectual mission, to save defenseless children, he came to the conclusion that being a Catcher in the Rye would be Hillary's vocation. Later, he was not so sure.[49]

Indeed, there was a deeply contradictory streak in this complex young woman. For all her exaggerated sense of responsibility for others less fortunate, she really didn't like people all that much. Well, she liked some people.

Exceptionally smart people, such as John Peavoy and Arthur Curtis and Don Jones. Maybe, she considered, she was innately a misanthrope—a hater of mankind.

"Can you be a misanthrope and still love or enjoy some individuals?" she asked. "How about a *compassionate* misanthrope?"[50] Compassion, she noted, was an important word in her reformer stage—a stage that in the spring of her second year of college she was already referring to in the past tense.

"My February Depression"

Hillary's identity crisis went on for four years. She frequently found the process of self-definition depressing. The fear beneath all her intellectualizing and organizing was that she might discover a void. Let's change the subject! Otherwise those damned inevitable questions kept resurfacing: *Why am I so afraid? Or why am I not afraid? Am I really not unique after all? Will I live a clichéd life? Is life merely absurd?* How do you define "happiness" operationally? she asked Peavoy.[51] She always set off "happiness" in quotes.

Happy, for Hillary, equaled getting A's, doing good deeds, and running for something. Or did it? In February 1967 she made an A in economics and an A+ in political science and turned in a good paper; she had gone skiing, met a new boy, and started tutoring in Cambridge—"a beautiful little seven-year-old Negro girl." But for all that perfection, she had sunk into "my February depression."[52]

She could hardly get out of bed. She was cutting classes, falling asleep in Bible class, and disappointing her professors, she feared, but everything was too much effort. So she sat alone in her room and thought. But "thinking is a dangerous thing for me," she admitted. If her mind was focused narrowly on some issue or idea—something abstract and challenging enough—fine. But random thinking usually led her straight back to the same frighteningly uncontrollable place: looking inside. And once she slipped into self-analysis, she found "my ego coming out on the short end."[53] The easiest way to avoid all that, she discovered, was to turn her attention to advising others on how to live *their* lives and thereby halt any thoughts approaching introspection. This became a lifelong pattern.

Peavoy wrote to Hillary describing the depression he had felt, coming from a "sheltered suburban life," when he had been confronted with the grim realities of city life on his holiday visit to New York. She commiserated, having visited Chicago's Loop on her vacation and returned to Park

Ridge with "my usual big-city depression."[54] She complained that Wellesley was almost as "unrealistic" an environment as Park Ridge. Even after having walked through the slums of Boston and worked in Chicago, she still didn't believe she had touched "reality." In the mind of this idealistic sophomore, the ultimate reality was far away in some African village on the equator where life is a day-to-day struggle for survival.[55]

THE "RADICALIZATION" OF HILLARY RODHAM

In 1968, Joan Didion famously quoted Yeats: "The center was not holding." Even Hillary the "moral Methodist" ran up against Sixties radicalism. Over Christmas vacation she had felt so alienated from Park Ridge and her parents' home and "the entire unreality of middle-class America" that she had to admit her perspective was shifting.[56] She had begun referring to herself as an "agnostic intellectual liberal" and "an emotional conservative."[57] The head was being further separated from the heart. But not without self-doubts. When she used the irreligious abbreviation for Christmas, "Xmas," it gave her pangs of guilt. She told Peavoy she felt even further apart from her father, although her mother seemed to be becoming more aware and tolerant. But with the Vietnam War raging and scenes of America's turmoil-ridden ghettos becoming unavoidable, she was coming to think that "the whole society was brittle."[58] Hillary's response was to work toward change by keeping her peers in line as they protested the status quo.

In her senior year, her letters became more and more ponderous and existential. In a midnight epistle to Peavoy she described the dilemma of how to deal with Wellesley's idealistic honor system. Since the college's library had lost $100,000 worth of books, Hillary saw the honor system as a farce. She favored door checks, including turning in those who were guilty of breaking rules. To Peavoy she posed a rhetorical question: "Is there really a place for situational ethics in such a setting as Wellesley?" It was a particularly revealing dilemma for a woman of absolutist ethics who would later marry a man one might call "Mr. Situational Ethics." Even then Hillary described it as a "quandaric problem." That was a word she had made up, a more esoteric way of saying "quandary"—a dilemma as to what to do—*a choice.*[59]

By her senior year she had "played around" with psychology (which she found dull), sociology, philosophy, and geology ("How excited can one get about rocks?").[60] French was her Achilles' heel, yet she stuck with it. She found reading Greek literature a glorious waste of time. No two ways about it: despite her disdain for political science as a major, she loved it. She did well in it. But could she hope to capture one of the few hundred jobs available to the thousands of poli-sci majors who would be unleashed on Washington after graduation?

She never did get to New York for a big-city experience with John Peavoy. In fact, in their four years of college correspondence, she never actually saw him. She joked about saving his letters until *he* became famous, imploring him to forgive her mercenary instincts. In her final letter to him, dated March 25, 1969, she proudly described her pseudo-hippie costume: a work shirt that had never seen an iron flopped over dirty denim bell-bottoms, her head bonneted in a purple felt hat and a polka-dotted scarf floating Isadora Duncan style to her shoulders.

"My problem now is choice of lifestyle."

The old Wellesley tradition of hoop-rolling in May still rewarded the winner by designating her "first to marry." Would graduation take Hillary out of dirty bell-bottoms and put her into Pucci pants? she wondered. "Such decisions," she wrote, gently mocking herself, "we of the pleasure class must make."[61]

In her junior year she ran for the presidency of the student government. But this time, to avoid any repetition of the painful defeat she had suffered in high school, she spent three weeks going dorm to dorm "spouting the usual platitudes."[62] She still considered herself a Republican, which was not exactly congruent with the radical chic of the times. She admitted feeling like William Buckley, who would have asked for a recount if he had won in New York City.

Was politics even necessary? She and Peavoy clashed on that question. Peavoy told her he was inspired by individual relationships and favored less government and more individual liberty. Hillary politely scorned his view. Basically, she argued, "Man is a political man."[63] He is not capable, she felt, of either the selfless compassion that would make communism work or the commitment to self that would make the "I" philosophy of Ayn Rand practical in a real world, she told Peavoy. Finally, she dismissed her friend's faith in individual relationships; they certainly would not be capable of operating the huge bureaucracies of modern society or the complexities of international relations.[64]

In this ongoing debate Hillary revealed a view of humanity that was far more Hamiltonian than Jeffersonian: Mankind was born selfish and unruly and must be channeled and controlled. Politics was the means. She even admitted that she couldn't identify with the "faceless masses."[65] She sounded almost like a Tory—elitist, privileged, distrustful of the people. Her stance might have come straight out of Alexander Hamilton's *The Federalist* papers, the message of which was "No happiness without liberty, no liberty without self-government, no self-government without constitutionalism, no constitutionalism without morality—and none of these great goods without stability and order."[66]

Professor Alan Schecter was a man ten years her senior, like Don Jones, with whom she communicated more passionately than with most of her male peers. He spotted Hillary as a pragmatic leader who shunned extremism and seemed to get along well with students as well as the starchy administration. Schecter was aware of students who called themselves "radical" but who were radicalized not so much in a political sense as in a psychological one, feeling alienated from their family and society. "Hillary's role amidst all this was not really radical," Schecter notes. "It's what I call 'instrumental': What can we do about these problems in our society?"

Hillary and the other two candidates for president, Francille Rusan and Nonna Noto, staged a debate for the benefit of the *Wellesley News*. Rusan was one of Hillary's black friends and far more liberal than she. Hillary looked formidably serious in her black turtleneck and white sweater-vest. Unsmiling, un-made-up, with her thick black-framed glasses, she stated her opinions in an articulate and unemotional way. "Her ability to speak in full sentences and paragraphs with introductions and conclusions—a highly developed skill—was a skill she had then," says Dr. Schecter. As usual, she projected maturity well beyond her years.

The election was decided in February. "I can't believe what has just happened!" Hillary was jubilant as she took aside one of her professors to tell him the news. "I was just elected president of the government. Can you believe it? Can you believe that happened?"[67]

The adult president of Wellesley, Ruth Adams, was impressed with Hillary Rodham: "She was, as a number of her generation were, interested in effecting change, but from within rather than outside the system. They were not a group that wanted to go out and riot and burn things. They wanted to go to law school, get good degrees, and effect change from within." Indeed, Hillary had begun to think about applying to law school.[68]

But the world outside Wellesley was far more barbarous.

The Killing of the King

The *Aha!* moment—when a shock pulls the gauzy curtain off everyday existence and throws a sudden floodlight on what our lives are really about[69]—occurred for Hillary Rodham on an April evening in 1968. She burst into the room of Fran Rusan. BLAM! Flinging her book bag against the wall, Hillary screamed, "I can't believe this! I can't stand it anymore." She was yelling and crying and shaking. "I can't take it!"[70] Martin Luther King, Jr., had been gunned down in cold blood while addressing his followers from the balcony of a Memphis motel.

So much for stability and order.

The killing of King horrified Hillary, recalls Schecter. He knew that she had met Dr. King, but the professor had also been passionate in presenting the class's study of King's leadership in the fight for voting rights and community organizing for the poor. "Hillary also by then had good black friends, peers on campus—and she'd had no black friends growing up," he adds.[71] That night she called the head of the black student organization, Karen Williamson, to express her sorrow.[72]

After her *Aha!* moment Hillary developed the reputation of one who possessed sharp elbows. She became much more outspoken. When Wellesley students called for a two-day strike during the school week, an assembly was held at which Marshall Goldman, professor of Russian economics, held forth: "Let's give up the weekends, something that we enjoy. Don't give up classes—that's not a sacrifice." From the audience a brusque voice shot back, "I'll give up my date Saturday night, Mr. Goldman, but I don't think that's the point." Students turned to admire Rodham's boldness. "Individual consciences are fine," she continued, "but individual consciences have to be made manifest."[73]

Some were shocked at the way she challenged an esteemed professor. In class, too, Hillary could be cutting, recalls classmate Gale Lyon-Rosenberger. Her good friend and dormmate Jan Piercey acknowledges, "She is not someone who suffers fools gladly." Even her mother recognizes high-handedness as characteristic of her daughter. "Maybe she does get impatient once in a while when she's on a course and knows it's going to work. Maybe she needs to work on that. She simply doesn't have the time to walk people through everything," says Dorothy Rodham.[74]

Hillary and other students did eventually stage a two-day strike on campus a month after King's assassination. Hillary helped to organize workshops and teach-ins, but she later told the *Wellesley News* that she had been disappointed with the day's activities: "I didn't learn anything new, as far as the specific issues were concerned, although I did pick up some ideas."[75]

Always the instrumentalist.

By late spring Hillary was campaigning for Eugene McCarthy, the pied piper of antiwar students in the 1968 presidential race. Although President Johnson had soothed some of the agony by signing the Voting Rights Act a week after King's assassination, that same spring he was stepping up his commitment to the war in Vietnam. Before people had quite grasped the new level of violence both foreign and domestic, Senator Robert Kennedy was brutally murdered immediately after his triumphal win in the California presidential primary. "With the war and the assassinations, I think it bred a level of almost a desperate commitment on the part of many people in our class," says Eleanor Dean (Eldie) Acheson.[76]

By their senior year Eldie, the yellow dog Democrat, had become one of Hillary's cohorts. "The world was not progressing as we hoped it would," says Eldie. "We had to sound the alarm." An idea was born to petition the college president to have a student speaker at the graduation. It had to be somebody who was politically active. Hillary was the obvious choice. But Wellesley had never before entertained the idea of a student speaking at commencement. The administration had secured a black U.S. senator, liberal Republican Edward Brooke.

"We had months of battle with Ruth Adams," says Eldie. "Her fear was change. I was the big mouth. Trustees got into it." Ultimately, the granddaughter of Dean Acheson consulted her father, who was a great leverage politician. "We wore them down," remembers Eldie.[77]

By the time the great day came, Hillary had spent weeks preparing her remarks. She scribbled notes while Senator Brooke, the first black man elected to the U.S. Senate, tried to draw a distinction between the nonviolent tactics of the civil rights movement and the chaotic methods of some antiwar activists. "When protest becomes violent, you lose the effectiveness of your cause," he warned. Hillary rose to the platform and announced she wished to respond to some of Senator Brooke's points. A stiffening of apprehension rippled through the parental audience. She did not look particularly impressive, with hair straggling down from the bun tucked under her mortarboard. But she knew exactly the effect she wanted to create.

"We feel that for too long our leaders have used politics as the art of the possible," Hillary said. "And the challenge now is to practice politics as the art of making what appears to be impossible, possible." Then, using Senator Brooke as a foil, she cast herself as the progressive: "We feel that our prevailing acquisitive and competitive corporate life . . . is not the way of life for us. We're searching for more immediate, ecstatic modes of living."[78]

Still feeling the sting thirty years later, Senator Brooke told me, "She was to the right of me! I was a Rockefeller Republican and Hillary was a Goldwater Republican. She had an agenda, she knew what she wanted to say, and no matter what had gone before, she was determined to say it. I didn't see any spontaneity."

The electric effect was created not so much by Hillary's words as by her authoritative bearing. Some parents and administrators were appalled, but Rodham's classmates leapt to their feet, clapping and cheering, and jumping up and down in a thunderous seven-minute ovation.

It should have been the peak of pride for her father. But Hillary's father was competitive with his gifted daughter. Hugh Rodham had held the bar of achievement always higher than she could reach. The implied promise was that once she met his ideal, her reward would be the love, affection, and full approval he otherwise withheld. But as she had become more and more accomplished in her own right—without the benefit of her father's direction—he had withdrawn.

On this day, when his oldest child was being graduated from one of the top colleges in the country and making national history, Hugh Rodham was not seen hugging and congratulating his daughter. (A press spokesman for Hillary's Senate campaign later refuted this.) A dozen of her classmates were re-interviewed, including former college president Ruth Adams. None remembered seeing Hillary's father. Her cohort, Eldie Acheson, now a deputy attorney general, confirmed, "I never saw him in our whole four years at Wellesley."

A RING BY SPRING?

"In our view, we had transited from the 1950s to the 1970s in four years," says Eldie Acheson. "We were full of energy and very eager to get out there and *act*—to take the ideas of people like Bobby Kennedy and Martin Luther King of how America *should* be and make them a reality."[79] But to work within the system.

In the corridors of elite eastern colleges Hillary Rodham had already assured her recognition as a star. Her picture appeared in the June 1969 issue of *Life* magazine. (Prophetically, another star student featured in the issue was the man who would eventually share the fanfare and failure of the Clintons' attempt at health care reform: Ira Magaziner.) She had made many friends, won many constituents. But to them, as to herself, the real Hillary was still largely unrevealed.

When she and her classmates had entered college, black Americans were still called "Negroes" or "colored," women were still called "girls," and even those women with superlative college educations such as Wellesley girls were expected by graduation to produce—not plans to become lawyers or doctors or writers or artists or business or political leaders—but "a ring by spring."

In spite of all her precocious political activity, Hillary was not immune to the prevailing social expectations. In fact, she was spooked by the worry that she might have to settle for the stereotypical marriage to a U.S. congressman or senator: "Of course, when I live in Suburbia with my commuter husband and 2.5 children, there is always PTA, the Junior League and other distinguished ventures in which I could indulge," she wrote caustically to Peavoy. She pictured herself entertaining at her bridge table other nice Seven Sisters graduates who also would be throwing away their fine educations. But even as she mocked that distorted picture, she did not turn it to the wall.[80]

She preferred to gaze at Life in the Future through a kaleidoscope of different and endlessly possible patterns, never choosing for fear the next creation might be even more beautiful. But the moment she tried to grasp at an appealing design, the brightly colored glass chips of her imagination shattered.

A strong inner sense of her own identity had not yet gelled. Her father never seemed to grasp who she was or what she was about. "He never gave Hillary a sense of self-respect," says Nancy Pietrefesa, a close friend of Hillary's in their twenties. "Her father was always a kind of downer guy. And her mother just fluttered by." Hillary often commented with envy on how Nancy's father was so interested in his children and obviously loved them so much. By contrast, Hillary had to be the problem-solver for her family.[81] As a loner by temperament, Hillary felt backed into a corner by family and friends who constantly barged in and demanded she solve their problems. And because she was so good at handling other people's dilemmas, she was aware of "completely defaulting on my own."

Most intelligent people in their college years go through similar surges of idealism and depths of self-doubt and concoct grand dreams, but they don't necessarily follow through. Many drift into conformity. Consider how often class presidents go no further in real life than becoming president of the local bank or Junior League. For Hillary, her college years were not just a utopian phase where she was at liberty to explore herself and the world. This was where she first found the identity that would guide her life, although she would have periodic lapses of certainty and phases of rediscovery. Her choices would never be simple or consistent.

As the cheers of jubilation for her speech died down and the last hugs of farewell were exchanged, one friend lingered to tell Hillary she would have felt lost without her. Allowing herself a rare moment of introspection, Hillary Rodham reflected on the dependence she had engendered in others. "I could spend my life worrying about other people or the state of the world," she told Peavoy prophetically. It was a noble sublimation. As long as she could bury her own problems in solving the problems of the world, she would not be forced to reveal her innermost self. There was just one thing left out, and she noted it almost in a stage whisper:

"I wonder who is me. I wonder if I'll ever meet her. If I did, I think we'd get along famously."[82]

CHAPTER FOUR

First Love

"It was an intense love affair—they were two strong personalities who met in an overheated political climate, right at the time Hillary was mutating."

—NANCY PIETREFESA

She was wearing a jumpsuit. A silver lamé jumpsuit. It was hilariously inappropriate. All she was doing was driving to Boston's Logan Airport with two other women to pick up a man who was flying up from Georgetown, but this was a special man—a ruthlessly handsome "black Irishman" with dark eyes that he used to his advantage. He would become her first real love.

David Rupert was a government major at Georgetown University, a classmate of Bill Clinton, although Hillary had not yet met big Bill. Rupert says he was 150 pounds of pulsing hormones.[1] Their relationship was a tempestuous one.[2] She kept it secret from some of the people in her life; neither John Peavoy nor Don Jones knew a thing about it. Nor has Hillary's love affair with Rupert—pre-B.C.—ever surfaced in all the articles and books written about her.

The pair had met in Washington in the summer of her junior year, 1968, as two ambitious interns on the make—politically, not romantically.

Each year ten girls chosen from Wellesley packed their best suits and headed to the nation's capital to share a house at George Washington University with ten girls chosen from Vassar, all vying for the best intern jobs on the Hill. The responsibility for finding positions alternated each year between the two women's colleges. The summer of 1968 was Wellesley's year, and Hillary was, of course, the head of the Wellesley delegation. The head of the Vassar delegation, Leslie Friedman, sent her a letter suggesting they hold a social for the girls in the house. Hillary wrote back, "We didn't come to Washington to waste our time having tea with silly college girls."[3] The politics of dorm life was of no use to Hillary; she had national politics on her mind.

Rodham and Rupert attended a mixer for the new tribe of summer political wannabes on Capitol Hill. "There's a lot of interns, and you're working the crowd to see what you can do," recalls Rupert, when suddenly these two whip-smart high-tension activists ran into each other.

She asked whom he was working for.

"Charlie Goodell. Congressman from New York. Liberal Republican. He'll take Bobby's seat in the Senate this fall, you watch," boasted Rupert. (Senator Robert Kennedy's seat was still vacant after his assassination in June 1968.)

Hillary told him she was working for the Republicans, too, for the House Republican Conference. Rupert countered: he was Goodell's legislative assistant. Well, Hillary was working for the *head* of the conference. She had been assigned a prime spot as one of thirty interns working under the chairman, Mel Laird, a congressman from Wisconsin.

How had she managed to get that job? he wanted to know.

She was president of the Young Republican Club at Wellesley. Of course, she added loftily, party politics in college was a farce.

"Sounds like a chameleon act to help yourself get a job," he parried. Rupert was every bit as abrasive and competitive as Rodham. By the time they had drifted into a Georgetown nightspot and drunk some beer and argued about the war, Rupert wound up challenging Rodham in a way no peer had before:

"You're not a Republican. That's a bunch of crap. Why are you playing that game?"

She laughed it off. Aretha Franklin was belting out "Chain of Fools" from the jukebox.

"You're either a conservative Democrat or a Rockefeller Republican," he pushed her.

She was noncommittal. Then she one-upped him. She told him she was working on a speech for Laird. It was about Vietnam.

"That's bullshit," he said. "You're against the war."

So, maybe Laird wasn't a total hawk either, she suggested.

Rupert liked her spunk. "I thought she was attractive. I wasn't knocked over by her, like 'There's a knockout,' but that's not what makes me go anyway. She did have those big ugly glasses. The hair was pulled back. I don't remember any mascara. What I found attractive was the mix of her character, her intellect, and a physical attraction. And we laughed."[4]

"It was an intense love affair—they were two strong personalities who met in an overheated political climate, right at the time that Hillary was mutating," observes Nancy "Peach" Pietrefesa, a community activist who became a running buddy of Hillary's. "Hillary was always attracted to arrogant, sneering, hard-to-please men, like her father."[5] Rupert and Rodham dated for three years, right up through her second year at law school.

Melvin Laird, who later served as President Nixon's secretary of defense, remembers Hillary as a very active member of his intern group. "She was very, very bright, very dedicated."[6] She did indeed work on two major speeches for him, one of which, "Fight Now, Pay Later," was critical of the way the Vietnam War was being escalated without sufficient concern for its costs. When the appropriations bill for the Department of Defense came up, Laird used the speech on the floor of the House to demand funds to replace destroyed aircraft and weapons: "If we want the United States to be as strong as it was in 1964, this Congress can take no other action."[7]

In an interview later given by First Lady Hillary Rodham Clinton to mark the opening of the Melvin R. Laird Center for medical research in Marshfield, Wisconsin, Hillary spoke of how wonderful it had been to work for Laird. "It's essential in democracy that people who are in public life conduct themselves in a way that engenders the trust and faith of their constituents," she said. She complimented Laird on being a man who was "willing to engage in a back and forth with a kid who was only moderately well informed. . . . But at least he took me seriously." What had most impressed her about him, she said, was how fairly and respectfully he treated his young interns: "I have pretty good antennae for people who are chauvinistic or sexist or patronizing toward women."[8]

(Hillary made those remarks in an interview conducted, almost surreally, three days after President Clinton's deposition in the Paula Jones sexual harassment case. The next day the allegations broke concerning how Clinton had treated his own intern Monica Lewinsky.)

THE REVOLUTION IS US!

In the summer of 1968, when national political conventions were still high drama, Hillary went to Miami for the Republican National Convention. She was working as an assistant to Laird and hoped to see Nelson Rockefeller nominated as the GOP presidential candidate. To her, the governor of New York represented the moderate Republicanism she had come to favor; she also felt he was strong concerning issues of poverty. And one more thing: her father was a fervent supporter of Nixon.

It was a deep disappointment for her to witness the victory on August 8, 1968, of Richard Milhous Nixon. Who would have imagined that exactly six years later, on August 8, 1974, President Richard Nixon would resign in disgrace and Hillary Rodham would take pride in having played a small part in his demise?

Within weeks of her return to Park Ridge from the decorous Republican convention, Hillary saw on television the ominous buildup of tensions outside the Democratic National Convention in Chicago. Shaggy-haired student protesters goaded on by Tom Hayden, Jerry Rubin, and Abbie Hoffman were gathering in Lincoln Park to protest the war and a business-as-usual Democratic convention. She and a prim and proper high school friend, Betsy Johnson, decided to drive into Chicago, not to participate but to "observe." Both of their mothers ordered them not to go. The young women fibbed and said they were going to see a movie.

What they saw was students like themselves chanting the name of the North Vietnamese Communist leader, "Ho ho, Ho Chi Minh," in the faces of infuriated police, who were being jeered at as "pigs." TV cameramen, tipped off by Hayden that there would be a clash worth covering, turned their cameras on the student protestors, who, as if on cue, began chanting "The whole world is watching." When someone threw a beer can, it had the effect of a grenade. Police charged into the students, beating them with clubs and fists and dragging off some of the protestors, who had been trained to go limp as rags.

"We saw kids our age getting their heads beaten in," Betsy Johnson has frequently said of their experience. "And the police were doing the beating. Hillary and I just looked at each other. We had had a wonderful childhood in Park Ridge, but we obviously hadn't gotten the whole story."[9] For Hillary, it was proof of a transformation that she had taken in only theoretically from her studies of Ong and McLuhan. Now she was seeing in flesh and blood how the country's political consciousness would be reshaped by the clever manipulation of television.

Hillary returned to Wellesley that fall all fired up. Following on the heels of the Poor People's March on Washington during the summer, her senior year was to see a wave of student strikes and teach-ins sweep across the country. With her thesis adviser, Alan Schecter, she was direct: "I want to write my thesis on some aspect of the poverty programs of the Great Society."

"Well," said the liberal professor drolly, "you're not a Republican if you're going to write about the poverty program. It sounds like you're interested in the problem of poverty—not interested in the stock exchange or making money or the ideology of lower taxation." Once again, Hillary was noncommittal. She told Schecter that she had met the legendary political organizer Saul Alinsky that summer in Chicago. His reputation as a leftist organizer went back to the 1950s, when he had championed white ethnics against Chicago's landlords and big-business elite. By the mid-1960s, Alinsky was already very influential in teaching "the science of revolution" to the new generation of student activists (three years later he would publish *Rules for Radicals*). Using examples such as rent strikes and dumping garbage on the doorsteps of politicians, he argued that the best way to get action was to incite fear or rage in the opposition—or "mass ju-jitsu" as he called it. The Alinsky motto that found a ready ear in radical students was "Whatever works to get power to the people, use it." With the birth of the Black Power movement, "Power to the People" would soon be adopted as a rallying cry.

Hillary told her adviser that she was very interested in one of the great theories that Bobby Kennedy had espoused: "maximum feasible participation of the poor" in programs designed to help them. The basis of the theory, she explained, was Kennedy's belief that the difference between poor people and "the rest of us" is that we have control over our lives, but poor people have always been victims. What would help people rise from poverty and become effective citizens was to empower them. The burning question for her was how to do research into Kennedy's theory, how to write anything original.

"Look, you met Alinsky, why don't you lean on that?" Schecter suggested. "Why don't you study community organizing and the participation of the poor in Chicago through the Alinsky community?"

With her usual discipline and goal-directedness, Hillary did a thorough investigation of the Community Action Program in Chicago (CAP). It channeled federal money to states and local communities to help organize the poor politically. Hillary discovered in her research that Alinsky thought the CAP was a "prize piece of political pornography."[10] As she developed her thesis, she too became critical of the CAP's notion of participation by the poor. What happens in reality, she told Schecter, is that people would rise to positions of leadership within the poor community and then clash with one another. She observed that, as the black community on Chicago's South Side began to get organized, the white ethnics, who had already been activated, began to fight for the same poverty dollars.

Hillary's thesis, "Aspect of the War on Poverty," has been sealed away by the Wellesley administration. After Bill Clinton was inaugurated, Wellesley issued an edict: "The undergraduate thesis of any Wellesley graduate or alumna who is or becomes either the President or First Lady of the United States will not be made public." (There has been only one graduate of the college to whom this ban on freedom of information applies.) Alan Schecter, however, characterizes Hillary's conclusion: "The bottom line of her thinking was that community action programs could have short-term effects, but to have any long-term impact on the core problems you needed to have structure, organization, leadership, and a middle class willing to get involved." Hillary's adviser was pleased with his student's more complex and rounded viewpoint of Kennedy's "naive and idealistic" theory. It was a conclusion that indicated, once again, her pragmatic nature. "She was able to take a liberal program and analyze it pragmatically to determine whether it worked," says Schecter.[11] (Just as she would later do in analyzing liberal welfare policies and determining they did not work.)

She won from Schecter not only an A+ but also a glowing recommendation for law school; he secretly hoped that Hillary would become the first of his students to sit on the U.S. Supreme Court. "She is by far the most outstanding young woman I have taught in the past seven years at Wellesley College," he wrote. "Her papers are brilliantly executed, and I have learned from them myself. . . . She has the intellectual ability, personality, and character to make a remarkable contribution to American society."[12]

No such accolades were forthcoming from her father. "He showed no pride in Hillary's accomplishments," says her best friend in those years, Peach Pietrefesa. "He was not invested in her. His self-concept was fragile enough that Hillary's growing capacities were a threat to him."[13]

Through the spring of her senior year at Wellesley Hillary remained undecided about the direction of her life afterward. She did apply to Yale and Harvard Law Schools, and, as a fallback, she applied for a Fulbright Scholarship to India. On top of that, she was offered a paying job as a trainee in community organizing by Saul Alinsky himself. He spotted in her that rare concatenation of true believer and tough pragmatist.[14]

"It was a calculated decision on her part to go to law school," says Schecter, "to be more effective in terms of social change." Both Harvard and Yale accepted her. Schecter told her, "If you're going to put your shoulder to the wheel of how progress is defined in the future, you would be far more effective with a Yale law degree than if you were a community organizer." He also told her she didn't have to become a corporate lawyer, she could be a lawyer with the purpose of public service. She took in his argument.

Alinsky didn't mince words when Hillary turned him down in favor of studying to become one of a species he ridiculed: liberal lawyers. She remembers him saying to her, "Well, that's no way to change anything." At the age of twenty-one, Hillary already had the self-possession to hold her own against a powerful male mentor whom she admired. "Well, I see a different way than you," she told Alinsky. "And I think there is a real opportunity."[15]

An exploratory visit to Harvard quickly soured her on that school as a choice. A friend of hers who attended Harvard Law School introduced her to a distinguished older law professor. Her friend told the professor, "She's trying to decide whether to come here next year or attend our closest competitor."

Hillary later recalled the sorry end of the encounter: "This tall, rather imposing professor, sort of like a character from *The Paper Chase*, looked down at me and said, 'Well, first of all, we don't have any close competitors. Secondly, we don't need any more women.' That's what made my decision. I was leaning toward Yale anyway, but that fellow's comments iced the cake."[16]

By April 1969, she was enthusiastic about becoming one of about forty women in an unusually large group—204 students—admitted to the Yale Law School Class of '72. Many of them, like Hillary, had turned down Harvard in favor of its closest competitor.

What was to become of her romance with David Rupert? They had suffered pangs of loneliness as long-distance college sweethearts throughout their senior year. But Rupert discovered something unexpected about Hillary: get her away on a weekend, and she could be playful. He vaguely remembers them joining a march on Washington and spending the weekend there together. "Some of us were inhaling," he says with a you-know-what-I-mean smirk. The obvious question is, did Hillary inhale too? "I don't have to go there," says Rupert, "but you can read between the lines." He describes the young Hillary as never wild and frivolous, but she did have a passionate side: "Absolutely." He is very matter-of-fact about their relationship.

"We always used birth control," offers Rupert. "Abstinence is the absolute remedy here, but a fear of getting pregnant did not deter us in our relationship." He often stayed over with Hillary in the suite she shared with three roommates at Wellesley and knew her roommates well. He and Hillary traveled together to Kansas to attend the wedding of Jan Craigbaum, and on the drive back they stopped by Park Ridge. Hillary introduced Rupert to her parents as "my boyfriend."

"But there was never any formalized commitment," he says. "Neither one of us pressed for that." From comments Hillary made, Rupert was well aware that his girlfriend was seeing a couple of other people. "It was clear from her to me, and from me to her, that ours was a primary relationship but not an exclusive one."

Did he feel like he was her first real love?

"That's probably true."[17]

GETTING SERIOUS

Studious, solemn, dynamic, substantive—these are the adjectives her classmates use to describe Hillary Rodham at Yale Law School. She gave no thought to "getting herself up." Hillary was "*deliberately* unattractive," according to one male friend who first met her on line at registration. "I believe it came down to her self-consciousness about her own looks," says this source. Lanny Davis, who was ahead of Hillary at Yale and is now a partner at Patton Boggs in Washington, D.C., and one of Hillary's most loyal vassals, would often tease the first-year student about the way she dressed: "Lurking somewhere beneath that headband and those glasses and that dress is a beautiful woman."[18]

"I'm not hiding it," she would brush him off, annoyed. "I just don't care."

She still didn't care to compete in traditionally feminine ways. And for a woman at Yale in that era, it may have been a smart strategic choice. Lani Guinier, in her book about Yale Law, *Becoming Gentlemen*, said that the school trained everyone, including women, to be gentlemen. In the absence of female law professors who could act as role models, the women law students interviewed by Guinier described the culture of the law school as one that "emphasizes aggressiveness, legitimizes emotional detachment, and demands speed." The teaching style was one of "ritualized combat," which robbed many of the women of their voices.[19] In Hillary's case, it seemed only to encourage her forcefulness and defeminization.

Drucilla Ramey, today the executive director and general counsel of the Bar Association of San Francisco, entered Yale a year ahead of Hillary: "Up until 1968, Yale and most law schools took four or five women and four or five blacks. All the rest were white guys." With tongue in cheek she describes the atmosphere: "The black students had to have a father who owned some African country or was a brain surgeon or something very special. For women, it was simple discrimination. Then suddenly, partly because the school thought the Vietnam War would sap the pool of white male applicants, the numbers of both women and minorities who were admitted shot up in 1968. This was still a year or two before the women's movement really hit."[20] But for the women at Yale it was already a huge sea change—even though, Ramey chuckles, out of the forty-odd women admitted in Hillary's class, something like half were from the elite Seven Sisters schools.

Everything about Yale Law School, from its soaring Gothic spires and stained-glass windows to the massive classical stone columns of its famous library, bespoke male authority as well as gentility—the Anglophile tradition. This was obviously the training ground of the ruling class, and Hillary was pleased about being part of that.

The place was full of famous professors: Burke Marshall, the heroic civil rights fighter who had been assistant attorney general under Robert Kennedy; Robert Bork, a contrarian who taught constitutional law and would later become a figure of national controversy as a Reagan nominee for the Supreme Court; Alexander Bickel, an old-fashioned moderate who set himself against many of the decisions of the Warren Court; Kenneth Keniston, an activist scholar for whom Hillary would later work on his groundbreaking research on children's rights. To her, perhaps the most important faculty member was Marian Wright Edelman, an activist lawyer who was lecturing at both Yale and Harvard in the 1970s, advocating liberal social policy and building a public service organization that Hillary would later join: the Children's Defense Fund.

There were also more colorful characters, such as Tommy "the Commie" Emerson, a devoted First Amendment scholar who had earned his sobriquet by sympathizing with student protestors. Donald C. Pogue, one of Clinton's roommates, has an enduring image of Hillary arguing a point with Professor Emerson in his class on political and civil rights: "He had very high standards, and I remember her clearly being very successful at meeting them."[21]

"Hillary was one of those students you would know because she would speak up in class when she had a point to make," says classmate Ken Kaufman. "People thought of her as very bright, very quick, well-spoken, and intellectual. Even as a first-year student at Yale, she was committed to certain core principles of equal rights for all Americans, whatever their background or economic status."[22]

In a group interview with members of the Class of '73 at their twenty-fifth reunion, a more average portrait of Hillary emerged: "She was just like everybody else. Everybody was idealistic. . . . She went to class on a regular basis. She was a diligent student. She wasn't a wallflower. She was an active and involved student, as opposed to someone who was shy and reserved and just stuck in a cubicle. . . . It would be easier if we could all say that Hillary was the name on everyone's lips. We can't honestly say this. . . . But she is the first First Lady who had the background of public policy and public service."[23]

WEEKENDS IN THE COUNTRY

Her release from the unrelenting pressure of trying to prove herself in the fishbowl of equals at Yale came on weekends—weekends with Alphonse. It was a piece of junk, really, but Alphonse was all hers, her four wheels, her liberty. Hillary didn't have to ask anyone for permission to climb into the little car she had named "Alphonse" and make the 150-mile drive from New Haven to Bennington, Vermont, to spend a day and a half with David Rupert "shacking up"—still the vernacular in 1969 for premarital cohabitation.

It was literally a shack—or, more precisely, a two-room apartment that Rupert had nailed up in one corner of a barn, dubbed "the chicken coop" by Peach Pietrefesa and her boyfriend, John Danner, long-standing friends of Rupert. "We spent at least every other weekend together, basically the four of us in a little converted chicken coop," remembers Danner fondly.[24]

Welcomed by a roaring fire in Rupert's stove and his two huge dogs, the foursome would laze around reading and talking as if they had all the time in the world. They would play music, make food—except Hillary, who never has cooked—and cross-country ski—except Hillary, who seldom attempts things at which she knows she won't excel.

Rupert was very athletic. He liked to ski: downhill, cross-country, anything. He found Hillary to be naturally clumsy. She resisted even trying to learn how to ski. Rupert would tease her, "If you're going to be an athlete, you're going to have to be willing to fall down, a lot. You gotta practice.

You're going to have other people watch you. You're going to fail. You know, Hillary, to become perfect, athletes have to be imperfect a lot of the time." Hillary refused to accept his analysis of her resistance to new experiences at which she might "fall down."

"You know you're a perfectionist, Hillary, and you're just denying it," Rupert would say. "Stop kidding yourself."

She didn't like to be questioned. Rupert found that she was unexpectedly vulnerable and sensitive to criticism. "It didn't have to be a vicious attack," he remembers. "It could be any kind of a challenge. She would flush in the face or get angry or mumble about it." Sometimes she would retreat into an icy silence. "She didn't like not to have the upper hand with men," says Pietrefesa. "Don't forget, her father walked on her." Hillary might come out of her icy cave by evening to take a famous Vermont moonbath with Rupert. The two would stretch their necks to take in the vast starry hood that seemed to enclose Vermont in timeless safety, away from the riot of the world.

In fact, Rupert was subject to the draft at the time, as was his Georgetown classmate Bill Clinton. But while Clinton had won a Rhodes scholarship that took him to Oxford, where he continued to wangle deferments, Rupert had declared himself a conscientious objector. "So you know I'm stubborn and principled," he says.[25]

His declaration was not made out of religious conviction. He had been raised a Catholic in upstate New York, but by the time he met Hillary he was neither religious nor particularly spiritual. "I am a Christian, but by Catholic standards my Christian values are rather liberal," he says. He found Hillary, too, not in the least religious or spiritual. (She was describing herself at the time as an agnostic.)[26] The only time he can remember them going to church in three years was on a tour of the National Cathedral, "but it wasn't to pray and talk to God." Rupert did have strong political convictions, however, and he was appalled by the war in Vietnam. He wanted to do alternative service. He had selected his own alternative: the Head Start program in Bennington. Nice work if one could get it; few did. "If you had conviction, you had choices," he explains. In effect, he told his draft board, "This is your choice. Take it or leave it. If you say no, I'll go to prison." But in fact there was an appeals process, and Rupert knew he would probably win.

A hearing was held, and a week later he was given technical status as a CO. But then his draft board let him dangle. "I got out of college in June '69 and burned up a year and a half before my self-selected assignment was approved," he says with lingering bitterness. To kill time, he had volunteered to work for the new VISTA program (a domestic Peace Corps) and was sent to a poor rural area in Alabama. Hillary didn't make it down to visit him very often during that year. But once he moved to Bennington in the summer of 1970, he was entirely happy working for Head Start. Given Hillary's interest in protecting and empowering children, Rupert's work was another link that drew them close.

Culturally, it was a time of surging idealism with bards such as Joan Baez crooning in her crystal-pure soprano, "Come all ye fair and tender maidens" and doing the Lord's Prayer in calypso, and of course Bob Dylan whining, "Everybody must git stoned." Rupert was rather like an exaggerated mirror image of Hillary, or of the person Hillary wanted to be, as first loves often are. Northern upper-middle-class, smart, stubborn, and self-righteous like Hillary, he was also congenitally political like Hillary. But he seemed even more committed than she to the social causes she espoused.

Was Hillary a bit like the Holden Caulfield character in *The Catcher in the Rye?* I asked Rupert.

"I can remember her saying something like that," he recalls. "I didn't believe it. I think she might have wanted to see herself that way, but I don't believe that is her character."

What, then, was the central quality of her character?

"There was always the perfectionist, the drive, always the ambition."

As the Rodham-Rupert romance entered its third year, their differences became more apparent.

"I wasn't going to move to New Haven, and she wasn't going to move to Vermont," says Rupert. So, trekking to Yale to stay over with Hillary in her on-campus suite, he began picking on her for some of her friends there: "They're off the wall! Their values, their behaviors. Why are you wasting time with those schnooks?"

"I'm intellectually curious, David."

"But what are *you* getting out of it?"

"I'm trying to understand them."

"That's bullshit, you're wasting your time."

They also clashed over the worth or worthlessness of making one's political contribution through government service. "That internship in Washington," says Rupert, "validated my sense that the whole apparatus in Washington was all fucked up. I saw the roots then of what we know to be true today. I wanted to work with people at the grassroots level."

He did not need to be recognized as a star. She did. "I think that's what she wanted, but I never thought of her as a star at Yale," he says. She didn't talk about a political future for herself. "Or if she did," says Rupert, "it was masked—again a kind of self-denial. She didn't know how to be comfortable pursuing political ambitions for herself." Only in retrospect did Rupert realize that Rodham wanted *him* to be more ambitious.

"I think my lack of desire to be in a political role, having done that in Washington and then having gone to VISTA, was something of a disappointment to her." Stubborn to the end, Rupert told her, "I'm not going to play that game—it ain't gonna happen." By the spring of Rodham's second year at Yale, Rupert sensed that their love affair was cooling down but wasn't sure why. She never exactly spelled out the longing that he could not fulfill.

"I never stated a burning desire to be President of the United States," says Rupert. "I believe that was a need for her in a partner."[27]

CHAPTER FIVE

Prude Meets Passion

*"He wasn't afraid of me," Hillary said.
"But I was afraid of us, I tell you that,"
admitted Bill.*

Hillary's fate came walking into the Yale Law School library in the fall of 1970. It took the unexpected form of a tall, handsome southern boy with a wild shrub of hair and high-water pants revealing impossibly hickish shoes. Bill Clinton's hungry eyes, however, reached across the room for his fellow law student.

He had been following her around for weeks, having heard her speak up fearlessly in a class they shared on political and civil liberties. He had watched her in the cavernous wood-paneled dining room. She was magnetic, always challenging, arguing, drawing upperclassmen around her with her intellectual energy. So sharp, that Hillary Rodham. So big-city sharp and staggeringly confident. But there was more to the attraction: Hillary had come to Yale already a star, known to Clinton as the college senior who had delivered an extraordinary counter-commencement speech at staid Wellesley College.

Bill Clinton thought she was "the greatest thing on two legs."[1]

He had trailed her out of class, following her so closely that he could smell her hair. At one point he stopped dead in his tracks. No, this is nothing but trouble, he told himself. "I could just look at her and tell that she was interesting and deep."[2] He walked away. For the next couple of months he stared at her, he followed her, but he couldn't bring himself to make the first move.

One night, huddled at the end of the library, he watched the object of his gaze stand up and march the full length of the law school library until she stood face-to-face with him. "Look, if you're going to keep staring at me, then I'm going to keep looking back," Hillary said, "and I think we ought to know each other's names. I'm Hillary Rodham."[3]

"I was dumbstruck," says Bill Clinton. "I couldn't think of my name."[4]

They have been looking at each other with mixed feelings of fascination and apprehension ever since. When I asked Hillary what she remembered as the most ecstatic experience of her twenties, she pondered, then laughed as she conjured up the sunny southerner with Elvis sideburns who entered Yale Law a year after she did.

"Falling in love with Bill Clinton," she answered.

What attracted her to him?

"He wasn't afraid of me," Hillary said.

"But I was afraid of *us*, I tell you that," Bill Clinton admitted to me.[5]

Given his reticence, it became Hillary Rodham who pursued Bill Clinton. It was like exploring a hidden part of herself, an undiscovered country.

In many ways, however, Bill and Hillary seemed to invert the usual gender roles. Professor Burke Marshall remembers Hillary vividly: "She was even then forceful, very smart, very articulate. Some very good lawyers ramble, but that's not Hillary. Her mind is an organized mind."[6] Hers was the precise, disciplined world of the tort, the logical argument. She was all up in the neocortex, nonemotional, fiercely focused. Bill Clinton's IQ was at least a match for Hillary's—he, too, could be coldly analytical—but he could also work from lower down in the brain. He has what science writer Daniel Goleman has defined as EQ—"emotional intelligence"—the capacity to tap into one's own and others' emotions and use them as a source of power.[7]

Nancy Bekavac, the quick-witted daughter of a Pennsylvania undertaker, began dating Clinton after she bailed him out by lending him her class notes.[8] She was intrigued by his novelistic sensibility: "What he remembered about people was some human fact about their life not unrelated to sentimentality and emotionalism."[9] In contrast to Hillary's sharpness, Bill was "Mr. Aura"—a funny, intense, very quick study who loved a good time and relied mostly on his charm to attract others. Classmate Ken Kaufman remembers, "Bill Clinton was the one with the southern accent, which made him stand apart, certainly. He wasn't in the traditional mode of people at Yale." The common thread through recollections of his classmates is that "Clinton was always reading novels or off running some political campaign."

Among the cliques of northeasterners in the clamorous dining hall, Bill felt more comfortable sitting at the black students' table. He broke the unspoken color barrier with his easy warmth and sense of humor. But these were not the southern black kids he had hung out with in his grandfather's store; they were from the elite: women such as Lani Guinier, an imposing Euro-Jamaican scholar who was to become Harvard Law School's first tenured black female professor, and men such as William T. Coleman III, who was from a family of Philadelphia Republicans. Coleman had a theory about white southerners who transcend bigotry: "They feel some part of the soul that touches each other. Bill had the tempo of the South—he got it."[10]

For his first two years Clinton shared a beach house famous for its parties. Coleman, one of his housemates, remembers Clinton reading Camus and always dating several different women, including a beautiful African-American classmate who later became a psychiatrist. Nancy Bekavac marveled at his knack for "fitting them all [his women] into one semester. Simultaneously." One of his ploys was to spot the title of the book a pretty woman was reading and approach her with the line "You're reading my favorite book!" A married classmate caught Clinton trying to pick up his wife in Logan Airport when Clinton saw her reading *All the King's Men* (which really was one of Clinton's favorite novels, based on the quintessential old-style southern politician Huey Long). "He involved her in a very detailed discussion of Louisiana history," recalls the husband, adding philosophically, "Huey Long, Bill Clinton—aren't all great leaders flawed in some way?"

To Clinton, law school was just a credential. "He did not spend lots of time trying to master *Marbury v. Madison*," snickers Coleman. He had a single-track focus. "He was a very good student, he's very, very smart," says Burke Marshall. "But I never thought of Bill Clinton as law firm material. He was obviously going to be a candidate."

MOVEMENT GIRL

In the spring of 1970, Yale and New Haven succumbed to the Panther fever that had been sweeping larger cities since the founding of the militant Black Panther Party in 1967 in Oakland, California. Nine of the militant group's members were in prison in Connecticut, including the party chairman, Bobby Seale, all charged with conspiring to kidnap and murder a half-witted underling. A murder had indeed been committed and two men had already confessed to it, but New Left theorists were successfully peddling the line that "the facts are irrelevant." The Panthers were being framed. Indeed, most of the party's leadership across the country was by then in jail, in exile, or in coffins.

Jessica Mitford, a feisty left-wing daughter of British aristocrats, and her husband, Robert Treuhaft, a lawyer from the San Francisco Bay area, came to New Haven to raise money for the Panthers' defense. Mitford threw a party that Hillary attended. Among Yale students, that spring's showdown was seen as the buildup to the Bobby Seale trial. Behind the doors of the city's black middle-class families the phenomenon became known as "Panthermania."[11]

Hillary could no longer merely "observe" the active fault-line dividing America. The choice was grim: Those in the middle stood between the reactionary forces of J. Edgar Hoover—the cross-dressing white supremacist director of the FBI who branded the Black Panthers "the greatest threat to the internal security of the country" and threatened to rescind the civil rights freedoms so recently gained—and the stoned radical forces led by Huey P. Newton, the black son of a New Orleans sharecropper, and the white anarchist Abbie Hoffman, who celebrated "revolutionary suicide." America's whole legal system was itself on trial. Even the esteemed president of Yale, Kingman Brewster, issued a famous statement: "I am appalled and ashamed that things should have come to such a pass that I am skeptical of the ability of black revolutionaries to achieve a fair trial anywhere in the United States."

That spring, to Hillary's horror, the Parthenon-esque Yale Law Library was torched. An anguished meeting was called, and students packed the law school's biggest lecture hall. Two decades later, what most people remembered about the meeting was Hillary Rodham's finesse. Perched on a table in her usual bell-bottoms, swinging one leg back and forth, the first-year student assumed the role of mediator over the tumultuous crowd. "There was a lot of angry rhetoric being exchanged," recalls Abraham S. Goldstein, a Yale Law professor who had just been named to replace the outgoing dean. "Hillary showed extraordinary force for a very young woman. She somehow managed to keep the discussion calm."

When a speaker boiled over into radical rhetoric, Hillary would intercede: "I hear you saying this," or "If you could be in a room with Professor So-and-So, is this what you would say?" She was the cultural translator.

"Hillary did what would nowadays be called international summitry—fly-ing back and forth between both sides," says Kristine Olson Rogers, a class-mate at both Yale and Wellesley. "She's always been one who sees the need for balance."[12] Her mother's prescription—always keep the bubble in the middle—gave Hillary the ballast to keep from leaning too far left or right during those turbulent years.

On May Day 1970, Yalies initiated themselves into the Panther cause by staging a huge rally on the Yale Green and inviting students from any-where. That Saturday found ripe-bosomed coeds dishing up a soul picnic for the incoming Bedouins of the Woodstock nation. Rock bands sounded the welcome. State authorities were in a funk. Brown trucks bore down on Connecticut's softly knuckled hills and spilled National Guardsmen onto the city's streets. Long mute lines of boys in weekend soldier uniforms stood with their bayonets unsheathed, forbidden to speak to the milling rabble. Four thousand men of the 82nd Airborne and 2nd Marines were flown up from North Carolina to bases in surrounding states to await the revolution.

Hillary joined the superefficient student marshals who patrolled the campus, giving it the aura of a big-city emergency room. Fifteen thousand college students, almost all of them white, covered the Yale Green like budding revolutionary crocuses, ready to take up the rallying cry. Tom Hayden's words stunned them to attention: "The trial in New Haven is a trial of whether or not there is anything left in this country worth defending." The elfin Abbie Hoffman with his electrified hair shouted paeans to pot, revolution, and release from Whitemiddleclass Paralysis. "We ain't never, never, never gonna grow up," he promised. "We will always be adolescents. . . . Fuck rationality. . . . We got the adults scared to fuck anymore 'cause they know they're gonna have long-haired babies!"

Doug Miranda, a young Panther from Boston, promised, "We just may come back with half a million people and liberate New England!"

Things threatened to spin out of control when fifty or so white and black students massed across the street from the local jail and began shouting ex-pletives at the police and National Guardsmen. Suddenly, marshals from the local black community found themselves fighting across an iron fence with black Yale and Harvard students—dream kids, for God's sake! The middle-class black marshals pleaded, "Go home! When you leave, we've got to live here!"

Sanity prevailed. Panther hosts began driving their VW buses all over town and hollering through bullhorns, "This is not the time!" The Yale rally went down as a *good* political festival, just as Woodstock was the *good* rock festival.

Hillary was shaken into action. That fall she was named associate editor of *The Yale Review* and helped edit a whole issue devoted to the New Haven Black Panther trial. The lead article charged that one of the confessed killers in the case, Lonnie McLucas, had not received a fair trial. The editorial cartoons depicted policemen as pigs. Hillary set her cap for finding a "movement" law firm to work for the next summer. She contacted the Law Students' Civil Rights Research Council, a national organization based in Boston that assigned students to law firms involved in civil rights work and willing to take interns.

Since she had expressed an interest in the Panther cause, Bob Treuhaft's firm, Treuhaft, Walker, and Burnstein, was more than willing to take her. Treuhaft, an impish but brilliantly clever defender of the poor and downtrodden, was one of the first white attorneys to take an interest in defending both black and white militants. His office was in downtown Oakland, across the bay from San Francisco. All through the 1950s and '60s, when the million-plus citizens of Alameda County had no legal aid society, Treuhaft's firm was the only office in Oakland that represented the working poor.

"Hillary was only mildly interested in the Panther cause," Treuhaft later discovered. "But she did want to work for a left-wing movement law firm. Anyone who went to college or law school would have known our law firm was a Communist law firm," he says today. Blithely recounting his vivid history, he says, "Decca [Jessica Mitford, his now-deceased wife] and I both wanted to be members of the Communist Party, but when we met during the war in 1943, we were both working at the OPA [Office of Price Administration] and security checks made it impossible." So the couple had resettled in the more permissive environment of northern California, where, as Drucilla Ramey says, there were lots of people who were members of the Communist Party, but who were not exactly "burn-the-bridge Reds."[13]

For a long time, Hillary had been chafing against the confines of the East and Midwest. Oakland was a hotbed of urban radicals and the birthplace of the Black Panthers; it intrigued her. When the graduate student reported to the Treuhaft office in mid-May, she was thrown all at once into a densely populated street culture dominated by more black faces than she had probably seen in the entirety of her twenty-three years. The police, many of whom were recruits from the South, were notoriously hostile to blacks. "She didn't give any sense of being in an unfamiliar element, and I

would have noticed," says Malcolm Burnstein, the non-Communist partner who represented cases for the NAACP and CORE (Congress of Racial
Equality). Burnstein worked directly with Hillary. "The Sixties was a mar-
velous period" in his view. Interns were paid almost nothing; it was considered a privilege simply to be part of the action at a hip firm such as
Treuhaft, Walker, and Burnstein. Hillary lived next door in Berkeley. "She
was bright and eager and very interested in going to court," Burnstein remembers. "The biggest things we had that summer were Panther cases."[14]

In their benign face, the Panthers ran free breakfast programs for children, schools, and health clinics, and provided great street theater. As a de-
terrent to police brutality, Panther patrols carried law books—and
shotguns. But it was on May 2, 1967, that the California Panthers had
stunned the world.

Thirty Panthers, menacing in their black leather jackets and berets and
brandishing M-1 rifles and shotguns, marched on the California State Legislature in Sacramento to announce to the world that henceforth Africans
in America demanded the right to bear arms in self-defense.[15] The group
was protesting against legislation that would ban carrying loaded
weapons. Reportedly, as the Panthers approached the steps of the Capitol, a
shaken Ronald Reagan, then governor of California, turned and fled. News
cameras rolled in. Party cofounder Bobby Seale read aloud a mandate issued by Huey Newton, minister of defense: "A people who have suffered so
much for so long at the hands of a racist society must draw the line somewhere. . . . We believe that the Black communities of America must rise up
as one man."[16] Whereupon the Panther phalanx entered the Capitol and
roamed the halls of the legislature until, led by newsmen, they stumbled
out onto the floor of the state assembly with their heavy weapons. They
looked around, startled, and were quickly and easily ushered out.[17]

"It was a completely innocent error," maintains Burnstein. "They
thought they were going to the visitors' gallery. The legislators were panicked, of course, but the Panthers were even more unnerved when they realized what they had done. It was a funny scene."[18]

That was to become the high-profile criminal case that Burnstein remembers having worked on with Hillary during her internship summer.
Under California's relaxed gun laws of the time, the Statehouse episode
was all quite legal since the Panthers' weapons had been empty. The militants had been charged with an esoteric statute about disturbing the
peace of the legislature. "Hillary went with me when I met with the Sacramento County DA's office," Burnstein remembers. "She had done intelli-

gent research for me and seemed interested in the whole thing. She certainly expressed no distaste for what we were doing. Some of my clients from other cases were in the pokey—county jail—and she eagerly came along to see them. The Panther case never went to trial. We pleaded it and got everything knocked down to minor charges. Only a few people did any time."[19]

As satisfying as her success in the Oakland summer may have been, Hillary felt painfully conflicted. She did not share in the faddish romanticizing of the criminal element within the black power movement or the denigration of the values of the black middle class. These urban radicals had nothing but contempt for theorizing about civil rights or Martin Luther King's nonviolent strategies for civil disobedience. The system that so many of her contemporaries were damning as corrupt and beyond salvation was, to Hillary, sacrosanct. She kept trying to reconcile the reasoned, well-ordered world she had been studying with the human chaos she saw around her. She *would* find a way to use the law to advance her social goals. Her way. Working *within* the system.

LOSING CONTROL

Hillary welcomed the few visits Bill Clinton made to see her in California. She introduced her new boyfriend to her boss. The only conversation Mal Burnstein recalls from that summer more than thirty years ago was not with Hillary, it was with Bill. He had learned from the couple that Clinton had a high standing in his class at Yale Law.

"Gee, you must have offers from all these big firms," Burnstein mentioned to Clinton in a casually friendly way.

"No," said Clinton with dispatch, "I'm goin' back to Arkansas, and I'm going to be governor."

"Period. He didn't say he was going to *try* to be governor. Or that it was something he *hoped* to do. He was going to *be* governor. That was the plan," says Burnstein, who was more than a little taken aback. "At Bill's age, saying something that forward was noteworthy."[20]

So right from their first year of dating, Hillary knew Bill Clinton's game plan. If she went along with it, it would be like signing up with a minor-league baseball team and hoping to go on to the majors. And from her side there was another element in the attraction: she sensed something child-like and needy about this man. Desperately needy. It appealed to the mature den mother persona she had adopted so successfully in controlling her relationships with men in the past. But with Bill Clinton, suddenly it wasn't going to be easy to maintain control.

He was the wild card in her well-ordered cerebral existence. For her, head had always ruled over heart. She was conscious enough of the division to have spelled it out in a letter to Don Jones: "I'm a heart liberal, but a mind conservative."[21] Hadn't she relied on her mind for twenty-three years, and hadn't it worked to keep her a few steps ahead of her female peers? She had never let her emotions run away with her. Never.

When Bill Clinton entered her world, he kicked over the applecart. Using his well-rehearsed powers of seduction, he introduced pleasure, surprise, spontaneity. For the first time she was overwhelmed by something she couldn't explain, couldn't control. He found the passion beneath the prude.

Shortly after Hillary returned from Oakland, the Rodham-Rupert match was dissolved. Against the fire in Clinton's belly, as she saw it, Rupert's ambitions couldn't hold a candle. "The plot thickens," Rupert admits with a laugh.

"I knew Bill Clinton," he says cryptically. "I was not a friend. He was a year ahead of me, but we traveled in similar circles at Georgetown. He appeared to be ambitious, good, successful, worked on the Hill, got a Rhodes Scholarship, end of story." Of Clinton's manipulations to avoid the draft Rupert was unaware: "Certainly a lot of people were thinking then, 'How can I cleverly work the system and evade the draft?' People like Clinton and me, who lived in the political capital and worked in the congressional arena, knew more about how to do that than the average poor schnook from Little Rock." When Rupert learned along with the rest of the world, during the 1992 presidential campaign, that his classmate had lied about manipulating his draft board and failed to keep a promise to join ROTC, he says, "None of that came as any surprise. I knew this man."

David Rupert was headed toward a grassroots, nonprofit-sector life, all very noble but not where Hillary wanted to go. After spending five years revamping the Head Start program in Vermont and marrying a professional colleague, he was to earn a master's in management degree from Yale University and become a very successful businessman. His career has been in executive management, moving from public sector to private sector.

Rupert admits that the official ending of his long-term relationship with Rodham was painful, but in the next breath he claims that he did not feel "jilted," nor did Hillary. "My simplistic view of a relationship," he says, "is you either continue to put something into it, or you just say, 'Move on.' " With his customary asperity he told Hillary at the summer's end, "If you care for him, then go for it. End of story. Have a great life."[22]

RUNNING WITH BILL

In the spring of 1972, Hillary and Bill both joined the Barrister's Union. In preparation for the competitive trial before a real jury, she whipped Bill into shape as her partner. Alan Bersin, a fellow student, now a partner at Munger, Tolles & Olson in Los Angeles, chuckles as he remembers Bill, "who was superb at presenting. But Hillary was definitely the serious one about getting work done and thinking through the position." They did not, however, win the prize trial. "I just had a bad day," Bill Clinton told me sheepishly, adding that it hadn't helped when "Hillary wore this bright orange outfit."[23]

But the dynamic duo made a lasting impression on one of the judges, John Doar, a hero of the civil rights movement. Doar would soon play an important role in Hillary's future.

Hillary made herself indispensable to the very political animal in Bill. That summer he went to Texas as a volunteer in George McGovern's presidential campaign. Completing her mutation from Republican to liberal Democrat, Hillary wangled herself an assignment in Texas, working to register voters for the Democratic National Committee in San Antonio. Clinton was up in Austin at the McGovern headquarters, working under Gary Hart. Hart had left his wife and two children back in Colorado while he worked for the apparently hopeless cause. Liberated from the frozen dogma of a dark evangelical sect that had ruled his childhood, Hart was anything but a positive role model for Bill Clinton.[24]

"Hart had a real Don Juan complex," says Amanda Smith, then the women's issues person for McGovern. "Women weren't people to him at all." Hart would go to a college to speak for McGovern and often spend the weekend with a member of the political science club. Time and again, these breathless, brainy little buds would turn up on Monday morning to commit their lives to working for the campaign. They would find themselves stuffing envelopes and weeping as Hart passed their desk without so much as a hello.[25]

Hillary made it her business to get up to Austin just about every weekend. She ran around with Clinton, journalist Taylor Branch, and the slightly older, feisty champion of women in politics Betsey Wright. Wright became "obsessed" with pushing Hillary into the fray. "But about political aspirations of her own she was always noncommittal," Wright says.

Wright saw the fateful chemistry between Rodham and Clinton from the beginning: "Bill Clinton tapped into a part of Hillary that no one ever had. Everyone else saw her as a terribly serious woman, very intense. He saw the side of her that liked spontaneity and laughter. He found her guttural laugh: it's fabulous—there's nothing held back. The public never sees that side of her. When she's laughing, that's when she's free."

Hillary had the structure. Bill had the sensibility. The two quickly became symbiotic. Whenever Hillary could break away for an unscheduled visit to Austin, she found herself laughing, caught up in a realm of emotion and sexual passion. I asked Wright if small-town Bill had ever met anyone like Hillary before. She was emphatic: "*Nobody* had met anyone like Hillary before."[26]

MOVING IN—WITH DOUBTS

Neither Hillary nor Bill had cracked a schoolbook or attended a class during the entire semester they were working in Texas. They returned to New Haven after the lost election of November 1972 just in time to take their finals. Faced with an open-book exam based on a text by the professor, Bill ran to the bookstore and the two of them boned up on the required reading. They both passed.

In Hillary's third year at Yale, she and Bill moved in together. They rented a Victorian-style New England house with a pillared porch, just off campus. "I loved being with her," Clinton admitted, "but I had very ambivalent feelings about getting *involved* with her." Even when he seemed to be "totally consumed by somebody else's being," as former housemate Bill Coleman recalls, Clinton did not for a moment lose sight of his soaring political ambitions. As a result, doubts about the match lingered for both Bill and Hillary. Clinton insists that he warned Hillary from their earliest dates, "You know, I'm really worried about falling in love with you, because you're a great person, you could have a great life. If you wanted to run for public office, you could be elected, but I've got to go home. It's just who I am."[27]

Although Hillary had been scheduled to graduate in 1972, she remained in New Haven an extra year and lived with Bill until he finished in 1973. She began clinical work in child development at the Yale Child Study Center. Observing kids at play and then sitting in on diagnostic assessments with the center's nursery school teachers, Hillary came to appreciate the many variations on "normal" child development. Her work probably confirmed something about herself: she seemed to have been born an adult, while some of her contemporaries were still behaving like children. Susan Bucknell, who had first met Rodham at the beach house that Bucknell's future husband, Don Pogue, shared with Clinton, observed, "I think we were all people who came from close families and had a sense of how essential that is. It was obviously such a strong concern of Hillary's."[28]

"She was one of the best, if not the best student we've ever had from the law school," says Albert J. Solnit, then director of the center. "Yale gave her course credit, but no advanced degree," he adds.[29] But it wasn't to earn an additional degree that Hillary stayed on in New Haven. She stayed to hang on to Bill Clinton.

Of equal importance to her pursuit of Bill was the mission that she had begun to formulate as her own. Her work with Marian Wright Edelman she now calls a "personal turning point."[30] Hillary had picked her only female mentor out of an article in *Time* magazine. It was during her first year at law school that she had read about Edelman, a Yale Law graduate and civil rights lawyer, who was coming to speak at her school. At the lecture Rodham introduced herself to the passionate speaker and asked if she could work that summer for a public interest organization that Edelman had founded. Edelman said fine, but she had no money to pay the student. Hillary then went to the Law Students' Civil Rights Research Council and secured a grant that had enabled her to spend the summer of 1970 in Washington working on behalf of poor families, some of them in migrant labor camps.

Through her work with Edelman "the world opened up to me and gave me a vision of what it ought to be," Hillary has said. Under the tutelage of her mentor, Hillary published her first scholarly article in November 1973: "Children Under the Law." At the time, children had almost no legal rights. Hillary argued that "categorizing everyone under eighteen or twenty-one as a minor is artificial and simplistic; it obscures the dramatic differences among children of different ages and the striking similarities between older children and adults." She advocated abolishing the legal status of "minor," and with it the presumption that children are legally incompetent. Instead, she argued for a new concept of children as "child citizens" who should have all the procedural rights granted adults under the Constitution.[31]

This was the turning point at which Hillary declared, "I want to be a voice for America's children." A review of her article by one of Rodham's law professors, Jay Katz, deemed it "pioneering." He says, "She was amongst the first legal scholars to address the question of children's rights." Hillary's article, however, would later become highly controversial, attacked as "anti-family" by right-wing Republicans and praised by liberals such as historian Garry Wills, who referred to Hillary as "one of the more important scholar activists of the last two decades."[32]

SOUTHERN EXPOSURE

A few months before his graduation, Bill took Hillary home to Arkansas for the first time. The ostensible purpose was for Bill to take the bar exam in his home state and for Hillary to take it there as well, "just in case." His ulterior purpose was to show off his friends and family.

After a long, very long, drive in a compact car all the way from New Haven to Little Rock, Bill pulled up with his girlfriend at 801 Country Club Drive, the rented house of two of his best friends, Paul and Mary Lee Fray. He had stood up as the best man at their wedding. Mary Lee was from an aristocratic Virginia family; Paul was more of a homegrown Arkansas product. Both had gone to Ouachita Baptist College, and Paul was to join Bill and Hillary in taking the bar exam. The air was hot and sticky that day. In Arkansas, the custom was for visitors to jump out of their cars and walk right in. Clinton loped around to the Frays' back door. Hillary remained in the car.

Out flew Mary Lee Fray in bare feet, six months pregnant, wriggling and giggling in anticipation of meeting the girl Clinton had bragged about so often. He had built her up as "my future wife." He had rhapsodized to Mary Lee and Paul, "She has the biggest heart, the most beautiful eyes. Her middle name is Diane—that means loving and gorgeous."[33] Paul Fray pictured Hillary as he would *his* ideal woman: a bleached blond with batty eyelashes. Shock reverberated on all sides.

"There I was—barefoot and pregnant," laughs Mary Lee, imagining that her cumbersome appearance confirmed the stereotype of hillbilly Arkies that Hillary had probably brought with her. Hillary never got out of the car.

"She had a scarf on," remembers Mary Lee. "No makeup. She was exhausted-looking. They were on their way to meet Clinton's mother. If I was going to meet my future mother-in-law, I would have at least combed my hair. Even if I had to put a headband on it."[34]

The clash between this steely, plain-faced city girl and Bill's flamboyant mother was as inevitable as a tornado in the plains. Virginia Kelley worked hard at being glamorous. She habitually went to bed with her makeup on because it took her so long to apply it. With her eyelids striped in three shades of eye shadow and a silver streak dyed down the middle of her dark hair, she was as showy as a skunk. It was her trademark to drive down the main drag of Hot Springs in her Buick convertible, on the way to the races, her dangerously brown shoulders showing out of a tube top. In season she was at the track every day—she had her own box. "She loved it, it was in her blood," said her neighbors. "Virginia wrote her own rules."[35]

In her backyard "she'd put on tailored men's pajamas and mules and hang around with a cigarette in her hand, real Hollywood," says a former next-door neighbor, Carolyn Staley. "She was a good-lookin' lady and hilarious. One-liners were her trademark, like a walking Will Rogers." Virginia Kelley was one pleasure-loving lady—the antithesis of Hillary's disciplined do-goodism.

Virginia's rivalry with Hillary first became apparent to me when I flew to Arkansas to interview the candidate's mother in 1992. I phoned her before leaving my hotel to check on directions to her home. Virginia Kelley stopped me cold: "I've decided I don't have time for the interview. The ponies are running today." I pleaded, "But I've come such a long way, and your son *is* running for president." Mrs. Kelley was adamant. Her final brush-off was revealing: "Yeah, but your article's only going to be about Hillary anyway."[36]

Virginia thought of her life as a movie with herself as the star. What a shock it was to encounter the woman that her Bill had chosen! Although admittedly, Hillary sounded like the smartest woman Virginia had ever met, she was also a hippieish female who cared not one whit about makeup! Virginia gave Hillary an icy, decidedly nonsouthern reception.

A COUPLE OF FAVORS

Six months after he graduated from Yale, Clinton was thinking about Hillary as part of his life—and already calculating the impact of her career moves on his political fortunes. John Doar was shopping for crack young lawyers to staff the House Judiciary Committee inquiry that would prepare the impeachment case against President Richard Nixon. Clinton telephoned Doar and excused himself from consideration; he was already gearing up to run for a U.S. congressional seat in 1974. "But John, since you're putting together the committee, I want you to take a good hard look at Hillary Rodham," he told Doar, according to Paul Fray, who overheard the conversation. "Hillary and I are very close friends, and I possibly may marry the lady. She was in law school with me; in fact, she did better in law school than I did."[37] He ran down Hillary's résumé. At the time, she was working in Washington for Marian Wright Edelman's fledgling research and lobbying organization, the Children's Defense Fund.

"If he hadn't suggested her, I would have called her anyway," John Doar told me.[38]

Second-guessing himself in that same December 1973, Clinton asked David Pryor, the Democratic candidate for governor of Arkansas, whether he had made the right move regarding Hillary. "He talked to me about Hillary going to work for the Watergate Committee," Pryor told Clinton biographer David Maraniss. "He asked 'Is that a good idea?' It was a career consideration. He knew that his career would be in politics, and the question was whether Hillary's connection with the Watergate Committee might have political ramifications."[39]

Hillary was excited about her new job. In Washington, she looked up a wealthy feminist friend she had made during the McGovern campaign, Sara Ehrman. The somewhat older woman had been profoundly impressed with Hillary's intelligence, strength, and toughness. She invited her to stay in her town house on Dupont Circle. "I barely ever saw her," Ehrman recalled. Every morning that winter and spring, Hillary left the town house at dawn to begin a twelve- to eighteen-hour day in the Watergate Committee's makeshift offices in the old Congressional Hotel on Capitol Hill. Prisonlike bars covered the windows. The doors had thick steel locks. The sequestered staff was analyzing the Nixon tapes and diaries that the Judiciary Committee would receive from Sam Ervin's Senate committee as they dribbled out of the White House.[40] Her boss, Bernard Nussbaum, hoped the tapes would bring down President Richard Nixon on a charge of obstruction of justice.

Hillary's recollection is vivid: "I was kind of locked in this soundproof room with these big headphones on, listening to a tape." The tapes were of Nixon recording himself while he listened to previous tapes and concocted his defenses to what he heard. "So you would hear Nixon talk, and then you'd hear very faintly the sound of a taped prior conversation with Nixon, Haldeman, and Ehrlichman. . . . And you'd hear Nixon say, 'What I meant when I said that was . . .' I mean it was surreal, unbelievable, but it was a real positive experience because the system worked. It was done in a very professional, careful way."[41]

Hillary also had a world-class survey of the misdeeds committed by presidents throughout America's history. Doar directed her to work with

Yale Law Professor C. Vann Woodward to detail abuses of power by no fewer than thirty-four previous administrations. It would serve as a measuring stick that lawmakers could hold up to Nixon.[42]

In Hillary's opinion, Nixon was "evil." Tom Bell, who shared both Hillary's office and her opinion, says that she believed that Nixon should be prosecuted or impeached not just over Watergate but over his conduct during the Vietnam War, specifically his order for the secret bombing in Cambodia, which she saw as immoral and even criminal.[43] She argued forcefully for a broader definition of the legal justification for impeachment—a position that would come back to haunt her when her future husband was prosecuted for impeachment.

Bill Clinton was back in Arkansas, wholly concentrated on his congressional campaign. "He was broke, busted, begging—always trying to figure out ways to raise money," says Paul Fray, who became Clinton's campaign manager.[44] Throughout that summer Hillary kept her hand in the campaign, calling Little Rock daily, snapping orders at the young southern male volunteers, and attempting to lay out strategy. "They had to listen," says Rose Crane, a childhood friend of Bill Clinton, "because Bill was backing her up."[45]

"She'd always talk to Bill when she phoned from Washington," says Paul Fray. "He'd turn around and bounce it off me." Fray, then an unregenerate male chauvinist, says today that he was glad to have Hillary's input: "I never really had a problem with her. I knew it was going to be a close-cut deal. You're looking at a twenty-seven-year-old boy trying to take on the entrenched Republican incumbent. And we were running in a Republican haven." But, in fact, Fray saw Hillary as a rival. What did this big-city girl have to offer for a congressional campaign in the mountains of rural Arkansas? Fray amends, "Her advice was not all that germane."[46]

CRAZY DREAMS?

Even from a distance of 999 miles, Hillary did more than keep the faith. Nussbaum, her boss and mentor on the impeachment committee, was shocked by the depth of her identification with Bill Clinton.

"I'm driving her home—big car—I'm dropping various people off," as he describes the revelatory scene. "She and I are the only ones left. I'm dropping her at Sara Ehrman's. Hillary was a clear star, only twenty-six years old. She said she wanted me to meet her boyfriend."

"Who is he?"

"A guy I met at Yale. His name is Bill Clinton."

"Oh, really? What's he going to do, practice law?"

"Oh no, he's going into politics," she said confidently.

"Shouldn't he get a job and practice law for a while, before he plunges into politics?"

Hillary ignored the question as if it wasn't worth her time to consider. "He's going to run for Congress. This year."

"Run for Congress? That sounds foolish to me, I think he should get some experience first."

Again, Hillary continued her narrative as if Nussbaum's comments were white noise: "After he runs for Congress, he's going to run for governor. And Bernie, my boyfriend is going to be president of the United States."

Nussbaum looked at her incredulously. They had just been listening to the Watergate tapes. Nussbaum was feeling the strain, concentrating on how to come up with the arguments that could head off a partisan vote. Suddenly his star apprentice had revealed the fantasies swimming around in her head. He was exasperated.

"Hillary, that's the most ridiculous thing I've ever heard," Nussbaum scolded. "How can you be telling me your boyfriend is going to be president of the United States? That's nuts!!"

She flared up. "You asshole. Bernie, you're a jerk. You don't know this guy. I know this guy. So don't pontificate to me. He is going to be president of the United States."

She got out of the car and slammed the door.[47]

CHAPTER SIX

The Hot Springs Kid

The violence and dysfunction in our home made me a loner, which is contrary to the way people view me, because I'm gregarious, happy, all of that. But I had to construct a whole life inside my own mind.

—BILL CLINTON

William Jefferson Blythe II was a traveling salesman and breaker of hearts who passed through Virginia Cassidy's life for less than six months. He liked to drink, and one night in May 1946 he swerved across a wet highway while driving south from Chicago and staggered from his car until he collapsed in a rain-filled ditch and drowned. He was twenty-nine. The tragedy meant that a future president would be left fatherless in the womb of his mother, who was three months pregnant and living with her parents in the tiny town of Hope, Arkansas.[1]

With Cherokee blood and the fight of the Irish in her, Virginia Cassidy Blythe Clinton Dwire Kelley had a lot of living to do and four more marriages to go.[2] Her footloose lifestyle cast a pall of confusion over her first-born son from the time Billy came into the world in the summer of 1946.

Joe Purvis has been a friend so long he can't remember when he didn't know Bill Clinton—or rather, Billy Blythe, which was what he was called in Hope when their mothers pushed them in baby strollers side by side. "Bill never talked about his father. And I don't ever remember saying, 'Where's your daddy?' My folks probably told me he was dead. I'm not sure we knew what that meant. But by the time we got to kindergarten, some of us probably thought his grandparents were his parents."[3]

Billy was no more than a year old when his mother waved good-bye to her dull hometown of Hope and set off for advanced nursing training in New Orleans. Virginia left her son with his grandmother, Edith Cassidy. This iron-handed woman subjected the baby to a regular regimen that his less disciplined mother would describe as "unrelenting": he "napped, played, ate, burped, slept in an unwavering cycle."[4]

"Miz Cassidy—she was all business," says Purvis. The Cassidys were from Bodcaw, a jot of a town near the Texas border. They had moved up to the "city" of Hope when Virginia was in high school. Hope wasn't anything resembling a city, of course; it was a simple agrarian town based on cotton, like hundreds of others in Arkansas, where most folks got by on subsistence truck farms. "Industry" was limited to one brick plant and a factory that made handles for hoes. The Cassidys lived in a modest foursquare frame house by the railroad tracks in a lower-middle-class white neighborhood, although just behind their house were the homes of substantial middle-class people. The Cassidys' street was one step up from the poor black section nearby, where Billy Blythe's grandfather Eldridge Cassidy ran the gas station and general store. The South in which Bill lived as a toddler was still segregated.

"You didn't invite black children over to play," remembers Purvis, "but Bill would run into black kids in his grandfather's store. He learned from his grandfather that you don't judge a man by the color of his skin or the amount of money he has." Clinton himself has said, "My commitment to civil rights was basically inbred through my grandparents. They knew a lot of black people and thought they'd gotten a raw deal."[5]

Billy Blythe used to sit at the counter of his grandfather's store in Hope and feast on a jar of cookies. But there are also the hungry memories of a little boy who didn't think himself lovable enough to be able to hang on to a father *or* a mother—a little boy who used to sit in the darkened parlor of his grandparents' house and stare at the phone, waiting for it to ring, "always hoping that it was Mother calling from New Orleans."[6] Billy's grandfather died when the boy was eleven. From then on he was bereft of male family role models.

He once went out to find the place where Billy Blythe had abandoned him. Driving up and down Highway 61 in Missouri, he was trying to locate the exact vanishing point, trying to make sense of the thin story he had been told about his father. "He just slipped off the wet road," Clinton later related. "He fell into a ditch full of water, face down, and drowned. It was just a fluke." How to come to terms with this legacy of vast carelessness? "I guess I never permitted myself to admit, I missed my father terribly," Clinton has said.[7] In the winter of 1992, when I asked Bill Clinton who was the first man who had endorsed him as worthwhile, there was a long pause. He stared out of the window of his campaign plane at the bleak, snow-blistered New England terrain. After mentioning his grandfather, he spoke stiffly of his stepfather Roger Clinton. "He took me to St. Louis on a train once, I remember that." He dredged up one family vacation, one fishing trip. "Literally, all those years and I can count on one hand—there just weren't many times. It was sort of sad . . . I missed it."[8]

It is possible that the man we know as William Jefferson Clinton came into the world a lie. Or, at best, a guess.

Virginia had been engaged for four years to someone else when she met Blythe. The tall, handsome salesman brought a woman into the emergency room of the hospital where Virginia worked. It was a hot night in June. The man had a glow about him, the glow of a man who never met a stranger. Virginia was dying to know if he was married. She never asked. He did the asking. Blythe walked up to her nurse's station and asked what the engagement ring on her finger meant. She blurted, "Nothing."

"I was shameless," she admitted. After only six weeks she and her new boyfriend were sleeping together. It was wartime, and, as Virginia wrote, "We talked fast, played fast, fell in love fast." So fast that Blythe, an eighth-grade dropout, swept Virginia across the border to Texarkana on September 3, 1943, and, without any parents present, they tied the knot before a justice of the peace. But the salesman had neglected to mention that he already had a wife.[9] Two months later, Blythe was shipped off to North Africa. He served in World War II for the next two years and died in the car accident on May 17, 1946.

Clinton biographer David Maraniss began to question Bill Clinton's paternity in his 1995 book, *First in His Class.* Maraniss pointed out that in November 1945, nine months before the birth of William Jefferson Blythe on August 19, 1946, W. J. Blythe, Army Tech 3, was still in Italy. When questions about her son's paternity resurfaced once Bill Clinton was elected president, Virginia amended her version. "Her answer was that Billy was born a month early, induced weeks ahead of schedule because she had taken a fall and the doctor was concerned about her condition," Maraniss reported.[10] But in Virginia's memoir, published the year before the Maraniss book, she made no mention of a fall or the birth having been premature. Her ghostwriter, James Morgan, later told me that Virginia never spoke of an early, induced delivery. He acknowledged that he had never questioned or checked into Virginia's account of Clinton's birth.[11]

I found the one person still living who had been present at the birth of the future president: the delivery room nurse, Wilma Booker. Proud to quote Bill Clinton as saying she was "the first person to spank his butt," she recalls, "It was a hot day, real hot." The first words to greet the infant's arrival were shouted from the hall by his cousin Dale Drake: "Wilma, it's hot as holy Hell in here!"

I asked Nurse Booker if Bill Clinton's birth could have been premature.

"No, not at that weight," she replied unequivocally. "I remember he was a nice-size baby, between eight and nine pounds. [His mother noted he was 8.6 pounds.] Virginia got kinda big while she was pregnant."[12]

In 1988, when Governor Clinton unexpectedly backed away from announcing what would have been his first campaign for the presidency, he gave Chelsea as his reason: "I made a promise to myself a long, long time ago, that if I was ever lucky enough to have a child, she would never grow up wondering who her father was."[13]

Clinton, most listeners believed, had slipped; he had meant to say *where* her father was. They thought he was referring to his desire not to be an absentee father. But Maraniss heard a more telling and poignant revelation: Bill Clinton had unintentionally exposed the painful mystery at the center of his existence. "For years afterward, there were whispers in Hope about who little Billy's father was, rumors spawned by Virginia's flirtatious nature and the inevitable temptation of people to count backward," wrote Maraniss.

"His mother was his daddy," says Paul Fray.[14] Virginia was certainly a maverick. For a young married southern woman to go off and get herself a professional degree was highly unusual in that day and age. "I'm sure a lot of folks thought Virginia was far too flashy for Hope, Arkansas, in the Forties and Fifties," acknowledges Joe Purvis. "And Virginia was a flamboyant character. She loved loud clothes, loved lipstick, she loved life, and the older she got the more she became larger than life."[15]

Stories about Billy's mother's loose ways were always around Hope and later Hot Springs. "I've heard about four different stories on who his daddy really was, so who knows?" says Fray. "Only the good Lord knows."[16]

WILL-O'-THE-WISP

Bill's first steps toward independence were taken at Miss Marie's School for Little Folks in Hope. It was a three-dollar-a-month private kindergarten. With her snow white hair pulled back, Miss Marie Perkins resembled the Gilbert Stuart portrait of George Washington. She and her sister, Miss Nanny, another hunched old maid, ran the school and acted as its only teachers.[17]

Young Billy Blythe was not the least bit assertive. "Quite the contrary," says his childhood friend and later presidential chief of staff Mack McLarty. "He had a measure of reservation." Billy was embarrassingly chubby. Maybe it was genetic. Maybe it was all the cookies he ate as a substitute for mother love. Whatever the case, he was so fat that he broke his leg skipping rope in kindergarten.[18] During a bittersweet visit to his birthplace in March 1999, Clinton himself referred to this searing experience: "In the first of many major mistakes I was to make in my life, [I was] jumping rope in my cowboy boots."[19]

The little cowboy caught his boot heel on the jump rope and fell—hard. "He started screaming and crying and everybody crowded around and called Billy a sissy," relates Purvis. "When I got home from school that day, my mother told me, 'Little Billy Blythe broke his leg in about four places. He's in the hospital.' I felt real bad at how we'd made fun of him. I went to visit him in Julia Chester Hospital and brought him violets."[20]

Purvis, who is today chairman of the Clinton Birthplace Foundation, refers to a photo of Billy Blythe at the age of eight or nine to make the point that, chubby though he was in kindergarten, "Billy didn't really pork up until mid–grade school. There he looked like a butterball."

In 1950, Virginia announced her intention to marry Roger Clinton, a hard-drinking, high-living gambling man from Hot Springs whose nickname was "Dude." His brother, Raymond Clinton, had sent him down to Hope to open a Buick dealership. Roger ingratiated himself with Virginia's father when he began supplying Mr. Cassidy's grocery store with bootleg whiskey. But Miz Cassidy violently disapproved of the match.

Miz Cassidy, who had been Bill's surrogate mother for several years, threatened to sue her daughter for custody of the child. She even consulted a lawyer. The four-year-old Billy was caught in a power struggle between the two women in his life. In the end, his grandmother lost the fight for the boy, and her new son-in-law soon proved to be a loser. "Roger lost that

Buick dealership in a crap game," claims Paul Fray, who later hung out in Billy Blythe's house in Hot Springs.[21] The loss hardly dampened the newly-weds' high spirits; it meant they had an excuse to move up to Hot Springs, which in 1951 was "a happening place."[22]

Billy Blythe was seven when Virginia and Roger settled in the tingly town notorious for its Thoroughbred racetrack, illegal gambling clubs, plentiful whorehouses, and gangster glamour. Hot Springs could boast of being the largest illegal gambling site in the South. Every winter the high rollers would come from New York, Chicago, and Miami Beach, looking for action. The city's history was rife with boasts of playing host to vacationing gangsters such as Bonnie and Clyde and "Machine Gun" Kelly.

Bill spent most of his boyhood cultured in this warm bath of half-truths and hypocrisy, where petty crooks and celebrity fugitives found a resort just right for their tastes and where a proliferation of Baptist churches attempted to put proper Sunday faces on the bathhouses, betting parlors, and brothels that were supported by the local government. The bald truth was spelled out by a local prosecutor, Paul Bosson:

"In Hot Springs, growing up here, you were living a lie."[23]

Clinton's mother has said that she never did recognize any boundaries. Virginia told her brother-in-law, Raymond Clinton, that she was having trouble finding work. Her diploma was very new, and all the doctors already had "girls," as they called their nurses. Virginia disparaged them as mostly nonprofessionals "who would just drip a can of ether, so what was the point of paying me for what I said was a better way?"[24] Uncle Raymond was one of the boss dogs in town, according to Paul Fray, and he fixed Virginia up right: "He let her be the nurse for the girls in the cathouses. She was the one who did the checking on the ladies."[25] That was the beginning of Virginia's lucrative career as a "freelance nurse-anesthetist."

A famous Hot Springs madam known as Maxine bought cars for her lawyer and for her girls from Bill's Uncle Raymond. Whenever one of them would come into the hospital with appendicitis or whatever, somebody would whisper, "She's one of Maxine's girls," and Virginia would be ecstatic. She knew that the people who paid their bills best were prostitutes: "Mr. President of the Bank might not pay me on time, but I knew Maxine's girls would."[26] They paid *before* they left the hospital.

Uncle Raymond also operated the Belvedere Club, according to his close friend and political ally, former state senator Q. Byrum Hurst, who lived only a few doors from Virginia and Roger on Park Avenue. The club offered the full menu of wink-wink "illegal" pleasures: liquor, crap tables, waitresses who could be persuaded to get familiar with paying customers.[27] Virginia liked to drink and gamble at the Belvedere Club. "I'm not one for rules, and the only rule in Hot Springs was to enjoy yourself," she said in her memoir, *Leading with My Heart.* "You could carry your drink around with you downtown, even on Sundays."

Bathhouse Row in Hot Springs soon became a mecca for mafiosi in the midwinter racing season. Al Capone had a standing suite at the town's lavish Arlington Hotel, where the bathhouse masseur boasted of giving rubdowns to Lucky Luciano and Meyer Lansky.[28] The Arlington's lobby was tarted up in brothel pink with big round upholstered banquettes and a massive wooden bar and dance floor. The flouting of rules in Hot Springs was so prevalent, the gambling so wide open, it never occurred to Virginia that some of her favorite activities were illegal.

"When it came to a vote on legalization of gambling in Arkansas," Virginia admitted, "I never was so shocked."[29]

CONSTRUCTING AN AIRTIGHT BOX

Miz Cassidy had been dead right: the world of Virginia and Roger in Hot Springs did turn out to be wild and uncontrollable. During nights on the town, Virginia loved to "show off," as she put it. When Roger disappeared with the boys to throw dice in the Belvedere Club's back room, Virginia liked to make him suffer by flirting with other men. By the time Roger yanked her out of the arms of some stranger she would be dancing with, her husband would usually be drunk. Predictably, he would erupt in a jealous rage. "Our house was just bedlam," Virginia wrote in her memoir, "from the time we got home until dawn's early light, by which time Roger would usually have yelled himself to sleep." When the drinking and beating and shouting of obscenities became unbearable, Virginia would sometimes bundle up her son Billy in the middle of the night and take a room in town, where they could stay together safely. But after her second son was born, it wasn't easy for all three to share the same rented motel bed.

The family drama was all too familiar. Virginia's own mother had pierced the nights with screaming fits. She was "insanely jealous," according to Virginia. While the Cassidys' only child lay in her bed in the next room, she would hear Miz Cassidy shrieking at Virginia's daddy about other women. And these fits went on for years, until Miz Cassidy got herself a diploma and began working as a private-duty nurse. Virginia was living out the script all over again.

"The stories from Hot Springs are so true," says Reverend Ed Matthews, the retired minister of Little Rock's First United Methodist Church. "On nights when Bill's mother and stepfather would get into brawls and even wave guns at each other, young Bill would reportedly have to take little brother Roger over to another home across the street and stay all night. Virginia and her mother both lived a life of denial. Yet Bill had an unrelenting love for his mother and grandmother—so he had to almost deny who they were."[30]

"The Clintons fit in with the Hot Springs way of life," says Carolyn Yeldell Staley, the sweet blond daughter of the local Baptist minister who introduced herself to me as "Bill's 'girl next door.' " Bill never rebelled, she adds. "He had to be the shining light in his mother's life"[31]—and in his grandmother's life. Years later, Hillary Clinton consulted a psychologist who told her that for a boy, being in the middle of a conflict between two women is the worst possible situation: there is always the desire to please each of them.[32]

At home, Billy Blythe adopted the role of family peacemaker. He worked just as hard at school and on the playground, using his charm and facade of sunniness to make everyone love him. He talked a blue streak. He'd say almost anything to win someone over. Bill Clinton once told a gathering that his sixth-grade teacher, Kathleen Schaer, had instructed him, " 'If you ever learn when to talk and when to keep quiet, there is nothing you can't achieve. But if you don't learn the difference, I'm not sure whether you're going to be governor or wind up in the penitentiary.' "[33]

What his teacher didn't know about Billy was the imprint on his character that was being impressed at home. There were two things he could count on his mother saying to him every day when she came home from work, according to Staley, who was always over at Billy's house:

"Her standard opening line was 'You know, nobody has told me all day long how cute I am.' And we would say to her, 'You are adorable, Virginia, you are just so cute.' Virginia would fluff up and say, 'Thank you, I needed somebody to tell me I'm cute.' "[34] Thus did Bill learn how to flatter women and how to make them purr. From this home tutoring he developed the powers of alchemy that would allow him to be seductive to both women and men for the rest of his life.

Second, he would be told how unjust the world was to his mother. "Bill and I would hear about Dr. X or Dr. Y that she was not able to work with, or how 'They hate me,' " says Staley. As a freelance nurse-anesthetist who hired herself out, Virginia pitted herself against the medical establishment.

She was ahead of her time as a self-made professional woman, and she built up quite a thriving business—so good that when Billy would ask her to attend a school function, she would always say, "If I'm not working." She made an extraordinarily good living for that time and place—maybe $60,000 or $70,000 a year, estimates state trooper Larry Gleghorn[35]—but she did not have an M.D. and she wasn't a man. "Sexism played a part in my career from start to finish," she was convinced. "And it ended very sadly," says Staley. "She had to stop practicing." A change in the state licensing law outlawed freelance nurse-anesthetists and required that they work under the supervision of an anesthesiologist with a medical degree. Virginia refused to do it.[36]

The Clintons have introduced to mass culture the concept of "compartmentalizing" one's problems. With Bill it was a matter of psychological survival. He once told an interviewer he put the sexual misconduct accusations made by Paula Jones's lawyers "in a little box."[37] In this mode of defense he had been well tutored by his mother, who in her memoir describes herself as the innocent victim of a campaign by "various forces [that] tried for thirty years to destroy my career."

This worldview was internalized very well by her son. When bad things happen, Virginia drilled her boys, just brainwash yourself to put them out of your mind. Bill and his brother, Roger, were troubled by the term "brainwashing," so she came up with the idea of a safe white box in which to lock up one's sanitized reality, leaving everything else outside in the black. "Construct an airtight box," she schooled them. "I keep inside it what I want to think about. Inside is white, everything outside is black. . . . This box is strong as steel."[38]

Hillary Clinton has adopted the same strategy. "We do box it off," she said of her troubles, "because there is no way you can let people with their own agendas interfere with your life, private life, or your duties. And that's what my husband does every day."[39]

THE INVENTION OF BILL CLINTON

Until his early adolescence, Bill was still the little boy locked outside in the black. Up there in the bedroom of the Clintons' house on Park Avenue, with his hands over his ears to shut out the chaos, the young Clinton would focus on the snapshot of Bill Blythe he kept beside his bed. Staring at this shrine to a father about whom he knew next to nothing, he dreamed up an idealization to fill the empty place where others had fathers. "He always wanted my mother and I to have the best," Bill Clinton would tell his play-mate Rose Crane. Did the boy look like the man in the snapshot? "No," says Crane, "not to me."[40]

Night after night the boy and his mother would be in the kitchen at dusk when the grumble of tires on gravel would announce Roger Clinton's re-turn and dread would come upon them: *Will he be drunk again tonight? In a jealous rage?* It went on like that from the time Billy was eight or nine, when he would say, "Mother, what's the matter with Daddy?" until Bill grew into a forty-year-old at the age of fourteen and didn't need to ask anymore; then he had to be the adult and call the police when the abuse became in-tolerable.

"The violence and dysfunction in our home made me a loner, which is contrary to the way people view me, because I'm gregarious, happy, all of that," Clinton once told an interviewer. "But I had to construct a whole life inside my own mind."[41]

Against the foreground of moral and ethical confusion in the Clinton household, Billy retreated into novels, music, and the Bible. He found spe-cial relevance in the biblical stories of the Pharisees, who seemed to him a reflection of "the modern-day Pharisees I saw saying one thing and doing another."[42] Without encouragement, he sought solace in religion, making a profession of his faith and being baptized at the Park Place Baptist Church.

"He made a personal decision to become a Christian; none of his family was there," says Staley.[43] Clinton has described how he walked alone a mile or so to his church every Sunday: "It wasn't something my parents did, but I somehow felt the need. I came to see my church as a place not for saints but for sinners, for people who know they're weak."[44]

Bill later became president of his Sunday school class at the First Baptist Church of Hot Springs. Sometimes he would wander over to the Pente-costal Gospel Sing at Redfield and enjoy the exultation of shouting praises to the Lord and releasing his troubles through the medium of gospel music.[45] Religion for him became both an intellectual study and an ongo-ing spiritual journey.

None of the neighbor children knew what was going on behind the ap-parently normal facade of the Clinton household. Only in his teenage years did Staley notice that Bill had a Bible inscribed to "Billy Blythe, III." How odd, she thought, since by then Bill carried the name Clinton. But she said nothing. Billy's friends were shocked to learn the story in retrospect. None of them could remember Bill ever saying a bad word about Roger Clinton. He did not tell his friends that his "stepfather" had never legally adopted the boy who had taken his name. He never let on about the bedlam outside the white box.

Given the terrible truth, it was the better part of valor to lie. But it became the habit of a lifetime.

This boy who was never a boy became a blueprint for the man who would take the reckless chances that later put into jeopardy his marriage, his political career, his legacy, everything that matters. Years later, Monica Lewinsky testified to investigators that Bill Clinton told her he had led a life of lies and deception ever since he was a small boy.[46] Being a smart kid who knew the consequences of his actions, he had maintained that hidden life, safe in the knowledge that no one knew the true Bill Clinton.[47]

"Some of the mistakes I made later in life were rooted in all those things that were unsaid or unexplored when we were growing up," Bill Clinton told me. Virginia Clinton made no attempt to explain or analyze his parents' behavior: "My mother was trying to keep peace and survive in an explosive situation."[48]

At the age of fourteen, Bill stood up for his mother like a man. It must have been his age, because there was nothing unusually extreme about his parents' behavior that night in 1962 when a shocking confrontation took place that marked the turning point in Billy Blythe's adolescent life.

Roger Clinton had come in the door cursing to himself. He had been getting drunk nearly every day since the mid-1950s, according to Virginia, and she had been threatening to leave him for almost as long. This night, when Big Roger began screaming accusations of infidelity at Virginia in front of the two boys, Little Roger, only four, ran outside and dragged in a big stick to try to protect his mother. Big Roger trapped Virginia in their bedroom and locked the door. She was afraid he was going to beat her.

Something in Billy Blythe snapped. His little brother was crying and from behind his parents' door he heard what sounded like bloody murder. Big Roger spent himself on the tirade and was slumped in a chair beside the gaming table the Clintons kept at the foot of their bed. A weight heaved against the door and broke it open. There stood Bill.

"Daddy, stand up," he ordered.

But Roger was too drunk to stand up. "You must stand up to hear what I have to say to you," Billy insisted. His stepfather mumbled and snarled and wobbled, but he couldn't get his legs to support him.

"Daddy, I want you on your feet," the boy repeated. Virginia would remember the boy's gentleness as he lifted his stepfather out of his chair. It was an act of considerable courage, since there were bullet holes in the bedroom wall from one of Roger's previous drunken rants. This time Roger threatened to smash his face in if he took his mother's side. The boy told the bully that he was the bigger one now.

Quietly, very calmly, young Bill said, "Never . . . ever . . . touch my mother again."[49]

On April 9, 1962, Virginia told Roger she was divorcing him. With Bill behind her all the way, she packed up the two boys and drove to the Motel Capri. Fuming. All those years she had been turning over most of her paychecks to Roger Clinton, thinking he was paying down the mortgage, and then she found out they didn't even own the house! Raymond Clinton owned it. Within a few weeks Virginia put down the money she had been "rat holing" to buy—all by herself—a brand-new brick ranch house on Scully Street in a respectable neighborhood of Hot Springs. Six weeks later Bill swore out a deposition against his stepfather, cataloguing the habitual drinking, the beatings, the times he himself had summoned police to their house. By June, Virginia told her sons her divorce was final.

In the brief respite when Roger was out of their lives, something astonishing took place: Billy Blythe went to a lawyer and asked to take "Clinton" as his legal name. He thus assumed an empty identity as the son of a man whom his mother had just divorced and who had previously refused to give the boy his name.

Thus, at fifteen, he created the first of many Bill Clintons.

Bill then took the place of his mother's husband. Virginia shifted her needy affections to a boy who perceived himself as a fat, slow fifteen-year-old who couldn't throw straight. Now Bill had to be her date for nightclub-hopping with her rowdy drinking crowd. She began taking her teenage son along to the Vapors nightclub. During racing season the club ran fast and loose with lusty Vegas entertainers singing over the raucous *chi-ching* of slot machines and the squeals at the blackjack tables—an experience that seems to have simultaneously intrigued and repelled the boy.

"It was fascinating," Clinton told me. But he added, "I didn't like to be around dark smoky places where people were drinking too much. . . . I had a real negative association with alcoholism. I think subconsciously I was afraid it would happen to me."[50]

His respite from the chaos came in sharing the rapture of music with his "girl next door." Carolyn Staley had a pillowy figure and a voice like an angel. Bill liked to have her come over after school and play the piano while he practiced his saxophone. For once, life was calm.

But the violent Roger wasn't out of their lives. Sometimes he slept on their concrete front porch like a derelict or waited outside in his car, moaning like a lame dog until Virginia would go out and sit with him. For all young Bill's courage in standing up to his brutal stepfather and assuming the burden of protecting his mother—even having his stepfather arrested and filing affidavits to rid their family of this blight—Bill still lost. Three months after their divorce, Virginia took Roger back.

"Mother, in my opinion, that would be a mistake," Bill told Virginia.

"Thank you," she said, "but it's something I feel I have to do."[51]

FIRST PRAISE

Finding an identity that suited him was deeply challenging for Bill Clinton. He never did prove himself in any of the traditional ways boys did in the South. He played no sports. He wasn't a hunter. He wasn't even a ladykiller in high school. On the contrary, he had to be "fixed up" for proms. And, as we later learned, he avoided anything to do with the military life.

He was in the band.

"Arkansas was a powerful football culture," says Judith Hollensworth Hope, an Arkansan who grew up just ahead of Bill and later became chairwoman of the New York State Democratic Party. "To be in the marching band was the wrong place to be on the football field," she relates. "Those kids were the losers. I mean, they were big-time losers."[52]

The Clintons had acquired their first television set just before the 1956 presidential campaign, and the ten-year-old Bill had become absorbed by both parties' conventions. A sense began building in the boy that he was bound for a special fate. He decided to give up the marching band and put aside his dreams of becoming a jazz artist. He wasn't as convinced that he could reach "greatness" in a musical career as in his other passion—politics.[53]

Although Bill's grades in high school were excellent, he was offered more musical scholarships than academic ones. While Hillary was a National Merit Scholarship finalist from her high school, Bill made only semifinalist. But from the beginning he was the better actor. Hillary, as we know, failed to win the role of Martha in *Who's Afraid of Virginia Woolf?* Bill, however, did make the final cut for a school play that could have been written for him: *Gentlemen Prefer Blondes.*

Bill wasn't one of those long-haired country boys celebrated in hound-dawg hillbilly music, however; he was a serious musician and dreamed of becoming a jazz saxophonist. The closest thing he had to a mentor was his band director, Virgil Spurlin. Once Spurlin guided Bill into music competitions, Bill made first chair on tenor saxophone in the Arkansas All-Star Band. It was the closest he had come in his first fifteen years to being a "star" in anything.

But Clinton was developing a tropism for power almost as finely tuned as Hillary's. The turning point came shortly before his sixteenth birthday. He was selected to go to the 1963 Boys State, a program founded by the American Legion in which young boys play the role of legislators, first on the state level and then, if elected, on the national level. Bill went off to attend the state convention in Little Rock that June, but he was not elected "governor." That honor went to his childhood friend from Hope, Mack McLarty. But Bill was selected as the delegate from his state for Boys Nation. That put him on the road to Washington, D.C., where he positioned himself to be first off the bus to meet his hero John F. Kennedy. Only a few months before the idealized young president was assassinated, Bill Clinton had his historic Rose Garden handshake.

His first exposure to Washington had concentrated his mind on education as his ticket to greatness. He and Staley compared notes, since she had gone to Girls Nation, and she remembers well Bill's epiphany: "I have figured out that babies are all born the same. It is what happens to you along the process of your life that makes the difference in who you are. And education is a great leveler."[54] Clinton asked his high school counselor, Edith Irons, what colleges offered a good program in foreign service. The only one she knew offhand was Georgetown; she promised to look up others.[55] But once Clinton had toured Georgetown, he came back to Hot Springs ablaze with visions of his future. He told Staley, "Those students at Georgetown know so many languages. They have all traveled. They've had opportunities that we didn't have here." She remembers Clinton making a firm declaration: "I am going to go to Georgetown, and I am going to go on to grad school, and I am going to get the greatest education I can and come home to Arkansas and put it to work for the people here." His mother, who was earning $60,000 a year at that point, agreed to send him.

In 1966, Clinton began interning in the Washington office of Arkansas Senator J. William Fulbright. "That office became a mecca for the youth of the country who opposed the war," says Lee Williams, an attorney who hired the Georgetown junior. "He was just a big kid eager to learn, and he asked all the right questions." Fulbright, then chairman of the Senate Foreign Relations Committee, which held extensive hearings on the war in Vietnam, took Bill Clinton to lunch now and then. He also encouraged the budding politician to apply for a Rhodes scholarship to go to Oxford for a year.

Two momentous transitions took place in Bill during his time at Georgetown: he finally dropped his baby fat and became attractive to women, and his relationship with his stepfather underwent a startling alteration. Bill was now a senior in college, a big, strapping young man with his life ahead of him. Roger Clinton found himself in the cancer ward at Duke University Hospital in Durham, North Carolina, a pathetic, shattered man. Just about every weekend in that fall of 1968, Bill drove from Washington down to Durham, to visit with his stepfather as he lay dying. Bill later told writer Don Baer how much those visits had meant to him. He had applied for a Rhodes scholarship to Oxford and kept telling Roger how nervous he was, hopeful but doubtful that he would be selected. Surprisingly, Roger was reassuring. He kept telling Bill he was convinced that he would win the scholarship.[56] And indeed, Bill did.

Years later, when Baer interviewed Hillary Rodham Clinton about Bill's boyhood, she picked up the story and elaborated on its psychological significance. She said a "healing" had taken place between these two men who had had such a difficult, combative relationship. She talked about how meaningful it had been for Bill to receive that kind of comfort. These were words of praise that this boy growing into a man had never received from his stepfather, or from any other man. She emphasized how important it was that this understanding had taken place between the two men before Roger died.

All this occurred before Hillary ever met Bill. "It was clearly something they had shared and bonded over," says Baer. "It was part of Bill Clinton's life story that he had wanted her to share in. Tears came to her eyes as she talked about it. It was an emotional moment for her, and it was not manufactured. I found that very telling."[57]

Hillary Clinton's first book, *It Takes a Village*, shows her appreciation of the complicated emotional havoc that adults must deal with when recovering from a disordered childhood. But there may have been another reason why she felt empathy for the boy from Hope. Empathy was not characteristic of Hillary. Perhaps she could project onto Bill her own childhood injuries without having to feel the pain personally. It was once removed. Clinton was exactly the kind of brilliant, damaged "boy" who would have appealed to Hillary's maternal side. And because his troubles had happened to someone else, someone much more vulnerable, she could feel powerful by taking action on his behalf.

EVERYTHING'S SLICK

As with other events in his life, the god of luck shone on Clinton in helping him escape the draft. After receiving his draft notice on May Day 1969, Clinton asked Cliff Jackson, a fellow Arkansan whom he had met at Oxford and who was working for the state Republican Party, to help him get his draft notice killed. Jackson arranged for Clinton to enroll in the ROTC program at the University of Arkansas law school in Fayetteville in the fall of 1969. Clinton was too late to enter the current unit that fall, however, and would need a draft deferment so he could join ROTC the following spring and avoid being drafted in the meantime.

After a few calls were placed on the favorite son's behalf by Senator Fulbright's office, Colonel Gene Holmes, commander of the ROTC unit, and Clinton's draft board granted the deferment. Had Colonel Holmes not agreed to grant the deferment and reclassified him as 1D, Clinton would have been inducted in the summer of 1969 and most likely shipped off to Vietnam. Instead, his manipulations allowed him to return to Oxford for a second year. During that year he was accepted by Yale Law School. When the time neared for Clinton to live up to his end of the agreement and enroll in the ROTC program at his state's law school, he once again manipulated the system. He took his chances and asked to reenter the draft pool. He drew lucky number 311, a high number that assured he would remain out of harm's way.

By the time Bill Clinton entered Yale Law School in the fall of 1970, the considerable polish he had picked up at Oxford enabled him to keep up with Hillary Rodham. But his moods were far more volatile than those of the Rodhams' daughter, trained as she was to keep the carpenter's bubble inside always level. Clinton became depressed. Some think he was burdened by guilt. He wrote to Cliff Jackson expressing doubts about his "desire to reach my life's ambition as a world leader." He added, with what may have been accurate foreshadowing, "I am having a lot of trouble getting my hunger back up, and someday I may be spent and bitter."[58]

Upon his graduation from Yale Law in 1973, he held to his promise to return to Arkansas and put his sterling education to work. At Oxford everyone knew Clinton as the student who was permanently running for office, but back in Arkansas at that point there was no office worth capturing. So, driving home from New Haven to Hot Springs, Clinton stopped to telephone the dean of the law school at the University of Arkansas in Fayetteville and asked for a job. The dean, startled by the new graduate's presumption, told him he was too young. Clinton used his wiles: "Well, I'm that, but I'll teach anything you need for now, and I'm not interested in tenure . . . it's a one-year deal."[59]

He began teaching law in the college town in a remote northwestern corner of the state where the mountains overlooked Oklahoma. Most parents found it difficult to visit Fayetteville, which liberated students and helped the university develop its reputation as one of the country's biggest party schools. But Clinton wasn't as interested in partying as he was in politics. Early in the spring 1974 semester of his teaching year, he began running as a Democrat for a U.S. congressional seat in what was a Republican haven. He was all of twenty-seven. It would have seemed a race of folly, except for one thing: Clinton's girlfriend, who had inside information. Hillary had been chosen for a seat on the Watergate committee staff and was in a position to tip off her boyfriend that President Nixon looked mighty vulnerable. If Nixon fell, he might take a lot of Republicans down with him, including John Paul Hammerschmidt, the GOP congressman from northwest Arkansas whose seat was up and who was vocally supporting Nixon.

That spring, Clinton kept calling down to his political pal in Little Rock, Paul Fray: *Who's in the power structure? Who should I see?* Fray knew all the county judges and sheriffs on a first-name basis, he claimed, and he wanted to be Clinton's campaign manager. Bill took his friend up on the offer. Fray got the bright idea of putting their campaign headquarters up in Fayetteville and convinced Clinton that they could draw on an eager pool of college students as volunteers. No one anticipated just how eager these tadpoles would be, nor the other opportunities they would present for Clinton.

He was a young, single, good-looking law professor, and "of course, he was real flirty, that's his nature," says Ron Addington, a Vietnam veteran who was recruited to the campaign to neutralize strong suspicions that Clinton had somehow avoided the draft. Pretty young coeds were attracted to the Clinton campaign, partly interested in the cause, says Addington, but also drawn by the force of his sex appeal. He remembers Clinton sitting in the middle of a circle of girls at his headquarters, pointing from one breathless volunteer to the next and dictating letters for them to type.[60]

"There sure as hell were a lot of damn seekers and stalkers in that campaign who came around to see and touch and feel," verifies Paul Fray.

"They wanted to run with this guy who was on his way to Washington. Hell, it was a way to get out of the Hot Stove League real quick."

As long as Hillary was sequestered in Washington, behind barred committee room windows, Bill's campaign ran just the way he ran his life: chaotically. Whenever his manager would ask him, "Billy, is everything hunky-dory with the money?," he'd say, according to Fray, "Everything's slick." By May, Fray had to challenge him: "Billy, we're not getting enough money here." Clinton picked up the phone, called his mother in Hot Springs, and said, "You need to go get me X dollars." Virginia went down to Hope and in less than twenty-four hours brought back the required amount—in cash. "Bottom line," says Fray, who didn't have much use for Virginia as a mother, "that woman could do some miraculous shit."[61]

Of course, Virginia was also trying to fight off the shadow of Hillary. It was so nice having her Billy back home in Arkansas and that uppity Yankee woman in Washington, occupied twenty hours a day for six months. But in August, snared by the committee's work and punitive public opinion, Nixon resigned. Hillary Rodham had become a part of history. And now, with the committee disbanded, she was on the loose.

Hillary's Leap of Faith

Washington was steamy on the August evening when Sara Ehrman came home to find her friend Hillary packing her bags. Ehrman asked where she was going so fast.

"I'm going to Arkansas to marry Bill Clinton."

Ehrman asked if Bill knew this.

"Not yet," Hillary said.[62]

Ehrman's face registered her shock and dismay. She sat her younger friend down, hoping to bring Hillary to her senses. In law, she said, it was much more important to be a small fish in a big pond than vice versa. And the big ponds were New York, Chicago, Washington—certainly not Little Rock. Hillary said she wasn't going to Little Rock, she was going to Fayetteville—from bad to worse, in Ehrman's view.

During their heated conversation it came out that months before Nixon's resignation, Hillary had begun quietly taking the necessary steps to join Bill in the college town. She had a position lined up at the law school and a place to stay. Her friend Sara wouldn't have to worry anymore about Hillary tying up the phone all night. The only problem was how to ship her books, papers, and a bicycle down to Fayetteville.

Ehrman, hoping to work Hillary over like a hostage, offered to drive her there from D.C., a three-day hegira. They gabbed and snacked and laughed all the way through the Blue Ridge Mountains, the Great Smoky Mountains, and straight across Tennessee. Every so often, Ehrman would stop the car to admire the scenery and question Hillary's preposterous choice. "Hillary," she would say, "are you crazy? Are you sure you want to go to Fayetteville, Arkansas?" Hillary was uncharacteristically muted in her mumbled responses. Ehrman kept needling. As a professional woman who went to work in the Senate before the women's movement was born, she was offended: "I thought, I worked hard as a woman to help her get the opportunities she was entitled to. I thought she was throwing that opportunity away. I really didn't want her to go. She was so gifted and promising, I thought her life should be on a bigger stage."

"But *his* life," Hillary countered, "is there."

Crossing the Mississippi, their first glimpse of *there* was the swampy flatlands of eastern Arkansas. It is the most dismal part of the state and one that had detoured even the rugged homesteaders who opened up the West.

"He's just a country lawyer," Ehrman rubbed it in. "Why are you doing this?"

Hillary kept her cool while they traversed the state. Eventually they reached the green mountains of Fayetteville. It was a Saturday in football land. The town was swarming with college kids going berserk in anticipation of the Texas-Arkansas football game. The air was filled with the high-pitched sound of pigs in heat. Only the initiated knew it was the "call the hogs" rallying cry of the Arkansas Razorbacks. Hillary Rodham, Ehrman's brilliant hope for the country's future, was about to settle down in a town that was antipodal to Washington, D.C.

"And that," Ehrman says, "is when I started to cry."[63]

THE COLLEGE GIRLFRIEND

"Do you think she really wanted to come to Arkansas? Hell-*ohhh?*" Paul Fray speaks in a stylized southern vernacular bullet-ridden with curses. "That was Hillary's damn goal from day one—to get back to D.C. She didn't give a fuck about staying down here. Clinton and I talked about that one day. He told me, 'We've got to win this race. I want to get *her* back up there to Washington.' "

Fray said, "No problem."[64]

Hillary's vision was equally arrogant. "Without a doubt, she wanted to hook on with a political man," says her friend in those days, Nancy "Peach" Pietrefesa. "With Hillary the power tropism was already there. Her dream was *I can do it all*."[65]

Having decided to eschew living with Bill "because of the local mores," Hillary moved into a professor's house. Then she began dropping by Clinton's campaign headquarters to kibitz. Of those early days Paul Fray remembers, "Everything was hunky-dory between us. But there were some damn schoolteachers running the place like a kindergarten. They were stamping choo-choo trains across the top of his campaign newsletters. We needed some folks in there with political moxie."

Enter Hillary. "She made sure this choo-choo express bullshit was out the door," says Fray.

"The drill sergeant" had arrived, in the view of Addington, the Vietnam vet. Hillary took over the campaign, he said, and the mood at headquarters tightened up from jovial and carefree to dour and businesslike. At first Fray refused to relinquish control. "Hillary never really got involved in our office problems," he says. "Except for the big one."

Despite Hillary's presence, candidate Clinton continued to enjoy flings in towns around the district. Mary Lee Fray, the campaign manager's wife, was given the nasty task of running those girls off. "And there were half a dozen of them," says Paul Fray. "Anytime these girls brought up his name, Mary Lee would say, 'Bill really does love Hillary. I think I hear wedding bells. And you know, Bill believes in marriage for life.' It was like they got hit over the head with a damn hammer."

Clinton also continued to romance a volunteer from Fayetteville, known to everyone in the campaign as the College Girl. She kept pestering Paul Fray: "Hey, tell me if Bill is dead serious about me."

"Honey, you got the chance of a snowball in hell," Fray told her.

"You can't be serious," she protested.

The College Girl obviously had in her mind that she was going to marry Bill Clinton, says Fray. " 'Look,' I told her from day one, 'that ain't going to fly, darlin'. You got to understand Bill Clinton—he's going to have a woman, a different woman, every damn day. Don't get yourself caught up in that little stratagem.' She still wouldn't back off."

Then Clinton himself went to his campaign manager and said, "You need to get Mary Lee to get to know this girl. See what Mary Lee can do to slide her on off down the road. Do you think she could be your baby-sitter to keep her out of headquarters?"

So Mary Lee put on the old southern peach-pie style. In the vernacular, that is *peachpaahstaahl*, a syrupy smooth technique of manipulation perfected by well-born southern women. Mary Lee didn't like her new assignment any more than the College Girl did. "My wife and I had a lot of fights about this little girl," says Paul Fray. "There were times when Hillary would be coming in the front door and we'd be hustling the College Girl out the back. It was sad. It was horrible."[66]

Fray has often been asked if he was the one who started the rumor about the First Lady's sexuality. "Hell, no," he protests. "That was some crap put out by the College Girlfriend in the campaign. Like a lot of other people who were jealous of Hillary, the College Girl was looking for ways to create a question about her. And if you looked at her in that day and age, the sack-o'-seeds dresses she wore, you'd understand it wasn't that hard."[67] Soon enough, rumors about Hillary were circulating around the Gas Light Bar, where chicken king Don Tyson entertained his cronies. The easiest way to punish someone who offended the southern male's image of what a woman should be was to call her a lesbian.

"This rumor has to be faced," said Fray when he confronted Hillary one day. Bill had brushed off the issue.

"It's nobody's goddamn business," Hillary fumed. Fray insisted that the rumors were hurting Bill. "Fuck this shit," blurted Hillary. She refused to dignify the accusations with a denial.[68] Fray, who says, "I use strong language with women, especially when they try to play hardball with me," was equally profane. Following this fight, the competition between the candidate's manager and the candidate's Yankee girlfriend escalated into a full-blown turf war. Bill Clinton remained neutral, as if it had nothing to do with him.

Hillary had no trouble picking up signals that she was not welcome. Once, nosing around headquarters, she found a list of Bill's "special friends" and tore it to shreds. When it came time for the state convention in Hot Springs, everybody else elbowed Hillary out. The campaign office manager failed to reserve her a hotel room, and Virginia Kelley refused to let Hillary stay at her home with Bill.

The convention turned out to be a free-for-all. Mary Lee Fray, then a nursing mother, was slugged by some thugs thought to represent a rival faction in their own campaign. Rumors were flying about drugs, sex, and violence in the Clinton camp. Orval Faubus, who had dominated Arkansas politics for twelve years as governor, got hold of Mary Lee's story of her attack, and in high dudgeon he vowed that unless Bill Clinton cleaned up his campaign, no one in it was going to D.C. and drag down the reputation of his state—not if *he* had anything to say about it.[69] Orval Faubus, the infamous old segregationist, was standing in moral judgment on young Bill Clinton!

At this point, Hillary panicked. She wanted to take over. She came down hard on Fray, who then issued an ultimatum—"I will step down if you want to rework this whole campaign"—and went off in a huff for the first two weeks of October.

Between Bill and Hillary, the relationship was extremely volatile. "They would constantly argue, and the next thing you know they'd be falling all over each other with 'Oh my darling . . . come here baby . . . you're adorable . . .' then throwing things at each other, and then they'd be slobbering all over each other," says Peach Pietrefesa. "This emotional roller coaster went on all the time." The intellectual invigoration the two offered each other was unmatched. Their arguments were sometimes like a great tennis volley; they both had to play at a different level of game than when they engaged with almost anyone else. But it also wore them out. "They were always jamming each other," says Peach.[70]

"All we ever do is argue," Bill confided to Carolyn Yeldell Staley.[71] Betsey Wright had watched the same high-tension tug-of-war between the two when all three had worked together on the McGovern campaign. After a particularly nasty argument with Hillary, Wright heard Clinton complain, "I tried to run her off, but she just wouldn't go."[72]

"Oh, Hillary was going to get him," says Max Brantley, editor of the *Arkansas Times.* "You can't fake the chemistry you see between them in the good times—you just can't do it." How then, did Hillary deal with the evidence, early on, of his tendency to be a sexual predator? "Maybe he was just a good liar," says Brantley. Or maybe, Paul Fray speculates, "She doesn't want to know the whole story. Because if she did want to know the whole story, she could have found out and hung him out to dry."[73]

Hillary handled the problem of the College Girl in her own adroit fashion: she asked the older of her two brothers, Hughie, to come down to Fayetteville and start giving the girl the rush. "That's exactly what he did," says Paul Fray, enjoying a gravelly laugh. "Hughie stalked her every day, every way. She came to me and said, 'I want you to stop this son of a bitch bothering me.' I said, 'You're old enough to get rid of him yourself.' By the end of October she was gone. She jumped up and married some other guy."[74]

But the worst of the blowups was yet to come. It would be a two-hour tirade involving all four main characters.

WAR ROOM

11:30 P.M. Election night 1974 headquarters. Mary Lee locks the door behind Hillary and Bill and her husband, Paul. The boy she has posted outside the door, Neal McDonald, is six feet four. The keys to both campaign cars are secreted down deep in Mary Lee's diaper bag. She has brought all the provisions necessary for a long siege: bourbon for the boys, Dr Pepper and ginger ale for Hillary. "And a change of hose and panties for me, in case it's an all-out sweat-out."

The four of them take positions opposite each other in the twelve-by-twelve-foot room—the Clintons' first war room. One desk lamp and a fluorescent light. A blackboard with all twenty-one counties in the congressional district graphed out with vote counts.

"We're getting our butt kicked," mutters Fray.

Mary Lee is afraid some people in the campaign want her husband to go down to Fort Smith, the Republican stronghold, and "pull a political no-no—cheat, hand out money, steal votes." She notices Bill drinking bourbon and Coke, and she knows he's not a drinker. Paul is gulping Jack Daniel's. Mary Lee knows that if Paul drinks too much, he will get nasty and she'll have no control over him. That's why the keys to their Monte Carlo are in the diaper bag. She's afraid he'll jump out of the window and get in their car and race down to Fort Smith to steal the election.[75]

11:35 P.M. Hillary takes the part of Bill's attack dog. She goes after Paul: *How did everything in this campaign get so screwed up?*

Paul throws it back in her face, "We knew three weeks out that we had problems. If we'd just run a few more ads . . ."

Normal people would have sat down and said, "We have a problem in Fort Smith, but no one's going to jump the gun to clear it up," says Mary Lee in retrospect.

"You got to understand," says Paul, "when Jewish people get together and things don't go right, they get hot and go at each other's throats."

But Hillary is not Jewish.

"She tries to be Jewish."

They are all aware that votes can be bought in Fort Smith. It's a known fact. It's the old way of doing business. Somebody would call up and say, "Hey, I got seven hundred votes here, where's my apron money?" But Clinton knows better. And Hillary is present. They all know that Hillary does not like any kind of chicanery with the election process—*especially* vote stealing. "I told Addington there's no damn way we're going to do it," Paul tells the room. "I mean, my God, how would a campaign manager look going out and trying to hand somebody apron money? Besides, you can't buy something after the fact."

11:40 P.M. The conversation goes straight downhill. Hillary demands to know how the campaign money was spent: *Why the hell are we losing Fort Smith?* "You know Bill loves to go to shit-assed small places and palpitate his ego!" Fray yells. "I kept telling him, you and I need to go down and knock on every damn door in Fort Smith. He wouldn't do it. He doesn't like to walk into the mouth of the lion. He likes to be loved."

Hillary wants to know where the hell *Paul* was the first two weeks of October.

Now Mary Lee gets steamed. She complains about her campaign assignment: "I had to have Bill's girlfriend as my goddamned nanny!"

That stops Hillary for a second or two. Then she comes back at Paul with both barrels: *You found Bill a bedmate while I was in Washington!*

Paul leaps to the moral high ground: "I would *never* procure a woman for a man. The son of a bitch can get his own stuff!"

Outside the door, Neal McDonald, the staffer charged with keeping others out, can hear the chaos. "There was a lot of arguing and yelling and cursing about who was to blame for the fiasco," he says.

You bastard!

"Hillary can cuss like a sailor when she wants to," remembers McDonald.

"Bitch! Don't try to make me the enemy."

"So can Paul," says McDonald.[76]

Mary Lee is not one to be drowned out: "Hillary, I was never to have been used as a cover-up for females, but you have to understand, in a congressional campaign we have to make sure we never get sued. If there were any little girls who got involved, that we even suspected, then someone had to go and talk to them and ask what happened or didn't happen. We were fearful of a pregnancy!"

There is a gasp in the room.

One voice, noticeably silent in this melee until now, speaks up. Bill screams at Mary Lee, "No, you've heard nothing but lies! Not everything is true!"

Hillary never turns her fury on Bill. She vents it all on Paul.

"*Paul* is not the evil one," Mary Lee says, defending her husband. "He may be a foul-mouthed, no-count Southern Baptist, but he's not the Devil."

Hillary and Paul start throwing things: papers, books, furniture. McDonald, the door guard, remembers hearing stuff hit the wall. "I imagine more than a few ashtrays and other things have been thrown at Clinton over the years."

Fuck you, Paul Fray, you were setting him up with loose women!

Then a window gets broken.

"We should have shook hands, southern style, and gone to Bill's place or ours and had something to eat," says Paul Fray, somewhat chastened after all these years. "But this was not handled southern style."

1:45 A.M. Mary Lee locks up headquarters. She and Paul drive off together in the Monte Carlo. "I can't believe you said what you did," Paul snipes at his wife. She says, "It had to come out." Paul broods, "Well, that finishes us."

"So be it," says Mary Lee, as they drive to the International House of Pancakes to treat the surviving staff to comfort food.[77]

That night Hillary probably wondered if her friend Sara had been right. Was she throwing her life away on a man who couldn't control his lust even long enough to win an election? Hillary might have been more enraged had she known what that night's loss would cost her: an eighteen-year detour to Arkansas.

Character is what was yesterday and will be tomorrow. Over the years Hillary would do all in her power to change him, but short of transforming the substratum of southern country-boy culture she would never succeed. Bill Clinton, né Billy Blythe, was always going to need lovin' so bad he could never be fully good.

CHAPTER SEVEN

Arkansas Diamonds and Denim

My parents don't even know where Arkansas is!
They expected me to be doing something wonderful
on my own in Washington.

—HILLARY RODHAM CLINTON

Four years after his defeat in the congressional race, the wunderkind was back and running for governor, and suddenly he and his wife were the talk of political circles. *Have you heard of that fella Clinton?* "He was a totally new face—we hadn't had an attractive new figure in Arkansas since [Senator] Dale Bumpers" is the fond recollection of state senator Jerry Bookout.[1] And he had a smart lawyer for a wife. In fact, Clinton had been working in the trenches and gotten himself elected state attorney general in 1976, where-upon the couple moved to the state capital of Little Rock. But it wasn't until 1978 that the Clintons really exploded on the political scene. At thirty-two, Bill Clinton was elected the youngest governor in Arkansas's history with a stunning 63 percent of the vote. The Clintons promised youth and purity to a state with a soiled political history, but they also came on strong with the sensibility of a new generation.

Their inaugural gala was a carefully planned assault on the senses: four hours of rock and folk music and down-home humor. Ozark folk singer

Jimmy Driftwood set the Diamonds and Denim theme with an original composition about an old-timer who dug up raw Arkansas diamonds and grew enough cotton to dress everyone in the state in denim. "The whole theme of the evening was country come to town—we're just Arkansas folks, but we're kinda sophisticated," says Bobby Roberts, who later became the chief legislative liaison for the governor.[2]

There were plenty of diamonds in the rough who did their best to shine that night. The Greasy Greens sang a lachrymose rendition of "Over the Rainbow." Jim Dandy, a hirsute howler, used his long blond tresses as a lasso, winding up with his band members chucking their guitar picks into the audience. Their fans screamed, "Get it on!" "I think it's important for a governor to do what he can to support the arts," Clinton told the frenzied crowd. "But the real reason we decided to do this," he smiled, "was that all my life I have wanted to be like Jim Dandy." Clinton then performed what the newspapers called a "capable" sax solo. So young, so hip, so sexy, so Sixties. To youthful Democrats, the hope was that the Clintons would bring them a down-home re-creation of Camelot.[3]

Late in the evening "a very special" surprise guest was introduced by the new governor: Orval Faubus. An even more infamous segregationist than Alabama governor George Wallace, former governor Faubus had stood against the government of the United States in the Little Rock crisis of 1957. The shame he had brought on the state by ordering the Arkansas National Guard to block nine black students from entering Little Rock High School was still fresh in many minds. It had been the first test of the federal government's willingness to use force to implement the 1954 Supreme Court decision that outlawed school segregation. Bill Clinton was well aware of this dark history. He had been an eleven-year-old pupil at a segregated school in Hot Springs when a number of white parents pulled their children out of the tense Little Rock environment and drove them fifty miles south to enroll them in his school. For the new governor's gala, Faubus had come out of exile in Texas. The wraithlike figure was dressed in a gray three-piece suit and smoking a filtered cigarette, as eerie a character as the ghost of Hamlet's father. Only scattered applause greeted his appearance onstage. But Governor Bill Clinton was in a redemptive mood and welcomed Faubus back as if to say, "Come on home—all's forgiven."

Little Rock's Lovin' Sisters closed the show, featuring Bill's girl next door Carolyn Yeldell Staley singing to the new governor, "You Light Up My Life." With her final number she reestablished the purity of her friendship: "Lord, Help Me, Jesus."

The other touch of purity that evening was Hillary Rodham. She had permed her long hair. Her inaugural gown was a vintage Victorian design: high-necked, long-sleeved, with a tiered skirt, all done up in a dusty rose panne velvet to duplicate her wedding gown. Fans of the local designer, Connie Fails, were pleased. Others thought the dress "truly hideous." In the setting of a rock concert, it did look like a museum piece.

But the Clintons were full of themselves. After all, it had taken them four long years to put the bitter memories of Bill's first political defeat behind them and rise to the top. For some, those memories were still vivid.

"He was literally on our floor, in Berkeley, for ten days," says Peach Pietrefesa of Clinton's earlier congressional loss, "lying there moaning and groaning and counting the noses of everybody who didn't vote for him. He spent hours on the phone sharing vile stories about his opponent, talking about how the Republicans had stolen the election." It was his usual motif: *the unfairness of it all.* Hillary was very short with her husband. "During his moaning periods, she'd bitch at him," says Peach. Then Peach would get out the restaurant reviews, and she and Hillary would placate Bill by taking him off for the best Mexican food or even to Alice Waters's place, the yet-to-be-famous Chez Panisse.[4]

Clinton was at his least attractive at times like these. Yet after he and his wife would fight, yell, maybe throw things, he would come back to her, cooing and smooching. Hillary couldn't help herself; Bill Clinton would seduce her all over again.

How Hillary Won Bill and Bill Won Hillary

Getting rid of the College Girl and getting Bill over his first postelection blues in 1974 had been peach pie for Hillary compared to the resistance she faced from Bill's mother. That was one battle Bill Clinton had had to fight on his own. On one of Hillary's visits to Hot Springs, Bill waited until his girlfriend was out of the room to present his case to Virginia. As he later related to Staley, his argument went like this:

"Look," Bill told his mother, "I don't need to be married to a beauty queen or a sex goddess. I am going to be involved all my life in hard work in politics and public service, and I need somebody who is really ready to roll up her sleeves and work for me."[5] He asked his mother to pray that his dream would come true.

Virginia prayed and brooded, prayed and seethed. "I would grind my teeth and wish I could sit Hillary on the edge of my tub and give her some makeup lessons," she later admitted. "Show her how to bring out all that natural beauty she was covering up by going natural. None of that mattered to her, though. She was too busy getting educated and doing good things like starting youth advocate programs."[6] But Virginia's deprecations made no difference to her son. Bill was determined to win Hillary as his partner.

"Mother, pray that it's Hillary," he begged Virginia. "Because I'll tell you this: for me, it's Hillary or it's nobody."

Hillary simply played hard to get. After a year of trying on Arkansas life, she had told Bill she wanted to see what all her friends were doing that she might be missing. Off she went on a tour of Boston, New York, Washington, and Chicago to size up her future possibilities in bigger ponds. She made him pine and fret so badly that he poured out his heart to his pals Jim McDougal and the future Susan McDougal.

One night at Frankie's Cafeteria in Little Rock, Bill met Jim with his usual bear hug and said, "I've got something to tell you." McDougal expected to hear a rundown on Clinton's current campaign: early in that summer of 1975 he was running for state attorney general. But the minute they sat down, Bill began talking about a girl: "I can't get her off my mind. She isn't like any girl I've ever met before. Nothing like the girls I've dated around here. I'm seriously thinking for the first time in my life"—he laughed, as though he could hardly believe it himself—"about getting married to her."[7]

Jim, who was just beginning to date Susan, egged him on: "Don't worry about marrying someone different. You'll need someone stronger to support you."

Bill was jumpy until Hillary returned to Little Rock from her East Coast sojourn in mid-August. Bill picked her up at a small local airport near Fayetteville. He was fairly wagging with pleasure, his face pink under an awning of unruly hair. "You know that house you liked?" he said. Hillary looked blank. "What house?" As Bill tells the story, she had made a passing comment about a pretty little glazed-brick cottage. He'd gone out and bought it, feathering the nest with an antique bed and flowered sheets from Wal-Mart.[8]

"So you're going to marry me," he declared, winding up his pitch as he pulled into the driveway of the house. But Bill would have to propose more than once, and he kept working on his mother: Couldn't she treat Hillary with a little warmth, or at least show her fitting respect? Virginia was forcing her son to choose between the two women he loved, just as she had done in the traumatic battle with her own mother over the four-year-old Billy. Only this time, realizing that she was in danger of losing, Virginia had what she called her "conversion on the road to Arkadelphia." With tears of remorse, she sat down and poured out her heart to Hillary in a long letter. Virginia believed she had made peace with the other woman in Bill's life. But Hillary never answered or acknowledged the letter.

"I kept struggling between my head and my heart," Hillary once told me. Head said: gold-plated law firm in New York or public-interest law in Washington. Heart won, she said. And when she had moved to Fayetteville, she saw it as "a leap of faith. I just knew I wanted to be part of changing the world," she explained. "Bill's desire to be in public life was much more specific than my desire to do good."[9]

Even as the young lawyer insisted she knew exactly what she wanted, some serious cracks in her argument were exposed when she debated her choice with another young teacher at the law school. Ann Henry and Hillary had bonded over their activist role in raising a cutting-edge issue for feminists: rape. Together they had set up the first rape crisis phone line in Arkansas. Hillary told Henry she envisioned a marriage in which Bill would be the candidate and she would have an independent career as well as being his senior partner—rather like in a law firm. Her friend, already a political wife and mother, warned Rodham that as a wife she would have to choose: either push her own career at the risk of jeopardizing her husband's, or accept less independence.

The Clinton marriage "nearly didn't happen at all," Hillary disclosed many years later in her syndicated newspaper column. "Making the decision to get married took time for me. . . . I just could not bring myself to take the leap marriage requires. I never doubted my love for him, but . . . I couldn't envision what my life would be like in a place where I had no family or friends."[10]

She waited until the very last minute to make her decision. Two months after Bill's first proposal, ignoring all her friends' advice, she said yes. But Hillary wanted no fanfare, no engagement ring. The most formal event surrounding the Clinton marriage was an engagement party shortly before their wedding in October 1975. It was a chilly night in Hot Springs when Jim and Susan McDougal drove down from Little Rock to meet the woman Bill had been raving about. "Bill was sitting in a chair, and she was sitting on the arm," remembers Susan. "She looked different than anybody else at the party. She didn't have the cheerleader good looks. She had frizzy hair, the big glasses, no makeup—she wasn't all dolled up. But she was very down to earth, quiet, and kind. They were holding hands and looked very much in love at that party."[11]

A simple at-home ceremony in Fayetteville was Hillary's plan. Virginia Kelley dreaded the wedding. She, her fourth husband, and a couple of friends made the long drive up to the mountainous outpost, expecting to see the couple's new home all picture perfect. Virginia took one look— "they had paint buckets out and light fixtures to put in and all this mess everywhere"—and took her party off to the Holiday Inn in a huff.

Late that day, October 10, the eve of her wedding, Hillary's own mother asked her what her dress looked like. What dress? For Hillary, a wedding gown was irrelevant. Aghast, Mrs. Rodham rushed her daughter to the town square of Fayetteville, where the only dress store open was Dillard's. Hillary reached into the rack, pulled out the first dress, a Jessica McClintock Victorian lace gown, and said, "This will be fine."

"Whoever heard of a bride doing that?" was the reaction of Ann Henry, to whom fell the role of hostess for the Clintons' wedding reception.

Given Hillary's usual modus operandi as a long-range strategic planner, her wedding seemed strangely out of character: put together like an after-thought. The wedding itself was brief, unceremonial, dry-eyed, almost a nonevent. Dry-eyed except for Virginia Cassidy Blythe Clinton Dwire Kelley, who was distraught over Hillary's defiance of the most basic marital tradition: the bride refused to take her husband's last name! Bill had broken the news to his mother that very morning. Virginia had never conceived of such a travesty. All she could think was that this had to be some fad imported from Chicago.

Ann and Morriss Henry were prominent young Democrats in town, hence the choice of their home for a lawn party for two hundred friends and political supporters. The wedding couple turned their reception into a political pep rally. Conversation focused on Bill's next run for office in 1976. It was Hillary, however, who upstaged him at the reception with the breath-taking announcement that she would remain Hillary Rodham rather than take her husband's name. That fact was prominently mentioned in the otherwise brief, colorless wedding announcement in the *Arkansas Democrat-Gazette.* Paul Fray, representing the voice of southern tradition, warned Bill, "Hillary Rodham will be your Waterloo."

Most unusual of all, Hillary took her family along on their honeymoon. Father Hugh, brothers Hughie and Tony, and Mother Dorothy all went off to Acapulco and stayed in the same hotel with the newlyweds. It was all so prudish, almost like an arranged marriage. Don Jones, Hillary's youth minister and first mentor, who hadn't even been invited to the wedding, found it particularly odd that the couple would want to share their first married days sunning and supping with their in-laws. All he could figure was "It might have been ideological—part of the long flowered dresses and Coke-bottle glasses, not being glamorous or pretty—part of the antiestablishment ethos of the times."[12]

It is also possible to see in Hillary's struggle over this momentous choice a "step style"—the characteristic way a person engages the steps of adult development—that she would repeat at important junctures throughout her life.[13] She does not tolerate ambivalence well; it provokes too much anxiety. To stay with the confusion and indecision of *not knowing* is uncomfortable for anyone, but for a person who dismisses inner turmoil as a waste of time and who is driven to act, there is little inclination to explore the real source of inner conflict. So, given Hillary's inability to hold ambivalence, she often rejects the advice of friends and advisers, makes a firm choice, and dismisses any lingering doubts. If she later has second thoughts about her choice, she denies them.

Why did she marry *him*, anyway? That was the question that kept her Wellesley classmates, the McGovern campaign feminists, and many of her Park Ridge friends gossiping for months, years. Most of those who knew Bill thought he was terrific. But *move to Arkansas? You gotta be kidding . . .* the subtext clearly being *buncha redneck racists.* "We were quite shocked," admits Dr. Art Curtis, reflecting the majority view of Park Ridge society. "We figured she'd do something herself, not be the First Lady of Arkansas."[14]

"I was disappointed when they married," admits Betsey Wright, who had been crazy about the dating couple when they had come to her home state of Texas to work for the McGovern campaign. "Hillary has been absolutely critical to Bill's success, but then I had images in my mind that she could be the first woman president."[15]

Mack McLarty, the childhood friend of Bill who later served with Hillary on corporate boards in Arkansas, made an affectionate remark about the two men's choice of wives. "I married above myself in terms of intellect, like the President did."[16] The Clintons would later draft McLarty to serve in the presidential administration until he had outlived his usefulness and returned to the private sector halfway through the second term.

From Clinton's point of view, it is not surprising that he should have married "up." Many First Ladies have come from social backgrounds "significantly superior" to those of their husbands, according to historian Betty Boyd Caroli. They boost their mates' careers by helping to smooth their rough edges.[17] The attraction between Hillary's role model, Eleanor Roosevelt, and her ambitious husband was not so different from the qualities that drew the Clintons together. Franklin Delano Roosevelt was a fun-loving, loose-tongued, even frivolous mama's boy when he met his serious-minded, moralistic distant cousin. When Franklin proposed, he told Eleanor that with her help he "would amount to something someday." Her modest protests—"I am plain. I have little to bring you"—were ignored. The presidential hopeful knew that Eleanor, the favorite niece of then Pres-ident Theodore Roosevelt, who gave the bride away, would be the perfect political spouse.[18]

What her friends may have missed about Hillary was the strength of her moral absolutism. Once she is committed to a course of action, it would take wild horses to turn her around. Her old friend John Peavoy understood her decision. She had written to him years before, "I believe there are some absolute truths." She wasn't sure whether such truths were within man's grasp, she admitted, but she was dead certain they did exist. In fact, she had directed Peavoy to read John Stuart Mill's essay *On Liberty*, an exploration of the nature of individuality and its necessity for any social system that ex-pected to remain creative and vital.[19] "If you're the kind of person Hillary is," says Peavoy, "you see a road ahead and you're determined to go down it. It presupposes an absolutist mentality, in the sense that you're not ques-tioning the value of going down that road."[20]

Yet the man she married was the ultimate relativist. His infamous depo-sition of 1998—"It all depends on what the meaning of the word *is* is"—would make clear that Clinton is a lesson in semiotics made flesh. There were certainly no moral absolutes in Hot Springs, where he grew up. It was evident from the start that Hillary and Bill came from two different worlds. He gravitated toward her decisiveness and discipline. And for her part, Hillary had written to Peavoy asking "Just how alive are we?" Perhaps Bill Clinton brought something dormant in her to life.

It took an observer with a more cold-blooded, pragmatic worldview to assume, "They were both very explicitly focused on his ambitions, but Hillary regarded Arkansas as a place to go and then leave." This was the early impression of Dick Morris, a New York liberal Democrat then making his name as a pollster who would become the Clintons' longest-running po-litical strategist. He first went to work for Clinton in 1977, when Clinton was attorney general and preparing to run for governor. At that point, Mor-ris says, Hillary would only pop in and out of their strategy meetings. Mor-ris didn't pay much attention to Hillary at first, seeing her as no different from hundreds of other political wives.

Susan McDougal made the same incorrect assumption. Invited to the Clintons' house in Fayetteville with her husband, Jim, to toast Bill for winning the gubernatorial election, Susan approached Hillary all girlish and giggly: "Gee, your parents must be so proud of you, being married to a governor."

"My parents don't even know where Arkansas is!" Hillary said laughingly. "They expected me to be doing something wonderful on my own in Washington."[21]

THE HILL WOMAN

"Everybody recognized that Hillary was a partner in this operation from the beginning," says state senator Jerry Bookout. Not everybody liked it.[22]

"Arrogant" was the outcry of the establishment. On the bone-chilling day when Bill Clinton took office, a parade of the Clintons' liberal friends from Georgetown, Yale Law School, Boys Nation, and assorted Berkeley and Harvard types stuck out as pointy-heads in the crowd. "The Clintons immediately managed to offend a lot of people—immediately," says Bobby Roberts with regret. "You had three guys with beards coming in from outside the state—John Danner [the Berkeley lawyer], Steve Smith, and Rudy Moore—as the governor's troika of legislative assistants. This was supposed to be a new, progressive look for Arkansas, but it put an image out there that a lot of people didn't feel comfortable with."[23] This was a poor, conservative state where a country song then popular in the South ridiculed such people as "long-haired hippie-type commie fags who voted for George McGovern."[24]

Clinton had made no fewer than fifty-three specific promises before he took office. Two of them were supposed to be fulfilled the first day: a budget summary book and drafts of all his bills. It was absurd, what one adviser called "a pent-up idealistic agenda." His first state address was so tediously detailed that it even covered the legal time limit landlords were allowed to hold back security deposits after renters moved out.[25]

"Clinton is a voracious reader," says Roberts. "He's also a garbage brain. You spend twenty minutes with him doing a quiz session on the issues, and he'll just file away the information. Whenever he needs it, he'll start spitting out statistics and issue minutiae. His recall is remarkable." But to many plain folks he seemed too much the liberal intellectual with too many ideas.

The governor's spouse became the lightning rod for people's resentment. To southerners expecting a more decorative First Lady, Hillary Rodham was almost an eyesore. She rejected makeup, glared through thick glasses, drowned herself in big, shapeless fisherman's sweaters and bell-bottoms, and adamantly stuck to her maiden name. "The image she put out was Career Woman—acts as an equal, rather than as a submissive partner," says Roberts.

For Hillary, Arkansas was a different world. Even in Little Rock, women in general and especially political wives were expected to be content with curling their eyelashes and selecting china patterns. Well-educated people seemed to take perverse pleasure in speaking as crudely as the proverbial crackers. *That ain't gonna fly.* For a woman so severely self-edited that she was always questioning her own spelling and syntax, it was grating to hear her peers throw double negatives around: "I don't neither." They knew better. They just thought it was homey.

She had trouble finding friends she could consider her peers. "She is not a gregarious person by nature," says Bobby Roberts, who observed Hillary over the ten years he worked with the Clintons in Arkansas. "She's always played her cards pretty close to the vest, she doesn't expose much of her feelings. Some people take that as being rude and standoffish." The First Lady's aloofness was magnified in contrast to her husband's hyper-gregariousness. Clinton never confronts people. He is a master at never quite telling a person no. Hillary is very direct. "People down here don't know how to deal with a woman like that, which I think isolated her even more." says Roberts.[26]

"Hillary's hard to know," concedes Carolyn Staley, who considers herself a close family friend. "I never knew from one day to the next how I was going to be received by Hillary. She's always very busy, she knows exactly where she wants to go and how to get there. You're either useful or extraneous to her." Finally she blurted, "Look, Hillary's tough as nails. Bill has always deferred to women to fight his battles."[27]

Hillary did click well with Jim McDougal, however, according to his widow, Susan. "Jim thought Hillary was a rock for Bill," says Susan. "He knew that Bill did not have a serious mind about money and finances. Hillary was more interested in business and financial things than Bill." She laughs. "Bill could have cared less about money. Bill just liked Jim's jokes."[28] It was Jim who interested Hillary in a little land development scheme on the White River, not coincidentally on the eve of the 1978 gubernatorial election.

"He invited them in very casually," says Claudia Riley, widow of a former Arkansas lieutenant governor. "Jim was a tortured person, always caught on the wings of some destiny never to be fulfilled." Fancying himself a reincarnation of FDR, he drove around town in a baby blue Bentley, leaning back to draw on a cigarette from a long cigarette holder.[29] "With Jim, everything was the game, the quest," said Riley. "And everything was done on a handshake and friendship."[30] He desperately wanted to cement a friendship with the man who would be governor. By Jim McDougal's own account, he saw Bill and Hillary down at the Blackeyed Pea restaurant and said, "I've got this piece of land up on the White River I'm going to buy. Do you want to go in with me? I'll take care of setting the financing up. They said okay."[31] To be clean politically, all partners in the deal should have made an equal investment and shared equal risk. But the Clintons put up only $500—as against Jim and Susan McDougals' $268,000—yet the Clintons later claimed tax write-offs totaling $24,154 for interest payments they had supposedly made on three separate Whitewater loans.[32]

Years later, attempting to cast her entanglement in the sinkhole of this financial deal as totally innocent, Hillary recited for Barbara Walters a favorite children's rhyme:

> As I was standing in the street as quiet as could be,
> A great big ugly man came up and tied his horse to me.

This verse—a grand self-delusion—has been trotted out by Hillary many times over the years. As far back as 1978, she had flagged it in a book of children's poems she gave to Peach Pietrefesa entitled *A Great Big Ugly Man Came Up and Tied His Horse to Me*, which Hillary described as "a work of considerable philosophical importance."[33] Who was this great big ugly man? Jim McDougal, a dime-a-dozen political hustler? Bill Clinton, the man to whom she had tied her own horse? Or maybe it was the shadow self inside Hillary, disguised as a great big ugly man. In any case, she came to believe—or at least tried to convince some others—that Whitewater was a stupid land deal with Bill's Arkansas friends that he expected her to clean up.

"Hillary's view was 'If you want to throw your money away, go ahead, but I'm not part of this,' " claims one of the First Lady's attorneys in the Whitewater imbroglio, Jane Sherburne, a partner at Wilmer, Cutler and Pickering. "In moments of frustration, she made it sound as if she had strongly objected. Based on the paper record, she went along," the attorney acknowledged, "but she always thought, 'This is Bill's project.' "[34]

But McDougal himself described how "Bill's eyes glazed over" whenever the two couples discussed any details of the deal. "If there was any business to discuss, I discussed it with Mrs. Clinton and not with the governor." She understood every nuance, he has said. "I found her astute."[35] Why did Hillary even abide McDougal? I asked Jane Sherburne. "She's a political wife," was the obvious answer. "The South has a lot of colorful characters. The guy had a connection to Senator [William] Fulbright. He was a political player in the state."

Wanting to ingratiate himself more personally with the new governor, for whom he briefly worked, McDougal encouraged his wife to be friends with Hillary. Susan tried calling her. They went to the movies and saw *Network.* "She loved it, I hated it," says Susan. They shopped together for raincoats. "She went for London Fog. I looked for something, um, less, um, tailored. We just had totally different tastes. I made an effort because Bill was Jim's friend, but we never had the sort of friendship where you exchange deep confidences or anything like that. It was very surface."

One wonders if Hillary ever tried to lure her husband away for a romantic weekend, just the two of them. "She and I went to Hot Springs once to look for a lake cottage with a boat dock, so she and Bill could get away together," remembered Susan of her days as a real estate agent. "We talked about it several more times, but we never found a place."[36]

Probably Hillary's closest friendship at that time was with Peach Pietrefesa, the principal of an elementary school in Tiburon, California. Peach had come to Arkansas with her husband, John Danner, intent upon joining their friends in the mission of bringing Arkansas into the 1970s. Peach remembers the intensity of a friendship forged by two bright nonsoutherners who felt isolated in an alien culture: "I remember one time we sat at a hearing on abortion, holding hands, because we couldn't believe what was being said." To most Arkansans on the governor's staff, Peach was just another uppity Yankee female and Hillary's cohort in retaining her name as a married woman. "Being with Hillary brought out the arrogance in me," admits Peach with a chuckle. "We were two smart women feeling our oats. It confused me that Hillary intimidated other people. But I did, too."[37]

Everyone who worked on the governor's staff was terrified of Hillary, says Peach. But with her few chosen friends, she was both affectionate and indulgent: "She had this very flattering way of talking about her friends as the smartest, most wonderful people in the world who were doing the most clever, important, terrific things." She sent Peach and John some seventy books, one signed, "To the Peach Woman. Love, the Hill Woman." She had a wonderfully wacky, playful sense of humor, says Peach. "I think Bill engaged that. They were both very good observers of the absurdity of human nature." The Danners had actually slept on the Clintons' couch during their gubernatorial election campaign. At night the foursome loved playing Pounce, "a wild card game conducive to cheating, lying, aggression, and other forms of social mayhem," as described by Peach.[38]

One day Hillary pranced into the living room, tossed Peach a fistful of bubble gum, and announced to the two husbands, "Okay, we're going out cattin' around. See ya, guys." They jumped into Hillary's little yellow Renault and drove to an arcade in Little Rock and played games.

Publicly, Hillary was perceived very differently.

"A lot of people thought it was not a good idea to have a woman who was equal to a man, especially in the South," says Ann Henry. "And Hillary didn't pay as much attention to her clothes as people thought she should. People really began to pick her apart, which she found hard to understand." Hillary did not see any reason to appease such people. On the contrary, she reverted to her role as a "pseudohippie," fiercely stubborn about not being a "face girl" who wastes time on her appearance. She was a woman determined to change the world.

SUPERWOMAN

Hillary wanted to put some distance between her career path and the slimy sexist sewer of Arkansas politics that her husband had to inhabit. In 1977, she had been one of the first women in the state recruited by a mainline law practice, the Rose, Nash, Williamson, Carroll, Clay & Giroir firm. Rose, with twenty-one lawyers, was the number two firm in Little Rock (overshadowed by the larger Wright, Lindsey and Jennings firm). But Rose could have fit into one department of Williams & Connolly, a prestigious Washington, D.C., firm that had expressed an interest in Hillary. In Arkansas terms, however, Rose was synonymous with corporate power and old money. Its client list was topped by the three biggest employers in the state: Stevens Inc., Tyson Foods, and Wal-Mart.

Vince Foster, an old friend of Bill's, had recruited Hillary to Rose. A tall, courtly, rectitudinous man, Foster fairly worshiped Hillary from the start. He pointed out to a few of the partners her quick mind and the way she had set up the first legal aid clinic in the state; they, too, were impressed. "I think initially there were some [clients] who might put her into a stereotype—the pushy, Yankee female," according to Webster Hubbell, another Rose partner at the time, "but I don't think anybody after fifteen minutes with Hillary would think that."[39] It was certainly not irrelevant to her recruiters that Hillary was married to the most powerful law enforcement official in the state, Attorney General Bill Clinton.

She considered her position at the Rose firm a day job. Income and prestige were necessary but not what made Hillary Rodham run. She had her own political agenda: improving services for women, children, and the poor.

Even Bill Clinton had been astonished at the way she had rolled up her sleeves within her first months in Arkansas and set up the legal aid clinic at the university where they taught. Her head, however, was still back in Washington, to which she would fly every few weeks to attend board meetings of the Children's Defense Fund (CDF), even though it meant standing by for cheap flights. She also traveled to regional meetings of the American Bar Association (ABA). In 1977 she helped found a lobbying group called Arkansas Advocates for Children and Families. That group was credited with creating the Governor's Commission on Early Childhood, which secured state money for new child care programs.

For Hillary, the first year of Bill Clinton's governorship was a banner year. Not only did they take occupancy of the governor's mansion, with all the free rent, staff, and perks that position entails, but Hillary was also showered with gifts in kind and recognition of her own rising star. A month before her husband's election, she gambled a thousand dollars on a high-risk investment in cattle futures that would bring her an amazing 10,000 percent profit before the end of the year—"amazing" if one bought her original story that she had done it all by herself with a little help from *The Wall Street Journal*. In fact, it was more like an inauguration favor from Jim Blair, the corporate attorney for the heavyweight political contributor Tyson Foods. Jim Blair's wife, Diane, had taught with Bill and Hillary at the law school, and Diane and Hillary had formed a friendship. Jim Blair's guiding hand in Hillary's opening moves in the complex commodities markets cemented the bond between the two couples.

Only a few months after she became the state's First Lady, the Rose firm named her a partner. She had been with the firm only three years and had a "BV" rating by Martindale-Hubbell (meaning high to very high legal ability and very high ethical standards). She was thirty-two years old.

Her pet project as First Lady was educational reform, which was to grow into the signature of the entire Clinton reign in Arkansas. "We've got some really bright, talented students in this state, we've just got to build their self-esteem," she told Skip Rutherford, then an aide to one of the state junior senators, David Pryor. While teaching at the state university, Hillary had been saddened by how limited the students' experiences were. She told Rutherford, "We have to offer them more classes, broader exposure, more internships."[40] After informal consultation with South Carolina's governor, Richard Riley, Hillary launched an Arkansas version of the Governor's

School, a summer program for gifted high school juniors. It was mildly reminiscent of the University of Life program of her own girlhood, where Reverend Don Jones had introduced Park Ridge students to existentialism. But Hillary's Governor's School was not for preppies. Students studied the anticapitalist theories of sociologist Herbert Gans, who explained how America's powerful kept the poor in poverty in order to make a market for heroin, cheap wine, faith healers, prostitutes, and pawnshops.

With her husband's public career well launched, Hillary could now redirect her energies to creating a national presence for herself as a social reformer. Her successful efforts caught the eye of President Jimmy Carter, who, in 1979, appointed the First Lady of Arkansas to the independent Legal Services Corporation (LSC) board, a group of politically connected lawyers that distributed money to local programs nationwide. Within months the White House advanced Hillary as its candidate to chair the board, and soon after she was elected to another "FW" post, as she called it: First Woman in the organization's history to hold the chairmanship.

She was an indefatigable networker. Through her activism with the CDF, the LSC, and the ABA, Hillary kept in close contact with her East Coast colleagues from Wellesley, Yale, and the Watergate committee. It was truly the feat of a superwoman to forge all these activist links around the country from a remote home base in Arkansas and to direct the efforts of LSC's five thousand lawyers spread across 335 legal services offices and handling a million cases a year—all the while continuing to practice law at the Rose firm.

As if that weren't enough, Hillary was gearing up to do battle with yet another American president. Richard Nixon had tried to kill off the Legal Services Corporation in the mid-1970s before it got on its feet, but he had failed. By 1980, Carter's presidency was fading and Ronald Reagan, the popular California governor who was chasing the GOP presidential nomination, had slashed his state's legal services for the poor. Hillary's struggling organization was imperiled. She went into battle mode. Legal Services funded a drive to turn out a "no" vote against a California proposition designed to endorse Reagan's cuts. It was defeated. But the fight was not over.

Once Reagan became president, he announced his intention of eliminating funding for the LSC altogether. Even Arkansas senator Dale Bumpers, who had formerly been considered a friend of the Clintons and of LSC, signed off on amendments that would have debilitated the organization. Hillary launched a nationwide lobbying effort to ensure the survival of her first political platform. As the Reagan administration prepared to

anoint an all-new conservative board, Hillary and her executives circum-
vented the Reaganites by transferring their organization's imperiled grant
money into shell corporations. But defensive moves are not the Rodham
style. She also went on the attack, suing the Reagan administration to prevent the president's appointees from even holding a meeting. She hired
Vince Foster, her recruiter at Rose, to represent her. They orchestrated a
press effort that ensured that the Reagan appointees would be skewered as
heartless bigots. All eight nominees were rejected by the Senate and replaced by moderates who didn't dare mess with Hillary's policies. Ultimately, the thirty-two-year-old Hillary walked away having used the legal
process to tie up another president.

CHELSEA MORNING

Hillary had an inordinate fear of being swallowed up by domestic life. It was
the one discordant note in the otherwise joyful news she shared with her
friend Peach in the summer of 1980—at last, she was pregnant! After
sharing in her friend's pleasure and pride, Peach began to raise what she
called "the gray area": How would motherhood change what Hillary was
capable of accomplishing? How would it affect her relationship with Bill?
Would they still be equals? On and on rambled Peach about the problems of
self-definition faced by women who want to do it all.

"Hillary denied any concerns whatsoever on that front," says Peach.
"Raising the gray area, I discovered, was horrifically threatening to her.
She denied having any ambivalence. She'd say, 'I am absolutely sure, and I
don't even want to discuss this.'" Despite severe problems that would develop with her pregnancy, notably endometriosis, she was adamant about
having the baby. As she once told Peach, "I don't think I could ever be a
woman without having a child."[41]

She never quit working. "It was nothing for her to come back to the
mansion from work at eight, nine, ten at night," remembers Captain Larry
Gleghorn, head of the Clintons' security detail at the time.[42] Night work
was not the only strain she put on herself in maintaining her superwoman
pace throughout her pregnancy. In her eighth month, she flew to New York
City with officials from Arkansas's Children's Hospital to make a presentation to underwriters who would determine the hospital's bond ratings. Dr.
Betty Lowe, the hospital's medical director who later became Chelsea's personal pediatrician, remembers that Hillary was quite uncomfortable during the trip. But she was also gallant. "Hillary made a wonderful

presentation to the money people at the bond house," says Dr. Lowe. After listening to the "elderly primiparous"[43] governor's wife speak passionately about the need for a neonatal nursery, one of the bond raters said it was the most fascinating presentation he had heard in years. He remarked that the hospital's financial backing (roughly $5 million) was poor, but given such a dedicated group, he was going to recommend it receive an "A" bond rating[44]—an impressive rating in view of the hospital's lack of assets.

Having trained in the Lamaze method, Hillary planned to have natural childbirth. It was not to be. According to Carolyn Huber, Hillary's mansion coordinator and close confidante, Hillary believed the baby came three weeks early because she was under the emotional stress of litigating a tough child custody case.[45] There were harrowing hours until Hillary underwent a cesarean. Bill paced outside. Diane Blair remembers Bill emerging from the delivery room in green scrubs, cradling a seven-pound baby, saying he was "bonding" with his new daughter, and generally acting "like he'd invented fatherhood."[46] The proud parents named their daughter after a Joni Mitchell song they both loved, "Chelsea Morning."

When the newspapers reported that "Governor Bill Clinton and Hillary Rodham had a daughter," voters were outraged at the blatant feminism of their First Lady who was *still* going by her maiden name. Ignoring the backlash and ever more determined to prove that the demands of motherhood would not slow her down, six weeks after her baby's birth Hillary was up and off to Memphis. She left her newborn daughter with her friend Peach. "The feminist I considered myself to be did not think a child of six weeks should be left with anyone else," says Peach. "Especially to go to some second-rate junko regional bar association meeting. This was her denial of emotional circumstances—by getting out there to fight what she had decided was going to be a terrific fight, it was a way to make what she was doing heroic."[47]

Hillary was breast-feeding her baby daughter in the next board meeting of the Legal Services Corporation. She continued to commute from Arkansas to Washington on a monthly basis and to run the corporation's two-day board meetings. Later in the year, Bill flew with Hillary to Washington and took care of Chelsea while his wife exercised her executive functions.

She was also trying to wean her husband away from the Arkansas good ol' boys. Carolyn Staley observed, "When they [sic] were first elected [as governor], Hillary told him, 'Think about who you really want to have dinner with, because now anyone will come.' She was probably always afraid that he was going to continue to suffer his old friendships way too long past their value stage" (Jim McDougal, for instance, who would become competitive with the woman he called "Auxiliary Hillary"). Staley recalls Hillary telling her husband, in effect, "There is a whole 'nother world out here, Bill Clinton. Let me introduce you to a network of very smart, very competitive, wealthy achievers. We're going to make that the staple of our life."[48]

But she made her peace with Clinton's mother—or rather, a silent pact. Carolyn Staley confided that "Virginia and Bill and Hillary have taken what might otherwise have been made out to be a debilitating background and they've carefully developed a spin to their lives to make Bill the conquering hero."[49]

With Hillary plotting his trajectory, Clinton's star rose rapidly—too rapidly.

TAKING CARE OF "BABY"

The new governor made the naive assumption that his resounding win in the election was a mandate to revolutionize his state—a mistake that he would later repeat as a first-term president. With a potpourri of ideas from progressive policy thinkers around the country filed away in his photographic memory, Clinton came on like a whirlwind. He created new departments, revamped the health care system, reorganized school districts, and speeded up the action agenda on educational reform previously set by Governor Winthrop Rockefeller.

And he continued to campaign. He couldn't wait to get out and around the state to meet and greet strangers and revive the alchemy that had seduced them into voting for him. When they spilled their problems, he would say, "Come by my office, let's talk some more." Too many of them did. Of course, he didn't have time to see them all. Operating on what his staff called "Clinton time" drove everyone, especially his wife, a little crazy. Even Clinton would complain, "I have no time to be governor!"[50] Staffers would fib to him about the time he was due at the next event, yet at the end of the day he'd still be running an hour or two behind. But he basked in the adulation.

Some saw a certain infantile narcissism in this behavior. It was unforgettably captured by a beloved Arkansas cartoonist, George Fisher. He began caricaturing the new governor as a baby in a buggy. Clinton protested. That only encouraged the cartoonist. He graduated "Charming Billy" to a tricycle and put him into a little sailor's suit. Clinton was thirty-three, and his nicknames were regressing from "Wonder Boy" or "The Boy" to the infantile "Baby."[51]

"His attention is focused on himself a lot," acknowledged his longtime gubernatorial assistant Bobby Roberts. "But he can also be very caring—as long as it doesn't cost him very much."[52] Along with legions of other Clinton observers, I have watched the man continue to work a ballroom even after the help has begun stacking the chairs on the tables and Hillary has gone to bed. His mother wrote, "Bill and Roger and I are all alike in that way. When we walk into a room, we want to win that room over. If there are one hundred people in that room and ninety-nine of them love us and one doesn't, we'll spend all night trying to figure out why that one hasn't been enlightened."

"You can say either he has a great, sympathetic imagination, or you can say he's a sociopath," comments Gene Lyons, a senior columnist for the *Arkansas Democrat-Gazette* and well-known Arkansas novelist. "He understands where people are coming from, he grasps who they are emotionally—how they *feel* about what they think. And that's one of the reasons people are drawn to him."[53]

"Bill was the one everybody loved," says Susan McDougal. "Hillary didn't need to be loved the way Bill did. She didn't need the campaigning, which is where he gets his needs met."[54]

"It was awful watching him so-called govern," laments Peach Pietrefesa. "He never committed himself to anything. His word couldn't be counted on." The governor became enthralled with polls. He called in his polling wizard, Dick Morris, to ask if he should fund highways or education. Morris pronounced education to be the real magic. Clinton decided to fund highways instead—"partially, I would imagine, because there were more campaign contributions to be gotten from highway contractors," says Morris. "And partially because the good-ol'-boy network wanted highways."[55] Morris conducted polls to determine the most palatable way to raise taxes for the new roads. The fastest method was to raise annual license fees. Two powerful lobbies, the trucking and poultry industries, raised hell. Clinton settled on a compromise that upset everyone: the licensing fee would be determined by the weight of the car or truck. Thus, middle-class owners of spiffier, lighter, newer cars would be taxed less than poorer citizens who were still driving heavy old jalopies or pickups. Morris watched the compromise turn into a disaster.

Reenter Hillary the drillmaster. "Hillary was always the one who came in to clean it up," says Susan McDougal. "She would make the plan, draw the lines of battle. That was her forte, it was what everyone expected from her."

Hillary once said jokingly, "If I didn't kick his ass every morning, he'd never amount to anything." But, as Susan McDougal points out, "There's always a grain of truth in humor. It was Hillary's way of saying 'I'm pushing him. Everybody help me.' She'd look around as Bill dallied to meet and greet more voters and say, 'Help me—help me get him out of here and on to the next thing.' You always knew that Hillary was about the business end of it, and Bill was about being loved. That was just the way they were."[56]

Some saw greater promise in Rodham than in her malleable husband. "Bill Clinton knows what's right, but he won't ever commit one hundred percent if the political damage to himself is too great," says Max Brantley, the longtime Arkansas journalist. "And I guess that's the thing about Hillary; there are times when she just might."

But on one thing, Bill Clinton and Hillary Rodham were in sync right from the start: anybody who worked for them, paid or volunteer, had to be willing to devote their lives to The Cause. "And as they have proved through the years," says Brantley, "if someone turns out to have flaws, they just jettison them. They don't look back."[57]

As the 1980 reelection drew near, Hillary's antennae picked up danger signs. A conservative tide was swelling in the land, led by California governor Ronald Reagan and his attacks on Sixties "anything goes" liberalism. President Jimmy Carter was not going to offer coattails worth riding for a liberal Democrat running for reelection in a conservative southern state. Hillary became more heavy-handed with Friends of Bill (FOBs) who worked for the governor. "She began giving them marching orders—who was to report to whom, what was to happen and not happen," recalls Susan McDougal. "She was trying to straighten them up. Suddenly, it was no longer just the boys having fun at the governor's office. That was resented."[58] With the election around the corner, the atmosphere grew tenser and tougher-minded until Jim McDougal bolted, taking two other Arkansas staffers with him. The McDougals were never again invited to the mansion as social friends.

Paul and Mary Lee Fray had been casualties of the first Clinton juggernaut. They were now followed by Pietrefesa and Danner. "The internecine warfare and degree of chaos [in Clinton's first gubernatorial administration] were just the same as you've read about in all the books on his presidency," says Pietrefesa. Southern staffers pitted themselves against the two outside staffers, often taunting them, "I know you think we're stupid, don'tcha?" Disenchanted and somewhat bitter about having believed so fervently in Hillary and Bill, Peach observes today, "This guy has evolved zero. Einstein's definition of insanity is doing the same thing over and over again and expecting a different result. Panetta [Leon Panetta, chief of staff to President Clinton from June 1994 through December 1996] got him into a real straitjacket and to some degree disciplined him. But you can't change a man who gives you his word and it means nothing."

About her once-bosom-buddy Hillary, Peach says, "She thinks everyone needs to understand that she's about such important business, other people are all expendable. There is no traction in their lives with other human beings."[59]

In the last week and a half before the election, the governor's reelection race began biting the dust. Hillary hit the panic button. She dialed up Dick Morris in New York. Eileen McGann answered, startled to hear from the Clinton camp for the first time in the year since Bill had fired her husband. "Is Dick there?" trilled Hillary. No, McGann said, he was traveling. As if no water had passed over the dam, Hillary rushed on, "We need him to come down here *immediately.* Bill's in trouble and we need Dick to do some ads for him." McGann said her husband was busy working on other campaigns and she seriously doubted he would be able to go to Arkansas. But Morris did answer Hillary's S.O.S. When she gave him the dreary poll numbers over the phone, he flew to Arkansas, arriving six days before the election to find the governor reeling from a barrage of negative advertising.

"They were nasty ads that really cut into him pretty hard," recalls Bobby Roberts. The rap against him by his opponent, Frank White, was basically "Cubans and car tags." White blamed Clinton for accepting Cuban refugees expelled by Castro, which the governor had done in part to please President Carter. The car licensing fees hit the raw nerve that Republicans would use so effectively for the next ten years: no new taxes. The coup de grâce was "a hippie wife and bearded chief of staff," says Roberts.[60]

Morris recommended some negative ads attacking Frank White. "Hillary was very prominent in the meetings at that point," says Morris. "She would be nodding. She was always the tough guy in the meetings. Always the one who wanted to take the fight to the enemy, attack them."[61] But Clinton demurred. He was afraid that if he let Morris and Hillary convince him to run counterattack ads, it would be tantamount to admitting that he was worried that White might beat him and would increase his opponent's credibility. More to the point, Clinton was not naturally comfortable with negative campaigning.

Bobby Roberts was astonished to find that the Clinton team had not even done opposition research on White. "Talk about a person who learned not to let her guard down again," he says, referring to Hillary. "They never, never made that mistake again. I think they literally looked out there and said, 'We're going to remake ourselves. And one of the things we're going to do is get in the mainstream.' "[62]

After only one term, Arkansas voters turned their backs on the Clintons. In exit polls many said they only meant to "send a message" that the Clintons' arrogance was not appreciated. But White, a former savings and loan president, interpreted his win as a divine intervention—"a victory for the Lord."[63]

On election night, Clinton was supposed to arrive at the state capitol by 9 P.M. to meet the assembled crowd. His arrival time was pushed back to ten, then eleven, then midnight. Clinton never did show his face at the capitol. Instead, he dropped in on the election party at the Camelot Hotel, where the mood was funereal. He made a five-minute statement, refused to take questions from reporters, and quickly ducked out the back door.

It was left to Rodham to speak for him in defeat.

CHAPTER EIGHT

The Rodham Regency in Arkansas

*Well, fellas, it looks like we might have
elected the wrong Clinton!*

—ARKANSAS STATE REPRESENTATIVE LLOYD GEORGE

The Clintons had furious rows over why he had lost. Hillary lashed out at Bill for his many mistakes: an unfocused agenda, the tax increases, caving in to pressure from President Carter to dump his Cuban refugees in Bill's backyard, failing to respond to his opponent's negative ads, being too damn soft for his own good. One friend arrived at the Clintons' door to see Bill, his head sunk in his hands, walking outside with Hillary behind him bellowing, "Wake up! People believed it was wrong! Can't you see that?"

Some said Hillary took the political defeat harder than her husband did. She withdrew into reading, playing dress-up with baby Chelsea, trudging off to the YWCA to work out. And erupting in anger. When she pops off, it is stinging. "The person on the receiving end never gets over it," shivered Hillary's mansion manager, Carolyn Huber.[1]

Try as she might to pin the blame entirely on Bill and others, this defeat also represented to Hillary the first failure in her own adult life. She blamed the press for creating the issue around her maiden name. "But it wasn't the press," says the journalist Max Brantley. "That was the creation of their political opponent, Frank White, and it happened to play into plenty of suspicion in Arkansas against meddlin' Yankees who don't take their husband's last name."[2] Although conventional wisdom blamed Clinton's loss on "Cubans and car tags," exit polls done by Clinton's own people had produced evidence that the main beef of Clinton's turncoat supporters had been Hillary's feminist stance, which had not registered with voters until the couple had a child.

Hillary was now faced with the natural contradictions of the Catch-30 passage: no matter what career and personal choices one has made during the twenties, in the early thirties the fit feels different. Some inner aspect that has been left out is likely to insist upon being recognized.[3] Hillary wanted to expand her public life, but as a new mother she was already fearful about possibly having to sacrifice some of her career goals. Now this unexpected rejection of her partner by voters only exaggerated her inner crisis. How could she do it all? The whole life structure she had helped to build with her partner was suddenly shaken. In two months, she, her husband, and their eleven-month-old baby would literally be turned out of their rent-free home.

Clinton himself was bleeding and in disbelief for weeks after his reelection loss. He could not bring himself to face any reporters. He kept canceling interviews with John Brummett, the political correspondent for the *Gazette.* It was almost a month after the election before Clinton would see Brummett, and then he brooded, "I loved being governor, probably as much as anyone has ever loved it. And it does seem it was much too short."[4]

"There are a couple of periods in my adult life that were pretty tough," Clinton told me in 1992, acknowledging that this was one of them.[5] Observant friends think that Bill also felt as if he had failed Hillary. "The mutual admiration that creates the closeness in their marriage also produced difficulties," observed Jan Piercey.[6]

Bill Clinton sank into depression and lassitude. He lost focus. "When you would see him walking downtown and offer him a ride," recalls Brummett, "you wouldn't go two blocks before he'd be wanting to know 'Don't you agree that I should have listened more? That I tried to tell people what was good for them? That I tried to do too much? What do you hear about my chances for a comeback?' " At every backyard barbecue, his conversation would circle obsessively around his loss. He would appeal to friends and strangers alike to tell him what had gone wrong. Bobby Roberts, who was then an academic, could afford to be frank with Clinton: "It was mainly a perception problem—you looked like you were going too far too fast, and you'd brought in a bunch of outsiders and a wife who didn't fit the mold. That's what beat you." The beaten governor didn't like to hear that. "If you told Bill something he didn't want to hear, he'd argue fiercely, but he wouldn't hold it against you," says Roberts. "He'd be fine the next day. I was never really sure about Hillary. You might lose her ear."[7]

During the hiatus after he lost the election, the Arkansas press enjoyed kicking Clinton around. One day, Carolyn Staley stopped by and mentioned an unflattering story about how Clinton had commuted a high number of life prison sentences in his last days as governor. As Staley recalls the conversation, Clinton said, "Oh, the people of Arkansas know I'd never do such a thing." Hillary was within earshot. She came flying into the living room, scolding, "See Bill, people believe what they read! If you don't correct it, then people are going to give the press the benefit of the doubt, instead of you."[8]

In fact, Clinton had done just what the papers said he had, and he and Hillary had fought up and down about it. A notable feature of dinner at Governor and Mrs. Clinton's mansion was being served by lifers. When one such poor devil was especially sweet and solicitous of the governor, Clinton would inevitably say, "You know, he's a lifer. I'd love to pardon him." If Dick Morris was at the table, he'd say, "Whoa, wait till you're reelected." And Hillary could be counted on to pile on: "Bill, he's right. You can't do that." Clinton might say, "I guess ya'll are right." Sometimes they joked about Bill being the softie of the operation. But in January 1981, shortly before he and Hillary had to vacate the governor's mansion, the lame-duck governor had indeed commuted the sentences of no fewer than seventeen inmates, including twelve men sentenced to life for rape or first-degree murder.

"Bill, you're out of your mind!" Hillary had railed at him. "You can't do this, you just can't do this."[9] But he had done it. And when confronted on it by a tough opponent in the next Democratic primary, he used classic Clintonspeak: "I never released a single first-degree murderer from prison. I did not do that." No, Clinton did not *release* the murderers; he allowed for parole consideration by commuting their sentences.[10] But the facts would catch up with him and cost him dearly, when his future opponent would hammer him on it with ads foreshadowing the infamous Willie Horton ad campaign that sank Massachusetts governor Mike Dukakis's presidential bid in 1988.

At the time of Bill's disorienting loss in 1980, Hillary's own career at Rose was soaring. She had become a partner and produced a perfect child in the same year. At the same time, according to Betsey Wright, Clinton was truly scared that he was stuck. Herb Rule, one of Hillary's Rose partners, sympathized with Bill Clinton: "You always want your friends and spouse to do well. But not at a time when you're failing. Subconsciously, that's hard for all of us." For the next six months, according to friends, the governor "went a little crazy."[11] As Wright retells it, "He got crazy in the incessant quest for understanding what he did wrong."[12] Clinton began walking up and down supermarket aisles, asking voters "What did I do wrong?"

Hillary and Betsey were appalled by this masochistic exercise. Clinton himself recalled that during this dark period he was so haunted by a sense of imminent death that "I would seize everything."[13] That included the soothing arms of anonymous women. Hillary told me she thought that "he viewed his father's death as so irrational—so out of the blue—that it really did set a tone for his own sense of mortality. . . . Not just in his political career. It was reading everything he could read, talking to everybody he could talk to, staying up all night, because life was passing him by." Uncharacteristically, her narrative began to skip as she talked about it: "I mean it was— it was an intense sense of—what he might miss at any moment."[14]

TEACHING BILL TO FIGHT BACK

The 1980 election represented the first serious flash point in their marriage. It was probably then that Hillary Rodham realized the full import of her husband's weaknesses. When he's down, says former presidential assistant Bill Curry, "he has the passivity of a Buddha."

Bill Clinton is a classic *puer aeternus*, the eternal boy—a Jungian archetype who remains stuck in an adolescent orientation toward life, often prompted by an exaggerated dependence on one's mother. Seductive to men as well as women, the prototypical eternal boy often hopes to redeem mankind. In the archetype he is meant to replace an old king as a symbol of the renewal of life (as Clinton would later replace the tired George Bush). But this "wingèd youth" often falls psychologically and in crisis turns to strong female figures to raise him up again. "Bill has achieved enormous success, but he's still reaching," I was told by Diane Blair, one of Hillary's closest friends. "It's the young man who's been a star and who is, I hope, not locked in adolescence. We don't know that yet," she said in early 1992; "he's only forty-five."[15]

His boyishness was a strong part of his appeal; after all, in terms of world history, America is an adolescent nation. But George Fisher was onto something when he depicted the governor as "Boy" or "Baby," and Clinton must have sensed it when he expressed resentment at the caricature, snapping at Fisher in public, "Draw me ugly, but get me out of that baby buggy." Fisher continued to draw Bill Clinton in the guise of a boy for the next twelve years, later graduating him to a tricycle and then a ten-speed bike, and ultimately, in a striking drawing, capturing Bill Clinton's dependence on his delivering angels. That cartoon shows three wingèd, spear-carrying women—Hillary, Betsey, and Joan Roberts, Clinton's former press secretary—lifting their barefoot boy from the battlefield. They are meant to be Valkyries, "awful and beautiful," who gather up the worthy and fly them to Valhalla, where the souls of slain warriors are waited upon.[16]

Hillary was the one who drafted Betsey Wright, the rough-and-tumble McGovern operative, to be Bill's next campaign manager. Wright would devote the next ten years of her life to protecting him and getting him reelected. "I have always thought it was Betsey Wright who cobbled Bill Clinton back together," says Bobby Roberts, "with the help of Hillary."[17] Wright had her own investment in Clinton's comeback. She moved into the basement of the governor's mansion and spent six weeks surrounded by cardboard boxes trying to sort out his contributor lists before the First Couple of the state was evicted. Hillary and Betsey were indeed his Valkyries for the next six years. Whenever the "wingèd youth" would fall from the heights, psychologically or politically—and it was always a sudden, drastic, engine-on-fire nosedive behind enemy lines for Bill Clinton—he would have to depend on them to rescue him.

But it was Hillary who would have to teach him how to fight—or take on his enemies herself.

"She decided he lacked the discipline and toughness," observes Dick Morris. "He was too idealistic. His head was in the clouds. He wasn't a pragmatist. He needed a tough-as-nails manager." Morris saw Hillary make a bold choice: "In 1978, they were a two-career couple; in 1981, Hillary became the manager of their joint political career."[18]

She picked her target: Governor-elect Frank White. Even before his inauguration, White was scheduled to appear in mid-January at a symposium at the University of Arkansas at Little Rock to recap the election upset. Clinton was invited to debate with him. But Clinton didn't show; Rodham did. White recounted how he had directed his advertising agency to exploit the Cuban refugee crisis. Over the objections of those on his campaign staff who felt that the TV ad was too harsh, White had ordered its continued use, and now he could point to its effectiveness.

Rodham stopped short of calling White's ad "racist," but she noted that all the refugees shown in the ad were black. To many in the Clinton camp, the not-so-subtle subtext of White's ads was "Do you really want to vote for a black-loving tax-and-spend liberal with a hippie Yankee wife?" "The ad was not fair or accurate, but it was very effective," Hillary commented dispassionately. She mentioned that various suggestions had been offered within the Clinton camp on "how to turn around emotional feelings on the Cuban issue" but that Clinton had rejected them all. The implication was that he had refused to take her advice and confront the negative ads. She acknowledged that Clinton's own TV ads had been ineffective in offsetting White's negative ads. Concluding her analysis of the loss with clinical detachment, she commented, "I think a political campaign has come down to a thirty-second war on television."[19] But something in the way she said it reverberated with vengeful purpose. "She was fiery in comparison to White," says Brummett. Max Brantley still remembers her effect: "Her spirits were up, she was eloquent, and her presence said, 'We've been defeated, but we're not through.' "[20]

A CALCULATED METAMORPHOSIS

During their two-year interregnum out of office, the Clintons bought the first house they had ever owned together. It was a small house but in the toniest section of town, the Heights, a mixture of upper-middle-class and bohemian residents. Hillary bought heavy Victorian furniture: "lots of red plush," remembers Morris. Victorian was her natural style.

Clinton got the only paying job he has ever held outside of politics. He was taken on by the premier Little Rock law firm, Wright, Lindsey and Jennings, with the title "Of Counsel." In 1982, his salary was $33,792, considerably less than his wife's earnings of $56,744 at the Rose firm.[21] But Bill Clinton did very little work. Basically, he was given a tiny office where he squeezed his ample six-foot-four frame behind a small desk and used his time to do what he always does—run for reelection.

Having decided to pick up the pieces of her husband's shattered political career and put it back together, Hillary had to ask herself if she were prepared to mark time on her independent career track. It would mean cutting back severely on her efforts to build a record as a legal activist, not to mention losing opportunities for income as a corporate lawyer. But there was an important compensation: the inner aspect of Hillary Rodham that had been left behind with her marriage was that of political leader. Now there was an excuse to live out that part of her identity, but without subjecting herself directly to the pummeling of a political candidacy. She could live it out as Bill Clinton's doppelgänger.

The essential equation in their partnership had been laid down years before. Claudia Riley, who had known Clinton from the time he had returned from Oxford and volunteered in her husband's campaign for lieutenant governor of Arkansas, remembers watching Hillary become the driving force behind Bill's rise as a political star.

"I know these people," says the wise widow. "Bill was ambitious, but he's pretty laid back. I don't think he ever really believed that he was going to be president. Hillary knew where they could go." Although Clinton could think on his feet better than anybody Riley had ever seen, she also saw that he was undisciplined, without boundaries, gregarious to a fault. "He loses himself with the people," she says. "Hillary has always been there to take control. She saw the potential in Bill Clinton, and she was going to take his future and mold it."[22]

After a year of stewing, Hillary made the choice to transform herself. Her husband didn't ask her to do it. If anyone talked to Hillary about the political liabilities she had brought to the defeat, it would have been Betsey Wright. "I certainly wouldn't have wanted to be on that delegation," chuckles Bobby Roberts. "But it was a smart, calculated change."[23]

Without a word from Bill, Ms. Rodham shed her name for his. She also lightened her hair, traded in her thick glasses for contact lenses, and feigned an interest in fashion. Choosing Chelsea's second birthday as the emotionally appealing occasion on which to reenter the fray, she stood beside Bill Clinton on February 27, 1982, as he formally announced his candidacy for the 1982 gubernatorial election. Clinton said he was "finished apologizing" and was now looking forward to a "good and hot" campaign. When he was asked at the press conference about rumors of a name change, he relinquished the podium to his wife. She was defensive: "I don't have to change my name. I've been Mrs. Bill Clinton. I kept the professional name Hillary Rodham in my law practice, but now I'm going to take a leave of absence from the law firm [which she never did] to campaign full-time for Bill, and I'll be Mrs. Bill Clinton." She added tartly, "I suspect people will be getting tired of hearing from Mrs. Bill Clinton."[24]

Brummett addressed a question to Hillary: "Did you change your name legally?" She responded awkwardly. He followed up: "For instance, is your name Hillary Rodham on your voter registration?" Annoyed, Hillary tried to brush him off. Asked if she was planning to change that, she said no. "And that was the end of it," says Brummett. "It was considered such an inappropriate question to ask the former First Lady."[25]

In fact, Hillary did not take formal steps to change her name until May 3, 1982, when she registered to vote in Pulaski County for the first time.

Some of her eastern friends still wondered why she would forfeit her independent identity. After all, it was as Hillary Rodham that she had already earned national recognition.

"Her name just wasn't more important to her than returning Bill to office and making a difference on education and health care," says her former Wellesley roommate Jan Piercey. "It wasn't a sellout or a giving up; it was a trade-off."[26] Her former friend Peach Pietrefesa is far less charitable: "The deal was, she gave up her name and her integrity in exchange for his promise to take them where she wanted to go—to be president together."[27]

Whatever her motives, Hillary managed to campaign flat out for her husband over the next year and still maintain her job at the law firm and fulfill her mothering responsibilities. Once again, she brought in Dick Morris to help with repositioning Clinton. The pollster had been fired by Clinton when the first-year governor was riding high. Since then, Morris had changed his stripes from a New York Upper West Side liberal Democrat to an equal opportunistic hireling who had pulled off some flashy upsets for right-wing Republicans. A natural-born political street fighter who fancies florid colors and speaks in machine-gun bursts, Morris might appear an unlikely choice as Hillary's longest-running political cohort. But his mind moves with stunning speed.

Hillary found a natural symbiosis with Morris.

"Republicans of that era were perfecting attack ads and attack campaigning," says John Brummett.[28] Communications consultant Roger Ailes had pioneered the technique to reposition Richard Nixon. Morris had adopted the practice and used it to stunning success for his right-wing candidate, Ed King, in a Democratic primary that had succeeded in unseating the liberal governor of Massachusetts, Mike Dukakis. "Hillary was intrigued by the technique," says Morris. "Her reaction was not at all ideological, it was purely pragmatic: 'We need to learn how the bad boys do it.' " Thus was Hillary an eager and receptive student of the School of Attack Politics: *You must create an enemy. That is the best way to define yourself. It's all for a good cause, but you have to target a whipping boy.*[29] Having already codified this approach and proven its effectiveness, Morris was able to mobilize Hillary's naturally confrontational impulse.

"I watched Hillary turn the world into Us versus Them," says Peach Pietrefesa. "That's how she looks at the world: she and Bill are good people with the grandest intentions who keep getting screwed."[30]

Hillary waited until Bill had squeaked by in the primary to go after the man who was now her husband's opponent. Governor Frank White remembers well that Memorial Day in 1982: "She ambushed me."[31]

White, who was running for reelection, was the first speaker at a civics club meeting in North Little Rock. Clinton was expected to attend, but again Hillary showed up in his place. When White saw the wife of his vanquished predecessor in the audience, he headed for the exit the minute he finished speaking. Having tangled with Hillary once before, he was not eager to repeat the experience. But Hillary rose and started shouting questions at him.

"She was yelling at me as I left," says the former governor. "I didn't stay to hear it, but she was screaming. You couldn't win, confronting the former governor's wife. She was a woman, and this was the South. You'd look like a bully. But that was Hillary's style—ambushing campaign opponents of her husband."[32]

"*Hillary* beat Frank White when Clinton ran against him in '82" is the unequivocal opinion of former Clinton campaign manager Paul Fray. "She would find out where he was speaking and show up and eviscerate him— in public. Frank White told me point-blank, "I began looking for her. Because I knew whenever she showed up that I needed to leave. She'd put the trial lawyer face on and chop me up." Fray adds, "She gets up there on that stump, and she could kick the dog shit out of you. Frank is still reeling from it, I don't mind tellin' you."[33]

SOMETHING IN COMMON

Five years into their marriage, the dynamics of the Clintons' relationship were all but opaque, even to those who saw them almost daily. Clinton went back to his true love, life as a perpetual campaign. Between 1980 and 1982, he was on the road most of the time. Bill's idea of a schedule was to start as early as human beings arise and stay out as late as there was anyone awake to shake his hand, usually midnight or later. Bobby Roberts would stop by the house about seven in the morning and find Bill and Hillary in the kitchen. Hillary wouldn't be making breakfast, she'd be making lists. She wouldn't play hostess to Roberts, who had taken a leave of absence from his job as a legal aide to drive Bill around the state in his ten-year-old Oldsmobile. If anyone wanted juice or coffee, it was catch as catch can. Bill's gustatory habits were as erratic as his nonschedule; he could go for hours without eating and then wolf down a diner meal and eat the leftovers off his aide's plate.

In the mornings there wasn't much conversation between Mr. and Mrs. Clinton, not even exchanges of a political nature. Bill's nose would be stuck in the newspaper. He did little more than grunt if anyone talked to him, no matter if that anyone was Hillary. "Clinton expects people to attend him at all times," says Brummett. "He is not cognizant of others' needs, except, sometimes, Hillary's."[34]

Hillary's presence on the campaign was like that of a backseat driver. She once directed Roberts to move Bill up on the list of speakers at an event in northwest Arkansas, even though the aide warned her that it would bruise local egos and do more harm than good. Hillary was adamant. Roberts balked. She went ahead and forced the change herself, and, according to Roberts, it did make everybody mad. "But when you're dealing with Hillary, it's pretty clear that you're working for her."

The candidate might make twenty phone calls during a day, half of them to Hillary, who most of the time worked from Little Rock. But it wasn't a ritualistic "I miss you" nighty-night type of call; it was more like checking in with the dispatcher and getting fresh orders: "Bill, you need to call so-and-so *today*." He had no compunction about calling people at two in the morning. A chronic insomniac, he would usually be up and wandering around somebody's house where he was camping overnight. Bored, frustrated by the downtime, unable to fight off his demons until light broke and he could set out again to win people's love, he would read, find a pool table, or telephone a woman he had met that day and flirt over the phone.

"As God is my witness," says Roberts, "the whole time I traveled with him, I never saw him do anything other than be flirtatious. And no more flirtatious than a lot of southern males would be."[35]

John Brummett, who traveled with Clinton as a journalist, describes him as an "ogler"—the kind of man who couldn't walk through a Wal-Mart without running back to tell the reporter, "You got to go back to Aisle Thirty and look—she's a knockout." In those days, Brummett had no idea of Clinton's philandering and put it all down to juvenile male behavior.

Everything about the Clintons was a contradiction. Whenever Hillary joined Bill on the campaign trail, says Brummett, "she always seemed beleaguered, put-upon, like this was not what she had in mind." It wasn't much fun for an overworked mother to drag her toddler on a typical "fly-around" to half a dozen tiny airports, climb up and down the rickety steps of a little prop plane, stand and smile, trying at the same time to keep a garrulous husband on some sort of schedule and a child in the Terrible Twos fed and amused. Clinton liked to relax by playing Hearts. Late one day, when he was about to deal the cards, Hillary piped up from the back of the plane: "Bill, no." He froze. "We've both had a hard day, and you've got a radio spot to cut tonight," she went on. "You need to get some rest. The last thing you're going to do is play cards."

He chuckled and said, "Aw, honey, just one hand."

"We played one highly uncomfortable hand," recalls Brummett. "We couldn't wait to get through it. He cowered a bit when she laid down the law."[36]

But he also had ways of retaliating. For example, one Saturday morning the Clintons made a campaign stop at a hot-air-balloon show in Jonesboro. Like a dog sniffing out a bone, Clinton gravitated toward a bunch of meaty teenage girls in shorts and T-shirts. A female aide said to Brummett, "This is going to be interesting; he won't be able to resist flirting with them, and it's going to drive Hillary crazy." "That was precisely what happened," says the reporter. "And Hillary stormed off and sat in the car."

A garden-variety jealousy scene might be followed by a tender, loving moment that the Clintons had no reason to stage for the benefit of a couple of aides and reporters who were dozing off on the plane at the end of the day. "I'd look up and see them nuzzling," says Brummett. "She'd be saying, 'I love you,' and he'd be nuzzling back. It was a sweet moment, and they thought it was private."[37] Brummett wasn't the first reporter to scratch his head and think, "I'm not sure what this deal's all about."

RETALIATION IN THE BUSHES

"The frustrations I went through in the eight years of being his chief of staff," moans Betsey Wright, "of watching the groupie girls hanging around and fawning all over him. I always laughed at them on the inside, because I knew no dumb bimbo was ever going to be able to provide to him all of the dimensions that Hillary does." According to Wright, Clinton resisted the aphrodisiac effect of his powerful position more than many men. But, she admits, "Bill was always very careless, out of an unbelievable naïveté. He has a defective shit detector about personal relationships."[38]

But he showed a special knack for knowing which women were ripe for the plucking. "He had two levels of women: smart peers who he could tell were having trouble with their spouses, and of course the babes," says Peach Pietrefesa. "He knows human nature so well, he knows how to lay that little 'test' on a woman. Handfuls of women had their feelings hurt. Clinton would come on to them and then be distracted or interrupted. When he came back, he'd look at the same woman like he didn't know who she was. He'd already forgotten their exchange!"

Clinton also knew how to pretend innocence. "He was fucking a married woman in the bushes in the summer of 1980," continues Peach. "He'd go jogging and meet her. She was a former campaign volunteer who wasn't getting along with her husband. Bill would come home and talk about her to Hillary: 'Don't you think she's fabulous? She is such an incredible . . .' Hillary knew what he was doing and got pissed."[39] From a male perspective, however, Hillary revealed a sense of helplessness. She once asked one of Bill's men friends if it should be this hard to maintain fidelity in a marital relationship. "It was almost as if she had run into a problem that she didn't know existed," he says sympathetically. Instead of dealing with it, she developed a pattern of denial.

Bill's pattern was one of seduction and betrayal. And occasionally, when his behavior became too outrageously overt for Hillary to ignore or deny to herself, she would fly into a rage and Bill would add to his pattern another element: repentance. He would hang his head and sometimes weep with remorse, finally promising that he would repent. And then he would continue in the cycle of betrayal and back to seduction. What struck Pietrefesa most dramatically, however, was the Clintons' interdependence: "Her behavior and emotions were very much influenced by what he did and vice versa. Their emotional link was extremely strong."

Eventually, the rumors of Bill's affairs became louder than whispers. According to his biographer David Maraniss, Clinton would soothe his year-old daughter with the lullaby "I want a div-or-or-or-orce."[40] But divorce was not an alternative that Clinton pushed. "In an alcoholic family . . . you tend to try to keep the peace at all costs," he has acknowledged.[41] The fact that Clinton's reality as a child was completely defined by a woman may explain his later dependence on Hillary and other strong women. Bill had also developed the pleasing style of many children from alcoholic homes, who reason, as Betsey Wright describes it, "If I'm really nice and I make this person feel better, then maybe this [behavior] will stop.' " Wright adds, "I can see that in Bill now. He sees it."[42]

Once Clinton had acquired his reputation as a serial philanderer, Hillary's role in their marriage became a popular subject of conjecture: Was she his coconspirator? Did she keep cleaning up after him because she was so intent on holding on to her power? Was she the ultimate family-values conservative, holding her family together for better or worse? Or was she simply in denial?

The couple would go through periodic freeze periods when Hillary might sleep in another room. "But what was most interesting and unanswerable was who was pulling away from whom?" says Dick Morris's wife, Eileen McGann.[43] Carolyn Huber is one of the few people in the world who knows Hillary intimately. She served Hillary as her closest personal aide in the mansion, her day-to-day logistical helper, as well as surrogate grand-mother to Chelsea. Later, Hillary got Huber a job as administrator at the Rose firm but she continued to work on the couple's personal and financial records at the mansion. Huber, too, marveled at Hillary's powers of detach-ment. No matter how strained or explosive the atmosphere around the mansion, the watchful mother bird would be reassured when she saw Bill and Hillary smooching.[44] Their friends called the Clintons "soul mates," ac-knowledging that they confide fully in nobody else, not even family, only in each other.

"She also had an investment in this marriage and his career," the prac-tical Betsey Wright points out. No matter how out of control Bill got in his "crazy period" while he was out of office, and no matter how furious Hillary would get, Hillary never considered divorce, says Wright. "It ab-solutely was not an alternative that she gave him."[45]

HILLARY GOES ARKANSAS

No one who saw the thirty-five-year-old Mrs. Clinton on the night of her husband's 1982 reelection victory could mistake the triumph she felt. She was glowing, a whole new Hillary. She looked soft and wifely in her form-fitting silk print dress; her blond bob fell from behind a hair band, and she beamed a hundred-watt smile. Her eyes caressed her husband's face as he told the cheering crowd, with mock modesty, "I think what I'm supposed to say is that it appears that we have won the election."

On the night of the inaugural ball, Hillary was ready with her beaded inauguration gown, Chantilly lace over charmeuse silk. And for Easter she made sure to pick out the sort of cartwheel-brimmed hat that would stir whispers of "Very nice" and "Just right." The midwestern girl had also ac-quired a southern accent, which came and went as the occasion dictated. As her friend Jan Piercey put it, "Hillary made her trade-offs early on, and I think she steeled herself not to look back."[46]

The conventional wisdom later promoted by Republicans cast Hillary as a big-spending, left-leaning liberal. But in fact, all through the 1980s, much to the surprise of the Clintons' chief adviser, Dick Morris, Hillary was the conservative in the family. "She was more conservative than Clinton was," he maintains. "She was always pulling him back to the right."[47]

"She definitely has a conservative streak," confirms her youth minister Don Jones, who has maintained contact with Hillary. "Particularly on abortion, homosexuality, and capital punishment. Surely, she is for gay rights, there's no question about that. But I think both she and Bill still think of heterosexuality as normative. I think that she's probably pro-choice in general but would also see certain situations in which abortion is frivolous and wrong."[48]

Governor Clinton returned to office with a broad promise to improve education in the state "as the key to our economic revival." He and Hillary were mindful of a study which concluded that Arkansas's school system was the worst in the nation. In some parts of the state, teachers were earning less than $10,000 a year and qualified for food stamps. More than 90 percent of the state's residents lacked a college degree.[49] But Arkansans were so accustomed to being ranked at close to the bottom in any academic comparison of quality of life that they had coined a motto: "Thank God for Mississippi."

In Clinton's inaugural address, he made a case for educational reform: "Without competence in basic skills, our people cannot move on to more advanced achievement." He went on to announce a daring initiative: he wanted a committee formed to study the state's educational system and make recommendations. Then came the stunner: "I have decided to name my wife, Hillary, as chairman of the cause. I think she'll have more time to exercise a sort of leadership and direction the commission needs."[50]

The downside to this idealistic pledge was that it would require another tax increase. One of the reasons Clinton had been voted out of office was because he had raised taxes. Moreover, when he announced that he would ask for a big increase in teacher pay, conservatives in his legislature stiffened to oppose him unless he also pushed for higher standards for teachers.

Hillary snapped up the idea. "Why don't we have a test for teachers and fire the ones that fail?" she suggested to Morris. It was a radically conservative idea, he thought. The teachers' union and the blacks were the core of the Democratic Party in Arkansas. "It meant moving sharply away from the Democratic Left," says Morris. "It took tremendous courage to do that. The rest of Clinton's governorship was a single-issue governorship: teacher testing."[51]

First, as always, Hillary did extensive research. "Hillary read through the curriculum of every school district in Arkansas," says Skip Rutherford, a Clinton campaign adviser. "She became impassioned." Then she marched straight into the heat of public censure. Hillary barnstormed around the state for hearings, town by town, school by school, stopping in all seventy-five counties—an amazing feat of energy and determination for the cause. "I kept running over and over again into people who said, 'These teachers can't read, they can't spell, they can't do anything,' " she recalls. When she spearheaded a requirement for a onetime teacher examination, a school librarian called her "lower than a snake's belly." Ignoring such insults, Hillary pushed on to introduce a consumer rights approach to education, and the fresh but somewhat frightening concept of continuing education for educators.

Hillary lost no time in going up to the state capital to report on the hearings to lawmakers. She had to work fast because the Arkansas legislature meets for only sixty days every two years. In July 1983, she addressed a joint Senate-House legislative committee. Plainly dressed in a white suit and open-collared ruby shirt, her hair uncurled, Hillary did not stop to schmooze in the corridors as Bill Clinton would have done. She took her seat at a small desk in the center of the high-domed, wood-paneled committee room to face a horseshoe of male legislators who sat, unsmiling, in upright pews.

Mrs. Clinton outlined for the legislators the recommendations of her fifteen-member committee: mandatory full-day kindergarten, a twenty-to-one pupil-to-teacher ratio, testing students before they could be promoted, and more math and science units. She also reflected her own childhood training in clearly dividing work from play. "We've confused our students," she said in recommending that extracurricular activities not interrupt the school day. "When you play, you should play hard. And when you work, you should work hard. But you shouldn't confuse the two."[52]

"You could never tell that day she was an Ivy League law graduate," says state senator Jerry Bookout. She used her *faux* southern accent to full effect: "The good ol' boys weren't threatened. Usually in legislative hearings there are a lot of exits and reentrances. She talked, it seemed like forever—no notes—but she had us all mesmerized."

A fidgety figure appeared just outside the door of the committee room and listened in as Mrs. Clinton fielded the legislators' questions with ease and grace. Satisfied that she was doing fine on her own, Governor Clinton left and was mercifully absent when Hillary finished her ninety-minute presentation. The booming voice of Danville rancher Representative Lloyd George, who liked to play country bumpkin, boomed out: "Well, fellas, it looks like we might have elected the wrong Clinton!"

Laughter filled the rotunda. As Bookout says, "I thought it was a real stroke of genius."[53]

It also marked the beginning of the four-year Rodham Regency in Arkansas. From 1982 to 1986, as observed by Dick Morris and others, Hillary Rodham Clinton exercised the ruling power in Bill Clinton's kingdom, much as a European regent does when a sovereign is too young, absent, or disabled to rule.

Her husband massaged his legislature until Arkansas was eventually funneling seventy cents of every tax dollar into educational programs. Those improvements, plus the governor's hike in teachers' salaries, won over the teachers' union, which had been the Clintons' bitterest foe. It was typical of the way their political partnership worked.

RUNNIN' AND GUNNIN'

The more power Hillary assumed in the Clintons' political partnership, the more distorted became their personal relationship. Hillary was both chief breadwinner and political manager, while Bill continued his perpetual campaign. "They did have a man-wife relationship, but they were both so busy runnin' and gunnin' all the time, they hardly ever had dinner together," says Captain Larry Gleghorn, who observed the couple from his guardhouse on the mansion grounds as chief of the governor's security detail.[54]

"Hillary left early in the mornings in her own car," he recalls. "Some days you could feel they were upset, snarling and snapping at each other. They were pretty evenly matched in arguments. Clinton told me once that Hillary was the smartest person he knew." Hillary was not popular with the state police detail. "She never offered us a cup of coffee," says Gleghorn. "She was like a robot. Her actions were that way to anybody who wasn't on her level. You were just in her way."

The governor drove Captain Gleghorn a little crazy, too. A decorated war veteran, narrow-lipped with black hair raked scrupulously over his ears and shades with rectangular metal rims, Captain Larry Gleghorn did not appreciate Governor Clinton's erratic behavior. Clinton liked to go to Washington, and Gleghorn would accompany him. "At night, he'd say, 'I'm going out with friends for dinner,' and he'd order us away. Then he'd leave the hotel with three ladies and two men. He was a womanizer, no doubt about it."

Even in Little Rock, Clinton sometimes tried to ditch his security detail. "I ain't gonna tolerate that," Gleghorn eventually told the governor. "Then we done had a come-to-Jesus meeting."[55]

Baby Chelsea was the object of adoration by both her parents, but their first priority was Bill Clinton's political career. Bill was never happier than when he was campaigning, which kept him on the road most of the time. And when Hillary was campaigning for Bill or traveling the state for her education hearings, she committed herself to a similarly rigorous out-of-town schedule.

A series of baby-sitters was hired at taxpayers' expense to live on the governor's premises and be on twenty-four-hour call. "Everybody spent a lot of time with Chelsea—Hillary's parents and friends and the governor's staff," says Skip Rutherford, but he emphasizes that Bill and Hillary also devoted lots of time to their child.[56] Once their daughter began speaking at age two, I was told by her surrogate grandmother, Carolyn Huber, "Chelsea would say, 'I want my Mama, Where's my Mama?' " But she soon learned to answer her own question: "Mommy go make 'peech."[57]

Commonly, a chief of staff and a willful wife are natural enemies, but again "Hillary made herself absolutely indispensable," says Betsey Wright. She sat in on all of the governor's strategy sessions. "Her own performance in selling and implementing his government programs was extraordinary. There were so many ways he needed her."[58] Skip Rutherford agrees: "I've never seen a Clinton campaign or a major political decision Bill Clinton made without Hillary's conclusions."[59]

With the Rodham Regency running smoothly by the mid-1980s, Hillary was also able to take on some corporate board work. As a sort of resident sociologist on the board of Wal-Mart, a nonunion company with 380,000 employees, she contributed to the retailing giant's ranking in "The 100 Best Companies to Work for in America." Named head of Wal-Mart's environmental committee, she injected her ideals into the private sector and launched the company on a recycling program. She "saved us from a false start on environmental policy," says Rob Walton, son of the company's founder.[60]

But she couldn't save Bill from stepping on another landmine from his past.

It was 1984, toward the end of his second term as governor, when a colonel of the state police phoned Betsey Wright, who dashed out to track down Hillary in a nearby restaurant and tell her, "We need to talk to Bill." The state police wanted to inform Clinton about their undercover surveillance of his twenty-seven-year-old half brother, Roger, who had been spotted selling cocaine.

"It was," Hillary told me in 1992, "a much greater crisis than anything we had in the presidential campaign."[61]

But it shouldn't have come as a surprise to the governor. "Clinton knew since '78 that his brother was hanging out in honky-tonks and strip joints frequented by drug dealers," says Larry Gleghorn, who by then had become the state's head of narcotics. Gleghorn had an informant who lived with Roger's girlfriend, and he wanted to arrange a sting. The informant told the police that Roger was snorting sixteen times a day. Gleghorn called the governor and asked him, "What do you want us to do?"

Clinton said, "Let justice work its way. Treat him like anybody else."[62]

At the time, Clinton was preparing for another reelection campaign. Some people thought his decision was less than nobly motivated. "That boy is such a political animal," carps Paul Fray to this day. "Why did he let his own brother go to the penitentiary over a pissy-assed drug deal?" Fray answers his own question: "Just to make himself look good."[63] Clinton did arrange the narrative in his own mind to make himself a moral hero. After his brother's arrest, Clinton told the pastor Don Jones about the incident. "He said it was a good example of how the law works for the best, because if he had interceded, Roger might not have gone into rehabilitation. He cited the fact that he didn't step in as governor to protect his brother as a badge of honor."[64]

Virginia Kelley said she just couldn't imagine why on earth her boy would want to escape into drugs. "Virginia was sweet to me even when I was puttin' her baby in the pen," says Gleghorn.[65] Hillary stayed clear of the whole mess. Roger did more than a year in prison, then came out to discover that he was cross-addicted to alcohol. Only then did a drug counselor round up Bill, Roger, their mother, and even occasionally Hillary for intense family therapy and lead them through sessions on codependency. The therapist gave Bill a lot of books to read on psychology. Clinton later said the process had helped him to learn things he had never known about himself. The counselor told them that the line between wanting to be a rock star— Roger's dream—and wanting to be a governor is a very thin one.

During "the next two or three years of discovery . . . they all came to grips with having grown up in the home of an abusive stepfather," says Wright.[66]

"After my brother got into trouble in 1984, it really had a profound impact on me," explained Clinton. "I just couldn't imagine. . . . I kept asking myself, how could I not have known this?"[67] Maybe he kept it locked outside "in the black," as his mother had taught him to do. The unfinished business of his past again threw him into a period of disequilibrium. He feared he might not be able to live up to the great expectations of his political life and his life partner. Clinton's soul-searching, which coincided with his early midlife passage from the ages of thirty-seven to forty, also sparked a revival of the behavior that had earlier put strains on the Clintons' marriage.

HILLARY'S BLIND SPOT

Hillary had known about Bill's weakness of the flesh from the earliest years of their dating relationship. Initially, she had put it down to adolescent prankishness; it had nothing to do with her. She simply detached herself from all that. She told herself that it was a very small, unimportant part of her husband's life—a pastime, like when he'd get up in the middle of the night and go down to the basement and hang over the pinball machine for hours. In no way did she see a connection between his sexual escapades and their relationship.

She knew Bill loved her. She didn't feel she was letting him down in any way. Quite the contrary—she was keenly aware, and didn't mind reminding him, of how much she had given up to follow him to Arkansas, drastically limiting her own career and earnings potential, and putting up with a place she loathed, at least initially. She made the money. She gave him political ideas. She campaigned for him. She kept him in the channel. She gave him a perfect child. And when his vast carelessness caused a mess, which was not infrequently, she was always there to clean up after him. What more could a man ask for in a political wife?

And he knew that there is almost nothing Hillary Rodham Clinton can't make happen when she sets her mind to it. The mix of her mission to make a difference and his ambition to be president, warmed by the boil of emotional needs beneath each of their enigmatic exteriors, had combined to produce an alchemy of amazing power. One of the things she most admired about Bill Clinton was the way he could block out ugly attacks, seduce even his sworn antagonists, and arise, phoenixlike and apparently unscathed, from one devastating setback and scandal after another.

In late 1984, when a classmate of Hillary's brother Hugh visited the Clintons in Little Rock, he went back to Park Ridge saying that he saw their marriage as "more a political partnership than a romantic infatuation thing." Notwithstanding, the couple slept together in a standard double bed. Betsey Wright knew it because she sometimes had to wake Clinton up for an early-morning event. Chelsea slept in the bedroom next door.[68]

Hillary may have participated in some counseling sessions for Bill and Roger's benefit, but when it comes to herself she is ambivalent about psychological analysis. Some of her friends say she has little if any insight into herself, and she is quite dense about analyzing her husband's behavior.

"She can talk about the finer points of education policy but not notice her best friend might be suicidally depressed," says one colleague. And she hates it when other people try to analyze her. Later, when it became stylish to label Bill Clinton's characteristic psychological defense as "compartmentalization," Hillary's staff would balk on her behalf when the term was applied to her: "We call it focus."[69]

Hillary acted as Bill's conscience. She was a self-appointed Jiminy Cricket perched on his shoulder, night and day, a traveling superego as welcome as a wake-up call. "I think that there have been many times when he would have liked to go home and turn on the TV and escape or just read a book," concedes Wright, "and she would be in with a list of things people had called her about that day or that had to be done. He would be, 'Ah, couldn't you just be a sweet little wife, instead of being this person helping me be what I'm supposed to be?' Between Hillary at home and me at the office, pushing and pushing him, I know there was a point where he felt, 'These people need to leave me alone. I just want to do what I want to do.'"

Betsey saw the warning signs of a rebellion. Hillary did not.

CHAPTER NINE

Money Business

If Hillary were doing what she most wanted to do in this world, she would not be a partner in a corporate law firm. That's what she's had to do—she's been responsible for the revenue in the family.

—JAN PIERCEY

When Hillary's first mentor, Don Jones, visited the Clintons in Little Rock in 1984, he asked the governor what he thought was a hypothetical question: "If you were to run for president in the next election, who would you have as your running mate?"

Clinton immediately snapped out an answer: "Mario Cuomo."

"So my guess is, he and Hillary were talking about this, maybe since '82," says Jones, "and thinking the sooner they went the better, because they'd still be young when they got out."[1]

Clinton's run in 1984 for another term as governor was a lark—his opponent couldn't even ride on the coattails of President Reagan's landslide reelection. The major political issue that Clinton wrestled with in the 1984-to-1986 period was a feud with the state's giant utility company. In the end, both Bill and Hillary would figure out ways to profit from the feud.

Entergy Corporation is a rich holding company that controls electrical power in the state and utilities in three other states with which Arkansas shares power.[2] Entergy had built a nuclear plant called Grand Gulf, located in Mississippi. Governor Clinton was faced with an order by the federal government to share the cost of the plant with Mississippi and Louisiana. He and his state's utility commission said they didn't want or need the extra power and asked to be relieved from that burden. But Entergy and the federal authorities hung tough. Clinton was scared to death that, having run on lowering utility rates, he would now have to force higher rates on the public. The governor also had reason to fear political punishment from Entergy, which anticipated profits from the plant and represented the dominant lobbying interest in the state. The battle became personalized between Jerry Maulden, CEO of Entergy Arkansas, and Bill Clinton.

To take the heat off, Clinton brought a lawsuit against the Federal Energy Regulatory Commission, seeking an injunction against forced payment by Arkansas for the Grand Gulf nuclear power plant. So far, so good. Then he retained the Rose firm as state counsel. Or, put more simply, he hired his wife's firm to represent the state.

"You'll get killed for that," Dick Morris warned Clinton during a strategy meeting in the mansion at which Hillary was present.

"My firm is the only firm that can handle it," Hillary countered. "Anybody else will screw it up."

The governor echoed his wife: "I have to win this case. This is crucial. I can't hire just anybody. They are the only law firm competent to do it."

Realizing he could not win his argument on the merits, Morris suggested a way that Hillary could protect herself from the inevitable charges of conflict of interest: "Just say you will not share in the revenues your firm will get from Grand Gulf."

"How can I do that?" she balked. "I'm a partner in the firm. I share in all the revenues at the end of the year."

Morris offered the obvious solution: she could create a separate pot of money that would include the Grand Gulf fees and exclude herself from any part of those revenues. "By the way," Morris probed, "are you getting any other state business?"

"Yes, we get a lot of bond business," Hillary said.

There was a spike in Morris's usual monotone: "You mean the state of Arkansas hires the Rose law firm to do its bond issues?"

Angry and defensive, Hillary said, "Our law firm represented the state under Bumpers, under Pryor, under my husband, under Frank White, and it will represent it under the next governor. I have nothing to do with us getting that business."

"Just don't share in the fees," Morris persisted. "Take more from the rest of the pot if you want, but don't share in those fees."

At this point Hillary made it clear that she would brook no further debate. "I am going to share in those fees," she said. "It's business we've always had."[3]

When the Grand Gulf case was finally settled, it looked as if everybody had gotten most of what they wanted. Rose reaped $115,000 in fees for its representation of the state;[4] Hillary proved herself valuable to her firm, although she and Rose later claimed that the fees from the case had been segregated from other income and that Mrs. Clinton had derived no monetary benefit from Grand Gulf; Entergy got its plant, dubbed "Grand Goof"; and Clinton claimed victory on behalf of his voters—despite the fact that 80 percent of Arkansas's share in the cost of the plant plus the legal fees were passed on to them. Most important, Governor Clinton patched things up with Entergy's Jerry Maulden.

"His utility company was the Antichrist in '84 to '85," says Clinton's former legislative assistant Bobby Roberts. "But Maulden and Clinton are both pragmatists, and by '86 it was clear they would both be around for a long time."[5] When Clinton was ready to run for president, Maulden was one of his first big-money donors; Entergy made contributions of $20,000 in "soft money" to his 1992 campaign.[6]

Hillary knew this was the point. Everything they did now was building toward a run for the presidency in 1988.

CALLING E. F. HUTTON

In the 1980s, like so many yuppies of her generation, Hillary turned her attention to another great American obsession: making money. Her father had taught her to read the stock tables when she was a little girl, and she has trained her daughter to do the same.[7] Even in the spring of 1983, when she was traveling around the state to hold her marathon hearings on education, she found time to form an investment pool with her law partners Vince Foster, Jr., and Webb Hubbell. Hillary set up an account for them at E. F. Hutton in Little Rock. Although none of the three was even forty yet, Hillary dubbed their account Midlife Investors, suggesting her apprehensions of an insecure financial future. The two men were functionally passive partners. Hillary was in charge, and she wanted the fast action she was used to from her dealings with Jim Blair, the Tyson lawyer who had helped her make the windfall profit on cattle futures. Her stockbroker at E. F. Hutton, Roy Drew, would get calls from Hillary three or four times a week, asking about their stocks: "What's Firestone doing?" Drew would say, "It's up an eighth today." She'd complain, "Why isn't it doing anything?"[8]

"When the time came for [Clinton] to run for president—and they knew he would—that would limit their outside earning potential, by law," points out Max Brantley. "They had a kid who would need to go to college. It was always important to Hillary that their needs be met and that Chelsea would not be denied an Ivy League education, travel, whatever."[9]

The Rose law firm was housed in a squat brick building surrounded by an iron fence dripping with honeysuckle vine. In its parking lot Mercedeses and BMWs mingled with pickups sporting gun racks. But Rose represented the holy trinity of Arkansas business and industry: Stephens Inc., Tyson Foods, and Wal-Mart. All three firms were regulated in one way or another by agencies of the state Hillary's husband ran, which in and of itself provoked questions of conflict of interest for the First Lady of Arkansas.

Hillary was never known as a rainmaker. In interviews with *The American Lawyer* in 1992, William Kennedy, the firm's current chief executive, acknowledged that Hillary had great potential but delivered a lot less than desired in actual bottom-line business. "If she had ever quit having two lives and concentrated on the law practice, she'd have been a superb lawyer," said Kennedy. The man who was chief executive from the late 1970s to mid-1980s, Joe Giroir, said, "I was always mad at her for not doing more [legal work]."[10] She tried only five cases in her career at Rose. But she developed a very cozy relationship with two of the most dynamic and respected younger partners at the firm, Webb Hubbell and Vince Foster—the Midlife Investors.

THE ODD COUPLE

Vincent W. Foster, Jr., was a small-town boy from Hope, Arkansas. Suburbanites like Hillary would have called Vince a hick, but he was smart. He had graduated first in his class from the University of Arkansas Law School and received the top score on the bar exam. He had immediately been offered a job at Rose and settled down in the insular town of Little Rock with his wife, Lisa, a stay-at-home mom.

Vince had never met a woman like Hillary—whip smart and cocky, witty and ambitious—and it put him in awe of her from the start. The start had been in the 1970s, when they had met through their pro bono work for the Legal Services Corporation. After Vince brought Hillary into Rose, they became great friends.

Both were litigators, although very different in their styles. Hillary's pugnacity was nicely complemented by Vince's courtliness. They made a classic good cop–bad cop team and successfully tried several cases together. They frequently traveled together on business. Hillary was so impressed with Vince's legal skills that he became the Clintons' personal lawyer.

As her headaches over her husband's careless behavior became more frequent and painful through the 1980s, Hillary frequently turned to Vince for advice and comfort. "It was a very, very close friendship," remembers Thomas Mars, an attorney who was brought into Rose by Foster and Hillary in the mid-1980s and subsequently became director of the Arkansas State Police. "They had everything in common."[11]

The rumor that Hillary and Vince had been lovers first surfaced in *The American Spectator*'s infamous "Troopergate" story in December 1993, only to be raised again and again by one spurious or politically polluted source after another. Four state troopers, who lived cheek by jowl with the Clintons and grew to dislike the haughty First Lady, were able to wreak their vengeance by talking to David Brock for his "gotcha" article, though only two, Larry Patterson and Roger Perry, would agree to be quoted on the record. All four said that when Governor Clinton left town, Foster would turn up at the mansion and stay till the wee hours of the morning. Two of them said they had seen "open-mouth kissing." One of the troopers said he was often used to drive Hillary and Vince to a Rose firm retreat cabin in the mountains. Patterson even went so far as to suggest that at a birthday party with Rose firm law partners, Foster fondled Hillary's breast and squeezed her fanny.[12] Others who were at the party told me that was preposterous. Arkansas journalist Gene Lyons said, "The idea that Foster, whose reticence and sense of propriety were well known, would have done anything of the kind is almost as grotesque to his friends as the notion of Mrs. Clinton's permitting it."[13]

The article was engineered by Cliff Jackson, the fellow Oxonian from Arkansas who had turned into Bill Clinton's bête noire. Jackson had raised money from right-wing sources to reward the troopers for telling their tale to Brock. Four years after the incendiary article, Brock himself wrote a letter to the President apologizing for having written the story that introduced

Paula Jones to the world. He confessed that "the troopers were greedy and had slimy motives, and I knew it."[14]

Subsequently, another trooper came forward with more sordid tales about the Clintons. This time it was L. D. Brown, who claimed to be closer to the first couple of Arkansas than any other state trooper. In his account, once again splashed across the pages of *The American Spectator*, Brown claimed to have solicited "over a hundred" sexual partners for Clinton. According to Brown, Clinton would rate women on a 10-point scale and saw them as intended "purely to be graded, purely to be chased, dominated, conquered."[15]

"These vindictive troopers have been making this stuff up for a long time," says Betsey Wright. The Vince-Hillary rumors "exploit the belief of a lot of people that a man and a woman can't be very close friends without having a sexual component to their relationship."[16] No one I have interviewed who knew Foster and Hillary gives credence to these rumors that Hillary and Vince were lovers. Yet the story continues to be retailed by writers of sensationalist clip-job books and the tabloids that feed off them.

What is clear in the accounts of those who knew Foster is the fact that he worshiped Hillary. And Hillary was drawn to him as the antithesis of Bill. While Clinton looked most at home in a wrinkled suit with his pants legs stuffed inside cowboy boots, his hair mussed and his hands busy pressing the flesh, Foster was more comfortable in black tie and satin waistcoat, his hair short and his long arms pasted to his sides. He shunned the public spotlight—political life was his idea of purgatory. Socially, he was shy to the point of repressiveness. But there was another side to Vince, a persona very different from the buttoned-down lawyer. His friends saw it only on occasions when he'd had too much to drink. "He'd get wild and wacky," says an Arkansas political reporter. "There was a Christmas party in their neighborhood [the Heights], and he'd get a snootful. Then Vince would put on cowboy clothes and go out to country-and-western honky-tonks rounding up people to go to the shit-kicker bars."

A Thorn at the Rose

Hillary's evolution at Rose took her a long way from the midwestern purist who, in 1974, would not countenance any manner of political skulduggery. In the Eighties, she became involved in another controversial land deal with repercussions that would plague her for years. After another campaign season, Hillary had some catching up to do as a partner in a

then-booming litigation practice. In the spring of 1985, Bill Clinton interceded to help her out.

Jim McDougal had just finished spending money to spiff up his bank,
Madison Guaranty Savings and Loan, to make it look more prosperous.
One day his friend the governor jogged in and sat sweating on one of his
new leather chairs. McDougal ignored the stain because he was always on
the lookout for the main chance and hoped this might be it.

"How's Hillary doing?" McDougal asked Clinton.

"Well, she's trying to get her feet back on the ground at the firm," Clinton said.[17] McDougal later testified that it was he who had first broached
the subject of his bank sending some legal work to Hillary Clinton. At the
time, Madison was in financial difficulty and, like many S and Ls, was looking for ways to raise new capital.

Just how Hillary and her firm became the facilitators involved with
McDougal while he was looting money from his nearly bankrupt bank has
been the subject of numerous contradictory accounts. Hillary herself has
changed her story repeatedly. When she first gave a description of this
episode at her nationally televised news conference in April 1994, she said
she didn't bring in McDougal and his bank to the firm; she had only been
trying to help a bright young associate at Rose sign up Madison as a client.
The following year, talking to lawyers for the Resolution Trust Corporation
(RTC), she remembered her motives somewhat differently—"certain
lawyers of the law firm were opposed to doing any work for Jim McDougal
or any of his companies until he paid his bill" from a previous case—and
since she knew McDougal, she explained, she was the natural person to
work out a deal with him to settle his bill and set a retainer for new work.
Even this revised memory was disputed, both by documents and by the
Rose firm's chief operating officer, Ronald Clark, who told *The Washington
Post* that McDougal's outstanding legal bills ($5,000) had been paid off in
November 1984, several months before Hillary became the partner re-
tained to handle his Madison business.[18]

Indisputably, Hillary did become the billing partner for Rose in its repre-
sentation of McDougal and Madison on April 23, 1985—the day she called
on McDougal at his office and arranged for him to pay the firm a $2,000-a-
month retainer. McDougal continued to be a major source of political contributions to Bill Clinton.

In her first effort on behalf of Madison, Hillary opened herself up to the
charge that she was abetting the classic offense of S and Ls that ran amok
in the 1980s: using influence on bank regulators to keep insolvent S and Ls
afloat if they were run by political contributors. Madison was then under

investigation by the Federal Deposit Insurance Corporation (FDIC) and was failing fast. Rather than allowing it to go under or be taken over, as the FDIC had the right to do, Hillary was promoting McDougal's scheme of selling preferred stock in the bank to keep it afloat.

In April 1985, six days after her firm had been retained by McDougal, Hillary telephoned the state's banking regulator, Beverly Bassett Schaffer, who, as a law student, had worked for then attorney general Clinton. Mrs. Schaffer owed her new job directly to the intercession of Governor Clinton. Her predecessor, William Lyon, had shut the door on McDougal, telling the finagler he thought the plan to bail out Madison bank was "a rip-off of stockholders."[19] Just before Christmas 1984, McDougal had asked Bill Clinton to replace the obstinate banking regulator. And early in 1985, Beverly Bassett Schaffer was appointed to fill Lyon's hastily vacated chair.

The First Lady originally said she couldn't remember who she had talked to at the state banking agency. But Mrs. Schaffer recalled in detail their telephone conversation. Hillary told her that Madison had a proposal and what it was about: a preferred stock financing to raise capital to get Madison back on its feet. That idea had been suggested by the FDIC as an instrument that might save struggling S and Ls. But it was only a general recommendation, not specifically applied to Madison, as some Clinton spinners have suggested.[20] Schaffer's assistant Charles Handley opposed the proposal for Madison because of the bank's precarious financial condition. Hillary maintains that she made only a routine inquiry, she didn't pull strings with Mrs. Schaffer. The outcome of Hillary's call, however, is a simple fact: Schaffer disagreed with her predecessor, and her assistant, and approved the proposal. But the bank still needed to meet certain financial requirements by the federal authorities. Failing to meet the requirements, Madison never went ahead with the offering.

Whether or not Hillary knew that McDougal was using Madison as "his private piggy bank," as federal officials later determined, she was to involve herself in an even dicier transaction on behalf of the rogue banker. Madison was making deals without the financial resources to back them up. In the spring of 1985, a partner in Hillary's troika, Webb Hubbell, asked her to see his father-in-law, Seth Ward. Ward was a cantankerous wheeler-dealer who "treated Rose like his personal financier," according to Jane Sherburne, who later defended the First Lady in Starr's investigation of Whitewater and Madison.[21] He was also a crony of Jim McDougal, and together they had purchased about a thousand acres outside Little Rock for

$1.75 million. They intended to develop a microbrewery and a trailer park, among other things. They gave the trailer park land the grandiose name of Castle Grande Estates. Ward, it would be discovered, had been used by McDougal as the "straw" buyer to hold much of the property in Ward's name, rather than in Madison's name. Why? Because the bank, as a regulated institution, was restricted as to the amount of property it could own directly.

On May 1, 1986, Seth Ward showed up in Hillary's office and asked her to draft an option agreement. It was a piece of paper that would allow him to "flip" a small land parcel back to the bank at an inflated price and make a tidy profit in commissions for himself in the bargain. It was a twenty-two-acre parcel, out of the thousand-plus-acre Castle Grande package, that he was trying to sell back to Madison for $400,000. The RTC later valued Ward's parcel at a mere $47,000.

Hillary claims to have been unaware of what Ward meant to do with the option agreement she drafted for him. She has maintained in depositions that in all her dealings with Ward she did not know that McDougal might have been using Ward to circumvent the law. Indeed, Sherburne, her attorney in the matter, makes her sound like little more than a stenographer for Ward. "She wrote [the option agreement] based on a sample provided to her by Seth Ward. She didn't do that kind of work. She spent less than two hours on it," says Sherburne, "which doesn't mean she had any sort of comprehensive understanding of the whole deal into which this thing fit. And she didn't."[22]

Hillary dropped Madison as an account only days before federal officials moved in on McDougal. In July 1986, the federal government removed Madison's owner and placed the failed bank under its direct supervision.[23] The state's top banking official, Beverly Bassett Schaffer, wrote to federal regulators in December 1987 urging them to shut Madison down. But the players in the Madison bank had fifteen more months to play their shell game before the S and L was closed down in the spring of 1989. Real fraud was committed, which led to federal criminal convictions of Jim McDougal and former Arkansas governor Jim Guy Tucker. McDougal's savings and loan ended up costing the government $60 million.[24]

Amazingly, Hillary's dealings with Madison and Castle Grande did not surface as issues in Clinton's next reelection contest. But the first ominous signs of the public price Hillary was to pay for achieving her political identity through piggybacking on her husband did emerge in the 1986 campaign.

HILLARY'S ARMOR

It was a bitter race. "When two combative former governors decided to run against Bill, we knew we had to brace ourselves for a messy campaign," Hillary later wrote.[25] One opponent was Orval Faubus, who was not a real threat. The other was again Frank White, the Clintons' nemesis, the banker who had evicted them from the governor's mansion once before. The man she had "ambushed" so successfully during his two years as governor in the early 1980s was still steaming, and as a result Hillary's personal integrity came under fire for the first time. White had by now figured out how to attack a woman, even if she was the governor's wife. He attacked her as exactly that—for using her influence with her powerful husband to benefit her private legal clients and reap profits for herself.

Hillary counterattacked by retreating into the traditional role of woman as victim. She let the Clinton campaign go after the challenger for disparaging the governor's wife. The Clinton team put out bumper stickers and billboards ridiculing him: "Frank White for First Lady."

Webb Hubbell, a former Arkansas Razorback offensive tackle, ran interference for Hillary. Her law partner acknowledged that Rose's state bond work had increased since Hillary had joined the firm, but explained, "We try to avoid any situation where they're hiring the firm of the Governor's wife." He stressed that Hillary did not share in those fees.[26] The Arkansas Development Finance Authority confirmed that the Rose firm handled eight bond issues between 1986 and 1991. At the going rate, their bond counsel fees would have totaled roughly between $170,000 and $300,000.[27]

White expanded his assault and hit the First Family of Arkansas on the continuing investigation into half brother Roger Clinton's drug-dealing associates. Hillary fought off White's negative ad by lecturing the press on the rights of the accused. No matter how negative he got, White was no match for Hillary's "trial face." But despite his ultimate electoral loss, White had opened a chink in Hillary's armor that from then on left her vulnerable to further attacks on the ethical front.

The 1986 campaign also prepared the ground for a line of assault that would ultimately roll over the Clinton family like a regiment of tanks. The gossip about Bill's extramarital excesses had become rampant by this time—no surprise, since he was using state troopers as hooks for his nocturnal trolling. Hillary could no longer deafen herself to the obvious, not without leaving her child undefended against possible teasing and worse. It had not been a problem so long as Chelsea was young enough for her parents to monitor what she saw and heard. But now she was six and mixing with other children at school. And she could read.

Chelsea is the only area of vulnerability that Hillary cannot hide. The longest periods of silence she maintained were in hotel rooms, a phone cradled in her ear, often dead tired but listening without interruption to a stream-of-consciousness account of her child's day. Even in a noncampaign period, Hillary would be out of town on law or board work two to three nights a week. She did homework with Chelsea by fax.

Clearly, Chelsea was a good part of the glue that kept the Clintons' marriage together whenever the corrosion of betrayal and false repentance threatened to take it apart. I asked Melinda how often Bill and Hillary had gone out together in those years. "Just the two of them? Very, very seldom. . . . Hillary took Chelsea on vacations. Bill would promise to catch up, but usually he'd come a couple of days late or not at all."

On the rare weekend nights when both Hillary and Bill were at home, Hillary's favorite recreation was standing around the kitchen counter in the governor's mansion with friends, talking ideas. People helped themselves out of the fridge. (Hillary rarely cooked, and the state dining room was scarcely used.) She might mimic one of her hillbilly witnesses spitting tobacco from the stand while she cross-examined him. Or she would burst into a high-pitched Ozark honk—*hee hee hee*—over one of her husband's Bubba lines. But at 10:30 she would announce, "That's it for me, I'm going to bed." Bill was the night owl, the eternal schmoozer. Hillary was the emotionally disciplined one. And she wanted her daughter to be the same way.

She and Bill discussed damaging charges that might surface. They decided to prepare Chelsea "so she would not be surprised or overwhelmed if she heard someone say something nasty about her father." One night at the dinner table the Clintons began a role-playing game to teach their daughter the "harsh truths" of politics. Hillary told the child, "You know, Daddy is going to run for governor again. If he wins, we would keep living in this house, and he would keep trying to help people. But first, we have to have an election. And that means . . . other people . . . saying terrible things about him."[28]

"Why would people do that?" Chelsea asked again and again.

Hillary did not have a good answer then and remarked in her first book that she still doesn't. So she asked the six-year-old to take the part of her father and say why people should vote for her. Chelsea obviously had congenital political instincts. She role-played: "I'm Bill Clinton. I've done a good job. And I've helped a lot of people. Please vote for me."

Then her father pretended to be one of the nasty men running against him. As Hillary retells the scene, "Bill would say terrible things about himself, like how he was really mean to people and didn't really try to help them." Tears sprang to the child's eyes as her blissfully rosy view of life was smeared for the first time: "Why would anybody say things like that?"

After repeating this dinner-table drill many times, Hillary was pleased to watch her daughter "gain mastery over her emotions."[29] Mother Hillary had inculcated in Chelsea the same kind of emotional desensitization that young Hillary had been taught by her own mother, using a carpenter's level as a tool.

The rough-and-tumble of the campaign seldom seemed to dent Hillary's armor-plated determination. "Hillary is convinced the way she does things is the right way," attests her brother Hugh.[30] Carolyn Huber, for years Hillary's day-to-day logistical helper, affirmed that Hillary will simply not be deterred: "She wants to win as bad as he does." Is she tougher than he is? "I think so," said Huber with a laugh. "She's more clear about what she wants and the way she wants it done. I don't think there's ever been a time when Hillary set her mind to something she wanted to happen that it hasn't happened."[31]

KING OF THE MOUNTAIN

The 1986 victory put Bill Clinton back on top. It was solid proof of his staying power. At the same time, he had his legislature pass a four-year term for future governors. That meant he would not have to run again until 1990. And even before he had whipped White, the wunderkind was named chairman of the National Governors Association—a prime launching pad for his national aspirations.

On the thrust of these heady victories, Bill Clinton was transformed at the age of forty from a prince in training—under the protection of his Valkyries—to the powerful sovereign of all he surveyed. After the election of 1986, according to Morris, Clinton's mind-set was *Now I've got a four-year term, a decent salary, I've defeated my nemesis, I'm king of the mountain.*

Clinton's reward to himself was to kick over the traces of his Valkyries. He made it clear that Hillary was not particularly welcome at strategy meetings in the mansion. She stopped attending. Power had ebbed and flowed between him and his wife throughout their relationship. "After his '86 victory, he told both Hillary and Betsey, in effect, 'Get lost,' " says Morris.[32] Betsey Wright continued in her role as his chief damage controller, but Clinton paid less and less attention to her. Over the next five years the political power that Hillary had enjoyed during the four years of the Rodham Regency was greatly dissipated.

But Clinton was still dependent upon her financially. He had increased his salary from $25,000 at the age of twenty-nine, as attorney general, to the princely sum of $35,000 as governor. He never made more than that until he left Arkansas at the age of forty-six. Hillary, as one of the chief litigating partners in the Rose law firm earned $175,000 in 1991.[33] That was puny pay for a Yale Law School graduate ten years into her career as a corporate attorney. "She could command the top salary for a litigator in any law firm in New York or Los Angeles [where the going rate in the mid-1980s was $500,000 annually and over]," claimed her partner Herb Rule.[34] Instead, Hillary's choice to follow her love to Arkansas had drastically limited her earning potential. She tried to make up for it by becoming a director on five corporate boards (including a position as the only woman on the board of Wal-Mart). But she also continued to pursue her passion for social reform by devoting much of her energy to pro bono work, chairing the Children's Defense Fund (CDF) and serving on the boards of nearly a dozen other educational and social justice organizations.

"If Hillary were doing what she most wanted to do in this world, she would not be a partner in a corporate law firm," confided her friend Jan Piercey. "That's what she's had to do—she's been responsible for the revenue in the family."[35]

Hillary had a keen sense of being gypped. The Rose firm had tripled in size from around the time she had started, in 1977, to boasting of fifty-three lawyers by 1985. The firm was led by Joseph Giroir, Jr., whose securities section was pulling in the most business from the robust mergers and acquisitions of the go-go Eighties. Giroir, as chief executive, kept the lion's share of fees for himself—close to half a million dollars a year. Hillary and the other litigators felt that Giroir was shortchanging their section; their compensation ran from $75,000 to $175,000. What's more, Giroir was always riding Hillary for taking leaves and not bringing in more big-money clients. Another Rose partner defended her: given her very public role as chair of CDF and board member of some of the biggest clients in the state, not to mention her highly visible role as the governor's wife, Hillary was most valuable to the firm as a marketing tool.[36]

As it turned out, Giroir was to rue the day he went up against Hillary. She formed a cabal with her partners Foster and Hubbell and plotted to overthrow him. By 1988, Giroir was forced out of the Rose firm.[37]

The year before the 1986 election campaign, the governor's wife decided that she wanted a swimming pool put in at the mansion. Once again Morris warned her, "You'll get killed for that." Hillary was unmovable. It was really for Chelsea, she argued, and it would benefit all future governors and their families. Beside, lots of people had swimming pools. Morris was stunned by her political tin ear. Impishly, he suggested a poll on how many people in Arkansas had swimming pools. She became furious and complained, "Why can't we lead the lives of normal people?" She had chosen the life of a public person, yet in defending her position on the swimming pool, she compared herself to an upper-middle-class professional: "Vince Foster has one," she complained.[38] When he heard about the debate, the journalist Brummett was floored at Hillary's lack of understanding populist feelings. "It's like, 'Hey, we're in the second poorest state in the country, and lots of people hate my husband, but let's build a swimming pool anyway!' "[39]

A far more serious question was why the First Lady had done a favor for men such as Jim McDougal and Seth Ward when it should have been clear that they were looting the Madison bank. What did Hillary stand to get out of it? "I believe there was an increasing desire for her to make money," says Morris. "She would say it was for Chelsea and her future."[40]

Hillary kept the couple's books: she wrote the checks, paid the bills, made the investments, and engaged in ingenious accounting wherever possible. She even took a tax write-off on a donation of Bill's underwear to charity—twice. As her mother told *Money* magazine, "She has always been careful and wise with her money. Her father had a constant theme when Hillary was growing up, that everything was too expensive, and you have to save for your retirement."[41]

She would periodically battle with Dick Morris over his fee. "It was almost as if she felt that Dick should be so grateful to work for them, he should do it for nothing," reflects his wife, Eileen McGann.[42] Yet the Clintons lived in an environment that required little cash. They enjoyed living rent-free in the 11,000-square-foot governor's mansion; a $51,000 mansion "allowance," for gardening, catering, and utilities; meals made by a taxpayer-paid cook, Liza, who indulged Bill in southern specialties; servants from the prison system; round-the-clock baby-sitters; luxury transportation in a chauffeur-driven Lincoln Town Car (used even for their pleasure trips); and, just for extras, a $19,000 "discretionary account." Not to mention the franking privilege for their Christmas cards. Governor Clinton also gladly accepted perquisites such as membership in three country clubs and $1.4 million worth of admission tickets per year to the Oaklawn racetrack in Hot Springs—his mother's haunt—which he passed around to campaign contributors.[43] All the Clintons really had to do with their money was invest it for Chelsea's education and their own retirement. Bill never worried about money; Hillary never felt they had enough.

The fish-eye lens of Bill's presidential ambitions became more focused after his reelection triumph in the fall of 1986, and by early 1987, Hillary had begun beating the drum. In April, she had to fly to New Jersey on business for Rose. She dashed off a handwritten note to Don Jones, her former youth minister, suggesting that they catch up over a cup of coffee as she passed through Newark Airport. Jones sent word that he had a class to teach that evening, so they arranged for him to pick her up and, without stopping to eat, the two drove straight to Drew University, where Hillary addressed the professor's Business Ethics class.

What was most memorable for Jones was watching his former protégé's reaction when he introduced her as a "Future First Woman of the United States, because her husband will be running for president soon." Hillary, he says, did not blanch.[44] Indeed, she spoke like a First Lady in Waiting.

All pumped up from having just heard TV pioneer Norman Lear speak at a meeting of his activist liberal group People for the American Way, whose board she was on, Hillary expressed a fervent concern that corporate America was running amok and subverting bedrock American values. She cited a rogue's gallery of corporate raiders—Ivan Boesky, Carl Icahn, T. Boone Pickens—and bemoaned the environmental degradation caused by companies that had given America the Three Mile Island nuclear power plant near-disaster and the cancer-producing pollution in Love Canal. Foreshadowing her later fascination with "the politics of meaning," she talked about the excesses of yuppie materialism, hyperindividualism, and narcissism that were overshadowing concern for the public good.

"We are experiencing a crisis of meaning and a spiritual crisis," she said, describing "the hurt, emptiness, confusion, and loss of meaning that characterize much of our society."[45] She wound up laying primary blame at the doorstep of corporate America. Its obsession with short-term profit, she told Jones's students, was a major source of the subversion of democratic, family, moral, and spiritual values in America.

Ironically, the business that had brought Hillary east was going to New Brunswick to the headquarters of the giant pharmaceutical company

Johnson & Johnson, one of her many corporate clients. Don Jones acknowledges the contradiction. "Hillary does think like a lawyer much of the time," he says, "so the inner moral person sometimes gives way to the legal persona."[46]

BETSEY'S BLACK BOOK

For Clinton, the presidential primary field was clearing. Mario Cuomo indicated that he was not a candidate for the presidency. Dale Bumpers backed out in March. And in May, the popular front-runner of the Democratic Party, Gary Hart, accomplished a stunning feat of self-destruction. When a reporter asked about his alleged womanizing, Hart challenged the press to "put a tail on me." Then he arranged a tryst at his Washington town house with Miami party girl Donna Rice, to whom he had offered the chance "to sleep with the next president of the United States." Confronted outside his town house by a *Miami Herald* reporter, Hart was disheveled and his speech disjointed. When he phoned his wife that Saturday night, he told her to ignore the imminent scandal. Like Hillary, Lee Hart was not in the dark about her husband's proclivities.[47]

How and why Hart had killed off his presidential candidacy became the subject of intense media scrutiny and political repartee and presented the country with a new debate: Should adultery be considered a legitimate subject in determining whether or not a person would make a good president? The Hart scandal had special relevance for Clinton. The two had worked together and there was much about both their public and private lives that was forebodingly similar.

That summer, after Hart had dropped out, Clinton asked friends and journalists alike, "Is there ever a time that your past is past?" At a softball game one night, he tested the waters with journalist Max Brantley: "We've all done things that we'd be embarrassed about if they ever came out in public, but it's the nature of the game today," he brooded, "that you never can be sure you won't have to answer for them." Brantley figured Clinton was talking about drugs, not sex.[48]

Hillary bought a condo for her parents in Little Rock, where they would be on hand to baby-sit with Chelsea while Hillary took to the campaign trail. By early July 1987, Hillary was in full mobilization. She telephoned her former mentor on the Watergate committee, Bernie Nussbaum. "Don't commit yourself to a presidential candidate until I have a chance to talk to you," she told him from Little Rock. "I'm flying in to New York to see you." The call came out of the blue; they hadn't seen each other for years.

Hillary met him at a restaurant on Forty-ninth Street off Park Avenue, and they enjoyed a three-hour dinner over a bottle of wine. "She was glowing!" Nussbaum remembers. "She talked about Chelsea, about how happy she was that she had a child. And about Clinton she said with great conviction, 'I just want you not to commit to anybody, because Bill may run.' "

Nussbaum chuckled: "Hillary, we had this discussion twelve years ago. I recognize I was a little too cynical then." Nussbaum was being gentle; he didn't want another fight with Hillary: "But I still think, Hillary, look, he's only forty-two. Kinda young to be president, isn't it?"

"No," she said. "No, he's really thinking about it. He's going to make a decision soon."[49]

The day of Clinton's announcement was predicted by the press to be perhaps the biggest political event in the history of Arkansas. A few days before, Bev Lindsey, the wife of his constant sideman, Bruce Lindsey, had begun working on elaborate plans for the press conference. *Newsweek* had already reported that Governor Clinton had made the decision to run. Everything was set for noon on Wednesday, July 15, in the ballroom of the Excelsior Hotel. Friends expecting to be given big jobs on the Clinton presidential team—California attorney Mickey Kantor; Sandy Berger, a fugitive from the Hart campaign; and other political big shots—flew in the day before. On the eve of his announcement, Clinton hosted a dinner for about six close friends, including Bruce Lindsey and Webb Hubbell, at the Capitol Hotel. But the Governor pushed past reporters hovering in the hope of a pre-announcement quote and disappeared into the Cherokee Parlor.

The next day, reporters were eagerly awaiting confirmation that a son of Arkansas was running for president. Clinton's top lieutenants and Hillary gathered along with friendly members of the press for a private luncheon in the official residence. The lettuce around their chicken salads began to wilt while they waited for the missing governor and two of his closest cohorts. Clinton was huddled on the back-porch steps with pals Carl Wagner and Mickey Kantor, having a last discussion of his options.

No one was prepared for the abrupt, bizarre words they were about to hear. Bill Clinton came into the dining room and told them, "I'm not going." Everyone, including his wife, was stunned. He mumbled a brief, opaque explanation about the conflict between his head and his heart.

John Brummett raced to a telephone to notify the *Gazette* of the shocking decision. The receptionist at the governor's office put out an S.O.S. for help on the switchboard; people were calling in to ask if it was a hoax and she had no idea what to tell them. What on earth could have been so potent as to cause Clinton to back away from taking the plunge at the very last minute?

Betsey Wright knew the answer to the riddle, and that knowledge was as bittersweet as Eve's apple. A couple of nights before, she had sat Clinton down in her home on Hill Street and done what psychologists call an "intervention": she had confronted him with irrefutable evidence of his sexual profligacy. It was not the first of their confrontations, but it was the most brutal.

"You have to absolutely crush his skull to get his attention, because his mind is on so many things at once," Wright told me. "When it was something as important as this, you had to shake him and say, 'You stop, pay attention to this, this is what's important right now, guy.' " She had already had several heated debates with her boss over the lessons of the Hart case; she argued that for Hart to be so reckless in flaunting an affair while he was a candidate raised questions about his mental stability. Clinton disagreed, and Wright could see that her boss had not taken in the warning. So this time she was blunt as a bailiff.

"Here's the list," she said. "I want you to tell me everything you can tell me about . . ." and she began ticking off the names of women with whom she had good reason to believe Clinton had been intimate.

Clinton's nose began to go red. He did not want this subject put on the table.

Betsey Wright didn't want any explanations, she said. She wanted to know about each one: just yes or no. How often? Where is that woman now? How likely is she to talk? About Gennifer Flowers she wanted to know, "Did you go to her apartment?"

Then she went over the list a second time.

"He didn't try to hide anything," says Wright. "He appeared contrite. Did it last? I don't know. It seemed genuine—at the moment."

After they had discussed each woman, Wright told her boss he could not run for president. She pointed out the terrible self-destruction it might cause his political career if he were to get into the race with this sordid record.

He put up a mild resistance. There really weren't that many people who knew about the women on Betsey's list, he said. He didn't think that much would have to come out. He still wanted to go forward. Betsey had to personalize her argument in order to penetrate his nonchalance.

"I don't care what comes out, this is going to be bad for Hillary and Chelsea!" she shouted.

Clinton finally put his tail between his legs and sulked. By the time Betsey let him out of her sight, he had given her his word that he would back off. She believed him.[50]

But the next night Clinton was back to weighing his options, according to Carl Wagner, another McGovernite, who had been asked by the governor to fly in a day early to "help his friend think this thing through." Wagner sat for hours with him and Hillary around the kitchen table at the mansion, analyzing the economy and the strengths and weaknesses of other possible candidates—nothing personal. Only after Hillary had gone upstairs to their second-floor bedroom did Clinton turn to Wagner and ask, "So, what's the bottom line?"

Wagner has described his own little intervention. "When you reach the top of the steps," he said, "walk into your daughter's bedroom, look at her, and understand that if you do this, your relationship with her will never be the same."[51]

The next day, while Wagner was sitting with Clinton and Kantor on the back-porch steps before the final decision, the Governor's seven-year-old daughter caught his attention for a moment. She wanted to know about their summer vacation. As Kantor retold the scene, Clinton told Chelsea he might not be able to go because he might be running for president.

"Then Mom and I will go without you," Chelsea said.[52]

Two hours after the private luncheon at the mansion, Clinton stepped to the podium in the Excelsior Hotel to face a ballroom full of expectant and bewildered faces. Hillary stood slightly behind her husband, schoolmarmish in a long white skirt and white stockings. Clinton said, "If people had told me five years ago that I would ever have a serious chance to run for president and not take it, I would have told them they were crazy." People began to go misty-eyed.

The Governor himself looked like a scolded boy trying not to cry. With his lips pursed, he went on, "Our daughter is seven. She is the most important person in the world to us and our most important responsibility. In order to wage a winning campaign, both Hillary and I would have to leave her for long periods of time. That would not be good for her or for us."

Clinton went on to talk about the magic that exists between a politician and the people. He said he thought he had the message and he knew he could deliver it. In the audience Brummett was thinking, "This is so weird.

He's making a great speech to kick off a presidential campaign. He's saying 'I'm not running, but if I were, this is what I would do.' And it sounded pretty good!"[53]

Clinton continued, "I hope I will have another opportunity to seek the presidency when I can do it and be faithful to my family, my state, and my sense of what is right." No one noticed whether Hillary winced at the words "be faithful to my family."

Betsey had not told Hillary about her intervention with Bill. "That was part of the awkwardness," Wright said later. "I worked for him at that point. I doubt Hillary even knew about the meeting we had, but I do know that she was deeply disappointed that he couldn't run. I don't know how they handled it between themselves. I don't have a clue."[54]

His eyes puffy, his face colorless, Clinton wound up his non-announcement with an emotional confession: "When it came time for me to step up to the bat, down deep inside, my head said, 'Go,' and my heart said, 'It isn't right for you now.' " In one of the only instances the Arkansas press could remember, Bill Clinton seemed to be in control. The crestfallen one was Hillary. The blood seemed to have drained right out of her. From the boil of anger and dashed hopes, a trickle of emotion leaked out. In public she wiped a tear from her cheek.

"Oh, it was a real emotional event," says Brantley. "Everybody was crying. I thought it was one of his great moments. And he was believable—at that moment, anyway. I remember being deeply moved at his consideration for Chelsea. Looking back on it later, I thought what a fool I'd been."[55]

Exactly when Clinton finally searched his soul and came to his decision, nobody knows. No addict likes to be cornered. A year later, Betsey Wright quit. The woman who had devoted much of her life to being Bill Clinton's strategist and apologist was burned out and in a state of deep depression.[56] Only after the primaries in 1990 would Clinton appoint her state Democratic Party chairman, and when the Clintons finally did make their triumphal race for the White House, Wright was not given a frontline position.

One week after the drama at the Excelsior, Bernie Nussbaum received a call from a very different Hillary. In a matter-of-fact voice emptied of emotion she told him, "Bernie, you're released. He's decided not to run." No explanation. They never discussed "the women issue," says Nussbaum. "But I sensed that she wanted him to go, despite whatever Betsey had told him."[57]

Hillary's feelings were too chaotic to be allowed to surface. Associates believed she was furious and devastated. "Both Clintons developed a sense that his career [as a political figure] was going to end," says Morris.[58] Betsey Wright agrees: "He was thinking about running for president and being president, and now he thought it was gone—the only chance he would ever have in all of his life."[59]

Clinton had already been governor too long. But what else did he know how to do? He had spent his whole adult life campaigning for election. He might never earn a decent living. Most painful of all, Bill and Hillary had to sink into their pillows that night wondering if their shared dream, their cause, their raison d'être—to make Bill president—was lost forever.

CHAPTER TEN

Divorce or Rededication?

It's tough to be in love with both your wife and another woman.

—BILL CLINTON

After her husband's 1987 climb down from their shared dream, Hillary was in the dismal position of so many political wives: having forfeited much of her own independent identity, she was now faced with losing even her derivative identity as First Lady of Arkansas. They both believed that Clinton's political career was going nowhere. If a man who loses his dream feels like nothing, the dependent wife may feel like doubly nothing. By now Hillary knew that she probably could have no more children, a source of deep sadness for her.[1] (She suffered from endometriosis, an overgrowth of the lining of the uterus, which makes conception difficult.) Resigning herself to being the drone breadwinner for a faithless husband and stuck in Arkansas for the rest of her days was the furthest thing from her own dream.

The couple moved toward a momentous crossroads in their lives where it appeared their tracks were destined to separate. Restless and bored, given to brooding about his lost chance to become king of a much bigger mountain, Bill let his governorship run out of steam.

So did the Clintons' marriage.

"I always wondered if I'd want to be sixteen when I was forty, because I never felt like I got to complete my childhood," Bill Clinton has said.[2]

Forty was his age on that fateful day in July 1987 when he surrendered his lifelong dream. He was a wunderkind, a runner of the eternal marathon of political campaigning. What else could fill that terrible vacuum? Moreover, his dream was his solution to—or his escape from—the morass of personal traumas in his past. His other escape was to slip back into the pleasure-seeking *puer aeternus*—the eternal adolescent—and seek reassurance of his lovability in the arms of whatever women were willing and available. As the 1980s wore on, his marital delinquencies became more frequent and flagrant. The names and descriptions would float up later from various sources, some of them more reliable than others: Elizabeth Ward Gracen, a former Miss Arkansas and 1982 Miss America, at first denied and then admitted "I had sex with Bill Clinton, but the important part to me is that I was never pressured."[3] Dolly Kyle Browning, a childhood friend, claims to have had an affair with Clinton over the course of twenty-five years.[4] Beth Coulson, a municipal judge married to an oil company executive, was later named a Jane Doe in the Jones lawsuit and questioned because she was only thirty-two years old when Governor Clinton appointed her to a state judgeship in 1987, prompting complaints that she lacked experience and suspicions that she had been rewarded for her denial of a sexual relationship with the governor.[5] Clinton acknowledged under oath he visited Coulson at her home when her husband was not present, but both Coulson and Clinton denied having sexual relations.[6] Deborah Mathis, a beautiful black TV news anchor from Arkansas who was alleged in a lawsuit and in the *Star* tabloid to be one of Clinton's lovers, said on the record: "For whatever it's worth, the allegation is a lie."[7] Also referred to repeatedly in news articles as Clinton mistresses were the wife of a prominent judge and a staffer in Clinton's office[8] and even a cosmetics sales clerk at a Little Rock department store.[9] His tastes were ecumenical, covering all three branches of government and all social classes.

Gennifer Flowers had also surfaced in 1987, letting it be known she and Clinton had started an affair in 1978. "We knew that Gennifer was going to try to claim something," says Betsey Wright, "because when Bill was thinking about running for president that year, the story began circulating that she had come to town to make her claim to fame by asserting that there had been an affair with Bill Clinton." Gennifer blabbed so much that she ended up on the list of Clinton's alleged paramours in a 1990 lawsuit intended to run Clinton out of the presidential race. "Gennifer had to leave town in

1990," says Wright smugly, refusing to elaborate on her persuasive tactics.[10]

Clinton made no effort to hide his leering at pretty women around the state capitol or at public events. He left it to Hillary to cut off questions from reporters about their relationship, which she did by declaring "a zone of privacy." Hillary was usually able to convince herself that Clinton gave in to his sexual compulsions only in times of great stress. "She puts these transgressions . . . in a box called lust; it has nothing to do with his profound relationship and love for her," commented writer Lucinda Franks after interviewing Mrs. Clinton.[11] For years Hillary had grasped for rationalizations to explain her husband's behavior and avoid looking at her own role in perpetuating that behavior or the possibility that she was wanting in any way as a wife. Too painful.

In the late Eighties the Clintons' marriage hit its nadir. For the first time, Hillary became distraught enough to discuss with her friends Diane Blair and Linda Bloodworth-Thomason the possibility of divorce. "This was the first time she acknowledged knowing about his extramarital activities," says a close male friend of the couple.

And then the torment got worse.

"There was only one serious threat to that marriage—the only serious relationship he had with another woman," says Betsey Wright definitively, although she wouldn't name the woman. "All the others were as silly as the Monica Lewinsky one."[12] But this was a woman different from all the others. This was a relationship different from all the others. Clinton had lost his balance and fallen in love.

A WOMAN DIFFERENT FROM ALL THE OTHERS

She was a fugitive from a fifteen-year marriage to a junior military officer. Marilyn Jo Denton Jenkins had relocated to Arkansas in 1984 and taken a job at the Entergy Corporation. She may have met Bill Clinton through her kin among the Blands, one of the wealthiest families in Arkansas and prominent supporters of the governor.[13] Or it may have been later, through her boss, an old friend of Clinton's: Kay Kelley Arnold, a pretty Irish lawyer of Bill's age who was a major player in his administrations until she joined Entergy as a corporate communications manager in 1988.[14] Both women ardently admired Clinton.

Tall, slim, blond, a striking divorcée in her early forties, the mystery woman began turning up at Clinton's political fund-raisers and receptions at the governor's mansion in 1988. Marilyn Jo Jenkins's ex-husband began to have his own questions during joint custody visits with his two young daughters. "From their conversations, it seemed as though Bill Clinton appeared frequently in their lives," said James Jenkins. "They would say they ran into him while they were with their mother—in Wal-Mart, of all places!" Jenkins, who is director of the Flight Department at Johnson & Johnson headquarters in New Jersey, later read statements from Arkansas state troopers describing Clinton's nocturnal visits to a woman who lived on Shadow Oaks in Sherwood. Buttons lit up. His former wife lived in the Shadow Oaks condominium. And who lived in the same complex? Trooper Larry Patterson. "It becomes perfectly clear to me that if the dates the troopers gave were correct, those were times when my children were with me," said Jenkins. If that coincidence weren't enough, "it all came home to me when the *L.A. Times* was able to obtain Clinton's phone records and there were a surprising amount of phone calls to a number that I knew was not listed. It was my ex-wife's number!"[15]

"I don't know anything about all those women the other troopers have talked about," said Corporal Danny Ferguson, a state trooper who was assigned to the governor's security detail in 1989 (and who was not among those who were later to go on the record about Clinton for the infamous *American Spectator* article). "The only dealing I had was with Marilyn Jo— the only woman in my five years that I knew the governor really liked."[16]

Marilyn Jo Denton grew up in the tiny Arkansas town of Crossett with no grand ambitions. Her father was a bookkeeper for the railroad, her mother a schoolteacher.[17] A partial scholarship sent her to Henderson State College in Arkadelphia, where she met her future husband, James Norman Jenkins III. "Arkansas isn't renowned for its schools of higher education," he said, "but for a couple of postwar kids from simple families, it was the best we could do."[18] Marilyn Jo and Hillary graduated from college in the same year, 1969, but Marilyn Jo had a "ring by spring" and married in June of that year.

Not long after, the bride was left stateside while her husband, an air force pilot, was sent to Vietnam. Meanwhile, Marilyn Jo's sister, Kay Denton, had married into the influential Bland family, owners of a prosperous bottling company with franchises for Dr Pepper, 7UP, RC Cola, and Mountain Valley Water.[19] The Denton family was welcomed into the Bland family's compound in Paragould, a remote town in northeast Arkansas, where life was comfortable but lonely for Marilyn Jo. "The Vietnam War was tough on her," acknowledges her former mate. When he returned, Jenkins's military career kept them in perpetual motion through assignments in seventeen states and tours in Europe. Marilyn Jo tried to use her degree in education to teach, but life for her was largely a blur of setting up and breaking down new households and rearranging the lives of her two young children. In her early thirties she went back to college for a master's degree in business at Western New England College in Springfield, Massachusetts. Both she and her husband received MBA degrees there in 1983.[20]

By then, the accumulated strain of her husband's long absences and her own newly earned professional status made Marilyn Jo question her marriage. James Jenkins says, "Her faithfulness was not an issue, at all." There was mutual dissatisfaction that could not be resolved, and in February 1984 his wife left him and went home to Arkansas. A few months later she filed for divorce, contending that she had been treated "with such indignities that [her] condition in life has been made intolerable." She sought no alimony, and it was agreed that Jenkins would pay child support of $800 a month plus a cash settlement of $8,377. She would keep physical custody of their children, but he would have liberal visiting rights.[21] Neat, tidy, uncontested—but their divorce was not an amicable divorce, says Jenkins. Their two daughters were only six and eight when the couple split up. "They were thrust into a situation where now their mother was the breadwinner and I was not there all the time—it was traumatic on them," laments Jenkins.[22]

But Marilyn Jo seems to have landed on her feet quite quickly. With no work history to speak of, she found a job as a customer service representative for the state's major utility company, possibly through connections of the Bland family. She worked hard and rose to become a midlevel marketing executive at Entergy Arkansas, where she remains today as a senior customer service specialist.[23] When friends who grew up with her met Marilyn Jo at a school reunion in the Nineties, they were impressed at how she had bloomed. "She was rather studious and quiet at school," recalls a hometown friend, Mary Louise Clary. "She is far more outgoing, very attractive; she has changed more than the rest of us."[24]

For Bill Clinton, Marilyn Jo must have been like a soft summer breeze. She had the honeyed voice of a small-town southern woman. Yet she was an educated professional woman who, by the time they met, was surrounded by the gloss of a rich, politically active family. She didn't need a government job, and she was exceptionally discreet. I asked her exhusband what he thought it was about Marilyn Jo that made her so different from all the other women whose names had been linked to Clinton.

"Maybe she was the one person who didn't ask for some expected gain from Bill for being his friend," said James Jenkins.[25]

For a boy who had to be the shining light in his mother's life and a man who had to be president to satisfy his wife's expectations, Clinton now knew what it was like being loved simply for what he was rather than for what he could be.

In the fall of 1989, Bill Clinton had none of the drive a candidate needs to run a decent reelection campaign, this time for a sixth term as governor. He was rudderless. He and Hillary were close to separating. Clinton's telephone contact with Marilyn Jo during the summer and fall of that year bordered on the obsessional. He was calling her late at night and first thing in the morning. Using his mobile phone as well as his home phone, he would make contact with her up to eighteen times a day. The marathon conversations between the governor and Miss Jenkins stood in contrast to the brevity of his contacts with his wife. Once, while away at the Boar's Head in Charlottesville, Virginia, Clinton checked in with Hillary at her office for a three-minute call in the afternoon, but at 1:23 A.M. he phoned his other love at her home for a conversation lasting ninety-four minutes.[26]

The full contours of the relationship between Bill Clinton and Marilyn Jo Jenkins are, of course, known only to them. Both later denied they had a sexual relationship but neither disputed they had a close friendship.

"It was a period of great tumult," acknowledges Wright. Clinton was torn. He was still sleeping in the same bed with Hillary, as confirmed by one of his most trusted state troopers, Danny Ferguson. But one day after a function at the capitol, Clinton walked out on the lawn with Ferguson and pointed out the slim blond beauty to him. The heartsick governor confided that he loved both Hillary and Marilyn Jo. Corporal Ferguson later testified that Clinton had told him, "It's tough to be in love with both your wife and another woman."[27]

HILLARY'S ADDICTION

A spasm of divorce threats overtook the Clintons. The governor telephoned Dick Morris and reported that his marriage was in deep trouble. Clinton did not sound broken up. He did not indicate that he wanted any emotional support. He simply wanted to talk about what it would mean politically. Morris offered to let him use the Morrises' house in Florida. Clinton said he would consider staying there.[28]

Hillary seriously considered abandoning her role in saving Bill's career and attempting to fill his shoes herself. If he didn't want to run for governor again, she would. Hillary called up a friend and former newspaper publisher in the state, Dorothy Stuck, and asked, "What would happen if I ran for governor?"

"After all this time Bill's been in office, you'd be hung with his baggage," answered the veteran newspaperwoman. She pledged her support but advised Hillary to wait a few more years. "She thought she had a good chance," remembers Stuck.[29]

"She got very enthusiastic about the prospect of running for governor," I was told by one of Hillary's closest confidantes, Carolyn Huber. Hushing her voice as if telling a tale out of school, Huber said, "I think she'd like to be governor, but she wasn't about to try if Bill wanted to again."[30]

"Hillary made it clear that she wanted to run if he didn't," agrees Morris. He recalls vividly Bill Clinton telling him, "She feels we've done everything for me. My career and my needs have taken a front-row seat—now it's her turn." Morris sensed that Clinton was going out of his way to be supportive of his wife, as Hillary had by now built up a huge reservoir of resentment. Morris said he was sure that Hillary was telling Clinton, in effect, "I've made all the money for the family. If you'd been able to keep your cock in your pants, we'd be able to run for president. But you fucked that up. So if you're not going to be governor, I am."[31]

But now she would be confronted with the public price she had paid for being Bill Clinton's wife.

She asked Morris to add some questions to a poll in late 1989 to test the chances of her running as an independent gubernatorial candidate. After all her visible contributions during her husband's governorship—including travels all over the state to promote major education reform—she was stricken by the poll results. Voters saw her only in the role of the governor's wife. Bill Clinton was even more upset than Hillary. He sat down with Morris and rewrote the polling questions, incorporating a reminder of Hillary's contributions. The results did not change.[32]

"Things came to a head at that point," confirms Wright. "They entered into very personal negotiations—what each felt they had to have to continue the marriage."[33] The central mystery behind Hillary—why she stands by her husband although he wounds her again and again—came closer than ever to being revealed to both of them.

"I think we're all addicted to something," Bill Clinton told Carolyn Yeldell Staley in the mid-1980s. "Some people are addicted to drugs. Some to power. Some to food. Some to sex. We're all addicted to something."[34]

Hillary's addiction is Bill. He is her only rebellion, the one thing she can't logically explain. An addiction causes people to do things they would otherwise never think of doing. So addicted did Hillary become to Bill Clinton that she gave up the chance for a prominent career of her own, gave up her name (temporarily), moved to Arkansas, and stayed there for eighteen years. Bill was a taste of freedom, a flight from her Calvinist "shoulds," an escape from her father.

But as many of us do, Hillary repeated with her husband the central dynamic of her childhood. She had tried to be perfect to please her father—earning top grades, learning to recite baseball statistics, becoming a dutiful Goldwater Girl—but the dour Hugh Rodham had always withheld the unconditional love for which every child longs. "Her father was an impossible person to please," says Nancy Pietrefesa, Hillary's running buddy in her twenties. Pietrefesa was one of the few people who got close enough to see the Rodham family drama: "Her father was a deeply narcissistic man who saw her as competition and always tried to undermine her sexuality."[35] So Hillary tried harder, but the more accomplished she became in her own right—without the benefit of her father's direction—the more he withheld his love and approval.

In Bill Clinton, Hillary had found a substitute who did respect and admire her. For years she had tried to be perfect in pleasing Bill, hungry for the affection and approval lacking from her father. At times, Clinton lavished her with his easy love. But if Hillary needed real personal intimacy from her husband, it was not easily forthcoming. According to a formerly close White House aide who has been by Clinton's side in both public and private situations, "He is emotionally unavailable. He lives on campaign junk love and casual sex—where no long-term commitment is required."[36]

With the abysmal banality of neurotic patterns, Hillary seemed to be living out the same dynamic with her husband as with her father. When her accomplishments overshadowed Clinton's, he would punish her in his own way—by philandering.

By this time, the two had become symbiotic as political partners who also fulfilled each other's deepest psychological needs. Over the years Hillary had learned not only to rationalize but even to capitalize on her husband's weaknesses. When his misbehavior was flagrant enough to incur her wrath, this normally narcissistic man would of necessity show his wife some warmth, some physical intimacy—or merely pay attention to her.

Eileen McGann adds, "When Hillary rescues Bill, he invests her with a lot of power. Those are the few times he's able to be warm and emotional and just give something."[37]

She also found another compensation: when Hillary the wife lost, Hillary the political partner usually made gains. She took charge. And he let her. In 1988, when Clinton was caught up with Marilyn Jo and slighting Hillary the wife, he praised Hillary the politician all the more volubly in public. "Some say the wrong Clinton is in the statehouse," the governor drawled during a charity roast of Hillary in 1988, "and I wouldn't disagree with them."[38]

"Hillary has the most incredible ability to separate her personal hurts, her personal indignity, from a bigger picture, and a bigger goal, and a bigger love for him," Betsey Wright told me. "I was always so jealous of it, because I could not do it. I'd get so mad at him, it was hard for me to remember anything I liked about him or that he had ever done. Hillary would get mad at him, and yet she could sort through that within a matter of hours." Wright had become increasingly disturbed by Clinton's indiscriminate flirting; it offended the feminist chief of staff personally. As an excuse to "get in his face" about his misbehavior, Wright would lash her boss by pointing out, "You're jeopardizing my investment in you!"[39]

Hillary also had a thirteen-year investment in the marriage and her husband's political career, and there were other reasons she hung on. She would later suggest that her mother's desperate experience as a child who had been abandoned by divorcing parents had deeply affected her. "She had terrible obstacles," Hillary said of her mother, "but she vowed that she would break the pattern of abandonment in her family, and she did." Her mother had always advised Hillary, "Never get a divorce—endure everything."[40] Wright finds the explanation deeper in Hillary's camouflaged feelings: "Given her love for this man, there were worse things that could have happened than infidelity," says Wright. "Like being without each other or not having a marriage. To stay with him was, for her, a much bigger relationship than this little rotten, infested piece."[41]

Hillary's anger at her husband didn't just dissolve, however. It was diverted. Or it calcified into grudges against others she saw as betraying her. "He blows up and the next five minutes loves you again," says Robert Boorstin, a political public relations man who worked closely with Hillary on health care reform. "She gets angry at you and doesn't forget it for twenty years. Hillary is capable of carrying a grudge like almost no one I know. You're either with her or against her—black and white."[42]

But—and it is a hugely important but—Hillary can contain her anger in service of her greater life goals. It is a deliberate alchemy and arguably the secret behind her relentless drive and noblest aspirations.

"She was always more conscious of their future," says Boorstin. "He was a creature of the moment—the future would take care of itself. This is a woman who clearly knows where she wants to go and has for years and years, and has compromised herself to get there."[43]

THE RE-SEDUCTION OF BILL CLINTON

The Clintons' personal negotiations dragged through the summer and fall of 1989. From the start, Hillary took divorce off the table. Wright is clear on this point: "It absolutely was not an alternative that she gave him."[44] At some point, probably early in 1990, Hillary called Bill to a Come-to-Jesus meeting. In the South this means a day of reckoning—confessing your sins and asking to be forgiven.

But this time it was Hillary who would have to seduce Bill back into their marriage. They shared something that was really important to both of them, and that was Chelsea. And hadn't they made a terrific political team? Indeed, for his rebellion against Hillary and Betsey following his 1986 re-election victory, Clinton had paid a price. He is superb at absorbing information and superb at regurgitating it—articulating a line. But in the middle phase, his mind often jams. Given to overstuffing his brain with data and information and other people's opinions, he often suffers from a serious backlog of analysis. He needs someone on hand whom he can trust to help him wade through the raw data and digest it, so that he knows what to do with it. "Every night or two he would call up and just regurgitate eight or ten summaries of magazine articles, books, conversations, thoughts, and observations he'd had," says Morris. "He would be asking, in effect, 'Where do I put these in the puzzle? How does this fit into our strategic design?' "[45]

While Hillary had performed that role, Clinton had done particularly well. But in the late 1980s she was otherwise engaged in making money, spending more time with Vince Foster, and considering her own future. Now Clinton's political momentum was desperately in need of resuscitation. He never considered a nonpolitical life. "I don't ever really think that he thought he could have a *life* without Hillary," says Wright.[46]

Moreover, Hillary could offer Bill what no other woman could: she could give him a pass on the transgressions that had kept him from running for president. She could give him what F. Scott Fitzgerald bemoaned was impossible in American life—a second act.

But she would not condone any ongoing affair. Bill would have to 'fess up, admit how desperately he needed her, and together they would rededicate themselves to each other and to capturing the presidency.

"I have a strong feeling that Hillary would have been confrontational with her husband on these matters," says Ed Matthews, the retired minister of Little Rock's First United Methodist Church who became Hillary's pastor in June 1990. "At that time, the more respected friends of the Clintons were anxious that he and so-and-so had had an affair, and that Hillary was now aware of it," says Reverend Matthews. "I would guess the affair went back at least a year to eighteen months before that." Hillary never mentioned names to her pastor, but she did discuss confronting her husband. Matthews told me, "Clinton admitted it, and at that point maybe they did get some counseling."[47]

Hillary also took the part of child development expert and explained Bill to himself. She told him he had been scarred by the early abuse he had suffered when he was only four years old—when his footloose mother had come back from New Orleans to Hot Springs and fought with his grandmother to reclaim her son. Hillary probably didn't see the parallel situation caused in 1987 when Clinton had been pulled and tugged between his wife, who desperately wanted him to run for president, and his surrogate mother, Betsey, who scolded him and scared him into withdrawing.

"In the end, they made a commitment to work on and save their marriage," says Wright. Clinton vowed that this was the last time. He would start over. He promised to straighten out. He didn't *want* to be unfaithful. He wanted to make their relationship his central priority. He wanted forgiveness.[48]

The upshot of the Come-to-Jesus meeting was that Hillary insisted her husband work on himself until he conquered his weakness. He promised to try. Friends hint that one of Hillary's conditions of recommitment was that Bill get professional help for his philandering. That may be why Clinton has never released his medical records from that period. He was obviously out of control and dangerously reckless with his marriage, his career, and even Hillary's health. (There have been unconfirmed reports that Clinton caught a sexually transmitted disease.) Hillary thought that she and Bill now had an understanding. In subsequent years Reverend Matthews came to think, "Maybe there is some denial going on in her mind."[49]

Hillary's remark in an interview in 1999 suggested something of the sort: "I thought this was all resolved ten years ago," she said in the wake of the Lewinsky affair. "I thought he had conquered it; I thought he understood it, but he didn't go deep enough or work hard enough."[50]

BACK IN THE GAME

Almost as an afterthought, Clinton himself backed into the 1990 governor's race that spring. He first had to square off against four Democratic rivals in a primary, and his staff hadn't even prepared campaign buttons. Even Hillary may not have known his disposition. "Halfway through his announcement speech, some people weren't sure whether he was going to run or not," says Brantley.[51] Clinton may not have been sure himself. As George Stephanopoulos has observed, "Clinton never knew exactly what he wanted to say until he heard himself say the words."[52] Amazingly, the governor admitted before five hundred people in the capitol rotunda that "the fire of an election no longer burns in me."

Once more, it was Hillary who went out to ambush her husband's opponent. Only if she saved him again could she hope for a return of even his meager attentions and emotional warmth.

Tom McCrae, Clinton's main challenger in the Democratic primary, called a press conference to lambaste the governor while he was out of town. He was in the middle of calling Bill Clinton a chicken "since the governor will not debate" when another voice chewed into his sound bite: "Tom, who was the one person who didn't show up in Springdale? Give me a break! I mean, I think we oughta get the record straight."

The camera swung around to reveal a yellow-haired woman in a bold houndstooth-checked suit—literally in his face. Having crashed the candidate's photo op, Hillary began reading embarrassing passages from McCrae's own earlier handouts in which he had praised Clinton's policies. The camera spun back to reveal the man's grit-eating smile, his eyes bobbling around in his head. The local Eyewitness News man wound up his thrilled coverage with the tag line "Hillary Clinton showed again that she may be the best debater in the family."[53] On primary night Bill looked weak enough in the early returns that CBS predicted there would be a runoff, but he squeaked past McCrae to take 54 percent of the vote.[54]

The 1990 general campaign was the nastiest yet. The Republican challenger, Sheffield Nelson, had sprung up from the same small-town background as Clinton, but he had not been nearly as publicly successful. He ran Arkla, the Arkansas-Louisiana Gas Company, the largest gas company in the state (later headed by Clinton's close friend Mack McLarty). The two men hated each other and took pleasure in uncovering and spreading unsavory information about the other. That year, Nelson tried to nail Clinton to the cross of miscegenation—spending his own money in a futile effort to prove rumors that his nemesis had fathered a child by a black prostitute.[55] (The charge was finally disproved by DNA evidence in January 1999.)[56] Weeks before the election, a right-wing malcontent by the name of Larry Nichols, who had been fired as an Arkansas state employee, filed a lawsuit against Clinton. He contended that the governor had used state monies to entertain at least five of his lovers, including Gennifer Flowers. The case was thrown out soon after, but Nichols remained an irritant, accusing Clinton of an assortment of improprieties including running drugs from Central America. (Flowers, too, kept hounding Clinton for a state job, which she eventually landed in June 1991, when Clinton would be poised to try a presidential run.)[57]

As tensions mounted on the campaign trail and inside the mansion, Clinton took out his frustrations on Dick Morris. On a humid night in 1990, the two were scheduled to have an early-evening emergency meeting to discuss the governor's dismal polls. His number was down to 43 percent. He was losing a campaign for which he had no heart in the first place.

Morris had gone straight from a dentist's chair to the mansion at dinnertime and sat around fidgeting until midnight. No one fed him. When the governor finally joined him in the breakfast room, along with Hillary and his campaign manager, Gloria Cabe, an alarm bell went off in Morris's head: the governor had had a glass of wine.

Exhausted, worried, unable to contain his frustration, Clinton tore into his strategist. "You got me into this race, so you could make some extra money off me," he screamed, ". . . I'm about to lose this election and you're too busy with the little legislative races for Betsey to give me any attention at all." Clinton's cloudburst of a temper was legendary, but in the thirteen years they had worked together he had never yelled at Morris. But Bill Clinton is hypersensitive to abandonment, and he took out his emotional turmoil on Morris: "I pay your expenses, and you come down here and you work on Betsey's races, not on mine. You've forgotten me. You don't care about me. You've turned your back on me. I don't get shit from you anymore. You're screwing me! You're screwing me!"

In the face of this blast, Morris lost his temper, too. "Thank you, thank you, thank you!" he yelled. "You've just solved my problem. I'm getting shit from Atwater [Lee Atwater, the Republican operative] for working for you. Go fuck yourself! I'm quitting your goddamn campaign." Whereupon he stormed out of the breakfast room and toward the back door.

Clinton charged up behind Morris and tackled him before he could reach the door. "He was above me on his knees," Morris remembers. "He had his fist cocked back as if to punch me. Hillary grabbed his bicep, screaming, 'Bill, don't do this! Stop this!' and pulled her husband off me." Hillary helped the shaken Morris to his feet. Immediately Clinton switched from expressing his hurt through anger and fell to pleading with Morris: "Don't go, don't go, I'm sorry." Ignoring him, Morris walked out and slammed the door behind him.

It was Hillary who ran after the shaken strategist to calm him down. She put her arm around his shoulders and walked him around the mansion grounds in the dark. "Please forgive him," she pleaded. "He didn't mean it. He's very sorry. He's overtired, he hasn't slept well in days. He's not himself. He values you. He needs you," she kept repeating. The most disturbing of her excuses was the one Morris would remember best:

"He only does this to people he loves."[58]

HILLARY'S BRILLIANT CHOICE

When Clinton won election to his sixth term as governor, Hillary had mixed emotions. During a debate he had been asked if he would serve out his full term if he was victorious. "You bet," he said.

If he was being truthful, that meant he had just taken himself out of the 1992 presidential race. Hearing this, Frank Greer, his media consultant, says he "died a thousand deaths. We had talked a lot about running for president. I thought perhaps it wasn't going to happen."[59]

Hillary was not so easily discouraged. It was at a girls' softball game in Little Rock in April 1991 that she began beating the drum again. She had carefully followed the polls on President Bush. Eighteen months earlier, he had seemed invincible. But after hitting a peak approval rating of 90 percent following the Persian Gulf War, Bush had ignored signs that domestic economic problems were seething below the surface; instead, he had rested on his victory laurels. Some of the best and brightest Democrats had given up the idea of challenging him for the 1992 presidential election. Bush's slow slide had suddenly become precipitous: only the previous month, his approval rating had dropped by 12 percentage points, to 78 percent.[60]

Hillary spotted the vacuum—or at least an opening.

"I sure don't think George Bush can be beaten," said Skip Rutherford, a political junkie like Hillary, who was sitting next to her at the softball game. "I think he's going to win again."

"I'm not so sure," he remembers Hillary saying as she watched Chelsea guard third base. "You know, what the Democrats need is a good message and a good messenger, and that's a winning combination."

"Can I read something into this?" Rutherford nudged. "She didn't say 'yes' and she didn't say 'no.' "

Hillary turned on her Scarlett O'Hara voice: "Oh, I don't know."[61]

She knew.

Two years before, she had helped persuade Clinton to accept a deal from Democratic activist Al From: if Clinton would take the chairmanship of the Democratic Leadership Council (DLC), a group of moderate Democrats who were seeking to redirect the losing leftist lean of their party, it would give him a national platform, together with some resources to travel the country and try out his own national agenda. The deal was sewn up for Hillary when From told her husband, "I think you'll be president someday, and that'll make us both important."[62]

All through the strained 1989 to 1991 period in the Clinton marriage, whenever Bill would be bouncing around the country in a six-seater plane for the DLC, From was surprised at how often he would call Hillary. She was like his personal modem; he dialed her up on his cell phone several times a day, and she would feed him whatever information he needed.

In May 1991, Clinton delivered what may have been the most important speech of his political life. The DLC held a national convention in Cleveland, where Clinton was the keynoter. He and Hillary worked together on his address all night, laying out the themes that would become hallmarks of the New Democrats' approach. In the high-adrenaline race to refine and internalize their message before morning, Bill and Hillary were once again bound by what they both love most—the belief that they are about to change the world for the better.

They were the only people in the world who could do that for each other.

Shortly before nine the next morning, Clinton wrote three words on a piece of paper—"Opportunity, responsibility, community"—and stepped up to deliver a knockout of a speech. From remembers, "People said it was the first time they'd heard a moderate Democrat speak with passion. They loved him."[63]

A few weeks later, at dawn, Bill Clinton was dropping Chelsea off at the Little Rock airport to go to a Concordia language camp in Minnesota with Max Brantley's daughter. As the two fathers walked toward the gate, the governor enthusiastically replayed what Hillary had told him when she arrived home from an international conference in Scandinavia at two that morning. Once their daughters were dispatched, Clinton had a cup of coffee with his friend who was not coincidentally a journalist, and they talked about what it would take for him to be a serious presidential contender.

"He laid it all out like a lawyer's case—like Hillary would do it," recalls Brantley. "At the end he said, 'Plus, Hillary thinks I should run.' That was obviously the clincher."[64]

It was a midsummer day in Arkansas, so hot and humid one could almost see the rampant growth of the kudzu vine, when the Clintons summoned to the mansion the people who would become their kitchen cabinet. Bill and Hillary sat around sipping coffee with Bruce Lindsey, Skip Rutherford, and aide Craig Smith, talking about "Can George Bush be beaten?" At the end of the forty-minute discussion, the friends asked, "What if we lose?"

"If we lose, we lose," someone said.

"But, Governor," said a concerned Lindsey, "what if we win?"

Clinton said nothing. Hillary smiled and spoke for him: "Then we'll serve."[65]

In October 1991, Bernard Nussbaum got a call from Ken Brody, then a partner in the investment firm of Goldman Sachs: "We're having a big organizational meeting to discuss supporting Bill Clinton for president. Hillary says you're on board."

"Well, if Hillary says I'm on board, I'm on board," said Nussbaum. It had been years since the two had spoken. All of eight people turned up for the "big organizational meeting" held at Tom Tisch's office at the Loew's Corporation building, most of them asking, "So who is Bill Clinton?" Brody said he had met the Arkansas governor once or twice, and he seemed like a good guy.

Why are we here? Nussbaum wondered. *We're supposed to be the core group, and none of us even knows this guy—he has as much chance of being president as the man in the moon!* But he gamely gave them Hillary's pitch:

"Bill Clinton has incredible political skills. He shares our Democratic values, of course, but that's not how you sell him. This guy got himself elected attorney general of Arkansas at twenty-eight. He got himself elected governor at thirty-two—the youngest governor they ever had. He's gotten himself reelected four times." Nussbaum wound up with Hillary's declaration from their Watergate days: "This guy is going to be President of the United States!"[66]

The other men looked at Nussbaum the way he had looked at Hillary seventeen years before—as if he were crazy.

The Herculean task ahead did not discourage Hillary. She was ready to take her own platform national, as a campaign letter would later describe. And she had become bored with the politics of Arkansas. "She didn't like all the duties of First Lady," confirmed her brother Hugh Rodham. "It was tiresome and too local."[67]

One morning in August 1991, Hillary woke up on the second floor of the Arkansas governor's mansion, looked over at her husband's sleepless face, and told him, "You almost have to do it." She meant run for president.

"Do you have any idea what we're getting into?" he asked.

"I know, it'll be tough."[68]

CHAPTER ELEVEN

Two for the Price of One

When you think of Hillary, think of our real slogan,
"Buy one, get one free!"

—BILL CLINTON

Nineteen ninety-two was heralded as the Year of the Political Woman. But the most controversial figure of that presidential election year— Hillary Rodham Clinton, lawyer, activist, author, corporate boardwoman, mother, and wife of Bill Something—was not even running for office.

Or was she?

In the space of one week in late January 1992, Hillary fast-forwarded from being introduced as the "wife of" (*60 Minutes*) to the victim of "the other woman" (*Prime Time Live*) to "Trapped in a Spotlight, Hillary Clinton Uses It" (*The New York Times*), the last illustrated by a picture that said it all: Hillary waving to a crowd and wearing a big campaign smile—out in front of her husband.

Eight years of Bill, eight years of Hill.

That was the dream. It was Hillary's private slogan, shared with one of her closest intimates, Linda Bloodworth-Thomason. Early in his 1992 presidential campaign, I asked then Governor Clinton if he was concerned about being upstaged by his wife. He was unfazed: "I've always liked strong women. It doesn't bother me for people to see her and get excited and say she could be president, too."

"So, after eight years of Bill Clinton?" I teased.

"Eight years of Hillary Clinton," he said. "Why not?"[1]

Flickers of the sweet ingenue smile of her college years were still evident in her now-forty-four-year-old face. She had whittled her voluptuous Victorian figure down to a fighting size 8 by touching little more than a lettuce leaf and water during campaign fund-raisers (while her less disciplined husband had piled on twenty-five pounds). When the cameras dollied in tight, however, one could detect the calculation in Hillary's eyes. Lips pulled back over her slightly jutting teeth, her public smile was by now a practiced and ever-present game face. A small but frequent frown established an air of superiority. Her long blond flip was lifelessly doll-like. Her wardrobe had the look of loving-hands-at-home-in-Little-Rock. But there was no mistaking the passion in her words or the impact of her presence.

THE ENABLERS

Even before Clinton announced his candidacy in 1992, he and Hillary appeared in front of the Washington media at the Sperling Breakfast and made a blanket acknowledgment that there had been infidelities in the past. They believed this would be an immunization. The Clinton camp had planned "a slow build for Hillary," according to her own campaign manager, Richard Mintz. That was until all hell broke loose—the day Bill Clinton was "deflowered" by a cabaret singer who had once headlined at the Pinnacle Lounge in Little Rock.

On January 23, Gennifer Flowers finally seized her opportunity to make a splash with the revelation of her sexual history with Bill Clinton. *The Star* tabloid had paid her a reported $100,000 to spill her smarmy tale of a twelve-year sexual affair beginning in 1977. "They Made Love All Over Her Apartment," screamed one headline. The candidate's young, inexperienced advisers hustled the governor up to their suite at the Holiday Inn in Manchester, New Hampshire, for a panicky strategy session. As they all read the *Star* stories, Clinton speed-read ahead, picking out details he knew could be disproved and giving his aides a running counterpunch. Being true believers, George Stephanopoulos and James Carville wanted to agree with their boss that it was all malicious fiction. They wanted to see Clinton as he liked to see himself—as the victim of unscrupulous political enemies.

Stephanopoulos has admitted that he needed Clinton to be dependent on him as his defender, "which made me, of course, an enabler."[2]

But no one surpassed Hillary in that role.

The Clintons asked *60 Minutes* to give them a TV interview that Sunday. The taping would be done in Boston. The night before their extraordinary "Checkers speech," the Clintons rendezvoused in a suite at the Ritz-Carlton and treated themselves to room service, Hillary indulging her husband in a cheeseburger. The couple ignored the obvious. When the television crew invited them to inspect the hotel room where the interview would take place, Hillary conferred with them on colors and camera angles. "My sense of it was that she was in control," says Steve Kroft, the interviewer. "We fiddled around with who should sit on which side, and they fiddled around with chair heights. If you didn't know she was his wife, you'd have thought she was his media consultant. She didn't do it in a dictatorial way. She was very delightful and charming. When they left the room, everybody pretty much said, 'Boy, she's terrific.' "[3]

Hillary's close friend Susan Thomases, a bright, belligerent New York lawyer, flew in to assert herself as Hillary's crisis manager. Thomases coached Bill not to explicitly deny having had an affair with Flowers or anyone else. When other advisers suggested that they be candid, both Hillary and Bill stiffened. Clinton swore that Flowers was lying. Hillary and Bill were a seamless wall of resistance against even mentioning the scarlet "A." Their media consultants offered polls showing that 39 percent of voters would have reservations about voting for a candidate who had been unfaithful— but that percentage diminished if the wife had known about it and accepted it. The obvious conclusion was that Gennifer's unforgettable slot-machine eyes, hydraulic lips, and black roots required a chaste visual challenge: Who better than the governor's apple-cheeked, moon-eyed wife? She was staggeringly poised, effortlessly articulate, primly silk-scarved, blond too, but with a good little Wellesley girl's hair band covering her brown roots.

They settled on a strategy of *appearing* to be candid about their past marital problems. Clinton would use his family as a metaphor for his character. The burden of their defense would rest on Hillary. The pattern was thus set. Satisfied, the candidate's wife adjourned the meeting about 1 A.M.[4]

The next day, before airtime, tension was reportedly running high in the control room, with producer Don Hewitt ranting to Clinton's advisers, "He's gotta come clean! He's got to say yes!" Once Bill and Hillary were seated, Mrs. Clinton stared intently at her husband as he responded to the grilling. This was no Nancy Reagan gaze—this was the look of a consigliere sitting vigil over a member of the Family.

Kroft's impression of Hillary was that "She's tougher and more disciplined than he is. And analytical. Among his faults, he has a tendency not to think of the consequences of the things he says. I think she knows. She's got a ten-second delay. If something comes to her mind she doesn't think will play right, she cuts it off before anybody knows she's thinking it."[5]

"I have acknowledged wrongdoing," Bill offered when the cameras were rolling. "I have acknowledged causing pain in my marriage." At another point when Kroft pressed him—"I am assuming from your answer that you're categorically denying that you ever had an affair with Gennifer Flowers"—he took the bait. "I've said that before," he replied quickly. "And so has she."

In jumped Hillary the litigator: "I don't want to be any more specific. I don't think being any more specific about what's happened in the privacy of our life together is relevant to anybody besides us."

It was a signal for her husband to button up. "Having made the mistake of denying Gennifer Flowers, he was undoing what they had decided to do," Susan Thomases told me. "So she was reminding him, 'Hey, buddy, remember our strategy: if you say you're not going to talk about any specific case, and then you talk about one case, you're blowing the strategy.' "[6]

Hillary's presence was so strong that, according to Kroft, "We found ourselves rationing her sound bites to keep her from becoming the dominant force in the interview."[7] Betsey Wright gave Hillary the highest marks for her performance on *60 Minutes*. "That appearance established that she was not a victim," says Wright, "and once she was not a victim as a result of any of Bill's behavior, then we could move on."[8]

INSULATING HERSELF FROM HURT

It was easy to mistake Hillary for cold and hard. When I referred to the Gennifer week as a "crisis," Hillary corrected me: "This is *not* a crisis, not a personal crisis, anyway." In all the time I traveled with Hillary in 1992 and in the sixty interviews I did that year with her friends, family, and associates for a *Vanity Fair* article titled "What Hillary Wants," there was only one hint of a deep emotional reaction. That was the week she phoned her confidante in the governor's mansion, Carolyn Huber. When Huber broke into sobs, a fissure opened in Hillary's studied equanimity. "I know, Carolyn, it's hurting so bad," Hillary said, referring to herself. "The press doesn't believe you have any feelings. They sure don't believe in the Bible." On further exposure, it seemed to me possible that Hillary's superficial brittleness hides a greater inner vulnerability than Bill's. "She never shows her personal feelings on the surface," says Huber.[9]

The Clintons confided fully in nobody, not even family—only in each other. One friend whom Hillary did occasionally allow herself to cry with, and had even debated divorce with, was Linda Bloodworth-Thomason. Being accustomed to life in the political fishbowl, Hillary did not talk to her friends about the skeletons in the Clintons' closets.[10] "She knew this day would come," said Jan Piercey, "and she wasn't going to put anybody in the position of lying."[11] It sounded like another excuse. In fact, Hillary remained silent about her husband's infidelities not to protect others but to protect herself. Another friend said of the media frenzy over Clinton's nocturnal peccadilloes, "None of this came as a surprise to her."

But Hillary was determined not to leave herself or the campaign vulnerable to any more of Bill's mercenary "rodeo queens." After Gennifer, Hillary and her sidekick Betsey Wright mounted a sub-rosa black arts campaign against the women. Hillary called upon her old friend Bernard Nussbaum to counsel Wright on how far she could legally go to stanch further "bimbo eruptions." But even Wright, Thomases, and Nussbaum were not tough enough for Hillary's counteroffensive.

"I am somebody you call in when the house is on fire, not when there's smoke in the kitchen," brags San Francisco private eye Jack Palladino. "You ask me to deal with that fire, to save you, to do whatever has to be done."[12] Hillary knew of Mr. Palladino from the summer when she worked in San Francisco on the Black Panthers case. Panthers Huey Newton and Eldridge Cleaver were clients of Palladino's. He had also helped the Hell's Angels beat drug charges. He is now middle-aged and portly with penetrating eyes and a shiny pate.

Wright told him there were nineteen women, by her count, being chased by the tabloids, led by *National Enquirer* editor Dan Schwartz, who admitted that his newspaper was willing to pay "top dollar" (six figures) for stories about Bill Clinton's private life.[13] Palladino was tapped to be the Clinton campaign's secret policeman, his assignment to wrest from the targeted women signed affidavits denying any sexual or romantic involvement with the rumored skirt chaser.

The counterculture private eye proved his worth right away. In April 1992 he killed off a nasty story concocted by another private investigator. Palladino tracked down an Oklahoma City woman who claimed to have had an extended affair with Clinton in the Eighties, and turned her around. When Palladino ran into resistance, he would visit relatives and former boyfriends and develop compromising material to convince the women to remain silent.[14] He would eventually gather affidavits from six of the Jane Does later subpoenaed by Ken Starr.

For his effective services, Hillary and Wright arranged to pay Palladino $100,000 out of federally subsidized campaign funds, initially disguising the payments as "legal fees." (The payments were laundered by passing them through a Denver law firm and then on to Palladino's agency.) After this practice came to light in a *Washington Post* story by Michael Isikoff, the campaign began publicly disclosing their payments to Palladino.[15] While Palladino was working his way through the names in Wright's "black book" on Clinton, Wright herself mounted what she called "a truth squad" to monitor the activities of reporters who were covering the campaign.[16]

Hillary turned a different face to the world. The stories of her husband's infidelities appeared to register, consciously at least, as having nothing to do with her or their marriage, but rather as evidence of the depths of degradation to which the hit men behind George Bush would stoop. Rarely did anyone in her audiences dare to bring up the question of infidelity, and when someone did, Hillary usually knocked it out of the ballpark and left people cheering. Her refrain became something of a mantra: "This is a much bigger issue than just Bill and me. I just hope for the sake of the country we'll set some boundaries for others coming along."

Not only was her altruistic defense politically astute, but it also served to buffer her psychologically from feelings that would send most women off on an emotional roller coaster. "It doesn't make any difference what people say about her," said her friend Dorothy Stuck, "whatever criticism or belittling, she doesn't take it personally, because the cause is always more important. It may very well be the way she insulates herself from hurt. And I think in the past ten or twelve years with Bill she may have done that to protect her sanity."[17]

I asked Hillary if she thought her husband had told her everything she needed to know. "Yes. I have absolutely no doubt about that," she replied, her blue eyes unblinking beneath the dark hedgerow of brows. "I don't think I could be sitting here otherwise. That's been, over the years, part of the development of trust."

Did she think Gary Hart was qualified to be president, or had his compulsive philandering revealed something disturbing about his character? "He was not yet at a point where he could be honest with himself, that's my perception," she told me. "People in his campaign said they confronted him and said, 'Have you ever?' and he said 'No.'"

She praised Bill for being honest with the people he loves, admitting his problems, and declaring he wanted to do better. "I think as he got older, as he became a father, he began to let his breath out a little bit," observed Hillary. She said her husband believes that trauma and mistakes are all tests that help one grow. For him, says Hillary, "it's a constant coming to grips with who you are and what stage of life you can grow beyond."[18]

All through the 1992 campaign the Clintons' friends fiercely idealized their marriage, painting it as a remarkable integration of strong personalities and sheer guts. Linda Bloodworth-Thomason told me prophetically, "Look, this isn't Lurleen Wallace. Hillary doesn't have to stay with Bill Clinton. She could get to the Senate or possibly the White House on her own—and she knows it."[19]

JUST MY BILL

After years of protecting the philanderer's secrets, Hillary had built so thick a guard wall that it seemed to paralyze her judgment when it came to revealing almost anything at all. When George Stephanopoulos raised the issue of Clinton's avoidance of the draft in December 1991, Hillary snapped, "Bill's not going to apologize for being against the Vietnam War."[20] She shut down any discussion about how they would deal with the inevitable questions when they did arise.

By the first week of February, the Clintons had survived the Gennifer story and Clinton was maintaining his lead in the New Hampshire polls. Suddenly, a reporter for *The Wall Street Journal* wanted facts about Clinton and the draft. The Clinton team had no strategy because of Hillary's lockdown. Clinton, ill with the flu, protested to his press secretary that he had nothing to hide. He fobbed the query off onto Gene Holmes, the ROTC commander at the University of Arkansas who had always covered for him. But Holmes had had a change of heart. A few days later, a devastating letter by Clinton to Holmes fell into the hands of ABC News. In it, Clinton thanked the colonel for saving him from the draft.

The campaign, according to Clinton, dropped "like a turd in a well." In three days he fell from first to third place behind former senator Paul Tsongas and Senator Bob Kerrey.

A crisis meeting took place in the men's room of the airport terminal in Manchester. Carville, followed by adviser Paul Begala, Bruce Lindsey, and George Stephanopoulos, crowded in with Clinton. Hillary marched in right behind them. After the group had passed around the pages of the photo-copied letter, Hillary spoke up first: "Bill, *this is you*. I can hear you saying this." Her tone was not censorious. It was nostalgic—as if she were getting a fix with all the potency of their early, passionately idealistic high.

Once again, Clinton's emollient personality smoothed over the crisis. Ted Koppel gave him a whole hour on *Nightline* to explain himself. He wound up with a winning sound bite, albeit a total lie: "Ted, the only times you've had me on this show are to discuss a woman I never slept with and a draft I never dodged."[21]

By now the Clintons had two strikes against them. But Bill's apparent sincerity about his draft manipulations and Hillary's nullification of the womanizing issue allowed them to remain in the game. Rather than being struck out in the New Hampshire primary, Clinton climbed back up to second place. He earned the sobriquet "The Comeback Kid."

The Clintons were euphoric—for all of a week.

FIGHTING GENNIFER WITH JENNIFER

Then Hillary went a little too far. It was not by chance that during a formal interview with me in the governor's mansion, Hillary departed from the subject we'd been discussing and purposefully planted a toxic tidbit in my tape recorder: "Why does the press shy away from investigating rumors about George Bush's extramarital life?" she complained. She told me a little story. "I had tea with Anne Cox Chambers [the heiress who is chairwoman of her media empire's Atlanta newspaper group] and she's sittin' there in her sunroom saying 'You know, I just don't understand why they think they can get away with this—everybody knows about George Bush.' And then she launches into this long description of, you know, Bush and his carrying on, all of which is apparently well known in Washington." Hillary continued, "I'm convinced part of it is that the establishment—regardless of party—sticks together. They're going to circle the wagons on Jennifer and all these other people."[22]

The Jennifer reference was to a decade-long Bush staffer who by then enjoyed a senior State Department position. She had been persistently linked with President Bush in rumors that had never been proved or printed. When I interviewed Jennifer in 1987 in Bush's Senate office, the amply built middle-aged woman, a born-again Christian, was discreet about her work and travel with Bush. Most of us who write about politics have long been mystified by how Republicans seem to escape exposure of their personal peccadilloes, even in the era of "gotcha journalism," while Democrats always seem to get caught. My guess is simple: Republicans tend to sleep with their own kind; Democrats tend to sleep with women who kiss and tell. For such women, sexual commerce follows copulation (or any variation thereof).

Anne Cox Chambers later confirmed for me that she had told Hillary, "I don't understand why nothing's ever been said about George Bush's girlfriend—I understand he has a Jennifer, too."[23]

Vanity Fair was still uncomfortable about using the incident in my article. Tina Brown, then the editor, sent me across country to catch up with Hillary at a Hollywood luncheon and go over facts and quotes with her. At the event Hillary invited me to sit beside her. She was warm and eagerly engaged in conversation. After her speech, I joined her in a van for a wrap-up interview on the way to her next event. The campaign photographer asked us to pose for a picture. Everything was chummy. When I came to the bottom of my checklist, I told Hillary that I had independently confirmed the story she had told me about Jennifer and Bush. "Anne Cox Chambers remembered the conversation almost verbatim the way you related it to me."

She gave me the glittery lizard eye blink. Her voice went cold as a courtroom witness: "I have no independent recollection of such a conversation."[24]

"Babs Bites Back" shouted the *New York Post* headline the day after the *Vanity Fair* story appeared. Barbara Bush took Hillary to task for stooping so low. It was only three days before the New York primary, and the Clintons were confronted with the headline as their campaign plane landed in Albany. For once, Bill Clinton had to step out front and defend his wife for making a major gaffe. He told the ravening reporters, "Well, you know, all of us make mistakes once in a while." A sweet, slow smile played at the edges of his mouth.

THE LOCKDOWN

"Hillary is naive about the press, both naive and sometimes hostile," says Lanny Davis, one of her most ardent defenders and the author of *Truth to Tell*, a book about his often frustrating tenure as the White House damage control spokesman. "It's this terrible combination of not understanding how the press works and the hostility which clouds her judgment about how to make it better." Over the years Davis has tried without success to counteract Hillary's knee-jerk instincts when it comes to the disclosure of anything about her—anything at all—that she has not approved. Looking back through the retrospectoscope from 1999 to 1992, Davis sees a tragic pattern: "One can speculate that the whole chain of events that led to the Whitewater investigation, then led to Ken Starr, which then led to the investigation of Monica and finally to impeachment can be traced back to the first Jeff Gerth *New York Times* story on Whitewater and the first instinct—to lock down." The decision (by Hillary and Susan Thomases) to make it difficult for Gerth to write that article was naive, says Davis, because the story was going to be written anyway and stonewalling only made matters worse. "It drove the journalism from that point on in the wrong direction, because it looked like the Clintons were trying to hide something. And there was really nothing to hide. But that's the pattern."[25]

The tenacious *Times* reporter had begun asking for information on Whitewater in early February, when Bill and Hillary had been in New Hampshire struggling to save their nascent campaign, under siege by reporters questioning his marital infidelity and avoidance of the draft. "Hillary thought this stuff was a nuisance. Ridiculous. Absurd," as the story is reconstructed by Jane Sherburne, the attorney who later became Hillary's White House defender on all scandals. "She began locking down because it was a complete distraction. So, screw 'em."[26]

Hillary would later reveal to Don Jones her distorted view of how the press works. When Jones brought up the *Times*'s breaking of the Whitewater story, Hillary groaned. "It's frustrating when you're dealing with an evidence-free zone." As a litigator, she felt deprived of an opportunity to cross-examine the reporter. She told Jones, "Bill and I decided not to retaliate in like manner."

"Just beat 'em?"

"Right," said Hillary.[27]

A whole subgroup was tasked with defusing this bombshell. Hillary put Susan Thomases in charge of it. Out in Little Rock, under Thomases hawkish eye, Hillary's two closest associates at the Rose firm, Webb Hubbell and Vince Foster, were assigned to examine all of the Whitewater records and those relating to the Madison bank, as well as Mrs. Clinton's contacts with the state banking commissioner on Madison's behalf. Thomases had free rein to go through all these records, and, after discussion with Hillary, they decided what to "give up" to *The New York Times*.

The decision became known as the "Fuck you, Jeff Gerth" strategy. Thomases stonewalled Gerth for weeks. "Hillary didn't want this to become the issue that brought the third strike against Clinton's campaign," says

Lanny Davis. "People were saying, 'Shut it down! You can't afford another one!' Everybody was overreacting, and that leads to terrible judgments about the press."[28]

Jane Sherburne, who only became involved with the fallout years later, acknowledges that Hillary and Susan should have worked with Gerth to get to the bottom of his questions. "A lot of Hillary's reaction originated with that very private nature of hers," says Sherburne. "Her attitude was 'What business is this of theirs? We want to be talking about education and health care. Why would anybody care about this?' I don't think she recognized the precancerous nature of the Gerth story."[29] The Clintons turned down requests for interviews. Finally, Thomases was dispatched by Hillary to New York to be interviewed by reporters and editors from the *Times* before they published their article. She provided fewer than twenty documents.

Gerth played out the Whitewater investigation in three articles during March 1992. Shortly after the first one appeared, a campaign lawyer working for Thomases discussed with Hillary tax deductions that had been double counted on the Clintons' 1986 and 1987 returns, as revealed in the *Times.* Now Hillary's partners took defensive action. After hours, in the dimly lit Rose firm offices, Vince Foster and Webb Hubbell scoured her records. Foster concentrated on Hillary's billing records, which revealed the work she had done for Jim McDougal and his shady savings and loan. Foster underscored potential problems in red ink.[30] Hubbell stumbled upon a jumble of receipts that were embarrassingly private in nature. He handed two or three boxes of documents to campaign aides sent by Thomases. *Newsweek* reported that one staffer pulled out American Express receipts for room charges at Little Rock's Excelsior Hotel, signed by Bill Clinton. The other aides laughed nervously until they found more receipts, also signed by the governor, for purchases from Victoria's Secret. The Arkansas troopers had complained of being used by the governor to buy gifts for his girlfriends at Victoria's Secret. How eerie it was to find cold-blooded documentation of his flagrant faithlessness among the financial records kept by his own wife![31]

Withheld were Hillary's billing records, which over the years were to take on the dark nimbus of a smoking gun. The firm's computer hard drives were later "vacuumed." The physical records were "found," under suspicious circumstances, only in 1996.

Mr. Clinton only conceded that, as governor, he "perhaps should have found a way to extricate himself from the financial relationship [with the McDougals], but frankly, at the time, it never crossed my mind because we were losing money."[32] Again, scandal did not stick to the Comeback Kid. Hillary's lockdown saved them from an explosion in the short term but kept the fuse smoldering. Hillary's hostility to the press would become her bête noire.

RUNNING MATES

"When you think of Hillary, think of our real slogan," Clinton promised unabashedly in his announcement speech. "Buy one, get one free!"[33]

What a novel idea—an egalitarian marriage and full political partnership such as the country had never seen. The Clintons promised a whole new generational shift: baby boomers coming to Washington to smash the old mold of patriarchal leadership and subservient First Ladyships. Was America ready?

At that time, fewer people seemed to have negative feelings toward Hillary than toward her husband. According to a national survey conducted in March 1992 for *Vanity Fair*, 41 percent of those surveyed had a generally favorable impression of Hillary, while 24 percent thought she was a liability. A whopping 84 percent said they would not object to a First Lady with a separate career. Those surveyed used the following descriptions of Hillary: "intelligent"; "tough-minded"; "a good role model for women"; "a feminist in the best possible sense." The negative descriptions were "too intense" and "dominates her husband." Most disturbing for the Clintons, however, was the skepticism over their relationship: 53 percent saw it as more of a "professional arrangement" than a "real marriage."[34]

The raised eyebrows were due in part to the way Hillary seized the stage at certain public appearances. On the evening of Super Tuesday, March 10, 1992, a crescendo of eleven state primaries held on the same day, Hillary and Bill basked in a triumphal glow. Even the normally unflappable TV newsman Tom Brokaw told me he had been startled when Hillary had shot past her husband to man the microphone in Chicago for their victory statement. "What I would like to do, in introducing . . . someone . . ." she began, while her husband danced in the background like a prizefighter trying to stay warm. Soon she was booming, "We believe passionately in this country, and we cannot stand by for *one more year* and watch what is happening to it!" Over the applause, Brokaw observed dryly on NBC News, "Not just an introduction, this is a speech by Mrs. Clinton."[35]

Hillary barely referred to her husband—and then only as "the messen-

A composed Hillary addresses world leaders at the World Economic
Forum in Davos, Switzerland, February 1998, twelve days after
the Monica Lewinsky story surfaced.

MIDWESTERN CHILDHOOD

Hillary at eleven,
the little adult.

Before ballet class,
Park Ridge, age seven.

In a flower coronet, March 1960.

R. Paul Carlson, Hillary's first history teacher, who taught "Communism must be destroyed."

Youth minister Don Jones, twenty-eight, introduced Hillary to the "University of Life" and Dr. Martin Luther King, Jr.

John Peavoy, high school classmate and devoted intellectual pen pal during her college years.

Hillary as firebrand: The Wellesley sophomore speaks
at a February 1967 rally.

"I won, I won!" Hillary runs for senior class president in 1968,
against Nonna Noto (left) and Francille Rusan.

Blossoming at twenty-one, during her "first love affair."

Hillary's first love— "a ruthlessly handsome black Irishman," David Rupert, a Georgetown University government major.

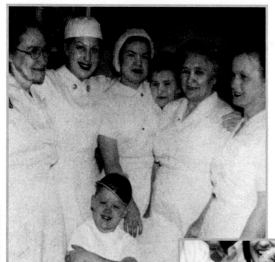

Virginia's butterball Billy Blythe (Clinton), age six, surrounded by his mother (second from left) and nurse colleagues.

COLLECTION OF NANCY BARR/RETNA

The "Hot Springs Kid" and his mother, Virginia Cassidy Blythe Clinton Dwire Kelley, the day after Clinton is elected the forty-second President of the United States.

CORBIS/REUTERS

Blinds drawn for secret Watergate committee work, Hillary
assists counsel John Doar (behind her), Harold Donohue (seated),
and chairman Peter Rodino (handing papers).

Clinton's first war room—election night 1974, Fayetteville, Arkansas.
Campaign manager Paul Fray studies the vote count in Clinton's
losing bid for United States congressman.

News Item: Governor Clinton wishes to be removed from Cartoonist's baby buggy.

ARKANSAS

New power couple: The morning after Clinton's 1979 inauguration as the governor of Arkansas, Hillary laughs at an editorial cartoon picturing Bill, the nation's youngest governor, in diapers.

New parents: Hillary and Bill hold newborn daughter, Chelsea, in 1980, the same year Hillary would make partner at the Rose law firm and Bill would be defeated in his reelection bid for governor.

Governor Clinton with his chief of staff, Betsey Wright, the woman whose list of names kept Clinton from running for president in 1988 and who would quash the "bimbo eruptions" in 1992.

Hillary cannot hold back the tears when Governor Clinton breaks the news that he will not run for president in 1988.

Marilyn Jo Denton Jenkins: Bill's feelings for her became a threat to the marriage.

BRAD MARKEL/LAISON AGENCY

The "hunks" playing
around during the
Clinton and Gore
bus trip.

Bill, Hillary,
Tipper, and Al:
the youthful
team eager
to serve.

SABA

COLLECTION OF THE AUTHOR

Author Gail
Sheehy and
Hillary during the
1992 presidential
campaign shortly
after Gennifer
Flowers's accusa-
tions surfaced.

The "two for one" presidential candidacy: Hillary reviews their press clips while Bill goes over a briefing book.

Bill and Hillary relax in a Chicago hotel suite after a late-night staff party on Super Tuesday, March 1992.

Swearing in, January 20, 1993.

The new President and First Lady with Hollywood friends
Harry Thomason and Linda Bloodworth-Thomason.

Jane Sherburne

Hillary
facing the
microphones
as the first
First Lady to
testify before a
grand jury.

Carolyn Huber,
who found the
long-lost
billing records.

Hillary beside her pro-
tector, Vince Foster, Jr.,
talking to President
Clinton after arriving
in Little Rock for her
father's funeral.

Susan
Thomases

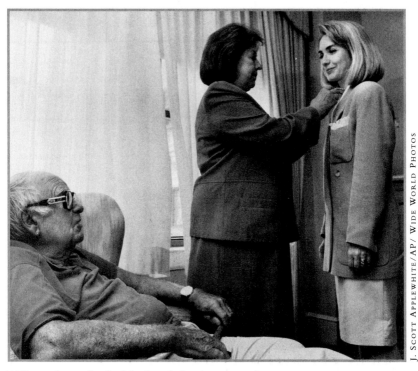

J. SCOTT APPLEWHITE/AP/ WIDE WORLD PHOTOS

Hillary always looked for her father's approval.

J. SCOTT APPLEWHITE/AP/ WIDE WORLD PHOTOS

Hillary coaching Bill for the twenty-third year, as yet
unaware of his playtime with Monica.

After helping Democrats win a stunning midterm election in November 1998, Hillary begins her rebirth.

On the cover of *Vogue*, December 1998.

VOGUE

The Extraordinary Hillary Clinton

Vogue's 12 Days of Christmas — THE ULTIMATE FASHION FANTASY

"I want to look sexy for Bill." At the National Medal of Arts dinner in the White House, November 1998.

REBIRTH

STEPHAN SAVOIA/AP/WIDE WORLD PHOTOS

Arriving at Martha's Vineyard in August 1999,
Bill steps aside. Hillary is now the rising star.

ger." If he was the messenger, she was the message. Those who kept asking "Why isn't *she* running?" missed the point. Hillary Clinton *was* running.

Still, Bill Clinton was caught by surprise when challenged on NBC's *Meet the Press,* and he had to demur when discussing his wife's possible role in a Clinton administration. But he remained certain that they could out-shine Eleanor and Franklin—which promised to make Hillary Clinton one of the most formidable women in the world, a model of a full partner in public life. Friends went even further, touting her as the next attorney general by pointing out that she would be better qualified than Robert Kennedy had been when his brother had named him to the post. Hillary's brother Hugh Rodham, a public defender in Dade County, Florida, told me he fore-saw even higher callings. "Attorney general is only local lawmaking," he said dismissively. "There's treaty negotiations she could do. There's labor stuff. There's secretary of state. . . ."[36]

When Hillary was asked at a public event if she wanted to be her hus-band's vice president, she brushed off the question with a wisecrack: "I'm not interested in attending a lot of funerals around the world." She got a laugh, but when she continued it was with serious intent: "I want maneu-verability. . . . I want to get deeply involved in solving problems." She later told me that she saw herself not as a Cabinet officer but as an all-around adviser.

She could also think like a long-distance runner: even if her husband lost, the campaign would be a splendid showcase for her own talents. And in the next presidential election, or one down the line, the other Clinton might be on the ticket. As Hillary told an audience in 1991, "We'll have a woman president by 2010." Would she consider running? she was pressed. "We'll talk later."[37]

When Hillary began to sense that she was becoming a lightning rod in her husband's presidential campaign, she dismissed people's reservations as sexist. "What they're trying to figure out is 'How will she be able to in-fluence him? Who is this person?' Well, Bill Clinton is the kind of person who asks advice from literally dozens of people. No one gives George Bush a hard time when he gets advice from Jim Baker," she complained to me. "Bush is advised by a coterie of men who are, frankly, all of one mind—a very narrow, all-white coterie of exclusively men."[38]

Even some who had been awed by her Super Tuesday speech commented, "There's something a little scary, a little Al Haig–ish about her" (referring to Reagan's secretary of state, who seized the moment of the assassina-tion attempt to tell the world he was now in charge). Hillary's closest counterparts, high-striving professional women, often reacted viscerally: she's "too intense," they'd say, or "She's missing something feminine"—as if they couldn't forgive her for appearing to have it all. Hillary raised the bar too high—it was a standard impossible for most mortals to meet.

To introduce her to the female Democratic power elite of Los Angeles, Linda Bloodworth-Thomason cohosted a luncheon on March 26 with Hollywood producer Dawn Steel. Hillary dazzled an audience that is usually ho-hum about stars and plenty impressed with themselves. "We need to be against brain-dead politics wherever we find it!" she thundered, looking fiercely pretty in a fire engine red suit. "We need to forge a new consensus about [our] new political direction . . . that doesn't jerk us to the right, jerk us to the left, prey on our emotions, engender paranoia and insecurity . . . but instead moves us forward together."

As in past campaigns, Hillary took on her husband's foes. In 1992, President George Bush was her favorite target, and she pilloried him mercilessly in her speeches. "When it's all stripped away," she told the L.A. crowd, "at the bottom what we see is a failure of leadership, rooted in a very hollow sense of what politics is and can be." As one listener put it, "She's unbelievably articulate and connects with her audience with a message that hits home."

The buzz was heard all over the room after she finished: "You can't help but think, Why isn't she the candidate?"

The hugely successful film producer Sherry Lansing (*Fatal Attraction, The Accused, Indecent Proposal*) pronounced it "an extraordinary speech, extraordinary."[39] Despite the heat of the controversy over Hillary's role in her husband's campaign, the sold-out luncheon raised $50,000. The gadfly candidate Jerry Brown had attacked her moneymaking ventures in Arkansas and elicited a snappish response from Hillary—"I suppose I could have stayed home and baked cookies and had teas"—that offended millions of women who chose to be full-time homemakers. That very morning, *New York Times* columnist William Safire had written about what he called "the Hillary problem," describing her as a "political bumbler" who suffers from "foot-in-mouth disease." It hurt.

In a private interview after the luncheon, I asked Hillary how she felt about being labeled "the problem." Uncharacteristically, she squirmed and stammered: "I don't know how I feel about it. . . . I think I'll just have to be more . . . careful in the way I express my feelings, so I don't inadvertently hurt anybody. I understand why some people thought that I was criticizing women who made different choices than the one I had—in fact, criticizing the choice that my mother and a lot of dear friends have made. Nothing could be further from what I believe."[40]

In fact, the careless remark had given her a bad rap. "I remember Hillary from the very beginning as a real advocate of tolerance," says Cynthia Schneider, an art historian who became part of Hillary's earliest network of friends at the annual retreat of movers and shakers known as Renaissance Weekend. Tolerance was the watchword at Renaissance Weekend, from the first small gatherings on Hilton Head Island in South Carolina in the early Eighties to the marathon seminar it has become, where the intent is to build bridges across traditional differences of age, religion, philosophy, and politics. Schneider remembers how the two women talked endlessly about the competing pulls of career and family life. Then an ambitious museum curator with a commuting marriage, Schneider was judgmental, while Hillary, then a lawyer with the toddler Chelsea wrapped around her legs, was the one who always said, "You have to give credit to the women who stay at home. They make a choice as much as the rest of us, and they arguably have a harder time."[41]

Barbara Bush had stirred up a hornet's nest at Hillary's alma mater, Wellesley College, when she had told students that a working mother should always put family before career. Did Hillary agree? I asked. "For me, I believe that," she replied fervently. "Personally, I believe that a woman should put her family and her relationships—which are really at the root of who you are and how you relate to the world—at the top of your priority list."[42]

The question that nagged at me then was never satisfactorily answered, until in 1998 it became the question everyone asked and that has pursued Hillary even into her 1999 Senate campaign: Why has she stayed in this marriage? Is she still helplessly in love with the boy in Bill Clinton, or is she in love with the power that he can offer her and unwilling to forfeit the years she has invested in managing his rise?

Hillary's protectiveness of her daughter, and her daughter's adoring bond with her father, was one strong reason she stayed. Chelsea merited considerable sacrifice from her mother. One evening at the peak of bimbo-mania, Hillary was facing a command performance as the "candidate's wife" before a backbiting Washington audience at a roast of Ron Brown, chairman of the Democratic National Committee. That same night, Bill was scheduled to take Chelsea to a father-daughter dance at the Little Rock YWCA. On the flight to Washington, I noticed that Hillary was unusually nervous. She needed some material. Fast. Her friend Linda Bloodworth-Thomason called Hillary on her campaign plane (provided by Linda's husband, Harry Thomason). Linda had an inspiration: "Let's do a live remote to Little Rock—it would be a nice image for your audience to see Bill dancing with his daughter."

Hillary didn't think twice. "No," she said. "This is Chelsea's night."

It is one of Hillary's philosophical tenets that children should be spoken to just like adults. This helped to explain how Hillary was able to pass a supermarket checkout in the company of her adored daughter without gagging. Hillary would be the first to point out the lurid tabloid headlines screaming about multiple affairs or a love child, instructing Chelsea that "this is what's to be expected in a political campaign." Chelsea followed the political horse race avidly, but "when they talk bad about my daddy" on TV, she would leave the room.[43]

During a lull in the campaign, Bill Clinton sat down with me and reflected on the personal journey he had made over the four years since his withdrawal from a previous presidential race. He told me that his fear of life running out at any moment had subsided: "It's all different now. I think—in the aftermath of my brother's encounter [his arrest and imprisonment for selling drugs] and all the stuff that Hillary and I went through, and where we are together now, and Chelsea—I'm so much more relaxed. I got into this race because I really felt I was strong enough to be president . . . and because the things that Hillary and I have worked on together were more relevant to what has to be done in the country than anybody else."[44]

Hillary also gave me her philosophy: "Life has become very unpredictable and scary for people. And the only insurance policy you've got against whatever comes down the pike is to be as ready as you personally can be. I think that's part of what the voters have been saying to me: 'Nobody could have predicted that all this would happen to you. You didn't ask for it. But you were ready. And, boy, we're glad you were.' "

If they lost, she predicted, "Bill and I have great opportunities. We'll always be able to make a good living, we've got a wonderful daughter—we'll be fine."[45] It doesn't usually work out that way, however, particularly not for two driven people whose every axon and dendrite had been tingling for months as they crisscrossed the country in matching campaign planes, eager to deliver political redemption to the masses. If suddenly they had landed back in Little Rock and awakened to the concern that their child had been necessarily neglected, and if Hillary had had time to thaw out the small, excruciatingly painful little package in the deep freeze labeled "Bill's Marital Mistakes," it might have been a devastating period.

But they kept going, even though the land mines from Clinton's past kept surfacing. Hillary never knew when they'd step on the next one. It was shortly before the last crucial primaries when Betsey Wright felt the heat again. A letter arrived at campaign headquarters from a man claiming to be Bill Clinton's half brother—worse, claiming that Bill Blythe, the man Clinton believed was his father, had been a bigamist. Henry Leon Ritzenthaler provided credible evidence that Blythe had married a Wanetta Alexander in Kansas City in 1941 and divorced her in April 1944—seven months after he married Virginia Cassidy, Bill's mother, in September 1943.

Wright had to call Clinton on the campaign trail with the bad news. To her surprise, Clinton was neither startled nor curious. It was Hillary who went into crisis mode, asking for all their files on Bill Blythe. Wright had to call back and admit she had given those files to Webb Hubbell and they couldn't be found. She called up some of the Blythe relatives she knew in Sherman, Texas. One of them told her, "I've been waiting for this call for years." In distress, Wright gave Palladino a new assignment: chase down Bill's father's marriages. "The first thing that I wanted documentation on was whether Ritzenthaler was a half brother or not," Wright told me. "We found marriage licenses without divorce papers." They documented Ritzenthaler's claims—now they knew the worst was true, Blythe was indeed a bigamist—but as they kept going, they kept finding more marriages. And more careless offspring of the traveling salesman kept turning up.

Wright had to call Virginia, who, like her son, showed no surprise. "Virginia didn't know how many marriages [Blythe had had], and every time a new child showed up, she would just tell the staff to have me return the call."

How many showed up?

"I don't remember the number," says Wright. "There were quite a few. I don't know of any that were bogus."[46]

Wright did her best to call each one and, in her down-home, deep-throated way, to soothe and sympathize with Clinton's putative kin. She was effective; none of them went public. Even though this patch of land mines wasn't Clinton's fault, it could have tarnished his candidacy just as the public was getting to know him. The loyal Betsey Wright has never disclosed this episode until now.

THE REAL HONEYMOON

The only thing sweeter for the Clintons than victory, on that muggy Thursday, July 17, in New York when Bill accepted his party's nomination for president, was the shock of a late-edition headline: PEROT QUITS RACE.[47] With H. Ross Perot's vaporization on the last day of the Democratic convention, the Clinton-Gore crusade was the only political game in town.

A novel road show had been planned to thrust Clinton and his new running mate and their attractive wives straight into America's heartland. There would be no resting on their lead in the polls. Clinton was determined to show he was a workingman with the energy to run a tough race. A convoy of eight buses was set to leave on "the first thousand miles" the morning after the convention. Hundreds of domestic and foreign reporters descended on the Inter-Continental Hotel in midtown, all clamoring for seats on the bus. Staffers agreed to give up their hotel rooms and sleep on the buses, and still they had to turn many away.

In the happy chaos, Senator Al Gore, Sr., was busy glad-handing around the lobby as ebulliently as if he himself were the candidate. His wife, Pauline, dragged him away and invited me to join them for breakfast. I asked Al Gore's father what he liked best about Bill Clinton. The garrulous, white-haired southern senator went silent for half a moment. With slight discomfort he said, "He's a warm human being."

His son did not know Clinton, he said. They had met only at political events. From my previous interviews with Gore's parents when Al himself had been running for president in 1988, I knew that they had emphatically not been grooming him to take second best. Now they were ambivalent. Gore Sr. said, "You understand, Al was *not* a candidate for this [the vice presidency]. Their first meeting [between Gore and Clinton] was a marathon. It began at ten in the evening and lasted until one-thirty A.M. Now, neither of them is a drinker, so it wasn't that kind of thing. They talked about the whole body politic. But the most important thing for Al is that Clinton had read his book."

Earth in the Balance was then number five on *The New York Times* best-seller list, and Gore, like most first-time authors, was flagrantly susceptible to flattery about his literary contribution. Clinton had focused most of their marathon discussion on Gore's favorite topic—the environment—and how, together, they could work on saving it both nationally and globally. Clinton's seduction had worked again.

Had Gore discussed with Clinton any of the personal charges that had been leveled against the Arkansas governor? I asked.

Senator Gore frowned. "That's not a role for Al—he can't get close to that." Pauline Gore looked pained. It was obvious that the Gores had considerable trepidation that their son might eventually be tarred with the same brush created by Clinton's character flaws. They changed the subject. Mr. Gore said he held Hillary in very high regard: "She and Tipper are different types. Tipper holds a master's degree in psychology—quite a difference from a law degree—but they're both educated." The senator then leaned over and shared his distilled wisdom on why the foursome would be a winning ticket: "Honey, you have here a young man from Oxford and Yale with twelve years of successful service as Arkansas governor, and you have a graduate of Harvard and Vanderbilt with sixteen years of successful service in Congress and the Senate, *and* they're both married to women who just may be better and smarter than their men are."[48]

Their first rally as a foursome took place in a light rain on Forty-seventh Street in New York City. The wives' hair was wilting, but Tipper Gore bounced up onto the platform and, like a perfect pom-pom girl, introduced Hillary Clinton, who emerged in a peony pink suit and white stockings, moving like a pretty automaton.

Hillary filled the time until Clinton and Gore appeared. "Tipper and I are really pleased to be on this thousand-mile tour—it's kind of like a rock tour," she said. "Camden is the first stop." She sounded as if she were already tired of the trip. Setting up the introduction of Bill Clinton, however, she regained her enthusiasm and whetted the crowd's appetite for her husband's economic plan to create jobs. "Bill and I have a personal interest in the plan," she said. "Our twelve-year-old daughter wants to build space stations."

The two heartthrobs appeared to rapturous applause. Gore's clear, uninflected tones gave way to the raspy lullaby of Clinton's voice: "This town has been good to me—New York luuuves you."

We piled into our assigned buses, named for characters in "Peter Pan." (I was in "Nana's Kennel.") The caravan traveled along the backroads through secondary towns and suburbs and flyover cities. Every stop was orchestrated for saturation coverage by local media. In a blazing hot union hall in a working-class Republican city Clinton walked around, sweat spreading on his shirt in dark blue blotches as he stroked his hand mike like a rock star. He crooned politics to the crowd with all the intuitive phrasing of a saxophone soloist. He was in his element.

While he made his music, Hillary and Tipper sat demurely, not saying a word. Bill was clearly the dominant voice now and Hillary the backup. It felt more comfortable to audiences that way.

High noon at the All-American truck stop in Carlisle, Pennsylvania. Harris Wofford, the newest wonder man of the Democratic Party, who had wrested a Senate seat away from a Pennsylvania Republican, hawked the good news: "There's an election surge spreading across through the country—we're hearing it from the truckers who have stopped here from all over the states." Bill turned on the magic: "I gotta say one thing about truckin'. I come from a state with a lot of truckers, and a lot of truckers here are from my state."

Hillary was signing autographs. She stopped to chat with a hard-core silent majority couple. The woman was a two-hundred-pounder in a sleeveless T-shirt who said she lets her husband decide who she should vote for. Hillary looked the husband up and down: a gravel-skinned middle-aged trucker with lips bitten down to slits. This was the target—blue-collar Reagan Democrats who were suspicious of a baby-boom draft dodger who said he hadn't inhaled. She asked the truck driver when he had become a Clinton supporter. "Only since I heard your husband's convention speech. I felt like he wuz talkin' to me."

"That's Bill," she said. "He *was* talkin' to you."

Hillary sometimes forgot her part in the tableau and stepped forward to articulate her positions on the issues. She would talk about "what we have done in Arkansas" and build up to "what I see as a message for America." After touching on everything from bread-and-butter economic policies to the most esoteric of foreign affairs, she would catch herself and revert to her *faux* Arkansas persona: "Ah'm just letting you know what *mah husband* will lay out for you."

Gradually, however, Hillary became "Tipperized." Learning from her counterpart how to melt into the backdrop as part of the blond blur of supportive wives, she wore only dresses and little makeup. Her headband was becoming her signature, like Jackie Kennedy's pillbox hats. She and Tipper would sit under a tent in their long-skirted milkmaid dresses circa 1958, their ankles crossed, spooning fruit cup and chatting about nothing of consequence while the hunks tossed a football.

"Guy shit goes over well at a truck stop," one of their aides observed.

Tipper the psychologist went to work breaking the ice between the "boys" on their customized bus. She laid the groundwork for an emotional relationship to flourish. This was a defining trip for the future administration: it would set the pace for the kind of working partnership that Clinton and Gore might enjoy. The two men were roughly the same age and forged by the same political generation. They both called their kids on cellular phones. Their relationship began to develop around friendly one-upmanship. On the bus, they played Sixties music on the tape system and competed at "brain basketball," bouncing issues off each other and competing with one-liners. Off the bus, they jogged together. When they played minigolf, Gore got a hole in one. When they threw a football back and forth, Gore made perfect, football-captain throws. Clinton's passes failed to spiral and dropped like a stone. It was poignantly easy to tell which man had had a father who taught him how to throw a ball. About the only thing Gore hadn't done better than Clinton was run for president.

But Gore was smart enough to adopt the role of the Better Brother. He began building a bond with Bill Clinton that seemed to caulk some of the great empty spaces inside the fatherless man. And some of Clinton's astonishing ease with all kinds of people began to rub off on Gore.

By the time they reached Utica, Ohio, Al had his role down—almost too well for Hillary's comfort. He came bounding out of a picture-perfect barn in jeans with his big shoulders and clean-cut good looks. "What's happening on this tour is absolutely amazing—we didn't expect anything like this crowd!" Gore always wore olive drab shirts because Bill, the star, favored hot pink or swimming-pool green shirts. As Gore became more relaxed, the Clinton team began running him down the rope line not once but two or three times, like a young stallion.

Now their campaign actually began attracting "jumpers"—teenagers who bounced with excitement—not seen since the Kennedys. Clinton would come out of the bus on the run, like a faster Gore, and throw Al a high five. With a big, hearty laugh, he'd ask, "Don'tcha think I made a good decision?" In a matter of minutes, Clinton would connect with the crowd. Gore would sometimes take the place of the adoring wife, fixing Clinton with a glazed look and nodding like a metronome at his every other line. At one point, Clinton made a careless promise: "Al, I'll give you an easy job: you've gotta pass a health care plan through Congress."

Hillary perked up. If she knew then that Gore would be real competition to her, she didn't show it. She was confident she still had the inside track.

The couple seemed to be forging a new closeness. Clinton was doing what he loves most—running the race—and every day leaving his opponent further behind in the dust. Hillary had her husband under her watchful eye, confined to a forty-foot-long rolling box on ten wheels. There was something boyish and even tender about Clinton's regard for his wife, as if he were rediscovering her after years of taking her for granted.

"Skylark" was her new name, bestowed by the Secret Service escort, as in "frolicsome as a skylark." Bill was "Eagle." The symbolism was gender perfect for a political campaign through Middle America. Seniors dragged their aluminum folding chairs down to the curbs of their main streets and waited for their glimpse of these dynamic youngsters who were telling a new story.

"Clinton's not a high-class guy who you ain't got nothing to say to," said an Everyman in West Virginia. "And Tipper and Hillary—they're real good lookers."

The bus tour turned out to be a stroke of genius. More than any other strategy, it put the Clinton-Gore ticket out in front. But more would be called for to keep them there in the general election campaign against George Bush.

The Republicans, having won three presidential campaigns in a row, knew the game by heart. The Clinton team discussed how to make itself "battle-ready." Carville said they would need a single strategic center for attack and counterattack. Hillary came up with the name and spirit: "What you're describing is a war room." Her imprimatur gave their young recruits the license to be mean and unpredictable, to counterattack before an attack hit. The war room never slept. It was crammed with high-tech toys. But the most revered icon of that stunningly successful operation was a crudely hand-lettered sign with Carville's dictates: CHANGE VS. MORE OF THE SAME; IT'S THE ECONOMY, STUPID!; DON'T FORGET HEALTH CARE.

VICTORY

The Clintons' last lap was a thirty-hour, nonstop marathon through nine states, with the candidate's voice turning toadish and Hillary propping up Chelsea while the three of them beat the bushes for the last of their 44,908,233 votes. Early in that endless day, an onlooker warned Clinton, "Take your vitamins!" He replied accurately, "*You're* my vitamins."

When the Clintons finally stumbled off their campaign plane at Little Rock airport, it was Tuesday afternoon—election day—and Bill still couldn't stop. Tears welling in his eyes, he reached for the hands of homeboys and -girls who had kept him alive politically for almost twenty years. Even after voting, Clinton couldn't keep himself from stopping by porches and hugging neighbors until he reached the governor's mansion. Hillary slipped an old John Wayne movie into the VCR. Clinton crashed into a chair, while Hillary and Chelsea snuggled on the couch. The little family slept for three hours.

As the returns rolled in that night, thousands of Arkansans—whom President Bush had called in a debate "the lowest of the low"[49]—were gaga with anticipation. More than fifty thousand of them swarmed downtown to party with bands and barbecue, catfish and cotton candy. A giant TV monitor displayed the parade of winning states.

"It's a landslide," announced Clinton communications director George Stephanopoulos—at which point James Carville's mother, Miss Nippy, burst into sobs.[50] At 10:48 P.M., as California put him over the top, all the networks declared Clinton the next president. But as midnight came and went, the Comeback Kid failed to appear for his victory speech.

When the Clintons emerged at 12:22 A.M. to stand under the soaring white columns of the Old State House and let the pent-up cheers wash over them, they suddenly looked different. Clinton was statesmanlike in a dark suit and knife-collared white shirt. Hillary, uniformed in royal blue with black stockings, had a monarchical air. Chelsea, in tartan plaid, looked like a footman to the royal couple.

All that work, all those miles, all those narrow escapes—it had been worth every minute of it. Hillary Rodham and Bill Clinton were now Mr. and Mrs. President of the United States.

One of the earliest and most enduring of Hillary jokes to make the rounds on the Internet caught the humor in this most unusual coupling:

President Clinton and the First Lady are out driving in the country near Hillary's hometown. Hillary wants to stretch her legs. Bill asks that the presidential limousine pull into the nearest gas station. The attendant comes out and asks if he can pump gas. No thanks. Suddenly, the attendant catches a glimpse of the First Lady. "Hey, Hillary, remember me? We used to date in high school." They chat for a few minutes.

As the First Couple is driven away, Bill is feeling very proud of himself. He looks over at Hillary. "You used to date that guy? Just think what it would be like if you had married *him*," he says smugly.

Hillary shrugs. "If I'd married him, *you'd* be pumping gas, and *he'd* be President."

Things Fall Apart

Turning and turning in the widening gyre
The falcon cannot hear the falconer;
Things fall apart; the center cannot hold;
Mere anarchy is loosed upon the world.

—W. B. YEATS, "THE SECOND COMING"

January 16, 1993. It should have been like Christmas morning for the Clinton family. This was the day they would fly from Little Rock to Washington, to prepare for Bill Clinton's coronation as the forty-second President of the United States. Clinton awoke unusually early. He slipped out of the double bed he shared with his wife, walked quietly past his sleeping daughter's bedroom, and sneaked down to the game room in the basement. It was five in the morning. He was expecting to have a special gift delivered.

The governor had told his new Secret Service protectors that a staffer would be arriving early. The game room had recently been converted to a secondary office, and anytime after seven dedicated campaign officials such as Nancy Hernreich might turn up to stoke the engines of the Clinton machine. Time was of the essence.

5:15 A.M. State trooper Danny Ferguson drove through the mansion gates. His instructions: to deposit his passenger at the basement door. Out of the official car stepped a tall, slender figure wrapped in a long coat, her face half hidden by a baseball cap. She quickly ducked inside.

6:00 A.M. Clinton emerged, giddy as a boy who has just played with his Christmas-morning toy. He turned the woman over to Ferguson. The trooper, who had often taken presents from the governor to this sugary blond lady, tucked her into his official car to drive her back to her condominium in Sherwood. The trooper and the lady chatted. She was not nervous.

"Marilyn Jo is a very nice lady, she always treated me very nice," says Ferguson. Unlike other troopers, who complained that Hillary would "cuss them out," Ferguson says he had no problems with Hillary. She was civil to him. But Marilyn Jo Jenkins wasn't at all like Hillary, in his opinion. "Marilyn Jo was real soft-spoken," he says. "She acted like a professional woman, but she was down to earth. No arrogance." She knew she was loved.[1]

Tensions between Bill and Hillary mounted during the two and a half months between his November victory and his January inauguration. Despite his vow to repent after their Come-to-Jesus meeting in 1990, Hillary must have suspected the resurgence of the Marilyn Jo relationship. The phone calls had not stopped; they had continued into 1991.[2] And since Clinton's ascendance to the presidency, he had had a certain swagger of insouciance that she must have recognized. It was reminiscent of his rebellious behavior after his victory in 1986, when he had pushed her and Betsey aside. He wanted to reward himself.

And he did. During this interregnum, while waiting to move to Washington, Clinton asked Ferguson to bring Marilyn Jo to his basement office on three other occasions. Their visits, twice in the same predawn hush and once late at night, lasted about forty-five minutes each.[3]

Rash? Brazen? The height of hubris? Yes, but Clinton was now virtually inoculated against any punitive action by his wife. She had little bargaining power; what could she do to him now that they were days away from occupying their dream?

Marilyn Jo Jenkins was also destined to suffer for succumbing to Clinton's charms. Five years later, when the Paula Jones lawyers tracked down a half-dozen alleged Clinton sexual partners with the intention of proving a pattern of behavior, she would be named as Jane Doe #1. Jenkins admitted being close to the President and said that he had helped her through "a personal crisis," but she insisted "there was no sex involved."[4] Despite a judicial gag order, her identity and that of the other so-called Jane Does was leaked to the press and made public in *The Washington Post* and elsewhere.[5]

O n the day of Bill Clinton's inauguration, after all their years of struggle to reach this penultimate seat of power, the couple was late. As usual, Clinton had left the serious shaping of his speech until the day before. Pumped up on adrenaline and anxiety, he had pushed himself and his speechwriters until four in the morning on the most memorable day of his life. He was grumpy when awakened at seven and still fretting about his speech. An impatient President-elect emerged from Blair House, scowling, and turned back to the door to shout angrily, "Chelsea, come on!"[6] His Lady in waiting to be First, Hillary Clinton, charged out next. The two principals were reportedly overheard by a shocked police guard exchanging words unfit for their child's ears. The Clintons were half an hour behind schedule. Tardiness on this day is not merely impolite; there is a statutory requirement that the president be sworn in on the twenty-first day of January at twelve noon.

Protocol dictated that the Clintons be driven from Blair House to the White House to pick up President and Mrs. Bush. The painful passing of the baton of power is generally cloaked in geniality as the outgoing First Family shows the incoming First Family around their new home. The Clintons showed up in a hurry and trailing two guests, their Hollywood pals Harry Thomason and Linda Bloodworth-Thomason. The Bushes were startled. The Clintons wanted to show their friends the Lincoln Bedroom, where they would be spending the night, seemingly treating the White House as a group share.

Nonetheless, Barbara Bush enveloped Hillary Clinton in a grandmotherly hug and waved at the horde of reporters and photographers spread across the South Lawn to record the moment. "Avoid this crowd like the plague," the veteran First Lady told her successor. "And if they quote you, make damn sure they heard you."

"That's right," agreed the media-hostile Mrs. Clinton. "I know the feeling already."[7]

Hillary's joy was further shadowed by her uncertainty about how she would carve out her own political role once in the White House. Throughout the nearly twenty years they had stalked the political jungles together, the couple had usually enjoyed a positive valence of power. True, there had been shifts, roughly every three or four years. But now, despite the Clintons' wishes to the contrary, there might be a monstrous disparity between a man who would be president and a woman who would unavoidably inherit the antiquated title of First Lady. Hillary was hardly the first First Lady to fear the shrinkage of her importance upon entering the presidential court in a capital city notorious for driving political wives into drugs, depression, or literary revenge. On election night 1932, her heroine Eleanor Roosevelt had been found in tears. "Now I'll have no identity," she had wailed.[8]

It was on Inauguration Day morning in a holding room in the Capitol, next to the library, where the tensions between the partners tore through even those thick, hallowed walls. Next to the holding room created for Bill and Hillary Clinton was a reception room where the congressional leadership was waiting before the ceremonies began. Several people among the Republican leadership reported hearing a loud fight next door. They couldn't make out the subject, but one source remembers hearing Hillary scream at the President-elect, "You fucking asshole!"[9]

Her irritable state continued to show right through the scrim of theatrics surrounding the inaugural events. Next, it was her pique over the portrait. The official presidential portrait is shot head-on from a fixed camera at the moment the First Lady holds the Bible for her husband to take the oath. The Clintons' Hollywood friends in charge of producing the inaugural were appalled to discover that no lipstick microphones were available, only a pineapple mike, a big bulbous monstrosity "probably left over from the Eisenhower era," they joked. As they did a walk-through of the swearing-in ceremony, they realized that Hillary's face would be blocked by the device. Rehearsing with a stand-in exactly her height, the producers had hit on the perfect solution: a riser.

"I'm not doing that," Hillary told the congressional producers on the day of the inaugural. They tried to explain that no one would know. The three-inch riser would be slipped out from under a chair when the big moment came: "That way, you can be seen full face."

"I don't care," Hillary said imperiously, "I'm not getting on that riser."

She didn't. And the producers didn't get the head-on official portrait. Afterward, Hillary apologized. She said she had been tense. But the word was already rippling through the members of the inaugural committee: *She's a pill.*[10]

Once the great moment of swearing in had passed, the new President brushed his lips past his wife's ear with an obligatory kiss, saving his emotional reaction for a warm wraparound hug of his daughter.

The couple seemed in better spirits as they led the inaugural parade down Pennsylvania Avenue. They strode on foot, waving at crowds on opposite sides of the avenue. Throughout the day they greeted hundreds of friends and countless thousands of supporters, and it pumped them up.

By that evening, the chill seemed to have worn off. Theatrics required the couple to traipse from one inaugural ball to another. They would arrive backstage, step out onto the bandstand to be introduced, then go down to the dance floor and take a few spins. But they had to reproduce this romantic scenario twelve times! One of the producers who followed them that evening remembers Bill and Hillary joking around backstage, giggling and tugging at each other and enjoying the absurd artificiality of it all.

Marilyn Jo Jenkins also attended the inauguration. The Entergy Corporation took a whole floor in the Hotel Washington, a block from the White House. Clinton's other love attended one of the inaugural balls, but she was not, nor would she ever be, the first woman in the President's life.

THE ASCENDANCE

I witnessed a typical example of Bill Clinton's style of seduction during the transition, when the President-elect and his wife were honored at a big banquet. Self-important men and women fluttered like moths outside a window screen, whispering "He's coming!" After he spoke, hundreds waited in line to greet the First Couple, fidgeting for exactly the right thing to say. But as each one passed into Bill Clinton's aura, it didn't matter. He was more eager to please than they were. He would look deeply into their eyes, massage an arm or squeeze a hand, and connect like a long-forgotten lover, and they would step away, transported, each one believing that Bill Clinton *knew* them. And would always know them.

Hillary's style was different, although also effective. As a sign of recognition, her eyes would pop open to f-stop 2.5 and she would say, "Gail! So good to see you again!" She would remember something personal, usually about a person's child, and make a polite inquiry. But the moment her duties on the receiving line were done, Hillary would normally leave the ballroom in haste. She preferred to receive a few chosen friends in her private quarters.

Bill would linger. And linger some more. Even after the banquet tables were denuded and the chairs upended, Clinton would still be trolling the corridors outside the ballroom, looking for someone else to win over. It was just as his mother had said: If there were a hundred people in the room and ninety-nine loved him but one didn't, he'd spend all night trying to "enlighten" that single holdout. A psychiatrist close to the Clintons pointed out to me that Bill had been accustomed to being abused and placating the abuser. When young Bill's stepfather had been in an alcoholic rage, the boy had had to be charming and ameliorative. People with this kind of background often make a greater effort to win over those who abuse them than those who are kindly disposed to them. It was an important insight. It would help to explain why, when Republicans would beat up on his administration, President Clinton would be more likely to invite them to the White House for dinner than his own loyalists.

Hillary is quite the opposite. I've heard her say more than once, "I don't care what other people think." And in January 1993, she was impatient to get beyond all the social events and down to business.

"I was worried about this co-presidency idea, about Hillary undertaking a major policy role," remembers Bernie Nussbaum. "She would be putting herself at a lot of risk—risk to her stature as First Lady." But uneasy though he was, Nussbaum wasn't going to challenge Hillary on her most heartfelt goal. "I didn't say anything to her."[11]

Dick Morris had deliberated long and hard with her during the transition period about the roles she might assume. "The important thing is to go counter to the image of a woman," he advised. "Go with the fiscally conservative stuff." Why didn't she run an effort to ferret out waste in the government? he proposed. She could call it the "Little Hoover Commission." (The idea was eventually taken up by Vice President Gore and became his Reinventing Government initiative.) Hillary wasn't interested, and it took Morris some time to understand why. Hillary more eagerly saw herself in the job of attorney general or even secretary of state. But in the administration's early days, a little research turned up the anti-nepotism law, which puts such positions out of reach for a president's wife. Hillary floated other ideas. "*Time* magazine thinks I would be a good chief of staff," she told Morris. To dissuade her, he compared that job to a baseball manager's: "The team's owner has to be able to ditch the manager if the team isn't winning."[12]

But Hillary was hungry and impatient.

"There was some fear that she was going to get gypped out of something she had paid a real price for," says Bill Curry, a former White House adviser.[13] Hillary felt she had been sidelined in Arkansas. After the poll that revealed that voters had seen her only as the governor's wife, it was painfully clear that for all her efforts she had not developed an independent identity. Even in Arkansas, she was just Mrs. Bill Clinton. Hillary was determined that Washington would be a different story. She wanted to have her own job, her own realm.

Back in 1989, when Clinton had been mulling over whether or not he wanted to run for another term as governor, John Robert Starr had taken Hillary aside. Starr, a longtime Arkansas political columnist who liked to think of himself as a kingmaker, opposed Bill Clinton on just about everything. But Hillary had long impressed him.

"Hillary, what do you want to do?" Starr had asked bluntly. "We're always talking about all the things Bill wants to do. What do *you* want to do?"

Starr remembers how stoutly she replied, "I want to run something."[14]

THE FIRST SIX HUNDRED DAYS

The Clintons weren't in the White House a month before Hillary got her wish. It was the President's idea to give Hillary the major policy initiative of his first term: health care reform. It certainly qualified as a powerful realm in its own right. The President's wife assumed responsibility for reforming a sector that represented one seventh of the American economy and on whose policy previous presidents had faltered and retreated.

By virtue of her assignment as head of the committee for health care reform, Hillary Clinton became the first First Lady ever assigned to a high official post.[15] With her sudden elevation to a position more powerful than those of some Cabinet members but free of any formal accountability, she began to throw her weight around. People who had known her in her earlier capacities as student or political wife found themselves unceremoniously demoted. In the weeks that followed the inauguration, almost every office in the White House was gifted with a giant picture of Bill and Hillary Clinton. (It had been customary in previous administrations for the President's and Vice President's portraits to hang side by side.) Moreover, in offices that had some connection to the First Lady, there were few, if any, pictures of the President.[16]

On the second floor of the West Wing, right above the heartbeat of the executive branch, Hillary created her own command and control center. Intent upon proving that she would be a full-fledged partner in policy making and execution, she hired her own staff, her own schedulers, and her own press secretary and created her own war room, known as the Intensive Care Unit.[17]

Right from the start, she took unprecedented steps to ensure the "zone

of privacy" that she claimed was hers and the President's. A corridor between the press room and the rest of the West Wing had always allowed
White House correspondents walk-in access to the presidential press secretary. Suddenly, the corridor was blocked off. It was a behind-the-scenes
edict from Hillary and her alter ego, Susan Thomases. According to George
Stephanopoulos, Hillary at first wanted the press corps unceremoniously
relegated to the Old Executive Office Building next door—a move that
would have been political suicide. She had yet to understand that some coddled White House reporters would bitch simply because they didn't get a
window seat on the press plane.

"There's a wall there," I was told by Helen Thomas, the respected thirty-
year veteran UPI correspondent who has covered every president from
Kennedy to Clinton and their wives. "Since she came to the White House,
she's had the biggest chip on her shoulder. It's more than just 'blame the
messenger.' We never had the chance. She's aloof. I don't understand how
we got off on the wrong foot."[18]

Accustomed to running beneath the radar of the media in Arkansas,
Hillary had been shocked and deeply scarred during the campaign by the
shark-infested ocean of national press coverage that had surrounded her
and her husband wherever they turned. In her mind, the mainstream press
was no longer distinct from the bottom-feeding supermarket tabloids, and
for good reason: the wildest allegations of *The Star* or *The National Enquirer*
were often picked up by respectable papers and networks. Journalists were
no longer merely observers of but players in the lucrative game of scandal.
The people in Hillary's office adopted her bunker mentality, or they didn't
last long. Her standard scold to anyone suspected of having given the press
any information not cleared with the First Lady was "Why did you tell them
anything? Don't tell them *anything!*"[19]

On the correspondents' end, "You take a deep breath before you call that
office," says Thomas of Hillaryland. Asking for the most routine information was—and is—interpreted as an invasion or, at best, ill-willed snooping. When the Clintons would walk across the White House lawn to their
helicopter, their every step recorded by cameras and reporters three rows
deep, Hillary would camouflage herself in dark glasses and proceed as
stiffly as a cadet, not acknowledging them with a smile or a wave. Her first
press secretary, Lisa Caputo, established a new rule: Hillary would not give
an interview unless the correspondent traveled outside Washington with
her. Reporters thought that was ludicrous. "Look, we spend thousands and
thousands of dollars traveling with the President," Thomas chided Caputo.
"Besides, Hillary and I are here in the White House every day." Hillary's

lieutenants wouldn't budge. Thomas later dubbed it Hillary's "two-hundred-mile limit." It took the most senior of White House correspondents six years to get an interview with the First Lady.

Hillary also stepped into the vacuum to run many of the White House operations. Bill Clinton, says a longtime ally, "likes to think, likes to talk, doesn't like to decide. Perhaps a myth had developed in their marriage that Bill Clinton was utterly detached from the practicum of life and that she was good at it. But aside from his own philandering, almost every problem the guy got into in his first term—Whitewater, the early appointments, Travelgate, Filegate, how she made money, cattle futures—all that was Hillary. She is awful at this stuff. Almost the worst I have ever seen."[20]

Hillary's chief of staff, Melanne Verveer, was candid with me in looking back at this chaotic initiation period: "Handling White House operations wasn't what Hillary cared to do. I think, frankly, what was happening in those early years of the administration was a sense that we couldn't get our act together."[21]

The tempestuousness of the Clintons' relationship was only heightened by the pressures of high office. The world read about a lamp-throwing episode overheard in the private quarters and apparently leaked by a Secret Service agent, but the occasions when senior staff stumbled upon Bill and Hillary acting like young lovers went largely unreported. "I just popped in on them in the Oval Office one day," recalls Bernie Nussbaum. "They were being a little intimate for a professional situation."[22] Another senior aide, entering the state dining room, supposedly emptied after a formal function, found the First Couple dancing cheek to cheek. And Betsey Wright was mightily embarrassed when she was asked by the President to meet him in a room; she walked in on the Clintons in a clinch.

It wasn't just the first hundred days that were chaotic for the Clintons; it was the first 657 days. Between the inauguration on January 21, 1993, and November 8, 1994—when the Democrats lost their hold on both houses of Congress for the first time in forty years—the Clintons' White House and their private world were rocked by revelations, humiliations, shame, smear, and personal tragedies following one upon the other in a breathtaking cascade that would have taxed the powers of any dramatist. Consider an overview:

February 1993: Harry Thomason, the Clintons' sole aviation consultant, begins his campaign to undermine the White House travel office in Hillary's name.

March 19, 1993: Hillary's father, Hugh Rodham, has a massive stroke. She takes Chelsea out of school and sits for sixteen days by her father's deathbed.

April 7, 1993: Hugh Rodham dies.

May 1993: Seven travel office veterans are accused of "gross misman-agement and fired," and a cousin of Clinton is put in charge. The White House brings in the FBI to do a criminal investigation of the employees, raising suspicions that they are using the Bureau for their own political purposes.

June 1993: News reports first raise the possibility that Bill Clinton's father, Bill Blythe, was a bigamist.

July 20, 1993: Vince Foster, Hillary's friend and protector, commits sui-cide.

October 1993: Both the President and First Lady deliver speeches to Con-gress to introduce Hillary's health care reform legislation.

December 1993: The New York Times and *The Washington Post* demand an investigation of the Clintons' Whitewater land dealings.

December 20, 1993: The American Spectator magazine publishes an article in which Arkansas state troopers spin sordid tales of procuring women for Governor Clinton and an affair is suggested between Hillary and Vince Foster.

January 6, 1994: Bill Clinton's mother, Virginia, dies of breast cancer.

January 12, 1994: President Clinton argues with Hillary and his divided advisers over whether or not to call for a special counsel to investigate Whitewater.

January 20, 1994: Attorney General Janet Reno names Robert Fiske as special counsel to investigate the rising wave of allegations surrounding the President's involvement in the Whitewater land deal.

February 12, 1994: The Washington Post runs a story quoting a woman named Paula Jones who corroborates at least part of the troopers' stories.

March 18, 1994: The New York Times details how Hillary Clinton made a $100,000 windfall in the commodities market in the 1970s.

April 22, 1994: Hillary gives her "pretty in pink" press conference to field questions concerning Whitewater. She denies knowing anything about a diversion of funds to Clinton's campaign, shredding of Whitewater documents, or any efforts by the administration to obstruct the investiga-tion. With one phrase—"shoulda, woulda, coulda"—she dismisses the idea that the Clintons should have been aware of any wrongdoing.[23]

May 6, 1994: Paula Jones files a federal lawsuit accusing President Clin-ton of sexual harassment and defamation of character and seeks $700,000 in damages.

August 5, 1994: Congress reauthorizes the defunct Independent Counsel Act, and Clinton signs it. A panel of three conservative judges appoints Kenneth Starr to take over Fiske's investigation. (The investigation led by Starr was to last five years and ultimately cost taxpayers close to $50 million. More than four hundred people would be caught in Starr's snare, at least one hundred of them White House officials. Friends and innocent bystanders would run up more than $23 million in legal bills. Henry Hyde's House Judiciary Committee would meet for more than two months before making a recommendation for impeachment. The Senate would be tied up for almost a month in an impeachment trial before deciding to acquit.)

October 1994: Hillary's 1,342-page health care plan dies on the floor of Congress.

November 8, 1994: The Democratic Party loses control of both the Senate and the House of Representatives, having controlled the latter for forty years. Most Democrats blame First Lady Hillary Clinton.

Thus did Hillary find herself turning and turning in the widening gyre of exposed secrets with the glare of public interest penetrating her most private zone. And as the rumble of lies and scandal grew to a roar, the symbiosis between the Clintons was shattered and re-formed, only to be shattered again.

WITH FRIENDS LIKE THESE . . .

The Clintons came to Washington with a clutch of kitchen-table friends who used to hang out at the governor's mansion and kibitz about running a state that spent a mere $1.7 billion a year on its 2.5 million people, compared to the federal Brobdingnag,[24] where $1.16 trillion had to be divided among the United States' 250 million citizens.[25] In 1990, Fairfax County, Virginia, spent more than the entire state of Arkansas. Put more simply, the Clintons had experience in governing the lives of just 1 percent of the throng they were now expected to lead.

Hillary made certain that her most favored Arkansas friends were named to high positions. Webb Hubbell became assistant attorney general. Vince Foster, Hillary's designated protector, was put in place as deputy to White House counsel Bernard Nussbaum. "If there was a legal issue concerning Hillary, you went to Vince—he and Hillary were very friendly," says Dee Dee Myers, the President's press secretary in his first term. "Vince had her ear, and that made him special from the start."[26] Hillary kept Foster right under her nose. He shared a suite with Nussbaum next door to

Hillary's office. And as her cohort in the health care effort she tapped a brilliant Oxford friend of Bill who was exactly the wrong kind of person for the job. Ira Magaziner had no standing in the health care community; he was a management consultant.

A key member of the health care team remembers having a sinking feeling about the Hillary-Ira axis. A week before the inauguration, Hillary called a meeting with about ten people at Blair House. The guardians of Hillaryland were present: Maggie Williams, her chief of staff; Evelyn Lieberman, Williams's top deputy; Melanne Verveer, then deputy chief of staff; and Donna Shalala, Hillary's choice for secretary of health and human services—along with Robert Boorstin, a special assistant to the President for health care communications.

Hillary told everyone that Ira Magaziner would be running the show. Then the ultraliberal management expert handed out a thirty-page, single-spaced document heavy with dates and flowcharts. "It was all about process and not at all about content," said Boorstin. "It had management consultant written all over it."[27]

When Dick Morris began to talk to Hillary about how to approach health care reform, he emphasized cost containment and came up with ways to cut Medicare spending. For the first time in their long partnership as pragmatic strategists, Morris found Hillary resistant to a middle-of-the-road approach. "She'd become quite a liberal and I didn't realize it until '93," Morris says. Mystified, he went to James Carville: "What's with all this liberalism?"

"These fuckin' liberals are all over the place!" exploded Carville. "They are like water damage. They seep in."[28]

Other staff members and FOBs—Friends of Bill—fought to establish their position in the pecking order by claiming "The First Lady told me . . ." or "The First Lady wants this done." Her word, invoked with or without her sanction and especially if it carried a threat, was tantamount to a cattle prod.

Harry Thomason was given a desk in the East Wing and asked by the President to employ Hollywood techniques to shape Clinton's image. The task became known as the "White House project." Thomason was the ultimate insider, and he traded on it. In late 1991, he had formed a company, TRM Inc., that had coordinated and provided all air travel for the Clintons' yearlong presidential campaign up through the inauguration. As one of his partners said, "It made for a unique, once-in-a-lifetime opportunity." Unlike most fledgling businesses, Thomason's custom travel service made a 15 percent profit in its first fiscal year.[29] Once inside the Clintons' court,

Thomason and his partners began angling to have their firm hired as consultants on a variety of projects. Thomason focused on the White House travel office, which handles the charter planes and buses for which reporters are charged on presidential trips. The White House charter business was worth an average of $40,000 a day. Thomason, who was competing with other FOBs to get a piece of the action by having the travel office privatized, found "discrepancies" and "sloppy accounting."[30]

"Harry ginned this thing up quite a bit," acknowledges Jane Sherburne, later Hillary's attorney. "Harry was representing to David Watkins [the White House administrator] how strongly Hillary felt about this and warning him that if something didn't happen, he would suffer the First Lady's wrath."[31]

Vince Foster initially told Hillary about this brouhaha and expressed his concern that it could boil over into an ugly scandal. According to Sherburne, "Her first direction to Vince was 'Get on it. Don't let this thing fester. Fix it. Deal with it.' Foster then told Watkins that the First Lady was very concerned about these abuses and wanted an audit done."[32]

Vince Foster would do anything for Hillary, anything. A night or two before the 1993 inauguration, the Rose firm had thrown a big party in the Grand Ballroom of Washington's Mayflower Hotel. Hillary was the only Clinton to appear. On the speaker's stand she looked as regal as a queen. Foster, standing beneath her, was almost overcome with emotion. As she was introduced, he breathed barely audibly, "What a remarkable woman." The Arkansas journalist and neighbor standing beside him, Max Brantley, saw tears in the eyes of this otherwise most reticent man. The jovial Brantley said it looked as if a late night of partying lay ahead. "Not for me," said Foster. "I've got to go back to work." Brantley looked at his neighbor more closely. "Already, he had a kind of hunted look."[33] After the swearing in, Vince went straight to the White House to work, leaving his wife and children at the curb of Pennsylvania Avenue. Lisa Foster was so angry, she didn't go to the inaugural ball.[34]

The dynamics between the two former peers and law partners were drastically altered by the elevation in Hillary's status. She was now Lady Hillary, while Vince was demoted to a mere vassal. Her tendency was to rely on someone who was known and indisputably trusted, but Foster was completely out of his element. For this rigidly respectable small-town lawyer, political Washington was terra incognita. Suddenly he found himself serving as all-purpose troubleshooter for the woman he worshiped—and failing miserably at every major task she gave him. After the lamp-throwing incident was leaked to the press, Foster had been told by Hillary to find the leaker among the Secret Service and weed him out. The Secret Service is a monolithic tribe; nobody invades it for political damage control. Foster was stopped cold. Having failed her on that assignment, he went all out to do her bidding on the travel office. Again, he made things worse.

"She was relying on Vince, especially on matters that were Little Rock–related: cleaning up all the Whitewater messes, the tax problem, and whatever was left over from the law firm," says another of the Clintons' former White House attorneys.[35] The more deeply Foster was drawn into mopping up behind Hillary's political messes, the less he pleased her and the more he implicated himself. But refusing her assignments would have alienated him from the person he wanted most desperately to please.

"Vince may have attached a lot of feelings to Hillary that she didn't return," says a first-term senior White House staff member. "Hillary wasn't going to risk what she had going in Washington by pursuing any sort of romantic thing with Vince, even if it was something they had going in Arkansas. So suddenly he was an employee. And he was the keeper of the hot potatoes—Hillary's legal records."[36]

Two months after Hillary moved into the White House, her father suffered a massive stroke. She took Chelsea out of her new school, Sidwell Friends, and the two flew to Little Rock and settled in for a long, unvarying vigil by the mute man's bedside. Suddenly, the woman referred to as "the czar of health care" found herself in the futile role of family member of a catastrophically ill person, faced with unimaginable costs, incomprehensible insurance coverage, and confusing forms. The St. Vincent Infirmary Medical Center in Little Rock gave the family an empty conference room in which to take their meals and make phone calls. Hillary and Chelsea often slept there on cots. "Hillary allowed no game playing," says her pastor, Reverend Ed Matthews. "She taught Chelsea a lot about death."

Identical hours oozed into identical days. Hugh Rodham remained comatose. He was eighty-two, but age had not tempered his gruff, argumentative personality, as observed by his sons. "When he turned eighty," said Hillary's younger brother Tony, "he figured out that he could say just about anything he wanted. Who's going to stop him?"[37] Meanwhile, Hillary's health care task force was at a virtual standstill. The May 1 deadline she and Magaziner had set faded into impossibility. After a two-and-a-half-week absence she was torn. "She understands as well as anyone I have ever met that we are all put here for a purpose," said her pastor. "She knows that she has been given many gifts and graces and she has greater obligations than ordinary people."[38]

Hillary returned to Washington a few hours before her father died. True to his persona to the end, Hillary's father was never able to give his daughter a blanket blessing or squeeze out a final expression of his love for her or his granddaughter. And Hillary was not able to express her love or her hurt.

She arrived only to learn that Bill Clinton had been entertaining Barbra Streisand. The lusty songstress had bragged about spending Saturday night in the Lincoln Bedroom. She had gone to the White House to play the demo cut of her yet-to-be-released album for the President, privately. While Hillary was attending her dying father, the President had squired Streisand, along with his mother, to the white-tie Gridiron Club dinner. In a giddy mood, Clinton had surprised the audience by appearing in a black sequined tux to sway with his saxophone to the Coasters' classic "Yakety Yak." At the end of the uproarious festivities, where the press and politicians roast each other, Clinton said in mock seriousness, "The opinions I will express tonight are those of my wife."[39]

Soon after Hillary's return, the President emerged for his morning jog with a mean claw mark along his jawline. "I'm the idiot who said he'd cut himself shaving before I'd seen him," admits Dee Dee Myers, his press secretary at the time. "Then I saw him. It was a big scratch, and clearly not a shaving cut. Barbra Streisand was clearly around at the time."[40] Hillary banned Streisand from staying overnight at the White House, the official explanation being that it would be improper for her and her then fiancé to share a bedroom.

Moving on from the personal to the philosophical, Hillary kept a speech date at the University of Texas in Austin a few days after her father's funeral. There she grappled rhetorically with the vexing questions raised by medical technology: When does life start? When does life end? Who makes those decisions? Then, she moved seamlessly into policy questions: How do we create a system that gets rid of the micromanagement, the regulation and the bureaucracy, and substitutes instead human caring, concern and love? She cast health care reform as critical to a broader search for a "new politics of meaning" in a society she said had failed to confront technological change and spiritual decay.[41]

Hillary would later be mocked for this expression by a young writer in a *New York Times Magazine* cover story titled "Saint Hillary." It was a particularly harsh assessment, since she was a forty-five-year-old woman facing one of the universal exit events of middle life, the death of a parent, and struggling with the "meaning crisis" that commonly arises at this stage. Typically, Hillary cast the personal as political. But politics can never make up for the loss of meaning between a father and daughter.

In late May, Alan Schecter, her college adviser, introduced her to the Wellesley student body when she spoke at commencement. "Hillary, I am disappointed in you," he said facetiously. "I had always thought you would be the first Wellesley alumna, the first of my former students, to be a United States Supreme Court Justice. And now it's not going to be."[42]

Her Little Rock pastor, Reverend Ed Matthews, went to see Hillary shortly after the magazine piece that sent her up as Saint Hillary. He told her that since the article had appeared, her enemies were demanding he kick her out of their church. He said he had even had threats on his life. "This is hard," she told him. "I'm having a more difficult time with this than the President is."[43]

The measure of her difficulties leaked out at least once, in a phone call between Hillary and Eileen McGann. As they talked over the mounting attacks on the First Lady, Hillary began crying on the phone. Eileen said to soothe her, "People just don't get that you have a regular marriage, and you love this guy." That remark made Hillary choke up. "She started sobbing. It was such a poignant moment. She was just all alone."[44]

Her Health Care Task Force was running into major obstacles. The first one was self-inflicted. Given Hillary's penchant for secrecy, she was easily convinced to sign a secrecy order suggested by the White House communications team. She and Ira Magaziner had originally set a hundred-day deadline. "The understanding was that we're going to come on like gangbusters in May and really do this thing quickly," the time management specialist told a reporter.[45] Instead, they behaved more like an exclusive underground cell. Doctors were shut out of the task force's deliberations, as was Washington's army of lobbyists and journalists. The First Lady refused requests for substantive policy interviews and ordered members of her task force to remain mum and guard all documents. Staff members were not even permitted to have the phone numbers of other staff members, for fear reporters might wheedle information out of them.[46]

Behind closed doors, Hillary began working toward her vision: universal coverage, cost containment, more primary care physicians, managed competition, and global budgeting.[47] In effect, Hillary was attempting to reform a system larger than the entire economy of Italy.[48] With the public left in the dark about essential information on which to participate in a debate that would affect every citizen, and health care reporters prevented from doing their job, the administration began to leak like a sieve. "Leaks are the inevitable by-product of unwarranted secrecy," wrote senior Washington political analyst David Broder in his book *The System.*

The other obstacle was systemic: Clinton was desperate to get a budget through Congress. On Monday, May 24, the First Lady and Magaziner finally got an audience with the President in the White House residential quarters but found him utterly preoccupied with his budget problems. He barely listened to them. The subtext of the meeting was to cool it on health care. Indeed, that was the last health care meeting Magaziner had with the President. And a week later, Hillary's task force was officially disbanded.

In June, the President was hit with another part of his past that he had always been afraid would come up. *The Washington Post* found the California man who had earlier claimed to be Clinton's half brother. Henry Leon Ritzenthaler offered evidence that their shared father, Bill Blythe, had already been a married man with a child when he had made his hasty wedding with Virginia Cassidy. The President did not react emotionally to this news in public. Only when the press kept asking if he was going to make contact with the man did Clinton phone Ritzenthaler. "He'd heard rumors in the past, but, being Virginia's son, he didn't deal with it until he had to," says Dee Dee Myers. "He didn't dismiss it. But he didn't want a definitive answer. He didn't invite the guy to come to the White House, and he never ordered a DNA test."[49]

Once again, friends of the President were unnerved by unpleasant taproots in Bill's background being exposed. As one senior adviser told me, "Clinton doesn't confide in anybody. So people who think of themselves as his best friends knew next to nothing about his past life."

LOSING THE LAST PROTECTOR

"It was a disaster."

Hillary's attorney, Jane Sherburne, was referring to the manner in which seven government employees in the White House Travel Office had been sacked.[50] FBI agents accused another of Hillary's Rose firm imports, William Kennedy, of pressuring them to take action on the authority of "the highest levels." Vince Foster felt responsible for the FBI contacts. Suppose Kennedy had, in fact, mentioned to the FBI "the highest levels"— whom could he have meant but Hillary? When Kennedy was reprimanded by the White House, Foster felt responsible for Kennedy's "fall" and wanted to take the blame.[51]

Then came the pressure to hide Hillary's Whitewater tracks. Foster is believed to have had one set of her billing records in his office and a duplicate set secreted in a briefcase back in his attic in Little Rock. He had annotated the set that wound up in the White House with red underlining where problems might be raised for the First Lady. Off the record, some of those close to Foster acknowledge that he was torn apart by his devotion to Hillary and his own code of ethics. That very May, he had spoken eloquently in his commencement address to the University of Arkansas Law School about the need for lawyers to maintain their integrity. In a private diary, Vince began compulsively jotting notes to himself to show why he was not guilty of everything that seemed to be going wrong. His references to "Hillary" became more distant references to "HRC" and finally to "the client."

"You could see that this man was just completely nonfunctional in trying to do the tasks she gave him," says a former senior White House staff member. "His entire life [for the previous six months] was spent trying to protect the Queen, and he wasn't able to do it. The cold reality became apparent."

On July 14, the Senate minority leader, Bob Dole, called for yet another special counsel—this one to investigate Travelgate, which he described as "this sorry episode of mistakes, misstatements, and downright wrongdoing." In distress Foster turned to James Hamilton, the distinguished Washington lawyer who had been deputy counsel to the Senate Watergate committee. The two men had spent a great deal of time together in Foster's last few months, vetting possible nominees for the Supreme Court. "I noticed that he was very taciturn," says Hamilton. "But I just figured that was his personality." Like Hillary, Hamilton was oblivious to signs that Vince was on the verge of serious depressive illness.[52]

Betsey Wright contends that Foster had been clinically depressed for years. "When he got to Washington, under all that extra stress and pressure—someone who is clinically depressed does not respond in a normal fashion," she says.[53] "Hillary and Vince were obviously very close friends and colleagues," Hamilton says. "In terms of the rumor about their relationship being something more, I will tell you that the family does not believe that. I know that when Hillary would get on the phone, Vince would certainly pay attention. He obviously had some involvement in Travelgate. He was involved with her on the Health Care Task Force. He had worked on the Clintons' personal issues. And he saw Whitewater as a can of worms. Much about Washington was difficult for Vince." Foster's wife, Lisa, stuck back in Little Rock, admitted, "I was angry at Vince about ninety percent of the time . . . for ignoring us and leaving us behind."[54]

Hillary made her last phone call to Vince sometime in the week before he died, according to Hamilton. It was not a consolation call.

There is a psychiatric term known as "flooding": When overwhelmed by personal tension, people often suffer from flooding with stress chemicals. A man like Foster, schooled to suppress his aggressive emotions to an extreme degree, would likely choose to flee rather than fight in an emotional confrontation. In retrospect Hamilton surmises that Foster experienced flooding: "To somebody who is depressed, everything seems to be a great trauma. He was being criticized personally and publicly, and, knowing there was a chance the investigation of the travel office was going to start, well, obviously he was stressed." Vince was losing weight, wringing his hands, unable to sleep, in torment. He stayed up until the wee hours on July 20, watching the movie *A Few Good Men*. In it, one character shoots himself in the mouth.

That morning, Vince Foster took the ultimate flight. He drove to a public park, took out a .38 special, and shot himself in the mouth.

That same day, phone records show a flurry of calls between Hillary in Little Rock, Susan Thomases in New York, and Maggie Williams in Washington. Months later, the revelation that Whitewater files had been removed from Foster's office—sealed off by the White House for almost forty-eight hours—suggested that he had been protecting Hillary's "Rosebud." A whole conspiracy industry was spawned on this news, fueling hate radio and cyberspace kooks and emboldening the Clintons' enemies to the point of circulating a videotape called "The Clinton Chronicles" accusing them of murder.

Two days after learning of Foster's suicide, Hillary, who was in Little Rock "on some business," made a scheduled appearance at Arkansas Children's Hospital. Dr. Betty Lowe, her compatriot in fund-raising for the hospital and Chelsea's doctor, says that Hillary did not mention Foster's death at all. "It's always true to me about Hillary," she observes, "Hillary does not talk about her personal things."[55] Instead, she clung to policy. In her speech she discussed the underlying principles of her health care reform plan: universal coverage, an emphasis on primary and preventative care, coverage for dental work and mental health, and fewer regulations.

The next day a somber President Clinton returned to Arkansas to say a personal good-bye to his boyhood friend of forty-two years. Under a sweltering midsummer south Arkansas sun, the memorial service left people half-witted and swooning. In his eulogy Bill Clinton called Vince "a complicated person." Hillary Clinton did not speak.

"We were all very sad and shocked, but I didn't see her boo-hooing or anything like that," says Philip Carroll, another partner at the Rose firm. "All of us at the firm thought it was going to be wonderful [when the Clintons won]. And now, it's hard not to say, sometimes we wish this election had never happened."[56]

One can only speculate on the complex emotions Hillary might have felt: sadness, loss, guilt, but also anger; yet another of her protectors had failed her and abandoned her. In a little more than a year she was to learn that her other partner and cohort at Rose, Webb Hubbell, had been padding his client billings and taking more out of the pot than his share. "Hillary really got socked," says Betsey Wright. "Her two best friends—one commits suicide and the other one shocks the living daylights out of her by having stolen money from her and their law firm. It was just awful. In a lot of ways, that had to be the same kind of blow as Monica Lewinsky would be a few years later."[57]

CHAPTER THIRTEEN

Down Hill

I'm feeling very lonely right now.
Nobody is fighting for me.

—Hillary Rodham Clinton

By the fall of 1993, at least some in the Clinton White House felt encouraged that the presidency had found its footing. An impressive Middle East peace accord ceremony had brought Israel's prime minister, Yitzhak Rabin, to the point of shaking hands with PLO chairman Yasir Arafat. Clinton had gotten Congress to pass NAFTA and the Brady gun control bill, and at last an economic plan was in place to begin stanching the hemorrhaging from the huge federal deficit. Now, Hillary believed, was her chance to propose the centerpiece of their domestic agenda: health care reform.

Hillary Clinton was thinking big. She wanted the federal government to guarantee health insurance to every American. Bill Clinton knew better. When he was asked by a columnist for *The Boston Globe* if the administration was really serious about demanding 100 percent coverage, Clinton's response was classic: "We'll take whatever we can get—this time around."[1]

But Hillary was more audacious. She rhapsodized about managed competition, which would band employers and employees into huge cooperatives with the bargaining power to challenge the insurance industry. It would force doctors, hospitals, and insurers to form partnerships in order to compete in offering the highest-quality health care at the lowest cost. This new competitive health marketplace would be overseen by a National Health Board. Hillary also threatened to drive a stake through the heart of specialists. She wanted to reverse the current ratio of the 70 percent of American physicians who are specialists and the 30 percent who are primary care doctors. "The American people did not stand on the street corners and say, 'Give us more thoracic surgeons,' " she told doctors in Georgia.[2]

Hillary's uncompromising style, an asset in the courtroom, proved contrary to the craft of capital politics, where compromise is a necessity. She had a tin ear for how to sell her ideas. "There was a sense of self-righteousness—'We're going to do it right'—that came through with Hillary," observed a senior White House adviser who sometimes worked with her. "She got defensive very quickly. So it came across as 'I know better. I have higher standards. I have better ideals. I have bigger plans.' One gets the feeling that Hillary thinks she is better than you are." As her own brother Hugh said, Hillary is convinced the way she does things is the right way.

Clinton called a joint session of Congress on September 22 to give Hillary's brainchild a grand send-off. The First Lady, clad in royal blue, was ushered into the gallery to great fanfare. This was to be the crowning moment that would prove what extraordinary value their co-presidency could bring to the Republic. The tension was unbearably thick, observed Robert Boorstin. Suddenly, Hillary froze. Clinton was standing at the podium, speechless. He turned around to whisper in the ear of his Vice President. More hesitation. Finally, he plunged in, but his words were not completely on script. The wrong speech had come up on the TelePrompTer.

"This health care system of ours is badly broken, and it is time to fix it," Clinton began. The rest of the way, he winged it, winding up with an inspirational coda: "But my fellow Americans, in a time of change you have to have miracles, and miracles do happen."

A week later, Hillary made her first appearance on Capitol Hill to sell her plan before a full committee room of lawmakers from both houses of Congress. She was greeted with all the incandescence of a starlet on opening night. A phalanx of flashbulbs created lightning all around her. "You'll blind me," she pleaded. As prearranged by the Democratic House bigfoot, Congressman Dan Rostenkowski, Hillary was supposed to testify for only an hour, and then modestly agree to extend her appearance so she could answer more questions. She gave them two hours and left the men of the Hill dazzled. Conservative Republicans realized they had another force to contend with, and it wouldn't be easy.

On the day the White House health care bill was to be introduced, the President escorted the First Lady into the Capitol's garishly majestic Statuary Hall for an unusual ceremony. Before an audience of 120 lawmakers from both parties, Hillary gave a short, lawyerly speech with a feisty conclusion: "And what this President and I and all who have worked on this look forward to is a vigorous debate that sheds light and not just heat. . . . And I am absolutely confident that if we do that, then in this Congress, in this next year, we will meet again to sign the kind of bill that the majority of us will be proud to have been a part of."[3] When Clinton stepped to the lectern, he used his vastly superior political skills to butter up the Republicans. Then he appealed to the raw politician in every heart: pass my wife's legislation, he said in effect, and we can slash the cost of health care so you all can argue over where to spend the savings. Finally, he cajoled them: "We could have had a bipartisan solution lickety-split . . . that would have reduced the deficit"—then, bringing one hand crashing down onto the lectern again and again—"if we were not choking on a health care system that is not working!" He swept members of both parties onto their feet, cheering and hooting.[4]

Ninety minutes later, the glow faded. The Republican majority went to work to cast the plan as socialized medicine and erroneously claimed that people would be prevented from choosing their own doctors. In early September 1993, a 238-page draft of Hillary's plan had been leaked to the news media by members of Congress. By the time the finished plan was unloaded on Congress later that month, it had ballooned to a tome of 1,342 pages.

In separate appearances before a number of Senate and House committees that fall, Hillary defended her vision of requiring employers to provide health care insurance to their workers. When she came before conservative Texas Republican congressman Dick Armey, he said, "We welcome you here."

Hillary quipped, "Yes, like Dr. Kevorkian."[5]

In December 1993, an odor floated up from the swampy land deals that Hillary had helped to facilitate back in Arkansas and mingled with the mystery still surrounding Vince Foster's suicide. *The New York Times* and *The Washington Post* were competing to be first to dig up the dead fish that they suspected the Clintons were hiding. Suddenly, the crisis was not Bill Clinton's alone. The glare of suspicion also fell on his wife. Hillary had always been the first to deny the philandering charges and defend her husband against them. Now she had a right to expect him to protect her from other people's snooping into her conduct as a lawyer and businesswoman who had handled the couple's involvement in the failed real estate venture known as Whitewater.

But he didn't.

Hillary was "paralyzed" with concern about media interest in Whitewater.[6] "It would be unusual for a person who was getting beaten up every day in the press and having to spend so much time with her lawyer trying to remember things that happened seventeen years ago, for that person not to be concerned," said Maggie Williams, her closest ally in the wake of Foster's death.[7]

Hillary thought she had the President convinced that to cooperate with the press or to accept an independent counsel would only open them to an endless fishing expedition. On a Saturday morning in mid-December, White House aide David Gergen and Stephanopoulos sat down with the President to persuade him that the only way to manage the story was to turn over the Whitewater documents. Clinton seemed to be leaning their way. Passively.

All at once his tone of voice changed, and he interjected Hillary's view. He sounded the way he had in 1991, when he had summed up for a journalist friend all the reasons why he should enter the presidential race against Bush. He sounded like Hillary. And out of his mouth came Hillary's anti-press venom: "The questions *won't* stop. At the Sperling breakfast, I answered more questions about my private life than any candidate *ever,* and what did that get me? They'll *always* want more. No president has ever been treated like I've been treated."[8]

Following that meeting, Hillary argued that no documents should be released unless and until there was a special prosecutor who asked for them by name and with the force of subpoena. Otherwise, the lockdown that she had established during the campaign would remain in force. But at one point during the rolling debate that took up much of December, Hillary felt a frisson of the same helplessness she had experienced during the campaign.

Foster's suicide had left her high and dry and Clinton could not be expected to get out in front and defend her. For a moment she gave in to her feelings and fears. She started to cry in the middle of a meeting. "We were out there alone [during the campaign] and I'm feeling very lonely right now. Nobody is fighting for me." Then, perhaps to escape the anxiety and aloneness, she went back on the attack. "I don't want to hear anything more," she snapped. "I want us to fight. I want a campaign now." She zeroed in on Stephanopoulos: "If you don't believe in us, you should just leave."[9] Then she walked out the door.

There would never have been an independent counsel to investigate Clinton had Bill Clinton not created it himself. In early January 1994 there was no statute in effect to create an independent counsel's office. It had lapsed. Stephanopoulos urged that the President order Janet Reno to appoint a special counsel "because *The Washington Post* wanted it, *The Wall Street Journal* wanted it, because we were getting hammered every day by the press," says Bernie Nussbaum. "Hillary's first instinct was to be totally against it. She understood the dangers."[10]

Hard Choices

One evening that winter, Hillary held forth before a small group of professional women on the subject of "Hard Choices." With her hair short and slicked back, she looked very soignée in a bathrobe-tied black pantsuit and lilac turtleneck. She said she had always assumed that the really hard choices came in deciding what you believed—about family, who to marry, how to raise your children. "Then I got to Washington, and I learned the hard choices were hairstyles," she said wryly. She repeated the advice a Washington hostess had given her: " 'You think these policy choices are the hard choices, but let me tell you, if you seat them wrong at a dinner party, you will *never* be forgiven.' "

Squaring her shoulders, Hillary said she preferred to remember what she had learned *before* she came to Washington: "To measure my choices not against the moment but against eternal values and *what is significant for my life*. Because that's what I'll be responsible for in the end."

She sounded as though she were giving herself a pep talk: "In the last year in Washington we've faced hard choices. It's been both exhilarating and depressing. You never know, when you make a hard choice, if it's the right one. It is most important to remain grounded in who you are and what you stand for. That's the only thing that saves you."

Who *is* she? I remember thinking then. What *does* she stand for? It seemed as if she would stand for almost anything where her husband was concerned. How did that square with her passionate concern—not for children in the aggregate but for the well-being of her own child?

Hillary was quite sanguine about her own choices. "Many people don't want to make choices at all," she said critically. "They look for elaborate rationalizations for why they can't make a tough decision." In the question-and-answer period, Hillary was asked how she had made the decision about whom to marry.

"When I was dating Bill Clinton in college," she answered, "people said, you can't go to *Arkansas*. I decided I could not make a decision *not* to marry this person I love because it wouldn't be good for my career to leave the East Coast. A dear friend drove me to Arkansas and told me, every ten miles, 'You are throwing away your life.' If I'd listened to everybody else or sat down and written out a balance sheet of my life, I never would have made the right decision for *me*." She added with great emphasis, "I think you can bloom wherever you're planted, if you put enough effort into it."

The two truly hard choices before her that winter she did not mention: first, whether to do full disclosure on Whitewater or continue to stonewall; second, whether to make a political compromise to get a health care reform measure passed or hold out as a moral absolutist for all or nothing. The second choice would determine the success of her co-presidency. The first choice would color the entire Clinton era.

New Year's 1994 brought no letup in the assaults against the bunker that the White House had become. Even the death of the President's mother, Virginia, on the sixth of January, did not give the Republicans pause in their renewed demands for hearings and the appointment of a special counsel.

Nussbaum was in Puerto Rico and the President was in Ukraine when a crucial meeting was held at the White House where the Stephanopoulos faction escalated its argument for a special counsel. "I heard about this meeting from Susan [Thomases] as I landed at JFK," says Nussbaum, "and that everybody agreed, *including* the Office of Counsel to the President—meaning me." Thomases told him that Hillary was furious.

Nussbaum immediately contacted his deputy, Joel Klein, who had agreed on his behalf. "Hillary's instinct on this issue is absolutely correct, and I totally agree with her," Nussbaum said. Klein tried to explain that he, Gergen, and Stephanopoulos all believed it was too late to release every document. Nussbaum was adamant: under no circumstances would he recommend a special counsel.[11]

In the final, climactic meeting, the President was only a disembodied voice. Hillary and all the players huddled around the speakerphone in the Oval Office to make their cases. It was two in the morning for Clinton in Ukraine, and he was not amused. He wanted the issue settled.

"You've done nothing wrong," Stephanopoulos emphasized to the President. "This will all be over in six months. Health care is coming up. Let's go with the special counsel and get this behind us."

Nussbaum argued vehemently, "This is an evil instrument. You could appoint me, Bernie Nussbaum, independent counsel, and the good Bernie would spend four years trying to turn over every rock. The bad Bernie would say to himself, 'Hey, this is a chance to affect history!' Many facts are ambiguous. Bad Bernie would twist anything to make his stupid case possible."

Hillary was nodding.

"There's nothing to Whitewater, that I know of"—Nussbaum was wound up now, speaking at his automatic weapons–fire pace—"but they won't stop there. This will be a roving searchlight. They'll search your family, your friends. I can't believe some of your friends down in Arkansas didn't do something wrong." His eyes fell on First Presidential Friend Bruce Lindsey. "Mr. President, a year from now your friend Bruce Lindsey will be under investigation."

Stephanopoulos overtook Nussbaum's monologue, calling him hysterical, and said he believed Attorney General Janet Reno would appoint a fair person.

"No matter who it is," Nussbaum bleated, "there'll be more things they'll dig up years from now, things we haven't dreamed of." (At the time, Monica Lewinsky was a junior in college.)

Clinton's voice suddenly screamed out of the speakerphone: "I cannot take this! You keep telling me all the dangers, but you're not telling me what you can do."

Suddenly Nussbaum realized that Gergen had been right: they should have released every document they had to *The Washington Post*. With hundreds of journalists vying to be the next Woodward and Bernstein plus a twenty-four-hour news cycle, everything would come out anyway. But it was too late. So the lawyer did a U-turn: "If it's that serious, Mr. President, you should ask Congress for a hearing on Whitewater. You and the First Lady should offer to go down and testify."

Clinton's fury boiled out of the speakerphone: "What? That is crazy. Do you know what the publicity would be?"

Nussbaum said he'd rather deal with a few days of bad publicity than months or years of . . . but by this point he had lost almost everyone. At that moment Nussbaum deeply missed Vince Foster. Hillary must be missing him, too, he thought; Vince would have stood with them. Now, only Hillary rose to his defense. She then efficiently summarized the opposing arguments for the President, who fell silent.

"The President and I will sleep on it," Hillary said. Discussion closed. She asked everyone but their personal lawyer, David Kendall, to leave the room.

The next morning she came into Nussbaum's office. "She's a very tough-minded person," he was reminded. "She said she understood and agreed with my arguments, but the President felt under such pressure. He needed to get on with his agenda, especially health care." The threat of seeing her bailiwick sidelined by scandal seemed to have won Hillary over, and it became apparent as the conversation went on that she had caved in. She told Nussbaum, "The President believes if he's going to get on with his agenda, he has to put this to rest."

Nussbaum assured her that he would take the necessary steps to set the process in motion for the appointment of a special counsel, but he couldn't resist warning of the inexorable path on which they were embarking: "This will haunt you and the President through all your years in the White House. And maybe beyond."[12]

By the end of January, Janet Reno had appointed Robert Fiske to be the Whitewater special counsel. The pattern of the Clinton presidency was set into motion. A month later, Paula Jones would hold her first press conference.

God, Why Me?

While Hillary seemed resolute under fire, Bill Clinton revealed a surprising self-image—that of victim. One evening in January I heard him tell a story that became his signature, retold many times:

"You know the story about the guy who falls off the mountain? He's falling down into the canyon to certain death. Then he sees this little twig coming out of the mountain and he grabs for it—his last chance. He's holding on for dear life, and the roots start pulling out of the mountain. He looks down at the drop of hundreds of feet below and he cries out, 'God, why me?' This thunderous voice comes out of the heavens and says, 'Son, there's just some people you don't like.' "

A member of the audience who was a junior Cabinet appointee snorted. "He's been telling that story all over the place. In truth, if there is a God, She's looking after the boy."

Clinton went on to say that he was "bewildered" by the hostility he had encountered in Washington, from politicians, the press, and special interests. He emphasized again and again how hard he worked, as if he were being paid by the hour. There were those in his audience who found it equally bewildering that such a charming, intelligent politician had failed to court the three Washington institutions most vulnerable to flattery: the Capitol press corps, Congress, and the Georgetown hostess matriarchy. By failing to court them, Clinton guaranteed that none of them would give him the benefit of the doubt. But he believed that he didn't need them, boasting that he could go over their heads to connect directly with the American people through his popular televised town hall meetings and chats with hospitable talk-show hosts such as Larry King and Don Imus.

Meanwhile, an aberrant new form of the virus created by the deceased king of the character smear, Lee Atwater, was being cultivated by an Atwater protégé, Grover Norquist. The Harvard-educated conservative started the Wednesday Group, which once a week brought together some thirty leaders of right-wing organizations from the National Rifle Association to the Christian Coalition, with writers, editors, and the newly popular hate radio talk-show hosts. "Sheer terror of Clinton's health care plan" was what galvanized the group, claims Norquist, but he also admitted to author James Retter, "The bottom line is we don't like Clinton. He steals our money, he steals our guns, and sends Americans overseas to die."[13] The Wednesday Group became the New Right's command center.

The self-appointed field marshal of the ongoing battle to discredit the new President was Cliff Jackson. He was the Oxford classmate who had helped Clinton circumvent the draft, but since Jackson himself had never served in the military, the lawyer's vendetta against his fellow Arkansan could not be explained by opposing views on the war. In the middle of President Clinton's first year in office, Jackson set up a nest of dynamite that would explode six months later and do severe secondary damage to Hillary's health care effort.

Five days before Christmas 1993, the sex scandal known as "Troopergate" was ready to explode in *The American Spectator* with stunning allegations by Arkansas state troopers that Clinton had used them to procure women for him. Cliff Jackson personally oversaw the Troopergate story. It was he who had sent writer David Brock to investigate the allegations and arranged for publication in a right-wing magazine. But Jackson didn't want the story weakened by a "right wing" label. "We needed the national TV hammer," he later said.[14] So he offered two of the troopers—live—to CNN, which aired the story worldwide two days before the magazine's publication. The *Associated Press* picked it up. From there it crossed the barrier that had once divided respectable mainstream media from tabloid journalism and spread like wildfire. Virtually the only national news media personality to challenge the troopers' veracity was Geraldo Rivera.

Too late, other news media uncovered the fact that some of the troopers were malcontents who had later been rewarded by Clinton's enemies for telling their damning tales. (As we now know, Brock himself later disowned his own story and apologized in a letter to the President for opening up the Paula Jones imbroglio.) Most people shrugged the story off.

Except Hillary. She believed it, according to a Washington power broker close to the Clintons: "Hillary gave him hell for months over that story. She beat up on him so badly, he just sat on his hands. He couldn't get near her. So he didn't do anything to advance health care. She had good cause to beat up on him, but it was at a crucial time when they needed to work together to sell the plan. That was one of the key reasons the health care project died." A respected Washington financial newsletter quoted an insider as saying "The state trooper sex scandal hit the President like a ton of bricks. It was at that point that you could almost feel Hillary's power coming back in full force. She now had the moral high ground, and the compromising spirit on health care evaporated."[15]

But the Whitewater scandal remained very much alive. In April 1994, Clinton presented the owlish gray eminence of Lloyd Cutler as his newly retained counselor on ethical investigations. "If there's a question here about conduct, we're open, not closed," the President assured reporters at the press conference. "I want the American people to see that this White House is different," Clinton continued. "There's no bunker mentality."[16]

But that was exactly his wife's mentality. She chose not to do "open kimono," as she and Susan Thomases jokingly called full disclosure. Abner Mikva, chief judge of the powerful U.S. Court of Appeals for the District of Columbia, who would later become White House counsel, had a more sober view of this mentality: Hillary, he observed, was "the center of paranoia" in the Clinton White House.[17]

Cutler met with Special Counsel Fiske and, finding him hard-nosed but honorable, strongly advocated giving him the documents he wanted—particularly the Whitewater files that had been removed from Foster's office. It was senseless to hold back nonincriminating material, Cutler told the President. But Hillary was of a very different mind. She didn't want to hear the argument that a President's right to privacy is often overruled by the public's right to know. Even if she couldn't agree that it was a right, others argued, it was *politically* right to disclose and dismiss some old Arkansas monkey business rather than make the Nixon mistake, since stonewalling was an invitation to constant harassment and the drip-drip-drip of suspicious news stories. Overruling his own good political instincts and deferring to his wife's worldview, Clinton went along with the lockdown on Whitewater. It split their staff and their lawyers down the middle and shook the presidency like a rolling earthquake that still has not stopped producing aftershocks.

Hillary's attitude, as she later explained it to Jane Sherburne, the attorney who represented her when Whitewater became a grand jury case, was that Clinton had gotten her into this stupid land deal with his Arkansas friends in the first place, and now he expected her to clean it up. She said she had told Clinton way back, "If you want to throw your money away, go ahead. But I'm not part of this."[18]

A very different version of Hillary's involvement is remembered by Susan McDougal. Whitewater was a shell corporation that Jim McDougal had designed as a tax shelter. When Governor Clinton was named in the Marion County newspaper as a delinquent taxpayer on the Whitewater property, an angered Clinton had called McDougal's office at Madison and squawked through the speakerphone, "You know that's political suicide. Hillary is mad as hell. This cannot happen." Susan, sitting with her husband in his office, was surprised, but came up with what she thought was a reasonable solution. Clinton seemed satisfied but told her to run it by Hillary.

That very afternoon, according to Susan, she went to the Rose firm. Congenitally flirtatious, she sashayed down the corridors, calling out to lawyers and secretaries alike, "Hi, guys." Inside Hillary's office she handed the formidable lawyer a stock transfer certificate. "What is this?" Hillary demanded. Susan explained that Jim wanted to help the Clintons get out of Whitewater. Jim had already talked to Bill, she said. They agreed it shouldn't become a campaign issue. "This is strictly for your and Bill's protection," said Susan. "You and Bill just sign it—"

"No!" snapped Hillary. Leaning over her desk to glare at the chirpy brunette, Hillary put her foot down. "Jim told me that this was going to pay for college for Chelsea. I still expect it to do that!"[19]

Ten years later Hillary would give Sherburne the impression that she had strongly objected to the Whitewater investment. Her attorney had to admit that, based on the paper record, she had gone along with the deal. But Hillary always told herself, "This is Bill's project."[20]

Clinton did not do for Hillary what Hillary had done for him. He didn't come up with excuses or get out front and take the blame for getting his wife mixed up with colorful rogues who were his friends.

Gergen thought these matters were Hillary's territory. "She was the one who had handled the finances," he says. "I never got the feeling from

Hillaryland that they felt the President was not pulling his weight." But Gergen was one of those sidelined and eventually dropped by Hillary: "The signals were pretty clear, you begin to be shut out of meetings. The true believers went ahead. I have never seen a White House divided up like that before—and I hope I never see another one."[21]

Clinton's attentions were also divided between his wife's agenda and promoting the interests of his old friends from Arkansas. Notably, he was eager to reward the Entergy Corporation for its longtime political support and, perhaps, because it would benefit his "other love," Marilyn Jo Jenkins. She was now an Entergy executive and had made several trips to the White House in the first two years of the Clinton administration.[22]

In June 1994, the Commerce Department chose twenty-four American executives to be part of a trade mission to China. Fifteen of the group were heavy contributors to the DNC, among them Entergy's Jerry Maulden. The trip, led by Commerce Secretary Ron Brown, would net $6 billion in new business contracts. Entergy came home with the lion's share: a $1.3 billion deal to manage and expand a power plant in northern China.[23]

BOTTOM OF THE HILL

"I used to describe her in 1993 and 1994 as Madame Mao," says Dick Morris of Hillary. He had become frustrated in trying to convince her that the Senate was clearly going to defeat her health care bill. Senator Bob Dole had offered a watered-down plan that was much less regulatory.

"Hillary, take half a loaf, go with the Dole plan, you can fix it up later," Morris coaxed.

"No, you can't do that," she said. "If you do that, it'll raise health insurance premiums. How would you like to have us running for reelection in 1996 and trying to explain away an increase in health care expense?"

"There are a thousand things that could happen between now and then. You can't think that way."

Hillary was adamant: "If you tinker with one part of this system, you screw the whole thing up. You've got to deal with all of it or leave it alone."

"You sound like a goddamned Stalinist!" Morris exploded. "Demanding that you've got to fix everything at once. Give me a break."

As Morris tells it, Hillary just tuned out.

Failing to persuade her politically, Morris tried to suggest a softening of her image. "One of the most appealing things about public figures is when they lead with their vulnerabilities," he told her. For examples, he pointed to Eleanor Roosevelt acknowledging her shyness and Ronald Reagan making fun of his memory lapses. "They talk about their defects and vulnerabilities, and people cut them a lot of slack."

"I can't think of any," Hillary said, making it clear she did not want to engage in any introspective exercise. "I'm not good at looking at myself that way."[24]

She paid a heavy price for her perfectionism: not only did it bruise the egos of the very members of Congress she needed to massage—such as Daniel Patrick Moynihan, her staunchest Democratic foe—but it turned even some among her natural constituency against her. Bob Boorstin, whose job it was to interpret the impenetrable plan to the public, said, "The real problem was there had been no really clear communication between Clinton and Congress on how to deal with this plan. The President's people hadn't prepared the ground. Somebody should have told us to bring in a broad outline of a plan, rather than this ludicrously complex thousand-page document. It had something in it to piss everybody off. So by the time the bill goes up to the Hill, it was DOA."[25]

Many people in the White House and in Congress faulted Hillary for being so self-righteous. "But there were a lot of people, myself included," says Boorstin, "who worked with her on the plan and who never had the guts to challenge her, who even encouraged her way of thinking. What we did made it seem like Hillary was saying, 'You do it my way or no way.' And that is a huge mistake in Washington—anywhere—but especially in Washington."

Hillary Clinton's Health Care Security Act never even came to a vote.

On November 8, 1994, Newton Leroy Gingrich became King of the Hill and spiritual leader of the first Republican majority of both houses of Congress. It was the debut of a new storyteller in the land. Cultural myths are what we live by, and Newt brought us a new myth: the angry white male striking back. Delivered in a voice with the swagger of John Wayne, Newt's message was pitched to the tenor of the times. He used words as weapons, perfecting the politics of personal destruction. The more outrageous his rhetoric became, the more hits he got on television and magazines. "We are engaged in reshaping a whole nation through the news media," Gingrich boasted to *The Washington Post*.

Oddly, Clinton and Gingrich understood each other very well. Both men had been abandoned by their real fathers and displaced at the age of three by harsh new stepfathers who had invaded their households and taken possession of their mothers.

Newt bragged that all presidential candidates for 1996 would have to adjust to a world in which his Congress was "relatively more important than the White House." The brand-new speaker did not discourage speculation that he himself might be available as a presidential candidate. But his second wife, Marianne Gingrich, had no appetite for the First Lady's job. "Watching Hillary has just been a horrible experience," she told me. "Hillary sticking her neck out is not working."[26]

Hillary was blindsided by the crushing defeat of Democrats in the 1994 congressional election. Yet it was the First Lady and her arrogant handling of the roundly rejected health care initiative who was blamed by many in her own party for their debacle. Dick Morris says that the only time he has ever seen Hillary Clinton "depressed" was after that 1994 election. He spoke to her by phone in November.

"You know, Dick," she said, "I'm just so confused, I don't know what works anymore. I don't trust my own judgment."

"Well, you know you had gone very far left," the guru chided her. "When I spoke to you in early September, you had just flipped out."

"I don't know what was getting into me that night," she said. Morris remembers her sounding contrite. By the end of their conversation she sounded lost:

"I don't know how to handle this. Everything I do seems not to work. Nothing goes right. I just don't know what to do."[27]

CHAPTER FOURTEEN

Tuning In to Eleanor

I have just had an imaginary talk with First Lady
Roosevelt, and she thinks this is a terrific idea.

—HILLARY RODHAM CLINTON

I ran into her in the ladies' room. She looked blanched, her blond hair flat on her head; she was dragging a comb through it. Her expression was rueful. Her body, camouflaged in a black covered-up pantsuit, was wider than when I had last seen her up close, during the inaugural. This was Hillary Clinton *après le déluge.*

In a speech she made at the end of 1994, reviewing the previous year, her voice was a monotone and she uttered not a word about the health care debacle. She made no reference to the challenges or accomplishments in her public life. Her remarks were concentrated on "my husband and my daughter." She told the large gathering that the past year had been important in bringing them closer together as a family. It sounded as if she were consoling herself.

Later, Bill Clinton did an imitation of Forrest Gump. It lightened things up. He didn't sound as hurt and angry as one might have expected. On the contrary, he expressed empathy for the "anxious white males" who felt threatened by the Clintons' commitment to change. He even dismissed the life-threatening incidents of a man who had crashed his plane into the President's backyard and another man, angered by Clinton's policy on assault weapons, who had shot up the White House. "They weren't shooting at me," he said forgivingly. "They were shooting at what the power of the presidency represents." He expressed frustration at being restricted from getting closer to people and then described how he tried to remind himself, "You fool, there are some things you have to give up to be President."

It struck me while watching the two of them that for all the stinging rebukes to his administration and his party, Bill Clinton seemed more optimistic as the new year began than Hillary Clinton did. "When you hit bottom, there's only one place to go—up," said a senior White House adviser whom I ran into at a newsstand. By contrast, I said, a great deal of pain was evident in Hillary's remarks. "Bill has always found it easier to let bad things roll off his back," the adviser continued. "Hillary takes everything much harder." But there was another reason for the contrast, beyond personality differences, a reason that went to the heart of Hillary's original choice. "No matter what kind of beating Clinton has taken electorally, he gets up tomorrow and has to lead the free world," the adviser observed. "What he says and does has a direct impact on two hundred fifty million people. Hillary gets up, and she has no clear job."

She had been stripped of her highly controversial and unofficial role as the President's domestic policy adviser. As the year turned, the Clintons were deliberating over what kind of role she could play from then on. "I don't know what she'll do, but I know for certain she'll be active," the adviser said confidently.

We agreed that Hillary was the lightning rod for people's fear of change: the change of generation, the change of political leadership, the change in the equation between men and women, the tremendous social dislocation brought about by moving into a new information-based economy. "When all else is stripped down, what people care about most is security," said the White House counselor. "I think it was brave of Clinton to talk about the anxious white males, but he's got to find a point of entry—a hook—to connect with them. Right now they look at Clinton and see him as a guy who cares about gays and women and minorities—and if there's some Clinton left over, he'll give it to them." The adviser drew a long sigh and tucked his papers under his arm. "If he doesn't find a way to connect to those men, it's going to be a long, long '96 campaign."

The next time I had an opportunity to speak to Hillary, her eyebrows shot up and she stretched out her hand and immediately made me feel important by making reference to my recent book *The Silent Passage*. "I thought of you when I heard a comedienne refer to menopause," she said. The comic had said, "I've decided I'm not going to do that."

"Yeah, right," Hillary laughed heartily, "let's do away with that."

I told her I'd had a discussion with the White House adviser after hearing the President's speech expressing empathy for anxious white males. "The whole theme of your campaign was one of change as good, as positive, as a chance to make things better," I said. "But most people don't like change. They fear change. They'll do almost anything to avoid change. Democrats expect their government to help them manage change. Maybe now what you could do as First Lady is connect with the wives of those anxious white males and offer them some ideas for helping their families manage change."

Hillary's large blue eyes glittered, and almost immediately she began spinning out a possible strategy. She recalled a recent study showing that most teenage American boys still saw their future as primary breadwinners; they wanted wives who would stay home and take care of them and the house and kids. The teenage girls saw their future in completely opposite terms: most looked forward to completing their education, getting good jobs, having the independence of a career, and, *if* they married, having a husband who would share the housework and child care. "So we're on a collision course," Hillary concluded.

Then, in an unusually candid self-analysis, she ascribed some of the white male backlash to herself: "I know I'm the projection for many of those wounded men," she said. "I'm the boss they never wanted to have. I'm the wife they never"—she caught herself—"the wife who went back to school and got an extra degree and a job as good as theirs. I'm the daughter who they never wanted to turn out to be so independent. It's not me, personally, they hate—it's the changes I represent."[1]

SAVING BILL—AGAIN

Hillary was right on target. Of all the areas of change she represented, she was most vividly a threat to centuries of patriarchalism. Don Jones, her former youth minister, says, "I think the United States would tolerate a woman president better than a professional, intellectual, uppity First Lady."[2]

"Patriarchy is characterized by the institutionally enforced authority of males over females and their children in the family unit," as described by Manuel Castells, professor of sociology at the University of California,

Berkeley. "Without the patriarchal family, patriarchalism would be exposed as sheer domination."[3] The most traditional version of patriarchalism—the married couple with children in which the husband is the only bread-winner and the wife is a full-time homemaker—has dropped to 7 percent of all U.S. households. Moreover, almost *one third* of the working wives in America (10.2 million women) now earn more than their husbands.[4] This arrangement is epitomized by the Clintons: in 1996, for example, the President of the United States earned $200,000. His wife made almost three and a half times as much—$742,852—from her own activities, writing and promoting a book. Hillary is also an international advocate for a woman's right to choose. Of all the struggles to preserve traditional family life, the antiabortion movement is the most militant, resorting to violence even as it has been losing sway with the majority of Americans and marking single-issue conservative candidates for almost certain defeat.

This is why the war between the two sides is so vicious. And Hillary is the poster woman for this revolution. Her mother, a castoff with no social position who was frustrated by a rigid and dictatorial husband, transmitted her desire to be autonomous to her daughter. And Hillary was not about to give up any of the autonomy she had fought to preserve in a marriage that was supposed to be a model of egalitarianism.

The human landscape of women's liberation is littered with corpses of broken lives. Would Hillary be another casualty of this revolution in progress?

In that defeatist period, however, the President never allowed her to be his scapegoat. "In every matter—political and policy—Bill Clinton was fiercely loyal to the First Lady," says presidential counselor Bill Curry. "He made it clear to anyone and everyone that he brooked no criticism of his wife."[5]

Hillary's support of her husband was just as unequivocal. Despite her "little depression when she had to kind of disappear and didn't know how to reshape herself," recalls a senior adviser then in the White House, "she was also very deeply involved in reshaping him at that time. She absolutely helped him get back the reins of his presidency. She was a rock."

Hillary made the call. In early December 1994, she arranged to have a short man with a flamboyant tie, who looked more like a car salesman than a high-level political consultant, sneaked into the East Wing. Bill Clinton's presidency had spun out of control. Hillary determined to put him together with his old adviser in the Treaty Room.

Dick Morris was so nervous, he deliberately hadn't prepared. He ducked Clinton's suspicious staffers, who referred to him as "Darth Vader." Hillary had been his tenuous link to the White House during the 1992 to 1994 period, when he had offered her advice once or twice a month on her own work and political style. During those first two years, he had not been in good favor with Bill. Morris was hoping now to strike a tough bargain with a beleaguered President who was already uneasy about his own reelection campaign two years down the road.

Morris's opener was obnoxious: "So, you want me to do basically for you what I did in 1980 or '82?"

"Yep," the President said.

Hillary lightened it up by joking with the President about the Svengali who had helped them with the "resurrection" of Bill Clinton when he lost his governorship. In a tone only half teasing, she said to her husband, "You're going to have to stop asking us to rescue you every time."

Clinton held up his hands and replied with the innocence of a dauphin, "Last time, I swear."[6]

In that little cameo was the thrust of the three personalities who would assure Bill Clinton's reelection: Darth Vader, Saint Hillary, and the Comeback Kid. The meeting ended with a pact to allow Morris to run a covert operation against members of the Clintons' own White House team. Morris himself would be as stealthy as a Klingon. His code name would be "Charlie." Not only would he be king of the polls and chief strategist, he would meet secretly with the President and Hillary.

The White House and its chief occupants began to function very differently. Bill Clinton stopped talking to Stephanopoulos, in whose judgment the Clintons had lost faith after the 1994 election debacle. He was now seen as a narcissistic kid too concerned with showing off to his friends in the media. But given his cozy connections with newspeople the White House feared, he was too dangerous to fire outright. "The idea was to put a bullet through his head and leave him standing, but with no power," says a White House adviser who remained under the new regime. But who was behind this new regime? "Nobody knew what this mystery man—Morris—was doing with Hillary, the President, and the Vice President. But the rest of us were all now out of the first circle."

Another inner circle had been secretly inserted. The weekend before New Year's, a bevy of inspirational New Age authors were invited by Bill and Hillary to Camp David to help them work through the traumas of their first two years in Washington. Both were in pain and feeling rudderless. In hours of consultations, the most meaningful for Hillary was their psychological counseling session with Jean Houston. A mature author whose foundation studies psychic experiences and mythic connections to historical figures and other worlds, Houston told Hillary that she was burdened with five thousand years of history of women's subservience. She analyzed the First Lady's sorrow and bitterness at being relegated to no-man's-land and described it as analogous to cutting off the hands of Mozart so he couldn't make music. She urged Hillary to hang on; the time would come when she would find a role in which she could express the fullness of her gifts. She represented "the new story."[7] It was the counterpoint to Newt's old story of patriarchy reasserted.

Hillary's season of despair would last for at least the first nine months of 1995. It was a profound identity crisis not unusual at her stage of life—facing the perimenopausal years and the approach of the empty nest—but it was presumably intensified by the continuing public scrutiny and her own recent policy failure.

Not so! protested her press secretary from those years, Neel Lattimore: "Nobody on her staff ever accepted failure on health care. And we *never pulled back.*"[8]

Both statements seem to have been true. She was the woman who had been constantly at the center of the strategy meetings during all of the Arkansas gubernatorial years, the woman who had kept Bill Clinton in the channel and saved him from drowning again and again until he had achieved their shared dream, the woman who had had the President's ear on just about every issue and on the hirings and firings of their first two years. By comparison, in 1995 and 1996, she became virtually powerless. "The trauma of the '94 defeat was so profound, no one even wanted to take a meeting about health care," says former White House policy adviser Bill Curry.[9] They went about fourteen months without meeting, and only after considerable nagging did a new policy group re-form. But Hillary made it her business *not* to attend their meetings.

Jeff Phillips, a brainy basketball player she had once dated in high school who was now a family physician in southern Michigan, had written to the First Lady during her health care reform campaign. Like most physicians, he knew it was a mistake not to involve doctors in discussions of what compromises they might be willing to make. Hillary had responded to him. But once her initiative fell through, Dr. Phillips's letters encouraging her not to give up went unanswered. "It was a death knell for her by then," surmised Phillips. "She didn't want to hear about it."[10]

A few weeks after Morris had been reinstated, he dropped some depressing polling results on the President. About one third of the voters were turned off by Clinton because of his "immorality." About the same number were turned off by his "weakness." Morris took it as a given that immorality was incurable. But the perception of weakness was correctable, he said. Then he risked doing something no one else had: he confronted Clinton on the political liabilities his wife presented.

"The more she seems strong, the more you will inevitably be seen as weak," Morris said.

Clinton didn't like what he heard. He didn't want to hear any more. Morris waited and later came back to the subject.

"Look, you and I know the reality of your marriage," he said. "Your strengths feed on each other. But people don't get it. They think either she's wearing the pants or you're wearing the pants." He suggested that Clinton simply show Hillary the data and explain the conundrum to her.

At about the same time, Hillary was dealt another blow. David Maraniss's biography of Bill Clinton, *First in His Class*, was published, and its revelations about Clinton's womanizing made Hillary livid. The scene he described of Betsey Wright going over the list of Clinton's women to persuade him not to run for president in 1988 came as a bitter revelation to Hillary. It reopened the raw wound of the previous year, and at a time when Hillary was already feeling more insecure and unloved than perhaps at any time since her college depression. And Wright wasn't the only insider who had revealed things to Maraniss.

Clinton called Morris in a cold fury: "Why did you talk to Maraniss? Can't I trust you anymore? Can't I trust *anybody* anymore?" When he screamed at his secret guru for telling Maraniss that Clinton and Morris had worked together on negative ads about Jim Guy Tucker, Morris was baffled. "That was in 1978."

"But he's now the governor!" Clinton shouted.

"What the fuck do you care?"

"He controls the state police!"

Hillary stopped speaking to Morris for the next four or five months. Not infrequently he would mention Hillary's freeze to the President, saying, "Look, I know you guys. And I know I'm not going to last here very long if I'm not in touch with Hillary. So if you want our relationship to proceed, you'd better repair my relationship with her."

The President's responses were always sheepish. "I'll try," he would say unconvincingly, or "I'm having my own problems." As the spring wore on, it became apparent to Morris that Clinton was in the doghouse with Hillary, too. At one point, the President encouraged Morris to talk to her on behalf of both of them: "She takes your advice."

"Yeah," said Morris. "I put the dog food out at night and in the morning the dish is empty."[11]

The Eleanor Channel

Hillary's psychological withdrawal from her husband and from running the castle day to day did not render her dysfunctional. On the contrary. She had to undergo "a little death" of the inappropriate identity she had assumed was hers for the asking and begin to search anew for another identity. Nobody, especially not Bill Clinton, told her to back off. The decision to withdraw was her own. She never attended a single one of the evening strategy meetings held weekly in the private residence with Morris, from January 1995 through August 1996, to plot Clinton's reelection campaign and money-raising schemes (although she always debriefed him in private).

What she did instead was seek out a new path through the wilderness. Her polestar was Eleanor Roosevelt. She had been communing with ER since the beginning of the Clinton presidency, on her own, addressing questions to her revered predecessor and drawing inspiration from her courage, both in surmounting the personal pain in her marriage and in pursuing the causes and convictions for which she had stood. But Hillary had not been successful in drawing out answers from her imaginary conversations. And she had conducted herself as First Lady in a very different manner that was far more invasive and obvious than ER's approach.

On January 26, 1995, two days after the President delivered the longest State of the Union address in history, Hillary delivered a keynote address at the dedication of Eleanor Roosevelt College in San Diego. It was an impassioned speech, but more of an inner meditation than her usual policy-heavy remarks. The focal point was choice: "Eleanor Roosevelt also understood that every one of us every day has choices to make about the kind of person we are and what we wish to become. . . . I would say that every day you have the opportunity to demonstrate courage. You have a choice. You can decide to be someone who tries to bring people together, or you can fall prey to those who wish to divide us. You can be someone who stands against prejudice and bigotry, or you can go along with the crowd and tell the jokes and point the fingers. You can be someone who believes your obligation as a citizen is to educate yourself and learn what is going on so you can make an informed decision. Or you can be among those who believe that being negative is clever, being cynical is fashionable, and there really is nothing you can do anyway."

It sounded like her own internal debate, her form of therapy. What would be Hillary's choice? Who to be? Hillary Rodham, co-president? Hillary Clinton, White House wife? Or Hillary Roosevelt?

Her core vision of herself as a policy maker had been shaken by the outright rejection of her health care reform plan. Her secrecy policy had even brought down a lawsuit charging the administration with unconstitutional actions and raising the sticky issue of whether the First Lady was or was not a government employee. Hillary consoled herself by reciting one of her favorite quotes from ER: "To undo mistakes is always harder than not to create them originally, but we seldom have foresight. Therefore, we have no choice but to try to correct our past mistakes."[12]

So while in withdrawal, Hillary set about attempting to create a new self. In early 1995 she began inviting Jean Houston to the White House. Picking up on Hillary's strong and intimate identification with Eleanor Roosevelt, the psychic counselor suggested that the two women might be kindred spirits. She urged Hillary to try harder to open herself up and connect with her archetype: "Talk to her."[13]

Hillary tried harder to connect with the fierce determination shown by FDR's First Lady in fighting against racism and sexism and for human rights. She asked how she had met obstacles and criticism and how she had lived with the loneliness. She was still not very successful in gaining answers, but Houston continued to visit and help her to channel ER—until somebody leaked the story and Hillary was in danger of being held up to ridicule. She actually handled the controversy quite well. In her formal statement, she described the meetings with Houston and others as an "intellectual exercise," and said, "The bottom line is, I have no spiritual advisers or any other alternatives to my deeply held Methodist faith and traditions on which I have relied since childhood." She also took to joking when she made a speech that "I have just had an imaginary talk with First Lady Roosevelt, and she thinks this is a terrific idea."[14] Audiences laughed.

The new self she was attempting to construct in the privacy of her thoughts and meditations was the antithesis of the passive helpmeet Hillary tried to project in public. In an interview in February with *U.S. News & World Report*, she said that "Whatever it takes to kind of be there for him, I think that is the most important thing I have to do. I want to continue working on health-related issues, particularly women's health and matters that affect the research that goes into women's diseases and problems; trying to be involved, as I am, on the mammography issue for older women." She mentioned having made a visit to a Washington, D.C., public school and said she would try to do something like that every couple of weeks, "so at least I can get out into the Washington community and be a presence there."[15]

It was a sudden shrinking of her domain.

I couldn't help but see the frustration growing in this woman's eyes," says a former White House communications adviser. "As Bill's career grew more and more, she had to take the back burner." During some of the President's speeches, the adviser would look over at Hillary. The fiery internal conflict she saw in the First Lady's eyes resonated with the adviser, who had also gone to a women's college. "How frustrating it must be to have your career diminished because your man—your bumblin'-head-in-his-zipper-husband—keeps literally screwing things up. And then on top of it, the world wants you to turn Barbie-esque. This goes against exactly what one learns at an all-women's college, which is to make your voice count and stay true to who you are."

Hillary kept moving ahead. She focused on Gulf War syndrome, a controversial health issue that had been swept under the carpet since the Bush administration. Quietly, methodically, she did research with doctors, the Department of Veterans Affairs, the Defense Department, building a coalition before she presented the President with a report. She convinced him that it was a worthy issue. The outcome was that the President created a blue-ribbon task force. Hillary was present for his announcement, but she was not appointed chairperson or even a member.

"So, have you learned your lesson?" "Doesn't the President trust his wife anymore?" "Is Hillary a liability for him?" That was the nature of questions from the reporters who called Neel Lattimore, Hillary's passionately loyal press secretary. "You're just kind of swatting it down, and you keep moving ahead," he recalls.[16]

When Hillary took up the cause of encouraging older women to get mammograms, the word was "Oh, so she's returning to traditional First Ladyisms, right?" Not exactly. Later in the term, Hillary had a brainstorm: "It struck me, as I watched the missile technology used in the Gulf War, that if we were able to send a missile down a chimney thousands of miles away, we ought to be able to do a better job of imaging a woman's breast."[17] She lobbied the Department of Defense, and by fall of 1996, Clinton was able to announce that the department was contributing $20 million to breast cancer research. Thus did the First Lady enlist military technology in the battle against invasions of the breast, which had increased alarmingly. It was pure Hillary: taking on a major social problem affecting women or children or the poor and pushing a novel policy solution—anything but "traditional First Ladyism."

To relieve her of the burden of guarding the White House against nosy investigators, a presidential adviser called on Jane Sherburne to take over scandal management. A feisty forty-three-year-old partner in Lloyd Cutler's law firm, Sherburne had already served during Cutler's six-month stint in round one of the Whitewater bout. Now she was asked to put together a team to respond to the Republicans' pledge to use congressional subpoena power to make sure they defeated Clinton.

At a meeting attended by Hillary, Sherburne identified no fewer than thirty-nine areas of investigation. Hillary was visibly exhausted by the prospect. Although both women were litigators, Sherburne introduced a very different theory on scandal management: Stop hiding. Get the information out early and often. She stressed how vital it was to respond quickly, before suspicions built and negative stories became inevitable.

"Our whole approach when I was there was to work closely with the press to develop relationships with folks, to gain credibility, and to put the bad stuff out," says Sherburne. "Hillary never resisted the approach, but she didn't express enthusiasm either." The First Lady's younger counterpart remembers being told, in effect, "Prove it to me. The scandal management around here has been fucked up for two years, and there are other issues we want to be addressing."

"She is a very direct, no-nonsense person," says Sherburne. "She forms her opinions quickly. She's fundamentally a problem solver. Hillary can be startling in the way she presents her response. It's quick, it's clear, it doesn't suggest room for collaboration."[18] Sherburne realized that an important part of her job would be to discipline the internal reaction to the ever-expanding investigations. As White House counsel Abner Mikva said, Hillary was paranoid, and her paranoia led to more secrecy and stonewalling, which led to more suspicion and adversarial relations with the investigators and the press. Sherburne was determined to contain the scalding pot of scandals with her own SWAT team.

That freed Hillary to begin establishing a new platform outside of her own country. In early March, in Denmark, she delivered her first speech to a UN World Summit, a forum that would become one of her most potent. Her audience was a natural international constituency, members of non-governmental organizations (NGOs)—mostly women—who were joining forces to share ideas for how to make their own countries' leadership—

mostly male—more responsive to the rights and needs of women and children.

Since she was going to have to hover in obscurity for a while, Hillary decided to use her remaining time in what might be her only term in the White House to see the world and expose her daughter to different cultures. Later that month, President Clinton announced that he was sending his wife abroad to show "a human dimension to politics, policy, and diplomacy." Chelsea, then fourteen, was on spring break and thrilled to travel with her mother to exotic places from India to Pakistan and Nepal to Bangladesh and Sri Lanka. They rode elephants, donned chadors to enter mosques, stood awed before the Taj Mahal, and enjoyed a moonlight dinner in the red stone ruins of the Mogul fort at Lahore. It was Chelsea's debut as a poised junior diplomat. Emerging from the gawkiness of early adolescence, Chelsea suddenly moved with the self-possessed posture and grace of a ballet dancer; the braces were gone, her crimped hair was very much in style, and she had an enviably close relationship with her mother. She got great press.

Far away from the detractors in her own land, "The First Lady has appeared both freer—and a good deal funnier—than she has seemed at home in some time," reported Martha Teichner on CBS. A Wellesley classmate of Hillary, Teichner dubbed it a "chick trip." Other women journalists described to me their excitement at being allowed to sit near the First Lady and her daughter on the long flights and engage in "girl talk." But, for all the sorority-sister atmosphere, the reporters were darkly warned that none of these conversations—not a word—could be used.

One of Hillary's precepts is that, to grow, one must constantly push oneself to do things one can't imagine doing. On that trip, Hillary addressed august audiences at Lahore University in Pakistan and at the Rajiv Gandhi Foundation in New Delhi, India. She was shocked when visiting the world's largest democracy to find that the prospect of the birth of a daughter in India could still cause family dread, that brides could be beaten if their families didn't meet the groom's family's demands for a more generous dowry. At an embassy luncheon she was given a poem called "Silence," written by Anasuya Sengupta, a New Delhi college girl; it resonated with Hillary's own despair at feeling misunderstood. "I read it, and I was just overwhelmed by it," Mrs. Clinton said later. That night she stayed up and rewrote large parts of the speech she was to deliver the next day in order to highlight the poem.[19]

" 'Too many women in too many countries speak the same language—of silence,' " Mrs. Clinton said before the Gandhi Foundation audience. She quoted the poem: " 'My grandmother was always silent, always aggrieved, only her husband had the cosmic right (or so it was said) to speak and be heard.' "

" 'They say it is different now,' " Mrs. Clinton read on, and now her voice clenched with emotion. " 'But sometimes, I wonder. When a woman gives her love, as most do, generously, it is accepted. When a woman shares her thoughts, as some women do, graciously, it is allowed. When a woman fights for power, as all women would like to, quietly or loudly, it is questioned,' " Clinton continued, still quoting the poem. " 'And yet, there must be freedom, if we are to speak. And yes, there must be power, if we are to be heard. And when we have both (freedom and power), let us not be misunderstood.' "

Students in the balcony erupted in unladylike applause and cheers. At last, Hillary's charisma had found an embracing environment. The glow lasted throughout the goodwill visit to five Southeast Asian countries. "Women flocked to see her and talk to her. They identified with her," recalls Teichner. "You saw real adoration wherever she went."[20]

Bill Curry recalls his earlier dismay "that she missed the point of Eleanor Roosevelt, who didn't insinuate herself into day-to-day affairs and who understood that there was an extraordinary amount of charismatic power that simply flowed from being the First Lady."[21] Now, belatedly guiding herself by the legacy of her heroine, Hillary's international prestige was growing. But never far away there was a man whose mission was to tear her down—if he couldn't bring down her husband first.

SKUNK AT THE GARDEN PARTY

One of Hillary's favorite homilies seemed to her more applicable than ever that year:

> *As I was standing in the street as quiet as could be,*
> *A great big ugly man came up and tied his horse to me.*[22]

The man was, of course, Kenneth Starr. The "I" was the way Hillary saw herself: working behind the scenes on issues and principles and selflessly helping her husband to regain the reins of a presidency run amok. Why, then, was this zealot chasing her down and trying to tie his subpoena to her? It was an infuriating distraction from her efforts to use the power of her husband's office to change things for the better for Americans and for women and children around the world.

One day in April, Hillary was the headliner at the Mother of the Year awards. A few days later, a paternal Bill Clinton had to reassure a shocked nation after a homegrown act of terrorism—the bombing of the Oklahoma City federal building in which 158 people were killed. Only a few days after that, the father figure of the country and the mother of the year faced their first deposition with Kenneth Starr. An eight-foot table had been moved into the President's study for the unique occasion. Clinton went first. He took a seat at the south end of the table. Already in place was a lineup of three prosecutors and a court reporter. At the opposite end Kenneth Starr faced the President. He wanted to take this deposition himself. Overeager to the point of carelessness, he was three or four questions into the deposition when he noticed the President's attorneys, Jane Sherburne and Abner Mikva, smirking. One of Starr's deputies passed him a note. The top prosecutor had forgotten to swear in the witness.

The contrast between Bill and Hillary's personalities was strikingly on display. The President, who believes that if he can connect with somebody he can always persuade him, couldn't have been more polite and helpful. He tried to put Starr at ease. After the formalities, he chatted with Starr and his deputies about the Oklahoma City bombing and then guided them around his office, showing off his favorite artifacts. "He's voluble, light-hearted, he's covering them with charm," describes Sherburne.

After Abner Mikva left, the President turned to Sherburne and said, "Will you show them the Lincoln Bedroom?" Jane followed the President's orders. Steeling herself, she toured Starr and his entourage around the Oval Office and the historic bedrooms.[23]

Next, Hillary walked in. Sat down. No chitchat. No "Can I get you a glass of water?" Just "Let's go." She didn't try to treat Starr like a friend or win him over. "She was just furious this man was in her house," recalls Sherburne. "She gave direct answers, said no more than she had to, got up, and left."

When Hillary later learned that the Starr party had been given a tour of her house, she made it abundantly clear that she would have preferred they had left and been done with it. The next time Starr turned up for another interrogation session in the White House, this time with a different set of deputies, he asked Sherburne, "Would you mind giving them the same tour?"

"Not on your life," said Sherburne. "No way. I'm taking you to the door, and you're getting out. We won't be doing any tours today."

Starr said, "You're making me feel like a skunk at the garden party."

Sherburne said, "That's a pretty good description," and ushered him out.[24]

Continuing to follow in Eleanor's footsteps, Hillary decided to write a book and to launch a weekly newspaper column, presenting a warmer, more personal side of the woman perceived at best as a policy wonk, if not as the "yuppie wife from Hell" or the "Wicked Witch of the West Wing." But the week before her print debut, the conservative Republican senator from New York, Alfonse D'Amato, launched his own Banking Committee hearings on Whitewater. With yet another "great big ugly man" in her life, Hillary's first columns carried an edge of anger and frustration: "The truth is, it is hard for me to recognize the Hillary Clinton that other people see."[25] Her column seldom took up the important political or policy issues of the day, as had those of her model, Eleanor Roosevelt, whose "My Day" column had evolved from a campaign-year diary in 1936 into a sounding board for Franklin Roosevelt's New Deal. Eleanor wrote her column not only to ease the sting of criticism but sometimes to openly oppose her husband's policies.

In July, Hillary had to turn her attention away from her column and from writing a book, which was about caring for children of the world, and fend off the latest Republican assault. D'Amato's committee was hammering her chief of staff, Maggie Williams, subjecting her to lie detector tests and saddling her with huge legal bills, which she, as a private citizen, would have to shoulder herself. On her first day of testimony, the tough young African-American aide broke down in tears.

Hillary trusted very few people by now, and she didn't trust Sherburne yet; it was only six months into their association. With the brio that astounds most people and shuts them up, Hillary stated her view on how to handle the D'Amato hearings. She wanted to take D'Amato on. He was a perfect target on which to vent some of her pent-up anger. She seemed to be almost salivating over the prospect of a spitting contest. Somebody had to take the risk. Few dared. Finally Sherburne took a deep breath and came back at Hillary—firmly.

"You can't show your face before D'Amato's committee," she insisted. "Your appearance would be a sensation. Why give D'Amato that much attention? His hearings are going to fail, eventually. We'll be successful at showing it's all part of a political exercise, and he'll be the one who ends up looking bad."

The formidable First Lady looked startled.

"Hillary wasn't accustomed to having people push back; it takes one to know one—people don't feel like they can come back and challenge me either," acknowledges the blunt lady litigator. "Hillary lacks self-awareness of this trait and how it affects people. When she says, 'Fix it!' or 'If there's a problem, fire 'em!,' she doesn't appreciate how she can make people jump. [Her impact] is a combination of her own personal style and the fact she's First Lady of the United States."

Hillary responded quickly to Sherburne's argument. "That makes sense, fine," she said.

"That's how I learned how forceful she can be and how people respond to that force," says Sherburne. "They don't realize she is open to listening to another point of view."[26]

But soon afterward, the decision blew up in Hillary's face. Breaking her habit, she read *Newsweek* the first week of August and found herself characterized in a column by Joe Klein as the "Daisy Buchanan of the Baby Boom Political Elite." Klein invoked the Roaring Twenties femme fatale from F. Scott Fitzgerald's *The Great Gatsby* to make the point that Hillary was throwing her chief of staff to the wolves. He wrote, "Why hasn't she come forward and said, 'Stop torturing my staff. This isn't about them. I'll testify. I'll make all documents available. I'll sit there and answer your stupid, salacious questions until Inauguration Day, if need be.' "[27]

Hillary was shaken by the column. When she called Sherburne, it was not to castigate her, it was to find an escape from the hideous mirror that was distorting her. How could anybody see in her a resemblance to that woman in the white dresses who sipped mint juleps while displaying a lethal indifference to the lives being smashed on her account? Hillary insisted she would have to testify: "Every bone in my body tells me that's what I should do."

"We're not at a point yet where it makes sense for you to do that," Sherburne said. The Clintons' personal lawyer, David Kendall, was also very much against it.

"How's Maggie?" Hillary inquired softly.

"We both know Maggie is tough. Maggie is not looking to you to come and save her."

Hillary returned to the depiction of herself as an insouciant Daisy Buchanan. She wasn't crying but was close to it. She said it was worse than a perception problem; it was about living with herself. If she stood by nonchalantly while one of her most loyal comrades in arms went down, she would be—she couldn't even spell it out. It sounded to Sherburne as if sobs were being throttled in her throat before they could escape.

"I'm not someone who just lets people suffer without offering any help," Hillary blurted out. *"I help people."*

What stuck in her throat was perhaps the deep contradiction she had first noticed in college: Was she really the catcher in the rye who saved children before they went over the cliff, or was she secretly a hater of mankind? She had always felt an obligation to help people—people in the aggregate, people with their millions of particular stories collected and bundled into a depersonalized mass, where they could be treated with a policy. But she didn't warm to many people personally. The streak of misanthropy was still in her. Now she was being accused of abandoning even those she loved, like Maggie.

"I'm not just someone who uses up people!" she wailed.

Sherburne tried to be as clear as the boundless summer sky. "Hard as this is, it is political, it isn't personal," she said. "Look at the attacks on you as a nasty game. That's the only way to insulate the center of your soul."

Hillary quieted down. She always felt more comfortable residing outside the privacy zone.

Sherburne reassured her, "We're going to stay close to this situation. Don't worry. We're on it."

If Hillary wished that Bill Clinton would do more to defend her, she never expressed it to Sherburne. "It's inconceivable she would have wanted the President to turn his attention away from running America," says Sherburne. "She was a lightning rod, to get at him. She understood that all along, intellectually. There came a point where she recognized that emotionally as well."[28]

Meanwhile, Clinton was dealing with the whole Whitewater mess by ignoring it and distracting himself. On August 9, only a week after the *Newsweek* piece that had laid Hillary low, the President was moving perfunctorily down the rope line of White House guests, enduring introductions forgotten on the spot before escaping on his helicopter, when a dark-haired beauty thrust herself into his sight line. She was wearing a light green suit that looked deliciously shrunk over her ample curves. The President gave the girl "the full Bill Clinton," undressing her with his eyes. It's the way he flirts with women—and not only with her, as the intern was to discover. But that day, on their first encounter, she was completely taken in: "When it came time to shake my hand, the smile disappeared, the rest of the crowd disappeared and we shared an intense but brief sexual exchange."[29]

Later on, when their sexual fantasies were being played out with abandon in his office, the President is supposed to have told Monica Lewinsky that he remembered that first moment vividly and said, "I knew that one day I would kiss you."[30]

GOING FLAT OUT

Hillary threw herself into writing her book. The deadline was Labor Day, 1995. Impossible. "If we had known how deeply involved she'd be and how much of a perfectionist she is, we'd never have set that deadline," says Rebecca Salatan, her editor at Simon & Schuster. Hillary had begun work on *It Takes a Village* in February and continued in spurts until summer, all the while fighting scandals and fighting for Bill. By mid-August the book was a welcome distraction, even though she wrote laboriously in longhand, even though it was difficult to find her voice. She had previously written only in colorlessly precise legal language.

From mid-August until the second week in December, she worked nonstop on the book. Salatan was invited to move into the White House. She could hardly keep up with the First Lady. At six in the morning Hillary would be up and working in her office in the residence. The editor found that Hillary inhabits the place. She fills it utterly. At the end of the day, while Hillary transformed herself from sloppy writer into hostess in high heels to make the requisite public appearance with the President, Salatan penciled in revisions. Normally, Hillary starts to fade by ten or ten-thirty. But every night she went back to her office, picked up the draft chapter left on her chair, and took it to bed with her. Sometimes she was still up at nearly midnight, responding to comments such as "This is hokey" or "This section is disorganized" or "This story is really not arresting." One night when Salatan padded down rather late to leave off another chapter, she bumped into Hillary in her bathrobe.

"What's up, buttercup?" said the First Lady, showing her hokey midwestern sense of humor.[31]

She couldn't stop herself. "She was relieved when she was working flat out on the book," observed her editor. When their separate staffs settled on Jackson Hole for the Clintons' summer vacation, Hillary took her manuscript along. It was a welcome buffer against the foul moods into which her husband would sink on holidays. Bill Clinton hates vacations. He thinks he should be enjoying himself, but he doesn't. Deprived of his maintenance dose of adulation, he starts worrying. Knowing that the President is in a notoriously bad mood when he can't offset his anxieties with work, his staff draws straws and the loser takes holiday duty. That summer of 1995, Clinton was on the phone all the time bellyaching about Bill Bradley and Colin Powell, certain they were both going to run against him for Pres-

272 / HILLARY'S CHOICE

ident, according to Morris.[32] When Israel's prime minister Yitzhak Rabin was assassinated, Hillary packed her manuscript for the funeral trip. By October, she was rewriting madly. The White House heating system wasn't working, and her office turned cold; still, at six on the frostiest morning she would be there, dressed for hard labor in a heavy sweater, leggings, and sneakers.

Bill took Hillary's book seriously, and his approval was important to her. He talked it over with her at night and sometimes popped into her office during the day. Hillary's moods fluctuated. It was plain from the first words out of her mouth in the morning whether she was upbeat or stressed out. When she wasn't upset, her editor found her to be a dream author. "She has a very strong point of view, but she listened and took feedback," says Salatan. "Each chapter went through many, many drafts."[33]

Hillary later told a bookstore owner in California that she almost hadn't set down the ideas she really wanted to get across; she had been too worried about giving her enemies a string with which to pull her down. Moreover, Hillary had no idea how to make policy arguments in a personal way. She admitted she had to fight with herself to reveal anything personal and did so only when she was persuaded it was for a good cause.

What the process of forced self-examination revealed was how profoundly her own experience of growing up in the home of an authoritarian father had colored her worldview. While working with her editor, she often mentioned the hard time she had had with her father. For Hillary, what happens between parents and children is not separate from what happens between government and governed. There is no dividing line between foreign policy and women's and children's issues, no hard and soft issues. Her book was a heartfelt manifesto meant to encourage broad support within communities for raising a child. No one knew better than Hillary how vital it was to have teachers and mentors as a counterforce to the limitations a child might be unable to escape at home.

But she never saw writing *It Takes a Village* as a retreat.

While his wife was wrestling with her muse, Bill Clinton entered his own season of high anxiety. He had to fight off Newt Gingrich. Such were the proportions of the Speaker's ego inflation, Clinton felt it necessary to declare that "the President is relevant."[34] Newt and the Republicans insisted on a balanced budget in seven years—with tax cuts and without regard to the slashing of the safety net of entitlements—or else they would let the government shut down. They were certain Clinton could be rolled. But he called their bluff.

On November 14, some 800,000 federal workers were sent home. The Republicans said that nobody noticed or cared. But government contracts worth billions were put on hold, choking many small businesses. The Grand Canyon and other national parks were closed to the public for the first time since Teddy Roosevelt created them. And with Thanksgiving around the corner, nearly a million government employees faced the prospect of no paychecks. They did notice.

Clinton kept to the high road. Gingrich, in a rambling tirade, revealed to reporters the very personal reason for the shutdown: the fact that he had felt snubbed by the President on their funeral trip to Israel had been "part of why you ended up with us sending down a tougher interim spending bill."[35] It was the first public display of Newt's dangerous thirst for power, but Clinton himself wasn't at all sure that his own strategy was a winning one. "He was scared to death, high-strung, constantly worried," says Morris. "And tremendously insecure."[36]

By the fourth day of the shutdown, things inside the White House were getting pretty dicey. The bathrooms were being cleaned only once a day instead of twice. The pastry chef was gone, the gym closed. Somebody was going to have to keep the infrastructure going.

Interns. It was discovered that a shutdown, which bars paid employees from working for nothing, did not apply to interns. So 135 of them were called in to work the phones, respond to mail, and keep the pizza coming.

As a prisoner in the White House, Clinton is often deprived of the kind of spontaneous up-close human contact that is his oxygen. His life had been Work, Work, Work for how many years? And what had it cost him? Didn't he deserve something to help him take the pressure off? A giddy snow-day atmosphere now prevailed around the White House. A former staffer close to Clinton, who saw him in workaholic mode day by day and for long periods during crises or campaigning, surmises, "When he turns to sexual predation, he's rewarding himself: 'I've been a good boy, worked my ass off—I deserve a little hootchie here.' "

"One night she brought me some pizza," Clinton would later testify innocently.

But even before that, Monica Lewinsky seized her chance to snare the attention of the President of the United States. On the second day of the shutdown, after flirtatious signals had passed between the President and the intern all day, she was waiting for him when he found her in an inner office. The thong that launched a thousand subpoenas was flicked before the President's hungry eyes. He paid attention. Later in the evening he beckoned the twenty-two-year-old into an empty office and began banal chitchat. "Where did you go to school?" he asked. Monica blurted out, "You know, I have a really big crush on you." Within minutes the President of the United States was kissing her, telling her she was beautiful and that her energy lit up a room.[37] The cheapest thrill was yet to come. With Monica down on her knees pleasuring him, he picked up the phone to talk to a congressman. "Clinton loves to degrade people without them knowing it," says the spouse of a high Clinton administration official. "I think that was probably the high point of their relationship."

On November 21, when the shutdown ended, the President thanked the interns for doing a "heroic job."[38] He and Dick Morris met in the residence to enjoy a brief gloat. Morris said he was eager to get back to Connecticut to see his wife. Walking the strategist to the elevator, Clinton pointed with a thumb over his shoulder back to the bedroom. "I'm going home to get reacquainted with my wife, too."[39]

CHAPTER FIFTEEN

First Woman of the World

Human rights are women's rights. And women's rights
are human rights, once and for all.

—HILLARY RODHAM CLINTON

Could the First Lady of the United States go to China and criticize its government for its authoritarian practices in dealing with women, children, and political activists? The very thought made traditionalists in the White House and the State Department shudder.

The United Nations Fourth World Conference on Women was being hosted by China in Beijing in early September 1995. It would be the largest UN gathering in history, bringing together women who stood for every religious and political tradition but who presumably shared the supra-ideological goal of achieving basic legal and human rights and the chance to participate fully in the political life of their countries. "This was one of those foundational events that Hillary felt strongly she should do," says her chief of staff, Melanne Verveer. "More people thought she should *not* go. The President was supportive, but he was also concerned—there were issues with Harry Wu and whether or not an appearance by the First Lady would advance the human rights issue or make it worse."[1] Beijing had refused to release from prison the Chinese-American human rights agitator Harry Wu, ensuring an international outcry.

"Wu is me" was the phrase of that summer in Hillaryland. The First Lady and her staff had been working the whole previous year to shape the American delegation and decide which issues should be on the agenda. Now they were all on standby. Madeleine Albright, then U.S. ambassador to the UN, was the official head of the delegation. Hillary was named honorary chair, but officials decreed she could go only if the Chinese gave up Harry Wu. Literally at the last minute, they did. The few staffers in Hillaryland not on vacation went into locked-down, heat-seeking-missile mode and planned hops from Hawaii to American Samoa to Cambodia, to Thailand, and to Mongolia before they arrived in China. The President's press secretary, Mike McCurry, issued a statement to the effect that the First Lady would not make news in China.

"If she goes and doesn't say something, I'll be hurt, because I work for a woman who plants her feet and speaks her mind," vowed Hillary's own press secretary, Neel Lattimore.

Hillary does not travel on Air Force One or Two or a 747. She's assigned an old 707 from the mid-Sixties that has had many mishaps. On this trip, she and her aides and her Secret Service detail were crowded in along with Secretary Albright, her aides, and the American delegation. All night long on the flight from Hawaii to American Samoa to Beijing, drafts of Hillary's speech were being passed around. Changes were tossed to Hillary's speechwriter, Lissa Muscatine, who patched up the phrases and tossed it back. The excitement was molecular; it bound the whole team together. When Madeleine Albright was looking for a place to fall asleep, she wandered the corridor between cabins and found Lattimore snoozing on a bench. "Do you mind if I sleep with you?" she teased.

"Make my day."

Chinese officials showed their fear of this event by putting Beijing under virtual martial law for several weeks. When the American president's wife was driven through Tiananmen Square, the Chinese security forces accelerated so fast that Hillary's head snapped back. "They made it perfectly clear she was not to stop and talk to anyone," says Lattimore.[2] Winnie Mandela, the estranged wife of the South African president, was barred at the door of the Great Hall of the People in Beijing and engaged in a shoving match with guards until forced to retreat. Meanwhile, the grassroots assembly of thirty thousand women from NGOs (nongovernmental organizations) had been pushed far outside the city into a muddy tent camp in Hairu. Inside the Great Hall, Chinese president Jiang Zemin mouthed an empty Chinese metaphor in tribute to them: "Women hold up half the sky in human society."[3]

In a hall designed to dwarf the individual, the figure of a blond woman in a pink suit moved across the stage, incongruously feminine against the stark backdrop. At the podium Hillary squared up and planted her feet. No one had to strain to hear her stirring words: "Women comprise more than half the world's population. Women are seventy percent of the world's poor and two thirds of those who are not taught to read and write. . . . Yet much of the work we do is not valued—not by economists, not by historians, not by popular culture, not by government leaders." She moved on to her favorite theme, choice: "We need to understand that there is no one formula for how women should lead their lives. That is why we must respect the choices that each woman makes for herself and her family. Every woman deserves the chance to realize her God-given potential."

With the audience spellbound, the First Lady lambasted China's Communist government for suppressing free speech and the right to assemble at the grassroots women's forum in Hairu. Then she launched into a fusillade of attacks on the abuses of women around the world. She condemned the Chinese practice of starving or drowning baby girls. She condemned genital mutilation and the burning to death of brides for the crime of having a small dowry. She inspired the women at Hairu to make their voices heard loud and clear against selling girls into prostitution, against rape as a tactic of war, against forced abortion or sterilization. Hillary evoked tears in the eyes of women and even hard-boiled male reporters as she wound up with a message as memorable for its time as Eleanor Roosevelt's original declaration on human rights: "Human rights are women's rights. And women's rights are human rights, once and for all."[4]

Her address was an epiphany for the UN delegates, who erupted in rapturous applause. The Chinese officials sat in rigid silence. For Hillary herself, it was a turning point. Her psychological withdrawal had ended. Hillary's comeback began in Beijing.

"Beijing unleashed something extraordinary: pressure by activists all around the world on behalf of women," says her chief of staff, Melanne Verveer, in retrospect. Verveer watched her boss undergo an evolutionary process following that conference: "She only lately came to understand that her office provides her with a way to move issues that she never thought she could do outside of the more traditional ways."[5] Over the next few years she would add to the foreign policy agenda the cause of women victims of rape by paramilitary forces in Bosnia, women refugees, women's access to microcredit, women's contributions to peace plans in Ireland and Israel, and on and on.

With each foreign trip, she gained greater international stature. Hillary Rodham Clinton was becoming known not merely as the First Lady of the United States but as the First Woman of the World.

"THAT LOVELY MEMO"

Back home, Senator D'Amato's hearings were now probing mundane aspects of Hillary's work while at the Rose firm, for the Madison Bank. The subject had reporters snoozing at the press tables. In November 1995, the New York senator began asking questions about Hillary's billing records. The White House response was "They probably are somewhere, but we haven't been able to locate them." D'Amato's ears pricked up: "What do you mean, they're missing?"[6]

Four days after Christmas during their file searches to respond to subpoenas from the committee, Sherburne's SWAT team turned up a damaging memo. It had been written by presidential administrative assistant David Watkins as a "soul cleaning." The Watkins memo blew the First Lady's cover wide open. It had not been he who had decided to fire the seven travel office employees, as he had previously stated; according to his memo it was Mrs. Clinton who wanted the travel office staff fired. Watkins wrote that there would be "hell to pay" if he "failed to take swift and decisive action in conformity with the First Lady's wishes."[7]

Sherburne was unnerved. "That lovely memo," as she calls it, might be the smoking gun D'Amato was looking for. Hillary was informed. The memo was passed around the White House lawyers for four days as if it were too hot to touch. On January 3, they turned it over to the committee and the story went out on the wires. The White House braced for another war.

The very next morning, the Clintons' closest personal assistant, Carolyn Huber, suddenly "found" Hillary's Rose firm billing records. They had been under subpoena for two years by a total of five investigatory bodies[8] (D'Amato's Senate Whitewater Committee; the House Banking Committee; Kenneth Starr's office; the RTC; the FDIC). A jittery Huber called the Clintons' personal attorney, David Kendall, to report her find. She said she had moved a table while cleaning up her office and found the records in a box of memorabilia on the floor. Later that day, three White House lawyers went to her office to quiz her.

"Well, here they are," Huber said as she handed over the fat roll of over-sized computer printouts to Jane Sherburne, Hillary's scandal manager. Sherburne immediately recognized the green-and-white-striped paper used by law firms for billing records. She opened them up and right at the top read "Rose Law Firm—Madison Guaranty Savings and Loan, Matter of." Flipping pages, she found the notations written in red ink by Hillary's deceased protector Vince Foster. It was even worse than Sherburne had thought; this would be seen by investigators as the evidence they suspected had been removed from Foster's office, raising the possibility of obstruction of justice.

"And where were these?" Sherburne demanded.

Distressed to the point of trembling, Huber stammered that she had earlier come across them on a table in the Book Room on the third floor of the residence. That set off more alarm bells for Sherburne. The Book Room was next door to a room Hillary sometimes used as an office. After a brief huddle with the other lawyers, Sherburne went back at Huber with more probing questions. How did these records get from the Book Room to her office? When? What was the sequence? Huber became very confused. She had brought them over from the residence three months ago, she said; no, maybe five months ago; no, ten months; maybe eight months.

The Clintons' attorneys were left without even the makings of good spin. Starr's deputies would seize on the appearance that key evidence about a suspect had been hidden in the suspect's private quarters. "Nobody knows the real story with the billing records," Sherburne maintained. David Kendall said that Hillary Clinton had been unaware that the records were in the White House. He did not know how to explain why records he had told the D'Amato committee, in effect, did not exist or couldn't be found, had suddenly surfaced. Kendall acknowledged that he had called Mrs. Clinton that morning to inform her of the discovery of the billing records. She was surprised, he said, but not alarmed.[9] Quickly recovering his élan, Kendall put out the story that Mrs. Clinton was relieved that the documents had been found. He argued that they were consistent with her testimony that she had done minimal work for Madison.

But the discovery of "that lovely memo" and the sudden surfacing of Hillary's documents revived the thorny issue of her involvement with Mc-Dougal's failed bank and brought to light further information about her efforts for Madison on the Castle Grande deal. The number of hours she had worked was not the issue. It was the fact that she had not only repeatedly claimed she did little work for Madison, but that she also had insisted she was ignorant of what was going on.

Twice, earlier, Hillary had been interviewed by federal agencies and claimed she knew nothing about the Castle Grande deal. Using a semantic dodge, she had claimed that she knew this real estate tract as IDC (Industrial Development Corporation). But evidence showed that from the time Madison's board members first discussed the purchase of these land parcels, the project became widely known as Castle Grande by most of the people involved in it. Arkansas newspapers consistently referred to it by that name, as did government officials.[10]

Hillary had just recently told Resolution Trust Corporation investigators that she did not have any recollection of having worked on the option agreement that she had in fact written for Seth Ward. The first report by the Resolution Trust Corporation on its investigation of the Rose firm, issued in December 1995, had accepted her story and said that "little was known" about what the firm did for Madison after the Castle Grande property was purchased, and that "the option . . . does not prove any awareness on the part of its author [Hillary] of Ward's arrangements with Madison Financial."[11] As late as January 1996, she told Barbara Walters on ABC-TV that "Castle Grande was a trailer park on a piece of property that was about a thousand acres big. I never did work for Castle Grande."[12]

But when Hillary's famously missing billing records were mysteriously discovered by her closest aide in the White House in January 1996—only a week after the first RTC report—it was revealed that she had put in sixty hours of work for Madison over fifteen months. And much of it involved the flurry of transactions around the thousand-acre Castle Grande swampland project. The records showed that Hillary had had fourteen meetings or conversations with Seth Ward, later found by federal regulators to be the "straw" purchaser in a "sham" real estate deal—Castle Grande—financed by Madison.[13]

The RTC issued a revised report in June 1996 saying "the firm in general and Mrs. Clinton in particular had far more contact with Ward than was previously known." Presented with evidence by the RTC of her many meetings with Ward in late 1984 and early 1985 concerning the whole thousand-acre Castle Grande or IDC property, Hillary admitted in a subsequent RTC interview that the records showed "there was a period of time when I had . . . intense contact with Mr. Ward on some matters. . . . He was Madison as far as I was concerned."[14] The billings also verified her call to the state securities commissioner appointed by her husband, Beverly Bassett Schaffer, who had the power to keep Madison afloat.

The obvious question left hanging is: Why didn't Hillary Rodham Clinton make it her business to understand the whole deal in which she had been acting as counsel for over a year? And why did she involve herself with such risky people as Jim McDougal and Seth Ward? It shouldn't have been hard for a sharp attorney to learn what a corrupt institution Madison was, along with the people who were using it to bilk money from the taxpayers. She had known the notorious McDougal for ten years before actively seeking him and his bank as her client. From her losses in the Whitewater land deal, she had painful personal experience with his overblown promises and erratic behavior; she knew he lacked any credentials as a banker; and she also knew that his S and L was already under close supervision by federal regulators since 1984 when it showed the first signs of failing. I asked Jane Sherburne, Hillary's attorney, why the First Lady of Arkansas had even abided Jim McDougal.

"She's a political wife," was the answer. "This guy had a connection to Fulbright [the powerful Arkansas senator]. He was a political player in the state."[15]

Perhaps she didn't know that Madison needed to be protected from looting by its owners, or she didn't want to know, or she believed Webb Hubbell would protect her. Hubbell was later to be found guilty of falsifying his own billing records and bilking his clients out of almost $400,000. He was sentenced to twenty-one months in a federal prison. In 1998, Hubbell was indicted two more times, for tax evasion and—more pertinent to Hillary— "that he schemed to conceal and obstruct the truth about the Rose Law Firm and its relationship with the Castle Grande real estate project."[16]

KEEPING THE CLOSET LOCKED

Doubt and mystification have been expressed by many sources as to why these records could not be found. Carolyn Huber was handed the Clintons' personal files that were removed from the White House office of Vince Foster office in the days after his July 1993 suicide. Two days after Foster's death, Hillary had asked Huber to transfer the documents to a locked closet in the personal quarters of the White House. They were kept in the Book Room next to a space that Hillary used occasionally as an office.[17]

Twelve days after Huber had stunned White House lawyers by telling them the documents had suddenly appeared on a table in the Book Room, Hillary's faithful retainer testified under oath before the Senate Whitewater Committee. Her small blue eyes were magnified by serious reading glasses as she stared up at the senators and told her story. Her nails meticulously lacquered, the administrator held up the bulky roll of billing memos. Yes, she acknowledged, she had gone into the Book Room in the first or second week of August 1995 to pick up some magazine and newspaper clippings. On the edge of a long table in the room she had noticed these documents.

Did she notice as she picked them up what kind of documents they were? Counsel asked her.

She stammered: "I just thought it was, it looked sort of like stuff. You know, billing memos . . . they were folded. I didn't open them . . . I just picked them up and clumped them down in that box that was already there with the knickknacks on it. . . . And I thought it looked like maybe computer printouts of billing memos. I didn't open it up to verify it. It was just from working in the law firm I thought that is what it looked like."

Next, she said, she called the usher's office and asked them to carry the box down to her office. She directed them to put the box on the floor under a table. She never opened it up or catalogued what was in it. It had been sitting on the floor in her office for four months before she noticed it again on January 4 and looked inside and realized what they were.[18]

Some committee members lauded Huber's appearance, but it was a rather bizarre account for an efficient administrator. Huber had been through months of searches with White House counsel David Kendall for these very documents, in response to subpoenas, even before she first came across them in August 1995. Some of the strongest suspicions surrounding the billing records were expressed to me by Hillary Clinton's own scandal-managing attorney, Jane Sherburne. I asked her what was Hillary's theory about the disappearance and reappearance of her billing records?

There was a long pause.

"You would die to have somebody keep your records the way Huber kept the Clintons' records," the lawyer began to explain. "She organized all their personal records, all the employment tax receipts, kept them all indexed. She had been doing this for the Clintons for years. She had been the office manager [in Hillary's law firm] for twelve years. She knew the format of Rose billing records in her sleep. She was the one who helped pack up the personal records for the Clintons when they moved to Washington."

Under the circumstances, Sherburne found Huber's story of how the documents turned up not credible. Sherburne suggested another possible scenario—that the records had been in one of the boxes of Clinton documents that were periodically sent to Huber from the warehouse for her review. If that happened, and if Huber had seen them, Sherburne suggested, "It's hard to imagine she wouldn't know immediately that this had some significance—to find billing records that had been subpoenaed a year and a half before that. Kendall had long since been through all the documents."

To suddenly have them turn up under Carolyn's nose, Sherburne postulated, could have shown the aide's carelessness. "She's a very proud and careful person. She would have been faulted for neglecting to locate and identify these documents. My speculation on how her mind was working is, she thought, 'Oh, what have I done?' So, not wanting to think about it, she puts the records on a shelf. They eventually end up in her East Wing office. That's where they were in January when she outed them."

Why, then, would Huber "out" them six months later, in January 1996?

The Watkins memo had surfaced or been leaked, Sherburne explained. "D'Amato is making an issue out of the absence of the billing records. Carolyn is no dummy. At this point she understands the significance of those records. So she then picks up the phone and calls Kendall and me and says, 'I've got something I think you ought to see.' "[19]

Sherburne seemed convinced in our interviews that Huber was responsible. But she never answered my question about Hillary's theory, and her speculation left out any mention of who could have prompted Huber to do this. Given the many accounts of how intimidating Hillary was to anyone on the White House staff, it is highly unlikely that Huber would have acted on her own. It is possible that when, as Sherburne said, the heat got turned up, somebody realized that the billing records had to be "found." Starr was considering calling Hillary before the grand jury. Also, Hillary was about to set off on a book tour that was supposed to rehabilitate her image. If somebody did direct the First Lady's faithful personal aide to "discover" the billing records, Hillary had to be given deniability.

Conceivably, Huber could have been made the fall guy. Most employers, if they learned an assistant had decided on her own that she was going to hide subpoenaed evidence to cover up her sloppy record-keeping, would fire her on the spot. Hillary never even criticized Huber, according to Sherburne. The faithful family retainer retired from the White House two years later, in February 1998, and went back to Arkansas. She has since moved to Texas. Huber did not respond to written queries about Sherburne's account of her actions.

All Alone at the Top

The first two weeks of 1996 were a low point for Hillary. All revved up to begin her book tour, she was slapped in the face by William Safire, a former Nixon speechwriter, who in a *New York Times* column called her a "congenital liar." If President Clinton weren't the President, said White House press secretary Mike McCurry, "he would have delivered a more forceful response to the bridge of his [Safire's] nose." But the President's attention was elsewhere.

On Sunday, January 7, Washingtonians awoke to find their city smothered in the biggest snowstorm of the decade. Pennsylvania Avenue was heaped with two feet of the white stuff as plows gave up and high winds shredded the air. The Clintons, appearing cheerfully devout, did not allow the blizzard to keep them from attending Sunday services at the Foundry United Methodist Church. The President was photographed playfully packing a snowball as he walked toward home with Hillary.[20]

That afternoon, Clinton called Monica Lewinsky at her home for the first time. He invited her to meet him at the White House; he was "going in to work" in about forty-five minutes. He had mentioned to Monica that people were already whispering that he had a crush on an intern, yet he was ready to entertain her in the sanctum of democracy.

The intern cajoled her brother into driving her from the Watergate apartments, where she was living with her mother, through the whiteout to the White House. Up until then, Monica had thought that her escapade with the President had been no "different from the millions of other women that he's been with or flirted with or seemed to be attracted to."[21] But this she thought of as their first date—and in the Oval Office! There they retired to the President's bathroom and were intimate for half an hour. Then Monica took a seat in what the lovers called "her chair," to the right of the desk of the commander in chief. The President chewed on a cigar. Monica saw him as like a little boy who'd had his sweets. She melted.

A week later Hillary got caught in another swirl of lies and cover stories. On Diane Rehm's popular NPR radio talk show, Hillary offered new information regarding the nettlesome 1992 Jeff Gerth story in *The New York Times* that had become the open sore called Whitewater. Hillary said she had sent her staff up to New York four years before with the documents pertaining to Whitewater and laid them out before *Times* editors. The newspaper got a transcript of that day's radio interview. Incensed, the Washington bureau chief called the White House press office to notify them that Mrs. Clinton was wrong and that they were going to run a front-page story essentially calling the First Lady a liar. Jane Sherburne recalls how "I called Susan Thomases and the other person who had gone to New York and done the open kimono. I told her Hillary made this statement. Susan said, 'We didn't do that.' Hillary was completely shocked."

Again, Hillary's defenders were making it sound as if she had been out of the loop when the most sensitive, potentially incriminating matters concerning her were being decided. I asked Sherburne how it could be that for four years—from the time of the Gerth story in 1992 to Hillary's interview on the Diane Rehm show in 1996—she had never discussed with one of her best friends, Susan Thomases, how and why the original Gerth White-water story had backfired on them.

"In '96, when I was dealing with this, Hillary did not connect the dots for me," she said.

The very same day, as the scandal manager was about to call her client, who was on the road promoting her book, another bombshell fell. It made the radio show flap look like child's play. Independent counsel Starr was about to drop a subpoena on the First Lady, requiring her appearance before his grand jury. No more favors, no more cozy depositions held in the White House Treaty Room; he wanted Mrs. Clinton alone. Sherburne thought it was pure evil.

"I can't take this anymore," Hillary moaned when Sherburne reached her on the road to tell her all the bad news. She would have to issue a retraction for her radio show gaffe. But how could she face being dragged into a federal courthouse as a criminal suspect? "How can I go on?" she wailed, her emotions spilling over their usual barrier. "How can I?"[22]

Since Starr was bound and determined to turn this into a circus, Hillary and Sherburne agreed on adopting a "head held high strategy"—like whistling when you know someone's mad at you. There would be no sneaking in back doors or ducking the press and debasing her office. The first wife of a president to testify before a grand jury would sweep in the front door of the E. Barrett Prettyman Federal Courthouse and slay the dragon.

Hillary made one big mistake, Sherburne admits. She wore a thick black felt cloak with a sequined dragon on the back—that made her look like the Dragon Lady. Inside, she and Sherburne stood in the doorway of a witness room and watched the grand jurors file in; they were mostly middle-aged black women, natural supporters of the Clintons. Then the prosecutors filed past: One white male. A second white male. A third white male. Hillary and Sherburne were both counting. Their lips moved in unison, "Nine white male prosecutors."

Looking at the twenty-three jurors, normal people who might be responsive to her story, Hillary found herself trying to explain and win them over instead of sticking to dry factual answers. That was another mistake.

In fact, in a grand jury room there is only one person with power. A well-worn defense attorney rubric warns that "A grand jury will indict a ham sandwich if the prosecutor recommends it."

One of the jurors came up to Hillary after her testimony and asked her to autograph his copy of *It Takes a Village*. She turned to Starr: Is this permissible? He said fine, go ahead. That juror was later dismissed.

During breaks in the four-hour testimony, Sherburne debriefed her client to learn what questions had been asked and how Hillary had replied. This is standard practice so the defense attorney can create his or her own record. Sherburne's notes were later subpoenaed. She couldn't believe it. She tried to reason with Starr's deputy, John Bates: "John, c'mon, my notes are only going to track your transcript. What do you need my notes for?"

Sherburne was incredulous at Bates's reply: "Well, if you wrote something down like 'Hillary said it's a good thing they didn't ask me this because I would have lied.'"

Coming from an established Washington law firm, Sherburne was well aware that she would have been obligated to come forward to the Justice Department with any knowledge of wrongdoing if she had any. But Starr would take the matter all the way to the Supreme Court, and in 1997 he would get her notes. Sherburne had left the White House by then and never heard another thing about it. "That led me to the conclusion the whole fight was political," she said. "They never had any serious or legitimate interest in the notes."[23]

The President looked in on Hillary and her attorney the night of her grand jury appearance. The two women were back in the White House solarium, still working. Still debriefing. It was dark. Hillary was dead tired. Clinton, by contrast, look handsome and fresh in a tux; he was on his way to a reception. How did it go? he asked. He gave his wife a hug. His manner was affectionate, concerned, but only briefly interested.

Late that night, Senator Christopher Dodd called the White House residence, intending to leave a message of concern for the First Lady. Dodd is a stalwart Democrat whom the President trusts as a friend and often calls upon as a golfing partner, knowing he will absorb Clinton's fits and fuming without asking questions. Dodd is more inclined to call when things are tough. "Most of us assume that high-profile people have important people calling them all the time, which I've found not to be the case," says the Irishman. "Especially when there's bad news, a friendly voice is very welcome."

To Senator Dodd's amazement, Hillary answered the phone herself. She sounded achingly lonely. Sitting up there in the residence all alone, she told him no one else had called.[24]

GLIDING ACROSS COUNTRY

Oh, how we love to see the mighty fall. Hillary had set herself up as a moral and ethical pillar, nauseatingly self-righteous, and people delighted in finding her feet of clay. In the midst of the unceasing attacks orchestrated by Bob Dole's unofficial campaign manager, Al D'Amato, it was predicted that she would be forced to retreat from her public role or face a hostile media and suspicious crowds.

But her book tour was a stroke of genius. She used it as a nearly shatterproof frame behind which to display her most heartfelt causes, from saving children to school uniforms to the V chip. As she sailed across the country, looking straight ahead, a hundred-watt smile ready to be switched on at the first sign of hostility, she would tell audiences her book was the result of a quest to learn "how we can make our society into the kind of village that enables children to grow into able, caring, resilient adults."[25]

The itinerary was arranged to put her in cities with key bookstores that report to *The New York Times* best-seller list, such as The Tattered Cover in Denver, Book Passages in Mill Valley, and A Clean, Well-Lighted Place for Books in San Francisco. By the time she reached that most liberal of cities, Hillary was able at last to let her breath out. They love her there.

Evereee day-yea is a day-yea of Thanksgiving!

A large swaying choir in bright blue robes and African kinte cloth sings out over the blast of rock music as hundreds pack into the pews of San Francisco's Glide Church. All at once Hillary materializes on stage in a brilliant red suit. Her eyes widen in flashes of recognition of friends in the audience. Behind her, projections of the publicity shot for her book show a laughing Hillary embedded in a multicultural cluster of smiling, singing kids.

The celebrity pastor, Cecil Williams, rocks over to the microphone and calls out, "We've got two women preachers here tonight: Hillary and Janice [his Asian wife]. We're going to send you out on fire!"

Hillary opens with a beautiful political touch. She tells how she and the President were at Camp David on Thanksgiving weekend: "We were just sittin' around readin' the paper when the President read that you here at Glide feed so many people on Thanksgiving. So the President picked up the phone and called Cecil to thank him. When I come to Glide, I'm coming to thank *you*. There are so many churches in America that could become Glide Churches."

Tell it! The audience starts rhythmically applauding.

"*All* these children are our children." Hillary sweeps her hand around the church. She segues into the theme of her book, community support: "It may be going next door and saying to that young single mother, 'Why don't you take a break and go out for a while and I'll look after your child.' "

Amen!

She launches into a very personal story to show she's not a know-it-all: "There I was, trying to breast-feed my baby [Chelsea], and all of a sudden she starts foaming at the nose. The nurse surveyed the scene and said, 'Mrs. Clinton, it would help if you lifted her head up.' " As the audience laughs, Hillary shakes her head self-mockingly. "All those years of schooling, all those degrees, it was no help." Then the windup: "For all the talk about family values in this country, we do so little to value families."[26]

Tell it, Hill-a-reee!

She is bathed in a wave of applause. Overcome by the embrace of unconditional love, a few chunks of her armor fall away, and before our very eyes Hillary Rodham Clinton—the purported cold fish—shudders and sobs.

Later that evening when she addresses an audience of 4,500 at the Masonic Auditorium in San Francisco, the feisty Hillary is back on display. She retells the story of how, as a four-year-old, she moved into a new house in a new neighborhood. The kids used to torment her, pushing her, knocking her down, until she would burst into tears and run back in the house. One day her mother took her by the shoulders and said, "There is no room for cowards in this house," and sent her back outside. This time, Hillary said, she shocked the kids by standing up for herself. In the retelling, Hillary gives the story a new twist: "I guess in every new house I move into, I have to hear that lesson again."

Her predominantly female audience roars with sympathetic laughter. But Hillary left out the most telling part of the story, the literal punch line: she had punched her tormentor—another girl child—in the nose.[27]

Hillary's book was a genuine hit, resting for twenty weeks on the bestseller lists. It would even earn her a Grammy (for the best spoken word on an album), which tickled both her and the President and allowed her an unusual star turn at Madison Square Garden in a gold gown by Oscar de la Renta—followed by the Smashing Pumpkins and the Fugees.[28]

OPEN NECKS

Hillary's rehabilitation was essential. It was a reelection year. The big issue was welfare reform, a hangover from Clinton's 1992 campaign, when he had promised to "end welfare as we know it." Since Clinton had begun talking about it again in late 1995, Hillary had stayed in the wings, but behind the scenes she told Dick Morris, "Our liberal friends are just going to have to understand that we have to go for welfare reform—for eliminating the welfare entitlement. They are just going to have to get used to it. I'm not going to listen to them or be sympathetic to them."[29]

In June, Hillary was asked by *Time,* "Do you think it makes sense to force a single mother of a young child to go to work instead of staying home and taking care of the child?" It was the choice question, again, on which Hillary had stumbled with her cookie-baking answer. But now it was even more perilous because they were talking about poor women.

"I've thought about that a lot," she told editor Walter Isaacson. "I think getting up and going to work, going to school, and having to make the same difficult decisions about who cares for your children that every other working mother has to make is a necessary step toward learning how to be self-sufficient. Yes, people who are physically able to work ought to work." Her backup was two other issues she has consistently promoted: "I think they ought to have childcare support, and they ought to have some benefits to take care of their children medically."[30]

In August, the President pushed the welfare reform bill through Congress and deprived the Republicans of a key weapon they had intended to use against him in the election. The Clintons were clicking together again. But Hillary's approval rating was at an all-time low. That's when Morris talked to her about "open necks."

Morris describes how he passed on "a lot of psychobabble someone had given me about women who wear open-collared shirts being seen as more open. I told Hillary they were critical of her for wearing closed collars and always wearing synthetic loud colors."

Hillary screamed at him, "I get colds! And I'm not going to get colds, so I'll wear high-necked things. I will dress how I please. I think I look *good* in these colors." Morris had touched a raw nerve. Hillary's final words on the subject were "If my husband can't get reelected as President of the United States with me dressing as I want, then I guess he's not going to get reelected."

Morris tried another tack, coaching her in how to pose for photos. "You should look warm toward the camera," he said.

"I do. But there's not one camera, Dick. There are four hundred cameras. All around me. Every angle. All snapping away pictures," said an exasperated Hillary. "Then they choose the picture that's the worst one they could possibly run. The ones where I look mean."

She went on to express her general dismay at the media in Washington. "You know, I assumed when I came to Washington there would be all these liberated feminist reporters, and I could be more myself," she complained. "But the Washington press corps is worse than Arkansas ever was."[31]

Later, when Helen Thomas was finally granted her first and only one-on-one interview with the First Lady, the veteran journalist reminded her that she had a reputation for being hostile to the press. Hillary said, "No, I don't think that is valid." But she was smiling. She acknowledged, "I think I had a big learning curve that I had to really catch up on, because I was not that familiar with the mores of Washington."[32]

In the summer of 1996, however, Hillary was not rolling with the punches. Feeling beleaguered, she was taking everything quite personally, even from her few friends in the press. Over the Fourth of July holiday she made a trip to Central Europe. The networks and CNN all sent reporters with her. "We were on scandal watch," says Martha Teichner, who was again covering her old Wellesley classmate for CBS-TV news. There was concern among news organizations that at any minute the First Lady might be indicted by Ken Starr. Teichner recalls, "Everyone felt very queasy, so we passed around the task of asking the questions our editors back home were hounding us to ask."[33]

In the Czech Republic, at a hospital founded by Václav Havel in memory of his late wife, it was Teichner's turn to ask the day's dirty question: "Did you hire Craig Livingston in connection with the FBI scandal?" (Livingston was a former bar bouncer, hired as director of the White House Office of Personnel Security, who obtained hundreds of FBI files on former Reagan and Bush administration appointees—the scandal known as Filegate.)

Hillary's face went blank. Maintaining her composure, she said she knew nothing about it. Later, her press secretary Neel Lattimore exploded at Teichner: "The First Lady was furious that you asked this question. Particularly since you have known her so long. She expected more of you."

Mortified, the correspondent stood up for herself: "Neel, I have to ask these questions. I was sent to ask these questions. How I use the information in my story is something else. Given my track record with you people—I've been with you in five countries—I would hope the First Lady would wait to see the story I do. If you want to yell at me, yell at me then." Knowing her ex-classmate, Teichner figured that Neel had been first in line to take Hillary's tongue-lashing and had passed it on to her.

"She was struggling with her own identity as First Lady and her identity with the press," says Teichner in retrospect. "On those trips she was doing things she passionately believes in—the issues she covered in *It Takes a Village*—and trying desperately to be taken seriously on that basis. She had learned to use the tools of the press and avoid any uncontrolled exposure. It was no different than what Ronald Reagan did—making people see one thing when the substance was quite different." At a dinner for the press in Prague, Hillary insisted that Teichner be seated beside her. "She even held my hand at one point. No mention of the incident, but she let me know she had rethought it, and it made me like her more."

At the end of the Central Europe trip, reporters asked for a wrap-up press conference. Hillary resisted but eventually agreed. As the session wound down, she said, "Okay, now I'm going to ask *you* some questions. Why does this keep happening to me? Why are people dogging me like this? What's wrong here?"

A White House correspondent for the *Associated Press* leveled with her: "If the public saw the Hillary we see in the back of the plane, you wouldn't have any problems."[34] He was referring to the relaxed, humorous, sarcastic, self-deprecating, down-to-earth person who would saunter to the back of the plane every time they took off and chat with reporters—a person the public never sees.

IGNORING MIDDLE AGE

A huge fund-raising extravaganza was built on the back of Bill Clinton's fiftieth birthday, an event the chief baby boomer was quoted as saying he'd "just as soon ignore." The gala at New York's Radio City Music Hall on August 18, 1996, featured a three-hundred-pound cake and netted $10 million for the Democrats' fall campaign. Hillary, as usual, did the introduction. But her tribute was more fulsome than ever. She described the President as the best man she had ever known.

Perhaps chagrined, Clinton responded, "I'm sure I'm not the best man she has ever known, but I sure have loved her and my wonderful child."[35]

Society orchestra leader Peter Duchin had been asked to play a cocktail dance for the heavy hitters at the Waldorf-Astoria. The minute the First Couple arrived, Clinton began working the room. "He's even better than Jack Kennedy," noted Duchin. "Clinton wants to fuck everyone in the room—but his way is 'Let's be buddies,' more of a common touch. Jack was more like the prince." Hillary, far less comfortable in such situations, made a beeline for the bandleader. They always chatted about Pamela Harriman, since Duchin's stepfather Averell Harriman had been among the great courtesan's husbands. Pamela had been given a plum appointment by Clinton: ambassador to France. Duchin teased Hillary about getting the beautiful grande dame out of Washington.

"I'm not stupid," said Hillary with her famously bawdy belly laugh.

The couple danced, not in a particularly graceful or fluid way. Observing them from his bandstand, Duchin realized he had never before seen them dance cheek to cheek. "What one notices is the way she looks at him, knowing that people are looking at her and totally aware of what they are seeing. It's much more studied even than Jackie," who had been a close friend of the musician. "With Hillary, it's as if she's entering his body, penetrating him. He says something funny, she laughs. You get the feeling there's an emotional closeness between them that is very unusual. But I don't get that it's sexual."[36]

Besides the pressure of the upcoming November presidential election, the Clintons had a more personal deadline to discuss: with Chelsea's departure only a year away, the Clintons would soon lose their most elemental personal bond, their one emotional oasis. Hillary was feeling the impending void. And she wasn't getting any younger either—she was forty-eight. A woman who had been told in her thirties that she could not bear another child perhaps could be forgiven for harboring a passing illusion in midlife that she might still be fertile. When Hillary told *Time* that summer, "I must say we're hoping that we have another child," she was asked if that meant a natural birth. "I have to tell you I would be surprised"—she laughed— "but not disappointed. My friends would be appalled, I'm sure." She went on to talk enthusiastically about adoption. It had been an off-and-on discussion between Bill and Hillary for a long time, she said. "I think we're talking about it more now. We'd obviously wait to get serious about it until after the election."[37]

For even floating the idea of bearing or adopting another child, she was mocked: too old. But her premonition of loneliness was to be proven accurate in the fall of 1997, when Chelsea flew three thousand miles away from her parents to enter Stanford University in California. Shortly after her daughter's departure, Hillary told a Miami banquet audience, "I'm looking for ways to divert myself from the empty nest. And I'll take just about any invitation to dinner that I can get."[38]

Characteristically, she would divert herself by assuming an even larger cause. She called Al From, director of the Democratic Leadership Council, the week after both of their daughters had gone off to college. After a long commiseration about empty nesting, Hillary told him of her plan to take their Third Way philosophy international. "Clinton had mentioned that maybe we could do an international conference, but Hillary is the one who grabbed it," says From admiringly.[39]

Two months after Chelsea left, Hillary would begin by spreading the word through Britain's newly elected Labour prime minister, Tony Blair. The two would hold a quiet, daylong conference at Chequers in November 1997 to discuss what the New Democrats and New Labour could do internationally to promote their common vision for a Third Way. "The President is spectacular on the subject, but other than him, there's nobody who comes close to Hillary's articulation of the Third Way message," says From.[40] An American who participated in the secret mini-summit at Chequers says, "With all due respect to the Prime Minister, Hillary was as insightful in both theory and political strategy as anyone there."

The Clintons held their place in the White House in 1996 with a landslide victory. The second time around, Hillary was not so defensive about appearing to be an independent woman. She was more interested in recapturing the magic between the Bill and Hillary who had felt a compelling magnetism from across the library at Yale Law.

Shortly after the November election, Oscar de la Renta, her court designer, was summoned to the White House to consult on the First Lady's inaugural ball gown.

"Tell me what you want to look like," the elegant Hispanic designer suggested.

"Oh, I don't know, you're the expert," Hillary demurred.

He tried again: "But you should be comfortable. How do you want to look?"

Again, Hillary backed off: "Whatever you come up with will be fine."

Back and forth they went, nine or ten times. Finally, de la Renta asked, "When you walk down the stairs with the President, how do you want to look?"

"I want to look sexy for Bill."[41]

CHAPTER SIXTEEN

Everything There Is to Know

It's like you go through a death and you can't live
for weeks and weeks and weeks.
And then the healing process begins.

—A CONFIDANTE OF HILLARY CLINTON

He lied to her. And she let him.

No one knows exactly what the President did and didn't tell his wife in private in January 1998 after he came home from denying, under oath, having had sexual relations with Jane Doe # 6. The Monica Lewinsky allegations didn't particularly shock Hillary; she accepted Clinton's dissembling and wrote it off as more childish behavior with a young woman who was probably just a groupie like so many of the others.

The real blow for Hillary in that conversation was to learn from her husband that he had acknowledged under oath and was now admitting to the world what he had denied to her, year after year, campaign after campaign, for almost twenty years: yes, he had indulged in a sexual affair with the lounge singer Gennifer Flowers. It might have seemed like "déjà vu all over again," in the immortal words of Yogi Berra, but to Hillary this came as new news, according to several sources.

"Hillary didn't believe that Bill had ever slept with Gennifer Flowers," said Betsey Wright, who is in a position to know what Hillary knew and when, since she was the governor's chief of staff and alter ego in charge of "bimbo eruptions" all through the Arkansas years. "I didn't believe he had. He told me and Hillary and Chelsea there was no truth to the rumors—and God knows, rumors about Gennifer had been dogging us for years." All through the 1992 campaign, Hillary had believed that this was just a shakedown, says Wright. "Absolutely. So much of what Gennifer said was patently false. And *provably* false. We always thought Gennifer Flowers was crazy."[1] In the wake of Clinton's admission under oath in 1998, Betsey still brushed off the matter: "It was not a major relationship—nothing like the twelve years she claims. They had a short-term fling at most."[2]

The woman on the Paula Jones lawyers' list who could have opened a raw wound for Hillary was Jane Doe #1—the beautiful marketing executive who had so captivated her husband, it nearly smashed the Clintons' marriage. If Hillary had cross-examined her husband on that Jane, she might have learned that Danny Ferguson, the Arkansas trooper who was Clinton's codefendant in the Jones case, had sworn under oath to delivering Marilyn Jo Jenkins to the governor for private trysts in the basement of Hillary's Arkansas home. Ferguson had been forced to spill all the details of the disguised woman's furtive farewell visit to Clinton, two floors below his sleeping wife and daughter, on the very morning of their departure for the glory day of the presidential inauguration.[3]

Clinton had denied to his own attorney, Bob Bennett, having had any sexual relationship with Jenkins. But Bennett believed that out of all nine of the Jane Does, Jenkins was "the real one," says another legal adviser to the White House. According to Bob Woodward's book *Shadow,* the night before Clinton gave his deposition, Bennett had boldly confronted him, saying "Mr. President, I find your explanation about one of the women frankly unbelievable." He had run down the 5:15 A.M. meetings with Marilyn Jo Jenkins, the gifts the two had exchanged, the phone records showing that Clinton had placed fifty-nine calls to Jenkins's home or office between 1989 and 1991.

Clinton sat forlorn and wistful through this whole drill, a "tipoff" to his attorney that there was a serious problem. Bennett tried to throw a scare into Clinton, warning "This is what impeachment is made of." If Clinton lied in his deposition, he would be dead. All the morose President would say was, "I hear you."[4]

Jenkins herself had been subpoenaed by the Jones lawyers to give a deposition on November 18, 1997. Wright's standard in deposing the "Jane Does" was that there must have been a connection to Clinton's governmental power, such as a state job given to the woman, or an allegation that she had been solicited by a public employee at Clinton's direction.[5] Jenkins's lawyers made extraordinary efforts to terminate her examination, claiming privacy, but after much legal haggling Judge Wright had ruled that the Jones lawyers could continue questioning Miss Jenkins. The reluctant witness refused to answer questions about sexual intimacy with Clinton or whether she had ridden in official cars with state troopers. Her lawyers filed a brief claiming that "Jane Doe has never at any time had sexual relations with President Clinton," and establishing that she had never been offered a state job or other benefits in exchange for having sexual relations with the President. The key phrase in their brief was that Marilyn Jo Jenkins "has no information regarding any *nonconsensual* touching or sexual advances made by Clinton against herself or any other woman."[6]

Clinton's attorneys made the same distinction in seeking to stop the judge from asking three of the Jane Does, including Marilyn Jo, about having sex with Clinton: "This case is not about whether President Clinton had female friends or whether he had a consensual relationship with any woman other than his wife."[7] Judge Wright's own husband, a distinguished law professor who advised her on her rulings, urged that a man still be permitted at least some personal prerogative: "From what I've heard, a lot of Bill Clinton's women have been satisfied customers."[8] As it turned out, Clinton had to admit to the gifts and phone calls and to visits with Jenkins, but neither the President nor the divorcee had to answer any questions about whether they had a physically intimate relationship. The judge ruled that since Jenkins was not a state employee, she was not a candidate for sexual harassment.

For Hillary, the worm of deceit must have been tunneling somewhere below the level of rational thought for many years. But she had apparently kept building walls, blocking off the doubts beneath her carefully constructed life strategy. Once the Clintons had taken up occupancy in that narrow-halled, overstaffed white house on Pennsylvania Avenue, Hillary had believed that Bill would be more or less exclusively hers, if not because of a change of heart, at least because of a change of opportunity. "Hillary liked living above the store," a friend confided. "He was under a kind of White House arrest, almost always home for dinner with her and Chelsea."[9] Hillary told friends she and her husband had grown closer because they were isolated in their public roles and constantly side by side dodging fire from all corners in a more or less constantly embattled presidency.

"It's very easy to get into a mind-set of 'you and me against the world,' " says Eileen McGann, a wife who knows from her experience with her own wayward husband, Dick Morris. "It creates an inherent paranoia, and it becomes self-destructive, because as long as you can make somebody outside be the enemy, you don't have to address the very difficult personal issues that have to be addressed if you want to have a real relationship."[10]

You poor son of a bitch," commiserated Dick Morris when he phoned the President before noon on January 21, 1998. "I've just read what's going on," referring to the Monica charges in *The Washington Post*.

Clinton's voice was lifeless. It conveyed the subtext *Oh God, have I fucked up this time*. "I didn't do what they said I did, but . . . I may have done enough so that I don't know if I can prove my innocence," the President brooded. "There may be gifts. . . . I gave her gifts. . . . And there may be messages on her phone answering machine." Clinton was unusually unguarded: "You know, ever since the election I've tried to shut myself down. I've tried to shut my body down, sexually. . . . But sometimes I slipped up, and with this girl I just slipped up."[11] When Morris phoned Clinton eleven hours later with the results of an impromptu poll, he gave his judgment that the President should not confess or even try to explain the situation. "Well," said the President, "we just have to win, then." In a heartbeat, Clinton seemed to recover his ability to shut the whole ugly mess outside in the black.

"It's as if a third party did it," Morris marveled, "as if it is some misfortune, like rain. It's totally unconnected with any of his causality."[12]

"He is not an integrated person; he has different personalities," agrees a formerly close aide to the President. "The guy who talks dirty on the golf course isn't the same guy who gives a great speech to the NOW convention."

That a man so dedicated to becoming President, a man who already had an independent counsel and lawyers in a sexual harassment suit breathing down his neck, would act out his sexual fantasies with a gabby, exhibitionist employee defied any rational explanation. The most popular theory among mental health professionals was that the President was a sex addict. He showed the classic signs: recklessness of monumental proportions, inappropriate choice of partner, disregard of the reality of consequences to himself and others.[13]

But in Clinton's case, there is much more to the story. He has an addiction, but only after interviewing a number of close observers, both friends and professionals, was I able to appreciate the subtly layered psychological construct that allows Bill Clinton to be both a convincing leader and a convincing cad. Once he was caught, it was his denial that threatened to destroy him. How could he lie to everyone and to himself for so long?

An intelligent trauma victim can often compartmentalize the psychological wounds of childhood if they are too overwhelming to confront. For Clinton, the shame and rage of growing up in a violent, alcoholic home with no real father to protect him may never have been resolved. Such explosive emotions sit there just below the level of consciousness, sometimes breaking out superficially in sudden thunderstorms of temper but continuing to shape one's life choices. In such instances one seldom learns from exposure. On the contrary, Clinton learned from disaster. He learned that he could always turn it around—provided he denied unpleasant realities and found someone or something else to blame and relied on his wife and friends to cover for him. Time and again he had been in a death spiral but had pulled out of the dive moments before impact. This, of course, had only fueled his fantasy that he was invincible.

FRIENDLY FLINGS

A pattern had developed. When his eternal-adolescent self would slip out and go off on a pleasure binge, Good Boy Bill had to prove that he didn't associate with that callow fellow. It was not he.

"His powers of denial are so highly developed, this is the way he appears to see the world," observes the Reverend Ed Matthews, Hillary's retired pastor in Hot Springs. "As long as no one penetrates his shadow side, he believes he can handle it, God ain't gonna get him."[14]

Bill Curry, an established Connecticut politician who has known alcoholism in his own family, gained special insight into President Clinton when he served as his adviser in 1995 and 1996. "One of the things that happens when you rocket through the social classes," Curry says, "is that the emotionally familiar disappears. In part, Clinton connects to his own emotional origins in some of his behaviors."[15]

His philandering is a secret excursion back to the warm bath of Hot Springs. "If your whole survival has been built on manipulating chaos and learning how to live with role confusion," Curry says, "then you don't know how to establish boundaries or enforce contracts. The chaos in the governor's office was later duplicated in the Oval Office. The way Clinton's White House staff functioned seemed to me rooted in his life experience. People didn't do things on time; they didn't keep commitments or honor contracts. It was a floating adhocracy." Curry sees in retrospect how the whole staff became a network of enablers for Clinton: "We were all living in Hot Springs, every one of us."[16]

Nobody surpassed Hillary in the role of enabler. Every addict or alcoholic needs one. The enabler is usually an intimate of the addicted person who allows him to persist in self-destructive behavior by making excuses or helping him avoid the consequences of his actions. Hillary seems to have no concept of herself as fulfilling this indispensable role in her husband's sexual addiction. The more she "understands" him and excuses his problems as the result of a "vast right-wing conspiracy" and rushes out to defend and protect him, the less responsibility he takes for his own misbehavior. She believes she is doing everything she possibly can to help the hero of their grand narrative. But as a result of her self-delusion, she is doing just the opposite.

Bill Clinton is in many ways the classic philanderer, like a little boy who comes back after being bad and looks for Mother's forgiveness. Hillary provides it. Thus encouraged, his sexual addiction became a craving so compelling, it turned self-destructive. When in 1992 Clinton went before the nation and reaffirmed his commitment to his wife on *60 Minutes*—"This is not an arrangement or an understanding. This is a marriage!"—he apparently did not mean that he intended to curb his enjoyment of other women.

Hillary may have looked the other way, but others did not. A former senior White House attorney confirms that Monica was not Clinton's first fling in the White House: "He'd been accustomed for so long to having the power of being governor and the sex appeal that goes with an official position. Then, too, he had those procuring troopers who were probably getting a little of their own on the side for introducing various women to Clinton. He just came to take it for granted. Then opportunities came at the White House. He didn't take advantage of all the opportunities, but some he did take advantage of. The great majority of them were women he had known for a long time, who were on the staff or from the campaign." The attorney did not want to mention names.

Clinton did do a great deal of open flirting during the 1992 campaign. Some of the women he flirted with ended up in the White House.

Marsha Scott—an Arkansas woman who refers to herself as "his old hippie girlfriend"[17]—was the first volunteer to show up at Clinton's Little Rock campaign office. She helped run his Northern California operation. The two had met through Jim McDougal when they were working on the Fulbright campaign and briefly dated. A former Clinton press secretary thought their romance was rekindled during the 1992 campaign.[18] Miss Scott was rewarded for her efforts with a job in the White House as Director of Presidential Correspondence, promptly firing a number of the older women who had been there for many years. Her self-important style did not cause her any job insecurity. In fact, one night in 1993, the single woman was bold enough to turn up at the door of the White House residence and demand that the usher, Chris Emery, give her and two of Webb Hubbell's daughters a tour of the private quarters. Emery told her the President wasn't home. When she insisted that he ring the First Lady, the usher protested that it was eleven o'clock at night, and the First Lady was already asleep. Miss Scott would not be deterred. The usher could see that she was tipsy. He gave her advice that most people would have taken as the door slammer: she could call the First Lady herself.

She did. Hillary refused to grant her a tour.[19]

By 1997, after holding five jobs in the White House, Miss Scott was earning in excess of $100,000. She was then promoted to chief of staff to the White House personnel director, where she remained as of fall 1999.[20]

Monica Lewinsky herself openly expressed jealousy toward another woman staffer in the White House, a sparkly little platinum blonde from Dallas with dollops of honey in her voice named Debbie Schiff, who Monica believed was a longtime girlfriend of the President.[21] Her name was outed by Starr when he released Lewinsky's tape-recorded phone conversations with Linda Tripp.

Clinton's flirtation with Miss Schiff, a single woman in her mid-forties, began when she was a flight attendant on his 1992 campaign plane, according to a female staff member who traveled extensively with candidate Clinton. "When Hillary traveled with us, which was about twenty percent of the time, he'd clean up his act," she recalls. "He'd stop the lascivious looks that communicated 'If I only had an extra hour . . .' " The Dallas-based girlfriend was later graduated to Air Force One. "When Hillary was along on the plane, the atmosphere was hugely different," says a former presidential adviser, "because he was on guard all the time." Later, Schiff was moved inside to a fancy-titled position in the President's office, where she remained before and after Monica as assistant chief of protocol for ceremonials.[22]

Ms. Schiff denied any sexual relationship with Clinton. But the President's interest in her was widely known around the White House. "She was a lovely woman," says the presidential adviser. "She worships him but had no illusions that he was going to marry her. She was perfect. Then he takes up with this brainless Beverly Hills floozy. Anybody who was already getting sexually serviced in the White House and who fully understood the implications for his presidency of getting caught—the only thing you can say is, he must be sick."

SMILING THROUGH SHAME

It has often been observed that Bill Clinton is one of the most self-obsessed baby boomers that his generation has produced. Yet he is also genuinely capable of feeling others' pain (as he often claims), and he can be passionately committed to alleviating the racism and educational and economic injustices that continue to dim America's shining record. How can one explain this split? Or the split between the adoring father and the supportive husband who can turn around, hours after attending church with his wife and daughter, and dishonor them both? One explanation is suggested by a ranking psychoanalyst in the military health establishment who works for the Clinton Administration and knows the President. "It appears that there is more than one person in him. His emotional reality is in Hot Springs. His intellectual reality is in his wife, who fosters his best self. The split is usually due to traumatic events."[23]

"He was so young, barely four," Hillary explained in an interview, "when he was scarred by abuse that he can't even take it out and look at it. There was terrible conflict between his mother and grandmother."[24]

"This kind of person, who was often abused as a child," explained the psychoanalyst who knows Clinton, "learns how to split off part or parts of themselves to survive." (Remember Clinton saying, "I had to construct my own world.") "When Clinton splits off into his other life, his Hot Springs identity—the one he associates with his mother and a permissive environment—he feels at home and comfortable. But it sometimes ends up being abusive [i.e., he may force himself on women]. When he's caught and lies, it's as if a third person did it."

This may explain why Clinton can cast himself as a victim and why he can become so righteously indignant at his lawyers when they corner him with evidence of sexual profligacy: *It's not him.* Even Bob Bennett was taken aback when the President reportedly sought to identify with his chief counsel as just another blameless dad: "What would you think if your daughter had to listen to this stuff about you?"[25]

Watching his wife on the *Today* show a week after the Monica story broke, seeing her once more step forward to defend his better self, was a second reckoning for Bill Clinton. He heard her tell the world that she and her husband "know everything there is to know about each other."

"The President realized then that he had not only betrayed her in their marriage, but also professionally, in a way that he'd never betrayed her before," believes Neel Lattimore. "That made it all the more difficult for him to be honest with her."[26]

And so, to keep from telling Hillary the full and awful truth, Bill Clinton spread his lies to everyone else.

"Nobody could ever prove it," recounts another former press secretary. "He'd already lied to his lawyer and his aides and gone in front of the American people and wagged his finger and vowed, 'I never had sexual relations with that woman.' I don't doubt that he realized when he saw Hillary on the *Today* show how deeply complicit he was forcing other people to be. But at that point he knew there was no going back."

Clinton didn't confide in Morris what he had told Hillary, but the political consultant is convinced that there are many questions the two don't ask each other. "It's part of the partnership," he says. "She doesn't ask him about the sexual stuff. And he doesn't ask about her commodities investments or her Madison Guaranty transactions."[27]

At this point, the obsessive question in the national conversation was: "Why doesn't she leave him?" The most practical answer was that if she left him then, *she* would have been blamed, along with Monica, for bringing down his presidency. Bill and Hillary Clinton were a team; this was *their* legacy; her self-interest did not lie in further tarnishing the record they had built together. The more pertinent question from her perspective was: How could she leave the White House after all she's endured to get there? Her life strategy, decided long ago, was to take the raw material of this brilliant, emotionally battered child with a good heart and a desperate ambition and shape him into a political star to which she could hitch her wagon full of dreams for changing the world.

It took a Hillary to raise a president.

By this time she had learned to look at the world the way men of power do: never allow the public to see your wounds, and in the face of all obstacles hold on to your life strategy in service of a larger agenda.

Another intriguing question: Why does Hillary often look her most glowing when her husband has shamed her most abysmally?

Every time he gets caught, Clinton concentrates his sexual magnetism on his wife for a change. Still insecure about her feminine attraction, she is once again courted and seduced. He promises (lies) whatever is necessary to get out of the doghouse. Whatever the exact words and body language he uses, they give credibility to her fantasy that everything will be different in the future. At last, if she captures this man who is magnetic to so many women, she will have won.

As Dick Morris says, "Hillary loves Bill, and Bill loves Bill. It gives them something in common."[28]

Hillary has been waiting almost thirty years to be the winner. She never lets it go as far as abandonment. Her fantasy is that eventually she will conquer him. And he fuels the fantasy. White House aides often puzzle over why the Clintons make a display of physical affection in front of their lawyers and staff; most long-married couples don't. "Even in offstage moments, Bill and Hillary would be physically affectionate, holding hands or he'd drape a hand over her shoulder," says one of their former press aides. "He'd stand close to her in an unconscious way. Maybe he does it to make her feel good, to make it look like he's turned on by her. The staff was always wondering, 'Do they do it? Only on her birthday?' "

As this folie à deux has played itself out over the years, Hillary the Wife has been repeatedly pitted against Hillary the Partner. The Clintons' relationship is a business, it's The Firm, but it is also a marriage. It used to be that Hillary the Wife suffered but steeled herself when Bill betrayed her. She had to put on her Hillary the Partner hat to defend and deny and sweep up behind him; she was a high-status abused wife. But it became increasingly apparent in their White House years that when Bill misbehaved sexually, it could be a win-win situation for both Hillary the Wife and Hillary the Partner. She is elevated to the iconic status of a secular saint and Bill looks like the troublemaker. Instead of her identity being subsumed into "Clinton"—vague, unrecognized, just the meddling wife—Hillary gets to be more "Rodham." Still feeling unrecognized for her myriad political contributions, she can assume greater power and step out front.

"It's absolutely true," says a former White House adviser. "Hillary the Partner gets her reward when Hillary the Wife is degraded."

"Hillary doesn't wait for the facts when it comes to his behavior," confided a lawyer close to the case. "She rushes to judgment and turns her anger on their external enemies." This attorney favored settling with Paula Jones, but the First Lady wouldn't have it. "Hillary held out," he says. Concession, even an inch, is not her style. Except when it comes to her husband. I wondered if, when she joined the President and his team for meetings on the Jones sexual harassment suit, the body language between Hillary and Bill had been hostile.

"Quite the opposite," said the lawyer. "It was hand-holding, arms around one another, lots of eye contact." It was the same in their initial meetings about Monica. The lawyer told me, "Hillary's clearly made a decision. She's going to rise or fall with him. So she's going to stand with him."

"She was really beginning to enjoy what she was making of the role of First Lady," says Don Baer, former White House communications director.[29] And then came the Year of Monica. The most ironic turn of the Clintons' twisted relationship was still ahead: As the world's most publicly degraded wife, Hillary, by choosing to stay with her husband, would levitate far above him.

HILLARY'S WAR

For the war on Monica, Hillary recruited Susan Thomases, Mickey Kantor, Dick Morris, Harry Thomason, and Betsey Wright—all combat experts with a tail gunner's focus on protecting the rear. Sidney Blumenthal was also assigned to the front lines "because he divides the world between the white hats and the black hats, just like she does," says a former White House colleague.

"People are always trying to show both of the Clintons they can be aggressive enough against the opposition to prove their mettle," says a former White House speechwriter who was also asked to reenlist in the damage control operation. "The sure way to be in Hillary's inner circle is to show a balls-out, go-to-the-mat mentality about taking on their enemies. Anybody who has a hang-up about fairness is cast out as part of the enemy camp. I find that a little unsettling." This speechwriter declined to do duty on the Lewinsky patrol.

Mike McCurry, who had been planning to leave his post as press secretary early in the year, couldn't bring himself to abandon the troops while they were under assault. "But McCurry was always making sure that he was doing a nudge-nudge, wink-wink about Clinton with the press," says the former speechwriter. "The subtext of his press conferences was 'Okay, I got to say this, but we all know he's a piece of shit.' "

For his part, the President met with Chief of Staff Erskine Bowles and his deputies and told them that there had been no sexual relationship between him and Monica and he had told no one to lie. "And when the facts come out, you'll understand," he reassured them. He told the same story to his Cabinet officers and party leaders. His approval ratings remained abnormally high.

In March, there was another shocker: Kathleen Willey, a widow with Junior League good looks, appeared on *60 Minutes* to describe an encounter with Clinton in which she claimed the President had groped her and placed her hand on his aroused genitals. She didn't mention the unusual circumstances surrounding her visit to the Oval Office. Gene Lyons, a skeptical Arkansas author and journalist, finds her story dubious: "Here's a woman who said that her husband came home one day and told her he had bankrupted the family and would have to sell everything to keep himself out of jail. So they had a big fight, her husband ran away, and the first thing she did was run up to the White House, where the President put his hands on her body, and then she came home and, whoops! her husband is dead. How much of a coincidence is that?"[30]

The day after the *60 Minutes* exposé, President Clinton said he was "mystified and disappointed" by Kathleen Willey's account, and administration officials released nine "admiring" letters she had written to Clinton after the alleged incident. Three days later, Speaker Newt Gingrich and Congressman Henry Hyde dispatched a group of congressmen to Starr's office looking for confirmation that the special prosecutor's team had enough evidence against Clinton to justify the House initiating an impeachment process.

Hillary remained stoic. Fittingly, she told her friend Sara Ehrman that her favorite new book was by an Arkansas novelist named Myra McLary who celebrates "the earthy stoicism of rural women."[31]

Was it an April Fool's Day joke? Out of the blue, on April 1, Judge Susan Webber Wright dismissed the Paula Jones suit. It had no merit, she ruled. Clinton, relaxing in Dakar, Senegal, reacted to the reprieve: "Unbelievable, fantastic." He let himself be photographed in a devil-may-care pose—sucking on an unlit cigar and palpating an African drum.

Starr began showing signs of desperation. He tried throwing his noose around other principals involved in Whitewater—Susan McDougal and Webb Hubbell—but even putting them behind bars would not enable him to squeeze either of them into incriminating Bill or Hillary.

Strangely enough, Hillary and Bill seem to allow themselves time to nurture each other, or to be nurtured, only when they are joined in battle against the rest of the world. In May of the Year of Monica, Hillary called up Steve Jobs and his wife, Lorene, to ask if the Clintons could use one of their several homes in the vicinity of Stanford; they wanted to visit with Chelsea. The founder of Apple Computer was delighted to oblige, and Lorene lavished their rather spartan Woodside house with paintings and plantings and staff. But the Clintons dismissed the staff and simply hung out together, the three of them. When the Jobses joined the family for lunch, they were impressed at the affection Bill and Hillary displayed—an impression that ran totally counter to the public's view of a strictly business-like arrangement.[32]

Word began to leak out of Starr's office in mid-July. The independent counsel had served Clinton's lawyers with the first grand jury subpoena for a sitting president's testimony in U.S. history. For the next ten days the White House went into information blackout. McCurry told reporters on July 24, "We don't talk about subpoenas." Reporters weren't the only ones infuriated. Even Lanny Davis, the Patton Boggs lawyer whose friendly face had become ubiquitous on TV as the President's most loyal spinmeister, could not get a truthful answer. He spoke privately to McCurry: "If Starr has issued one, it won't be news to him. . . . So why can't you confirm this for me—on deep background—so I don't appear stupid when I'm doing TV?"[33] McCurry repeated, "It's our policy not to talk about subpoenas." Now Lanny Davis knew what it was like to be a reporter dealing with the Clinton White House. Instead of trying to manipulate the press, he did a 180-degree turnaround in his own efforts. "Although it sounds a little bizarre," he told me, "I made the calculated decision to use the television airwaves to communicate directly to the President."[34]

When the President's own men resort to this dangerous tactic, it is a sign that the reality checks have broken down; a leader has become hostage to his own paranoia and the inner circle of loyalists who feed it, usually for their own purposes.

To stay above the encroaching mudslide, Hillary had her staff seek out a venue in the middle of the country where she could demonstrate her social concerns. The YWCA was opening its first battered women's shelter in Cincinnati and had invited the First Lady to preside. Since she was already scheduled to do a party fund-raiser in Cincinnati, she dispatched her advance people to look over the shelter. It was a Belle Époque mansion in the inner city that had been refurbished to guarantee a boost in self-esteem for up to fifty battered wives. It was perfect for Hillary. She agreed to go.

Francie Pepper, a dedicated community activist and Democrat, as well as wife of the then CEO of Procter & Gamble, John Pepper, was ambivalent about Hillary's appearance. The YWCA in Cincinnati is treated like a community shrine. Was Hillary's decision to visit evidence of her commitment or of her political opportunism? Francie Pepper had been unpleasantly surprised by two previous visits, when Hillary had whizzed in and out of Cincinnati to raise money for the 1996 reelection. "She stood behind ropes and delivered her perfect little speech like a Stepford politician," she recalls. "Then everyone stood in line, no talking with her allowed, no human con-

tact, just ten seconds—photo, photo, photo, like getting your license renewed—and she's gone!" But that was the phantom Hillary, subsumed by
one of her husband's campaigns.[35]

This time, Francie saw an entirely different woman: "She really believed
and cared about everything she said." Over lunch, Hillary talked with several of the women being served by the shelter and established an immediate rapport. She also made sure to stroke the CEO's wife. Having been
briefed that Francie Pepper had gone to Smith and had a daughter, Hillary
engaged her in conversation about women's education. "Where did your
daughter choose to go to school?" she asked. "Yale." Hillary wanted to
know if Francie had wanted her daughter to follow her to Smith. "Well, I
took her to see it," Francie said. Hillary sighed. "I wish Chelsea had considered Wellesley. I took her to see it, but I couldn't convince her. I think a female education is really important for women."[36]

In the midst of these pleasantries, the ugliness back in Washington
caught up with her. Hillary was called away for a phone call from the White
House. The President had surrendered to Starr's subpoena. And Monica
had won the immunity deal she wanted, so she, too, would testify. Now the
principal parts had been handed out, the Kabuki play was about to begin,
and the script would all be based on the most desperately private part of
Hillary's shadow life with Bill Clinton.

THE SUMMER OF HER DISCONTENT

When Kenneth Starr entered Monica's semen-stained dress as evidence
against Bill Clinton at the end of July, only two people in the world knew if
the stain was presidential. Bill Clinton was one of them, and he was still ob-
fuscating. Monica changed her story and testified that she did have a sexual
relationship with the President. Hillary's reaction went publicly undocu-
mented. With Starr's office spraying charges all around Clinton with the
crazy force of a fire hose out of control, the President's image was badly in
need of retooling, even among his natural tribal base: Democratic women,
gays, Hollywood, the New York literati, and many of Wall Street's elite.
Where better to gather them all under the same tent than East Hampton?

And so the Clintons made an OTR ("on the run") visit to the east end of
Long Island at peak lemming season, the first weekend of August. The plan
was to raise money for the DNC to help retire its debt before the rugged fall
election. Not incidentally, the First Couple appeared together attempting to

look relaxed and unconcerned, kicking back with their hosts, film director Steven Spielberg and his wife, Kate Capshaw, at their spread on Georgica Pond. They also dropped in for dinner with publisher Mort Zuckerman, comedian Chevy Chase, and their wives at a down-home ribs joint where the waitresses shrieked with delight—perfect.

Except that Hillary looked as if she had been hit by a truck. The President looked exhausted, the pinkish pouches under his eyes evidence of his insomnia. The pair entered a Friday-night event together, tense and metallic, and quickly separated, as if suddenly running on opposing polarities. They stood at appointed spots on financier Bruce Wasserstein's terrace, on a green grass brow leading down to the ocean, but Hillary wasn't working with him, not the way she'd always used to. One party official who was counting on Hillary to pull the President through—again—sounded worried: "She looks like a changed person."

On Saturday night, the Clintons looked colder than a poached salmon plate. And this was the big tent event at the home of actor-activists Alec Baldwin and his wife, Kim Basinger, in Amagansett. For the double bill of Hillary and Bill, a thousand ticket holders waited in a line half a mile long, rocking impatiently on their platform sandals, waiting to be shuttle-bused into the Stony Hill Farm. An unacknowledged undercurrent ran through the table buzz, but people were too polite to mention the Starr investigation.

Judith Hope, savvy chairwoman of the New York State Democratic Party and the weekend's organizer, was personally offended at the mounting evidence that Clinton had sullied the woman she most admired in political life. Also, she was from Arkansas; she knew his style. Judith made sure to sit next to the President. But he was eclipsed from the start by the starry glow around the First Lady.

A hush falls as the moment the crowd is waiting for arrives: Hillary the wronged wife rises to introduce the husband, who has repeatedly slapped her in the face.

She builds him up. She reinflates the President's dreams for the country, sending them up like bright kites. She speaks of his deep commitment. He appears visibly moved. Then she turns to welcome "My husband, President Bill Clinton."

Clinton leaps up and grabs her, not just a hug and an air kiss but a clinch, a prolonged Rhett-and-Scarlett clinch. Hillary swoons. At that moment Judith Hope has an insight: "He just keeps seducing this woman over and over again. This kind of chemistry can't be faked. She can't resist him."

The audience is smacking its hands together, tearful, out of its mind with exhilaration—it could be a wedding for all the emotion inside this tent. Hope turns to her husband, Tom Twomey, and says wryly, "I am ever mindful that a woman's heart takes her where her mind knows she shouldn't go."[37]

Inch by inch that August, Clinton painted himself into a corner. No fib, obfuscation, intimidation, or cockamamie distinction between oral sex and intercourse would allow the President to wiggle out of facing himself—or his wife—but it would be weeks more before he realized it. He should have known the jig was up on August 3, when Starr's deputies entered his house and literally drew blood for a DNA test against the stain on Monica's dress. Or at least by August 6, when Monica Lewinsky testified before the grand jury.

Friends who were staying over in the Lincoln Bedroom around this time told others of the horrific tensions in the private quarters. Clinton was reported to be talking to a young woman in the hall when Hillary popped her head out and screamed, "Are you sleeping with her, too?"

On August 13, Bill and Hillary had the dour duty of comforting bereaved families at a memorial ceremony honoring the return of the coffins of Americans killed in the African embassy bombings. Normally, at such emotional events, the First Couple holds hands. But that Thursday they stood apart on the rain-soaked tarmac of Andrews Air Force Base and "she seemed as cold as a fish to him," observed a former White House staffer. A tear leaked onto Bill Clinton's cheek, and he let it sit there as the cameras rolled. Hillary was stiff as a wooden soldier.

Right after the memorial, another knock-down-drag-out legal strategy session was set to take place. Hillary was more focused than the President, according to a knowledgeable source. Acting as his über-lawyer, she zeroed in on the bottom line, which was to save the presidency. She insisted that he must not lie to the grand jury. But at the time, says the source, she still believed there had been no sexual relationship with Monica.[38] According to most accounts, Clinton didn't tell her until that night or the following morning that Starr had a positive match on the DNA test. Thus did Hillary inadvertently force from the President the very confession that she had never wanted to hear from her husband.

CHELSEA EVENING

In the waning hours of that same dread Thursday, Clinton was bellyflopped on the floor of the solarium, absently playing Hearts with Harry

Thomason and a couple of other people, when the Secret Service radioed in that Chelsea's arrival was imminent. The President came to life. Twenty minutes later, when she entered the room, he literally leapt to his feet, climbed over the other players, and swooped her up in an adoring embrace. Although he never discusses his daughter even with his card-playing cronies, it is obvious to them that Chelsea is an overwhelming presence in her father's life.

Perhaps it was her appearance that gave him the courage to face his wife. That night, while Chelsea was out with friends, Bill Clinton finally stood by the bed and offered his wife a half-baked version of the truth. Until then, he had held to the fiction with Hillary that he had befriended Monica and that she had taken his attentions the wrong way. This night, facing his grand jury appearance, he had to admit he had lied. He told her that his involvement with Lewinsky had been long-running and that he had crossed the line. By some accounts, Hillary lunged at him and gave him a blow: "You stupid bastard!" Clinton became abject. He begged her forgiveness, but still he argued his case: he had never really had *sex* with that woman; fondling and fellatio, yes, but he hadn't *slept* with her. Perhaps most difficult for Hillary to accept was the fact that this was not an isolated incident but a relationship of sixteen months. And the girl was not much older than their daughter.

Their daughter.

They had to face the most noxious of questions: *How are we going to tell Chelsea?*

"Anyone who thinks Hillary knew what happened before the two of them had their conversation wasn't there that weekend," says Linda Bloodworth-Thomason, who was staying with her husband in the private quarters, where they could act as buffers. Linda, who thought it was great that Hillary "smacked him upside the head," says that in the few days following the blowup "the second floor of the White House was a somber place." Another friend elaborated: "Hillary learned only that weekend not just about the sex but that her husband was going to admit it—and humiliate her before the world. That was the epiphany. Public deniability would no longer be possible. Her nose would be rubbed in it."

It was only that Sunday, the day before he testified, that the President's lawyers were informed that he was going to change his story. Mike McCurry has since acknowledged that when the President's denials were scrapped at last, "it was devastating to all of us, from Mrs. Clinton on down."[39] A Washington attorney close to the case told me, "What made her more furious than anything was that he was still in denial, and she knew people would laugh at his legalistic explanation of sexual relations."

By some reports, Chelsea Clinton was so shocked and devastated by the revelation that her father had lied to her and to her mother that she fought with him. Chelsea's friend the Reverend Jesse Jackson, who often called her at college to pray with her, telephoned the White House to see if he could help. She was distraught and asked him to come over. On Sunday night, Jackson told me, he calmed Chelsea and Hillary Clinton with Bible stories:

"You ask, how can Bill with all his power make this mistake. Well, how could King David make it? David was a child prodigy. Slew Goliath. Israel's greatest king. And talented musician, just as Bill is. And yet he became weak when he saw Bathsheba. Samson, with all of his strength and abilities, in the face of Delilah, succumbed to the flesh."[40]

Jackson wound up his ministering before midnight, in time to join the President in the private residence, where he was preparing for his testimony the next day. The self-appointed spiritual adviser said, "What's different here is that Ken Starr is able to play God with government funding."

Hillary, according to Jackson, let out her whooping laugh. "Where did you get that line?"

"It has a trademark," said the ever self-promoting reverend. "If you use it, give me credit."[41]

Champions play with pain, they don't sit it out. "Hillary was able to do this," her mother told me, "because she had a commitment to her daughter—somebody outside of her own problems that she was being strong and positive for." In her book, Hillary wrote about her overwhelming desire to protect Chelsea, "to minimize the odds of her suffering at the hands of someone who didn't have enough love or discipline, opportunity or responsibility, as a child."[42] As it happened, she could not.

Clinton was to go before the grand jury for four hours on Monday, and in order to spin his testimony, he planned to make a televised statement to the nation that evening. Once again, Hillary turned her fury outward and kept it trained on Starr. Sidney Blumenthal boasted to his former journalist colleagues that he was a go-between who could help Clinton get on with his wife. Although Blumenthal was out of the country at the time, he faxed the First Lady reams of vitriol for the President to use for his statement to the nation. But she had her own ideas. She hunkered down with her husband's lawyers to lay out a defense of the indefensible. She was one of the last people to sign off on the statement before the President addressed the nation with his surly nonapology on the night of August 17. The address bore the unmistakable imprint of the First Lady: the anger, the outrage at privacy violated, the stubborn refusal to admit, apologize, or back down.

Once again, Hillary's political instincts proved flawed. Instead of coming clean in his speech, the President went back out and punched Ken Starr in the nose. Hillary had taught him how to fight too well.

How Could He?

In all the armchair analyses of "How could he?" I have never heard mentioned the three major personal marker events in Clinton's life that took place around the time he carried on his romance with Monica. The two most adoring women in his life both "abandoned" him in ways he could not prevent. Following a mastectomy, Virginia Kelley, the mother on whom he had an exaggerated dependence, suffered a recurrence of cancer in 1992. It spread to her spine, her skull, her pelvis. He lost her a year and half before he took up with Monica.

Even more agonizing for Bill Clinton was the long, slow slipping out of his arms of his daughter. For years Chelsea had been his Saturday-night "date" for dinner on the many weekends when Hillary was out of town. Who would play Hearts with him in the wee hours when insomnia would not let go its grip on his unquiet mind? Who, now, would love him unconditionally? Chelsea had one foot across the threshold of independence when Clinton turned to Monica, a girl only six years older than his daughter. Clinton himself was hurtling toward fifty. His hearing wasn't so good anymore, he needed reading glasses, his hair had long since gone wintry gray. And Chelsea was looking at colleges thousands of miles away.

A mental health professional who knows the Clintons takes the Chelsea connection even deeper. Adolescent children's sexual development often stimulates fantasies in their parents about their own, somewhat diminished sexual adventurousness. As they witness the emergence of a child's sexuality and her delight in acting on it, as well as all the opportunities young people have for the future, they may experience feelings of sadness for their own lost youthfulness. Men of fifty are especially vulnerable to having affairs or to starting new families when an adored daughter departs.

With Monica as his mirror, Clinton could recapture his lost adolescence. They talked as if they were fifteen, as if he were free, as if he didn't have a wife, as if he didn't have a daughter who was leaving him, as if he didn't hold the biggest job in the world or suffer any of the indignities of middle age.

Indeed, while he was still enjoying his secret sexual playmate, the third marker event occurred. Clinton stumbled down a flight of stairs at golf pro Greg Norman's house, and overnight he was hobbled like an old man, taking on all the accoutrements of decay and dependence: the wheelchair, the brace, the cane, the flaccid muscles. Unable even to play golf, he was deprived of almost all sensual pleasure. Except Monica. His final liaison with the intern was on March 29, a little over two weeks after his fall. Monica had to service her crippled lover while he was still on crutches.

Clinton had always believed he would die prematurely. He was haunted by Bill Blythe's fatal car accident before his own birth—the image of the car carrying that brash young man they said was his father careening off the road, out of control. Would he, too, careen off the road? Was his own flesh now suddenly a grave? "Sex is also a way of countering this death fear he has from his father," says the mental health professional who knows Clinton. "It's a way of reaffirming the life force."

When Monica constructed her fantasy about the two of them having more time together in the future, Clinton hinted that he might be alone in three years. Perhaps the thrill would be gone for Hillary once he was no longer President and could never be President again. Then another vision—one of crabbed old age—must have come upon him. According to Monica, he asked her an unexpected question: "What are we gonna do when I'm seventy-five and I have to pee thirty times a day?"[43]

While such impudent reminders of aging and mortality might be sufficient in themselves to send an ordinary man of middle age into a spiral of sexual impulsiveness, given Clinton's well-worn pattern of sexual escapism, they would have only added to his reckless need to reward himself.

HOLIDAY FROM HELL

During the darkest week in Hillary's dawning realization of the depths of her husband's betrayal, she remained mute. On August 18, after her husband's nonapology to the nation, she deputized her press secretary, Marsha Berry, to issue an opaque but politically safe statement: "Clearly, this is not the best day in Mrs. Clinton's life. But," the message continued, "her love for him is compassionate and steadfast." Did she forgive him? reporters asked. "Yes. She believes in this marriage." Did Chelsea forgive her father? No comment.

Everyone saw on the news the Daddy's-in-the-doghouse walk across the White House lawn that day, the President being led by his only sure friend in the world, Buddy the Labrador retriever. There was a sea of space between the couple, which their daughter tried valiantly to bridge by holding both parents' hands. With this seemingly endless journey across green grass, the shaken First Family set off for a twelve-day vacation from Hell.

On the helicopter ride to Andrews Air Force Base, the Clintons were frozen in silence. Hillary looked numb and Chelsea inconsolably sad. On the plane to Martha's Vineyard, Clinton read a mystery novel and Hillary dozed. When they arrived, the President climbed down the steps of his plane and fell into the huge, forgiving hug of Vernon Jordan. Hillary let the President cool his heels, alone, on camera, while she hung back, chatting up developer Richard Friedman about nothing more important than the weather.

Chelsea, out front, shook hands like a seasoned pol.

The unusually short official greeting line was the first clue that this, the Clintons' fourth summer holiday on the Vineyard, would be drastically different from others. The family quickly disappeared into Friedman's weathered nineteenth-century farmhouse.

This year Hillary didn't ask that there be candles and wine and soft music playing, as she had when it was only she and her husband snuggled in the guest house. The President even seemed reluctant to step inside. When Friedman stopped by to make sure his guests were settled in, the President was outside playing fetch with his dog, alone.[44] This year he wouldn't be dropping by the Bunch of Grapes Bookstore to pick up his stack for beach reading or sitting on the novelist William Styron's porch quoting from Márquez and Faulkner.[45] This year the Clintons would not be dancing on the beach and cavorting like kids in the surf. Bill didn't show his face in church or take out his golf clubs. Hillary didn't leave the house for the first two days. The press was on marital deathwatch.

In the Edgartown school gym, which was serving as press headquarters, a sweating Mike McCurry fended off restless journalists who asked why the Clintons were hiding.

"They've been out once or twice. We'll just see how it goes."

Was the President "hearing a lot from the missus"?

McCurry smiled wanly. "They're talking."

Did they sound hostile or calm?

"It changes."

Would they seek marital counseling? I asked.

"There is no marital therapy."

Hillary emerged at last on Saturday to have lunch with *Washington Post* owner Katharine Graham, another brilliant, emotionally abused wife whose husband had been unfaithful. Worried friends had been told that Hillary would give the signal when she was ready to be sociable.

That left the Rattners rattled. Steven Rattner, the media-savvy financial wizard at the investment banking firm Lazard Frères, had been wheedling for four years to get the Clintons over for dinner at their home on the Vineyard. It had been all set for Saturday night. Then canceled. At 5:30 P.M. on the very day word was sent that the Clintons would indeed turn up. Place cards were rearranged. Rattner's wife, Maureen White, raced to reseat separate tables for each of the Clintons. They didn't show up until after dark.[46]

The big man came in alone. "How lonely and forlorn he looked," recalled one sympathetic guest. "So unsure, as if he didn't know if anybody was going to speak to him or not."

The guests did seem hesitant. What opening gambit could possibly suit the occasion? "Hi, Mr. President, have a good week?" The White House photographer scurried around to find some young people, any young people, to have their pictures taken with the President. With the President of the United States, for God's sake! But the teenagers made themselves conspicuously scarce. "They were furious with him, outraged, male and female alike," said one mother. Eventually, the hostess rounded up her au pair and her au pair's friend, and they stood, eyes downcast, enduring the photo op like a forced kiss.

Hillary delayed her entrance until the President was safely below on the terrace. She had a snappy new haircut and was a study in animation, a marked contrast to the President. Guests smothered her in lingering hugs and, though their sympathy was unsought, some whispered words of support into her ear. A few muttered later to one another, "I wish I had the guts to tell him what I really think."

Although a few intimates confided that Hillary was rethinking her life, her personal feelings were hidden under a bright glaze of conversation about a dozen different topics. At another dinner party during their holiday, veteran newsman Mike Wallace innocently asked Hillary if she had ever had a stress test. "I'm having one now," she replied.

Martha's Vineyard, like East Hampton, was her crowd. "People feel very, very strongly about Hillary up here," said one Vineyard veteran. "She's Wellesley—she's one of us," remarked an attorney. "He's an Arkansas kid—up here, he's Hillary's husband."[47] Robert Kiley, a former Massachusetts and New York public-office holder seated at her table, said, "Her knowledge, her analytical skills, her passion were all on display; she was in fine fettle. That's her way of dealing with each of these crises. She admonishes him, beats on him, he makes promises he never keeps, and they go on until the next collapse."[48]

"Hillary was completely internalizing it, while Clinton had to externalize it," observed a guest from New York. At his table, Clinton couldn't help ragging on Ken Starr. The conversation was dominated by the bombastic lawyer Alan Dershowitz, who teaches a course at Harvard on law and justice in the Bible. "He had a very interesting analysis of the sinners of Sodom," Dershowitz said later. What was truly astonishing, given this President's need to seduce every man and woman at any party, was how Clinton stuck to his table like glue. Even when the hostess Maureen White coaxed, "Mr. President, there are a lot of guests here who'd like to meet you," he refused to budge.

After dinner, Hillary held forth with her own salon. "I saw her in battle mode," says Dershowitz. "She is first and foremost a tough lawyer and politician. The words she used were designed to get my juices flowing: 'Where do we go from here?'"[49]

THE UNREPENTANT

Astonishingly, Clinton hadn't called any members of his Cabinet or congressional Democrats before giving his speech to the nation and fleeing to the Vineyard. He hadn't been on the island for four days before he slipped back to Washington and ordered major military strikes on terrorist targets in Afghanistan and Sudan. Now he had an excuse to make a few phone calls.

"Joe? What do you know about Osama bin Laden?"

Senator Joe Lieberman was relieved to hear from the President. He liked the man. They went way back. As an itinerant student at Yale Law, Clinton had broken away to work for the Connecticut Democrat's first political campaign. Together the two men had dragged their marginalized party back to the political center when Lieberman had chaired the Democratic Leadership Council. And in 1992, Lieberman had been the most active Senate fund-raiser for the Clinton-Gore ticket. He was also an Orthodox Jew who fervently believed that one's faith should be an important frame of reference for political leaders.[50]

But Clinton made no reference to his faith in his fifteen-minute conversation with Lieberman. Not a word about his grand jury testimony or his statement to the nation. "The conversation was winding down, and he had not mentioned the eight-hundred-pound gorilla sitting on top of the Democratic Party, all because of him," recalls the senator. Lieberman was stung. Angry. Before the President could hang up, Lieberman told him, "Mr. President, I feel personally betrayed. When you made your finger-waving statement in January, I took you at your word. I believed you deserved the benefit of the doubt. But when you acknowledged that you weren't telling the truth, it unsettled me," he said. "And your nonapology to the American people was not ultimately an acceptance of responsibility."[51]

Clinton's curt response was a replay of his TV attack on Starr. End of call.

"It stewed in me after that conversation," admits the meditative Lieberman. "We had worked so hard to break away from the vision of the Democrats as the 'anything goes' party. My fear was that in this single act of irresponsibility, he was endangering all that he had helped to achieve for the Democratic Party. If some Democrats didn't speak out, we were doomed."[52]

The next day, a tired-sounding Clinton called Lanny Davis to ask what his spinmeister had thought of his speech.

"You sounded too much like a lawyer" was the critique by the lawyer turned media personality. "You have to be president, not a defendant. You need to get everything out." Davis made a bold suggestion: the President should release the transcript of his grand jury testimony, then invite the top news anchors to spend an evening with him asking all their questions. "Then it would be over for you and your family, and the country could move on." Clinton didn't bite. Davis found himself getting angry. He had been the diehard defender, sitting there in the TV studio all miked up on the night of August 17 waiting to put the best face on the President's speech to the nation. He had been disgusted to learn of Clinton's behavior. It had become harder and harder to defend him. Davis, a start-over dad in middle life, couldn't blot out of his mind the image of Clinton playing with Monica in Hillary's house—on Easter Sunday, after they had come back from church. He couldn't help wondering if Clinton was a sociopath, or at least amoral when it comes to sex. Like many former Friends of Bill, Lanny Davis found himself moving into Hillary's camp.[53]

Nobody, it seemed, could break through to Clinton. He had constructed an airtight box as strong as steel, just as his mother had taught him to do. He kept all the Monica ugliness locked outside in the black. Inside the white box of his consciousness he kept what he wanted to think about: the polls. After everything—the Lewinsky story, the information blackout, the hostility of the press, the blue dress, the backfiring of his speech—the public still approved of the job he was doing as President. Indeed, his job approval ratings were off the charts, 62 percent on August 21, 1998, way above his first-term average of 48 percent.[54] The economy was booming, the country was at peace, and he was still one of the most popular second-term presidents in U.S. history.

THE DEEP FREEZE

The irony was spectacular. Two years before, Hillary Clinton had been anything but popular with the American people. In a national survey by the Pew Research Center in the summer of 1996, the words most commonly used to describe her had been "strong," "dishonest," "intelligent," and "rhymes with rich." In late August 1998, when Pew repeated the survey, she received a superlative report card from the American public, who now saw her as "strong, intelligent, brave, loyal, and good." (Apparently, a strong woman must become a victim to be seen as good.) Two thirds of the public admired her decision to stand by her husband.[55]

But privately, Hillary was nearly paralyzed as their presidency appeared to be imploding. "It's extremely difficult and very painful" was as much as she would share with her former press secretary Lisa Caputo. When Mike McCurry tried to get her to open up, she revealed her emotional turmoil to McCurry only through a series of Socratic questions: "Do I feel angry? Do I feel betrayed? Do I feel lonely? Do I feel exasperated? And humiliated?"[56]

Hillary retreated to some sanctuary of the soul that was beyond the reach of her closest friends and even her mother. In the fall of 1998, I asked Hillary's mother if, when things become what most of us would think of as intolerable, Hillary calls her just to talk and get unconditional love and support.

"No," Mrs. Rodham said, sounding every bit as matter-of-fact as her daughter. "Hillary is really so mature. She always has been. . . . She's always thought things out for herself. Then, if she needs more help or direction, she'll discuss things."

Such as Chelsea?

"Of course, we've never discussed Chelsea," she said, except for obvious topics such as her choice of colleges.

Did she think that Hillary felt pain very deeply? "Of course she does—she is a very sensitive person," Mrs. Rodham said, her voice tightening. "But she is able not to overemotionalize it. . . . She doesn't go into one of these horribly overwrought kinds of tizzies. That's one thing I never did, either."[57]

Hillary's closest Arkansas friend, Diane Blair, asked the Reverend Ed Matthews, "Is she talking to you?"

"No, she's not talking to me," he said.

Blair was baffled and a little hurt. She told Matthews, "This is one time that Hillary hasn't shared the intimacy of her heart."

Mrs. Rodham told Reverend Matthews she knew there had to be lots of pain and she wished Hillary would let her in on it. When gently probed by those in whom she might normally confide, Hillary would say, "I'm not going to talk to you and get you subpoenaed." Her pastor believed that might be an excuse: "It's her nature. Hillary is a loner. She's an extremely strong and independent person and I think extremely spiritual." Hillary doesn't carry the Bible with her. "We don't wear our religion around," says Reverend Matthews, "but she does carry what I call a makeup kit—readings and inspirational material that she collects."[58]

"It was clearly a deep hurt and pain," one of Mrs. Clinton's closest associates told me. She described Hillary's state of mind: "It's like you go through a death and you can't live for weeks and weeks and weeks. And then the healing process begins. They are trying to work it through."

Once more, Hillary was faced with a choice: strike out on her own or bet on Bill? How many times had she faced the same choice? Scores of times? Only now she was fifty.

"Take care of your marriage. Don't worry about your image." That advice came from Mandy Grunwald, who, like so many of the Clintons' faithful former lieutenants, was sickened by the President's lies and betrayals and had strong ideas on what Hillary should do with her life. But the consensus among the masses was that Hillary must have known all about Monica. Many people believed that Hillary, too, had lied to them back in January.

Grunwald told me, "The public has for years had lots of misimpressions about Hillary. This one," she pointed out, "is based on an assessment of her that is true—that she's too smart, she must have known. It's in a way a compliment."[59] Privately, Grunwald thought it was sadder that Hillary *hadn't* known.

Friends of Bill in Arkansas seemed to feel a special sense of personal betrayal on Hillary's behalf. "Partly the hope of Clinton's candidacy was that it would erase the blot of 1957 [Governor Orval Faubus's segregationist campaign] and all the stereotypes which decent people in this state have been trying to live down since then," says the Arkansas writer Gene Lyons. "For example, jokes like 'What does an Arkansas woman say after making love? "Daddy, get up, you're crushing my cigarettes." ' " Lyons was struck by the vehemence with which his wife and her friends expressed their sense of personal violation: "They'd tell you, 'There's a lot of us who did a lot for that son of a bitch, and he let us down because he just couldn't keep it in his pants.' It was not fun being a fifty-year-old guy around town. You know, you'd get this kind of squinty-eyed look from the mothers: 'Would you sleep with *my* daughter if you got a chance?' "[60]

HUMILIATION ABROAD

In any lengthy marriage there are lakes of buoyancy, deserts of passive indifference, and sinkholes of despair. But between such drastic changes in the marital climate there are usually more than a few days. Not so with the Clintons. In this tempestuous match of motherly Hillary and mischief-making Bill, no one can predict the emotional weather.

Immediately after the couple's famous vacation from hell in Martha's Vineyard, the President and First Lady were expected in Russia. It was late August. A half-dozen members of Congress waited on Air Force One for the feuding couple to arrive for what their guests expected would be a long, tense flight to Moscow. Congressman Peter King, a working-class lawyer who is the voice of Irish Catholic conservatives on Long Island, recalls his amazement: "What struck me was that they acted like the two happiest people in the world. They were holding hands, telling jokes, laughing. Usually people are friendly in the public and fight in private. They were fighting in public, and in private acting like a totally normal, happy couple."

When the same couple appeared together a few days later in Northern Ireland, I was up close to see Hillary resume the façade of icy disdain; whenever the President tried to move close to her in public, she repelled him.

Hillary arrived in Belfast first, a day ahead of the President. The inevitable gray thunderclouds of an Irish afternoon sagged overhead as she hurriedly descended from her plane. Head down, all business, the First Lady was wrapped in a long military greatcoat. Fifty minutes later, when her limo pulled up to the new Waterfront Hall, a different Hillary swanned out like a movie star arriving at the Academy Awards. Sleek in a dark blue Oscar de la Renta pantsuit, she gave a queenly wave. It was her usual MO under fire: Look your best when you feel your worst.

The First Lady had come to Ireland for a Vital Voices women's conference saluting the nation's female peace activists for their pivotal role in the creation of the Good Friday peace agreement. Her speech was forty-five minutes of statesmanlike content. Breaking her unspoken rule, Hillary read from notes. She was coldly brilliant. Her words touched all the bases but revealed none of her humanity.

When Bill Clinton arrived the following morning, his spirit appeared broken. He didn't come to life even when speakers from all sides hailed him as the indispensable man in promoting the peace process. Members of the traveling press remarked that they had never seen him so down—"depressed" was the word used off camera by veterans such as CNN's Candy Crowley and NPR's Mara Liasson. An adviser to the President conceded that "Hillary has not forgiven him."

She arrived separately at Waterfront Hall before the President's speech, slipping in a side door just moments before he was introduced. The mere glimpse of her led to an ovation. Sitting with her friend the U.S. ambassador to the U.K. Philip Lader, she applauded mechanically and left the hall the moment her husband was finished speaking. For the next two days, she scarcely looked at the man. Whether onstage, in their limo, or walking the drear mile in Omagh where a car bomb had killed over thirty civilians, Hillary was separated from the other Clinton by a wall of ice. She kept her eyes hidden behind reflective sunglasses, her arms slung behind her back, hands clasped. Whenever her husband tried to move close, she repelled him.

In Dublin it was worse. The fear and loathing of fellow Democrats caught up with Clinton. He was standing next to Ireland's prime minister, Bertie Ahern, on camera, when reporters played back a withering critique of his behavior delivered by Senator Joseph Lieberman on the floor of the U.S. Senate. His old friend branded the President "immoral."

Even more astonishing was the President's reaction to Lieberman's tongue-lashing. "I agree with him," said Clinton on camera. "I agree with everything he said." And for the first time in public, Clinton said he was "very sorry" for the affair.

"Taken on the face of it, what he said was so humble, I was really touched and even pained by it," Senator Lieberman later told me. "The White House had called and asked me not to do it while he was abroad. But my kids wanted me to do it. Afterwards, some of my colleagues in the Senate thanked me, saying 'It lanced the boil.' "[61]

From Dublin the Clintons headed west to Limerick, and there the sun suddenly came out.

Crowds, pressed into the form of a massive human cross at the intersection of Thomas and O'Connell Streets, waited for hours through a drenching downpour before President and Mrs. Clinton appeared and the rare Irish sun shone full. Hillary, in a stylish yellow slicker, leaned over to whisper in her husband's ear several times. He nodded and made notes. When he rose to speak, looking once again youthful and handsome and wearing a bright red tie, her eyes followed him approvingly. Their old political symbiosis seemed to be switched back on. The crowd enveloped him in adoration unmatched since the visit of John F. Kennedy. And when the two stood to take their bows, Hillary's arm, almost absently, slipped around her husband's back. As automatic as a turnstile, his arm thrust out and circled her waist.

Was it their night at the romantic Adare Manor Hotel with moonlight over the lough and the vast gardens? Maybe they had just gotten a good night's sleep for a change. It wasn't exactly an embrace. But Hillary's signaling her public approval seemed to have resuscitated Bill Clinton—at least for the moment. Now it was back to Washington, where for weeks the long knives had been sharpening and Kenneth Starr was ready to dump his pornographic report on the doorstep of Congress.

Now Is the Time for Turning

On Clinton's return from Ireland, Erskine Bowles sat the President down and did a deliberate "intervention." His chief of staff told him the time had come to admit his misbehavior and start apologizing, one-on-one, to the Cabinet members and key party leaders he had misled.[62] Faced with public condemnation by the senior senator from New York, Daniel Patrick Moynihan, and even by a member of his own extended family, Senator Barbara Boxer (whose daughter is married to Hillary's brother Tony), Clinton's inner voice of self-reproach seemed to have overtaken his habitual survival mechanism of boxing off his personal problems.

"When he screws up, he knows it better than anybody," says Betsey Wright. "He's looking for the cat-o'-nine-tails."

Does Hillary provide it?

"Yes. She's a punisher. But not the dominant punisher. There's a multitude of people who do that for him."[63]

On September 11, Kenneth Starr made public his graphically detailed 354-page report on President Clinton and the Monica Lewinsky affair. There was no mention of Whitewater, the subject of the investigation he had originally been appointed to conduct. Instead, Starr laid out how the President had allegedly lied and obstructed justice in civil and criminal investigations concerning the Lewinsky relationship and totaled up eleven points as grounds for impeachment.

By all accounts, Hillary adamantly refused to read the Starr report. But once it finally confronted the country with the truth behind Clinton's lies, she bravely led her husband through the labyrinths of denial and anger to the point of self-examination. Responding, he invited more black brothers than ever to the annual White House prayer breakfast. "It was a terrible personal ordeal for him to be up all night, thinking about what he was going to say and what he had done," I was told by one of Hillary's closest aides. The President decided to amend his angry speech of August 17 with a full-bore Baptist-style confession.

He began quietly: "I have been on quite a journey these last few weeks to get to the end of this, to the rock-bottom truth of where I am and where we all are." He expressed his regret at hurting his family, his friends, his staff, his Cabinet, and Monica Lewinsky and her family. After asking for everyone's forgiveness, he said he believed that "to be forgiven, more than sorrow is required. First, genuine repentance, a determination to change and to repair breaches of my own making. I have repented. Second, what my Bible calls a broken spirit.

"And if my repentance is genuine and sustained, and if I can then maintain both a broken spirit and a strong heart, then good can come of this for our country, as well as for me and my family."

"He hit all the buttons in theological terms," commented Reverend Matthews, who was in the audience. "I'm persuaded that Bill is a good person at heart." Clinton even read a passage from Yom Kippur liturgy: "Now is the time for turning. For leaves and birds, turning in autumn comes instinctively, but for us it means losing face. It means starting all over again. And this is always painful. It means saying I am sorry. It means recognizing that we have the ability to change. These things are terribly hard to do. But unless we turn, we will be trapped forever in yesterday's ways."

He then turned himself from repentant sinner into Baptist preacher and prayed directly to the Lord on behalf of all Americans: "Revive our lives as at the beginning." Clinton wound up with a promise to seek redemption with the spiritual guidance of three Christian ministers who would meet and pray with him weekly to help him resist "the temptations that have conquered me" in the past.[64]

Hillary, who is normally cerebral about her religion, surprised her pastor with an emotional reaction to Clinton's speech. "She had tear-filled eyes," Reverend Matthews noticed. As soon as the President finished speaking, Matthews knelt beside Hillary and remembers her whispering to him,

"I never heard him say that before," referring to Clinton's oath of repentance. "And you know what we've been through."

Matthews spoke with her about forgiveness. "You know that forgiveness has nothing to do with human logic," he said. "Forgiveness has strictly to do with grace. And that's God's gift. I hope you are in touch with that. I'm praying that you are."

Hillary smiled. "I think I'm getting there."[65]

The leader of Clinton's three angels was Dr. Phillip Wogaman, since 1993 the President's pastor at the Foundry United Methodist Church near the White House. A white-haired Dutchman with a gentle manner, "Phil" clearly identified with the President as a victim of the conservative Right. Dr. Wogaman's approach in sessions with the President was to lead him toward "sanctification," which means "being made holy." "In the Methodist tradition, that is done by becoming more loving," he told me. "The heart of the problem with the baby-boom generation is a cultural one—a deep separation between sex and love and commitment. If that's the virus Clinton has, it's a very widely spread virus."

Later, Dr. Wogaman would publish a book about his encounters with the President, called *From the Eye of the Storm*. Strikingly, he never referred to Hillary by name—making only sparing references to "the President's wife"—and never addressed her role in the marital behavior. I asked Phil Wogaman if he thought it possible to restore the President's spirit or his shattered marriage. The senior minister told me, "Serious repentance is hard work, and it doesn't happen overnight." How long does it take? "Probably a lifetime."[66]

Could Bill Clinton be expected to devote the rest of his life to recovery? Based on her twenty years of frustration with Clinton's habits, Betsey Wright predicted, "I think he'll spend the rest of his life trying to convince people he was done wrong on this."[67]

The second of the President's spiritual advisers could relate personally to his difficulties. The Reverend Gordon MacDonald had also admitted to an extramarital affair and had had to leave the ministry. He had written a book about his rehabilitation that Clinton had read twice before selecting him.[68] The third angel was an old friend of Clinton from their Renaissance Weekend saturnalias for the soul, the Reverend Tony Campolo, a liberal Baptist preacher from Pennsylvania who believed strongly in the doctrine of forgiveness.

Clinton's spiritual advisers "would not hesitate to recommend some type of additional psychological counseling or treatment," promised Reverend James Dunn, executive director of the Baptist Joint Committee. "If they thought he needed the kind of help that was more than they could give, they would be the first to suggest it."[69]

Hillary may well have pushed this idea. In early October, she reportedly talked with a close friend who described another public power couple who had faced a similar watershed. When the wife had finally caught the man after a string of affairs, she had been devastated. But in the end, rather than throwing him out or surrendering him to another woman, she had decided it was better to fight for him and for what was precious about their relationship. Hillary said she was thinking along exactly the same lines. The key to saving the marriage, the friend said, was a therapist. Hillary reportedly responded that she and Bill knew that counseling was the right thing to do.[70]

Hillary's pastor was frank with me about this touchy subject: "It's a sickness of course, just like drug addiction or alcoholism, and he knows that. I have been told he is seeing a more professional kind of analyst."[71] Matthews was all in favor of it.

Hillary exempted herself from counseling sessions with Clinton's chosen spiritual counselors and avoided seeking help from both her past and present Methodist ministers. Don Jones wrote her in early fall to let her know he loved her but also loved her husband. He enclosed a sermon by Paul Tillich called "You Are Accepted" in which Tillich says, "Grace strikes you when you feel alienated from those you love the most. Grace strikes you when you have hurt those who mean the most to you." Hillary did not answer the letter. Instead, she passed it on to Bill, who wrote to Jones thanking him for being Hillary's friend "and mine." He closed with words that were to become ubiquitous: "We're working on it."[72]

Hillary refused overtures from Reverend Matthews as well. "I'm more pleased with the way the President has been looking for help than Hillary's reaction," he told me a year later. "Hillary is so blasted private, she could be seeing someone three times a day and we wouldn't know it. She's almost too independent for her own good. I, as a theologian, would say we are meant for relationships—we gain insights from one another."[73]

A folie à deux cannot be maintained if one person stops playing the game. "He's been doing this high-wire routine, and she's been his safety net," one friend observed. "If she decides to walk away, she could really do him in."

Of all the betrayals in their partnership, I asked a personal and political supporter of Hillary's, was this one of a different order?

"Oh, yes, it is, yes, yes, yes, yes—and on so many different levels," she said fervently. "On the professional as well as the personal level. If they'd made an accommodation to each other, it seems to me that he hasn't kept up his end of the bargain on any count, except perhaps"—she stopped abruptly—"I started to say, being a good father, but you can't even say that anymore."

Chelsea, whom the Clintons let fly thousands of miles away from Washington for college, was variously reported as being hospitalized for mysterious stomach pains and causing Hillary concern that she might be developing an eating disorder. A spokesperson at the Stanford University Medical Center said that Chelsea had never been there. But her refuge at Stanford had been invaded. Carolyn Starr, daughter of independent counsel Kenneth, had chosen to enter the same university that fall. The fact that Chelsea was now being dragged into this saga was the ultimate mortification for Hillary and Bill Clinton, portending a cycle of revenge that was almost Oresteian in scope.

Hillary was wretched. She could no longer reconcile her view of herself as a devout Christian with her complicity in this debauched marriage. Something would have to change. Drastically. For all Clinton's protestations of repentance, she could not count on him to change; she had heard it all before. No, this time the change would have to be in her.

CHAPTER SEVENTEEN

The Rebirth of Hillary Rodham

The cocoon has long since cracked open.
And I think it's going to be a beautiful butterfly.

—REVEREND ED MATTHEWS

All through the Arkansas years, friends had repeatedly told Hillary what the Little Rock newswoman Dorothy Stuck told me in 1992: "Regardless of what happens to Bill, the nation will be exposed to Hillary Clinton, and Hillary could—and should—be our first woman president." Hillary always laughed at such predictions. But she never brushed them off. David Rupert, the congressional intern who was her first love, sees a pattern in Hillary's life—grand ambition and denial of that ambition.[1]

She had, however, shown keen interest in running for governor of Arkansas in 1990. But Clinton couldn't surrender the title. Once her husband was president, she talked about "establishing my bona fides" in the first term so she could be considered for a Cabinet post as secretary of education if Clinton won a second term.[2] But she had been blocked at every turn by Hillary's original choice—to marry a man whose political ambitions were focused far earlier than her own.

In the fall of 1998, she began considering a Senate bid, but that would have to wait. First, as always, she had to clean up after Bill.

She started by rounding up a half-dozen Democratic congressional members to accompany her on a day trip to Puerto Rico in late September. The official purpose of the trip was to commiserate with the victims of Hurricane Georges. Her personal agenda was to school these gentlemen in how to oppose an impeachment inquiry. The congressmen were seated in a section behind Hillary's refuge on her plane when the First Lady, radiant in a white suit (referred to as "disaster chic"), plopped down casually and initiated a discussion of the inquiry—an issue on which the lawmakers would have to vote in a matter of days. About half the members of the group kept very quiet. Others, such as Congressman Jim McDermott, a Seattle psychiatrist, offered alternatives. Hillary listened, briefly.

"And then she blew our hair back," said one of the other congressmen. Adopting her lawyerly style, she said even if one stipulated that all the things Starr had charged were true, they did not rise to the level of an impeachable offense: treason, bribery, or other high crimes and misdemeanors. "She'll listen," said McDermott, "but she challenges you. You have to beat her down."

Was she intimidating?

McDermott sighs assent. "If I was going to war, I'd want her covering my rear. She's never going to run from a fight."[3]

The Clintons now faced the fight of their lives. On October 5, a House Judiciary Committee dominated by Republicans voted to trigger a formal impeachment investigation. More ominous for Clinton, several days later 31 Democrats joined the unanimous phalanx of 227 House Republicans in favoring an open-ended probe.

Hillary again channeled her anger into a political battle. Inside, she was bleeding; even her staff, with whom she rarely shares confidences, could see it written all over her. Her close friend Sara Ehrman described how Hillary had allowed herself while on vacation on the Vineyard to pull the covers over her head and pitch fits. Then, according to Ehrman, she had rallied herself: "I want to have a nervous breakdown, but I don't have the time now."[4] Hillary doesn't wallow. She perseveres, and never more intently than when she is in pain. But being human, she needs some ways to numb the pain. "She is hiding in her work and can't bear to be alone until she is so tired she must sleep," as Ehrman described her friend that fall of 1998.[5] Hillary was relying on the same healthy forms of escape that she had discovered back in college could combat depression: feverish work alternating with sleep of the sort that took her "back to the womb and away from the world."[6]

This time, Hillary found a way out of her funk that largely ignored Bill

Clinton, throwing herself into a nonstop campaign for endangered Democrats in the midterm congressional elections. Back and forth across the country she shuttled, stumping in New York for senatorial candidate Chuck Schumer, who found her impact "electric," and slamming Schumer's opponent, Whitewater committee chairman Al D'Amato, as a "Jesse Helms clone." In San Francisco she drew overflow crowds of women at events to help the shaky senatorial incumbent, Barbara Boxer.

The staff in Hillaryland was inundated with calls pleading for appearances by the First Lady. She outdrew Al Gore by a long shot. Only the President could be counted on to raise more money, but the tainted Clinton had to do it behind closed doors. Ultimately, Hillary hit twenty states, pulled in millions of dollars at some fifty fund-raisers, and spoke at thirty-four rallies. It was madness, but a heroic madness.

On election night, Hillary invited a few friends to a "girl's movie night" in the White House theater. They lost themselves in a lengthy melodrama, *Beloved*, the tragic saga of a black woman brutalized by men, but a story retold by powerful women—novelist Toni Morrison and actress-producer Oprah Winfrey. Bill Clinton was not welcome; he spent the night in his chief of staff's office surfing the Internet to follow the exit polls.

An astonishing reversal of the Democrats' fortunes defied historical precedent in a midterm election. On top of key Senate victories, Democrats picked up five seats in the House. It was the death rattle of Newt Gingrich, whose ads concentrating on Clinton's character and the Lewinsky scandal had backfired.

OPENING UP

Who was that dazzling woman on the President's arm at the annual awards dinner of the National Endowments for the Arts and Humanities? A plunging neckline revealed the First Bosom in a most flattering way—the first time that guests could remember seeing Hillary in décolleté. It was two days after the elections, and her table partners sang Hillary's praises for pulling out senatorial victories for Schumer in New York and Boxer in California. Hillary herself was not shy about claiming credit. In fact, she told Tony Podesta, then Senator Carol Moseley-Braun's campaign chairman, that she might have saved Moseley-Braun "if my team had gotten to Chicago a month earlier." He agreed.[7]

Thus the Clinton who found at least partial redemption in the fall of 1998 was not Bill, who continued to infuriate Republicans with his unrepentant answers to questions sent to him by the Judiciary Committee. It was Hillary, who erased the memory of her part in the Democrats' 1994 congressional defeat by emerging as the star of the party in its 1998 comeback.

Charlie Rangel, the hefty Harlem congressman with twenty-eight years in the House, heard Illinois political leaders salivating over the prospect of getting Hillary to run for senator from her home state. Rangel smacked his forehead and erupted in jealousy: "Jesus Christ, a superstar like this being a senator from Illinois, come on!"

"Why not New York?" he had pressed Hillary shortly after the midterm election.

She smiled. "It's interesting."[8]

Knowing that she likes a good fight (they had served together on the Watergate Committee) Rangel ratcheted up her enthusiasm for getting back at the Republicans who had mercilessly hammered her to get at her husband. Like many other former Bill Clinton enthusiasts post-Monica, Rangel had shifted his allegiance to the President's wife. Reviewing the couple's history, he was candid with me: "She saw the rascal running around Yale Law School. She cleaned him up, made him President, but now and then he falls off the wagon. I don't think the President deserves her."

Three days after the election the heavens opened up. Senator Moynihan announced he would give up his seat. "She started asking people right from the start, 'Should I run?' " says Rangel. But the pall over her husband's White House necessitated modesty. She asked Rangel, "Could we hold off on this conversation until after the President gets through this impeachment proceeding?"[9]

She had to wait.

Would Hillary always be seen through the invasive snooperscope of Monica's story? The intern was writing a book and negotiating to do a Barbara Walters interview, both of which would have the effect of producing a distorted image of Hillary. Hillary has a horror of others telling her story. When she traveled, her press and advance people maintained a *cordon sanitaire* around her; "nettlesome" reporters were confined to a "press pen" at least fifty yards away. No writer or sound engineer was going to record a spontaneous comment or stick her with a question about the presidential crisis.

She burned off her frustration on new gym equipment in the White House. She was like an Olympic athlete in training, waiting for the big event. And much to her delight the pounds began dropping off and a new, race-ready body began to emerge.

For a brainy careerist—for any woman who has passed fifty—it is important to feel pretty and sexy. On election night 1996, her young male press secretary, Neel Lattimore, had presented her with a "Hillary Is a Babe" T-shirt. Then forty-eight, she loved being told "You're hot, Hillary." But she was more often referred to as Hillary the fashion frump, so uncertain of and changeable in her appearance that she used to say, "If I change my hairstyle, I can knock anything off the front page of the paper."

Her uncertainty was only magnified by the Monica revelations. She asked Cristophe, the celebrity hairstylist who had worked on Bill Clinton, whom he could recommend for her. Cristophe gave her a petite young Swiss-French girl who didn't watch TV, didn't read newspapers, was totally apolitical, just interested in pleasing her clients. Isabel Goetz looked at Hillary's broad face and decided she needed a short, sexy, but feminine hairstyle. She showed the First Lady a picture of Raquel Welch: "This is the style now, you should try."[10] The cosmetic makeover of Hillary Rodham had begun.

On her frequent trips to New York she conferred personally with haute couture master Oscar de la Renta and came under the tutelage of America's reigning fashion cop, *Vogue* editor Anna Wintour, who shrewdly struck up a friendship with the First Lady. Her wardrobe became consistently glamorous: a uniform of neutral-colored suits with hip-hiding long jackets, topped off with a golden helmet of shorter, straighter hair and softer matte makeup. Gone were the dark dominatrix eyebrows and the barrel-bottomed suit jackets and the treacly pastels. More often she appeared in New York black. For evening events in the White House she began looking noticeably sexy. At one Governor's dinner she turned heads in a blue Bill Blass number with a thigh-high slit.

She was fifty-one before she found her personal style for the first time. "She definitely hit her stride late in life," acknowledges Lattimore, "but she has certainly mastered it."[11] At the same time, she had to live with all kinds of ugly characterizations of herself being floated in the media: Was she Hillary the enabler? Hillary the victim? Hillary the feminist sellout? The gossip on the Republican dinner-party circuit in Washington was even nastier, according to a Democratic wife married to a minority business mogul: Hillary was blamed as the cold, sexless, depriving wife whose husband had had to go elsewhere. In the glare of these depictions, Hillary became ever more vigilant about controlling her image. Ann Lewis, her handpicked White House communications director, was cooperative with a *Vanity Fair* article until it was mentioned that a picture of Hillary triumphant might be nice on the magazine's December cover. Alarm bells went off.

"If he's down by December, she can't look like she's up," said Lewis.[12]

Vogue had been working with the White House for months on a prosaic story about the First Lady's Save America's Treasures project. The scandal had put the story on hold. But Anna Wintour was intrigued. The editor saw the First Lady emerging as a considerable person in her own right: "attractive and confident in herself and in what she believes, in other words, very much a *Vogue* woman."[13] Wintour called the White House and asked if Hillary would agree to resume the story but shift the focus to herself—with glamorous pictures by star photographer Annie Leibovitz. Hillary agreed.

Regal was the look that Anna and Annie wanted. A picture was sent to Hillary of a burgundy velvet gown that Oscar de la Renta had done for the Balmain collection. She liked it. Oscar agreed to custom remake it for her since Hillary does not have a couture figure. She is a size 10, or, as the magazine's fashion director, Paul Cavaco, would say, "She's a woman. She has a full figure. She's got it all goin' on."

The stylists were surprised to find that she didn't treat fashion as fluffy, although her schedulers hovered about and she continued to work with them simultaneously during the shoot at the White House. Annie Leibovitz set up her equipment on the Truman Balcony and suggested that Hillary be shot having a cup of coffee and reading a newspaper. Her assistants recoiled. One of them replied, "The First Lady does not read newspapers."

In the end, both crew and subject were pleased with their work. "I've done a million celebrities—but she's the First Lady, and she was everything you'd want the First Lady to be," swooned Cavaco. "Her bearing was regal, her manners were impeccable. I was completely wowed and in love with her by the time I left."[14]

When she wants to be warm, Hillary is wonderfully warm. And funny. And she is often flirtatious. Lattimore had teasingly called her "my girl." He chuckles as he recalls a trip to Bolivia when he and the staff were dragged out by Hillary on some archaeological dig in the wind and rain. The guide turned out to be young and handsome; all the young female aides went gaga. Hillary swept past them, eyes twinkling, and took him over: "I'm the First Lady, this is *my* guide."[15]

WHY NOT NEW YORK?

The loyal denizens of Hillaryland echoed the official story that the First Lady had never given a thought to running for political office before the idea was planted by Congressman Charlie Rangel and Senator Robert Torricelli in late 1998. In fact, an invitation had been extended a year earlier.

It was actually December 1997, on the receiving line at the White House Christmas party, when Hillary's ear was caught by Judith Hope, the New York State Democratic Party chairwoman. "A lot of people think when you leave the White House, you ought to run for U.S. senator from New York," Hope had said. Hillary had simply raised her eyebrows in mock humility and laughed. But once this exchange found its way into print, Senator Pat Moynihan had gone ballistic; it was his seat they were talking about, and he still intended to keep it warm at least until the year 2000.[16]

"Please don't do that again," Hillary said the next time she saw Hope. "I just don't need this now." Judith kept the idea percolating among party leaders. "Everyone was telling Judith she was crazy," recalls her husband, Tom Twomey. "The White House went bananas. They shut Judith up fast."[17]

But the idea had legs, and by the summer of 1998 it was picked up by none other than the President himself. During the Clintons' tense on-the-run visit to East Hampton at the peak of the Monica revelations, the President was looking for ways to make up to the First Lady. At the gala fund-raiser thrown by Alec Baldwin, the actor lavished Hillary with praise in his introduction, calling her "the most effective First Lady in U.S. history. She stands alone in her contributions to the President's success." Hillary rose to speak first, sober in a brown silk pantsuit and noticeably untanned. She stuck strictly to issues and ideas. Sitting behind her, Bill Clinton's gaze bordered on Nancy Reagan–esque awe. When Hillary's remarks were continually interrupted by gusts of applause, the President became excited. He turned to Judith Hope and whispered, "She's really popular in New York, isn't she?"

"She *owns* New York," pronounced Hope.

He kept staring at Hillary—this was her crowd—and basking in the reaction to her, a narcissistic extension of his own need to capture every last heart and mind. He said with a proud chuckle, "Maybe she should run for office here."

"You said it, I didn't," Hope insisted. "I get in trouble when I suggest that."[18]

While Bill Clinton was under virtual house arrest in Washington throughout that fall and winter, Hillary went out of her way to establish a very public parallel social life—mostly in New York. (She went as far as

Bulgaria in order to be out of Washington on October 11, her wedding anniversary.) At the opening of Carnegie Hall's season in late September she turned up, unescorted, in a black velvet gown. She sat in the box of former Treasury official Frank Newman and his wife, Lizabeth, who had relocated to Manhattan and become prominent arts patrons.

"So, Liz, how are you adapting to New York?" the First Lady was curious to know. Sensing that Hillary herself was shopping for a place to relocate, Liz Newman said, "Hillary, what they care about here is the bottom line—they don't care about your private life."[19]

Hillary had always had an unfulfilled love affair with New York. All through her college years she and her pen pal, John Peavoy, had made plans to meet in the Big Apple. For her, having a drink in New York symbolized grown-up sophistication. But Hillary's father had refused to give her permission to go to rotten Gotham—it was too dangerous, too expensive, too draining.[20] Now she was free to kick up her heels.

New York City was where she planned to live after vacating the White House. She loved its pace and sophistication and its muscular liberal politics. What a relief it would be to say good-bye to public housing, she told an interviewer. Her only problem was—money. The Clintons were faced with legal fees running up to $5 million. Their solicitations for help in paying off the debts for Bad Boy Bill had become so desperately broad that one had been sent to Dr. Bernard Lewinsky—Monica's father.[21] The money that Hillary had systematically invested over the years toward the day when she could finally buy their own home had been depleted to pay for Clinton's Excelsior Hotel moment with Paula Jones. Almost half of the $850,000 settlement had to come out of the monies in the Clintons' blind trust, most of it earned by Hillary. Defending Clinton through months of impeachment proceedings was going to cost a fortune. And her husband's only plan for the future was building a Clinton Presidential Library—a monument that these days would cost well over $100 million.

When she began to think seriously about mounting a Senate campaign, those financial burdens were the least of it. The Clintons could form fundraising committees for just about everything except their personal living expenses. As much as she longed to live in New York City, its golden co-ops and pricey condos were beyond the means of a public servant with no independent wealth. As First Lady, she couldn't earn honoraria for her speeches. And as an elected lawmaker, she wouldn't have time to cash in on the multimillion-dollar book contract that was being dangled before her. Her salary as a senator would be $136,700 a year.

But wasn't it Bill Clinton's turn to be the breadwinner?

LET HIM WAIT

It would take House Republicans weeks of self-immolating tactics throughout October and November before they realized that the curtain had already fallen on this Shakespearean history play—and they weren't going to kill the king. "We have to get this [impeachment inquiry] over with as soon as possible," warned Wisconsin's Republican governor, Tommy Thompson. "The voters are sick to death of partisanship."

Hillary continued to levitate above the fray. Her valiant year was comparable to Jacqueline Kennedy's example of dignified grief after the assassination of her husband. "Hillary has moved to a new level as a public figure," Judith Hope told me after the midterm elections. "She is a person of enormous political authority in her own right—not derived from her husband."[22]

In late November, Hillary took a congressional delegation to the Dominican Republic, where she spent a weekend as the guest of Oscar de la Renta and his wife in their new plantation-style villa in Punta Cana. But Hillary didn't spend much time relaxing in planter's chairs. She was too busy cultivating the Dominican vote (New York City has 600,000 Dominicans) with baseball hero Sammy Sosa in tow. The First Lady was repeatedly asked if she was going to run for senator from New York. "Don't tell me Charlie Rangel's been all the way down here campaigning for me!" she joked. Of course he had, and of course she knew it. After dark, while beautiful people serenaded her with guitars on Oscar's beachfront loggia, Hillary sat with Rangel and the new president of the Dominican Republic and talked politics all night.

She told Rangel she was ready to step out and declare her own political identity—at last. He was thrilled.

She hated all the waiting. That had been plain the last time she had attended a service at her Little Rock Methodist church before her pastor had retired. She was asked to do her rotation as a steward and help take the collection. Glad for the excuse to greet everyone in the church, she had ignored the prodding of her security people and lingered for a long time after the service, gabbing and smiling. Finally, a Secret Service man told her, "The President radioed. He's leaving the Baptist Church, now."

"Just let him wait," she said, turning to Reverend Matthews. "I've waited all through our married life, he can just jolly well wait now." Then she broke into a grin. For Matthews's benefit she mimicked the way Southern Baptists do their roll call in order to give sinners one more chance to come forward.

"Just sing that last verse one more time," she drawled, "wonnnnne more time."

As her minister watched Hillary make her way to her car, a powerful image came to him: "The cocoon has long since cracked open. And I think it's going to be a beautiful butterfly."[23]

In December, the institutions of government began to defend their own integrity. Scholars and lawmakers engaged in intense debate over the standards for impeachment of a president. The indissoluble sticking point was where private lying left off and public lying rose to the level of criminality. The "agony" Clinton admitted having caused his family was no longer able to be "boxed off" from the mistrust of his presidential leadership. They were all of a piece.

In mid-December, I spoke to a lawyer close to the Clintons and made a very familiar note to myself: "She's still angry. She hasn't forgiven him."

Clinton was virtually friendless. The old FOBs had fallen away or turned on him, or at best were wary and keeping their distance. Weekends at Camp David had become torturous. Thanksgiving had brought together the family tribe, which consists of Mrs. Rodham, Clinton's widowed stepfather Dick Kelley, his brother Roger, Roger's wife, and their baby son, Toby; Hillary's brother Tony and his wife, Nicole, the daughter of Senator Barbara Boxer; and Boxer herself; along with the Bloodworth-Thomasons. It was a five-day endurance contest of playing games and watching videos.

The President was newly attentive to his wife's preferences in movies and jokes. When she vanished after the formalities at one White House dinner, Clinton anxiously asked his aides, "Where is the First Lady?" Told she had already gone upstairs to retire, the night-owl President said a hasty good-bye to the guests he was schmoozing with and followed Hillary to the private quarters.

Hillary was not sitting with his lawyers to deal with the impeachment challenge—"not at all," confirmed an attorney familiar with the case. He, like others, had heard rumors from within the Justice Department that Ken Starr was determined to bring an indictment against Clinton no matter what the outcome of the impeachment vote. The sagacious attorney gave me a grave pronouncement: the consequences of Clinton's private weaknesses would be hanging over his head for the rest of his life.

And for the first time, the woman who had taught Clinton how to fight, the protector who kept his "precarious little boat" in the channel, the Valkyrie who was always ready to lift her wounded barefoot boy from the battlefield and fly him to Valhalla had at last withdrawn her approval and support. The withdrawal of Hillary's approval helped to bring the President to an inner collapse in December. "This is passivity shading into immobility." That was Bill Curry's reading of Clinton's Buddha-like detachment from the lawmakers who turned thumbs down on him, day after day, during the week leading up to the final House vote. "Hillary is clearly less present, and it clearly saps him of the energy to fight," adds Curry. "He probably never knew until now just how great a difference she makes."[24]

NEGATIVE SPACE

The First Family fortuitously left Washington hours after the House Judiciary Committee adopted the first article of impeachment against Clinton on Friday, December 11. Hillary secluded herself in a separate compartment from the President on Air Force One. They landed in the new Palestinian-controlled Gaza airport, and Hillary kept a mostly separate schedule. In the sands of Gaza she was embraced with unambiguous warmth as a heroine of the Palestinians, one who had boldly spoken out the previous spring—on her own—in favor of an eventual Palestinian state. When the First Lady turned her back on the President and repulsed his attempt to take her arm, their body language interrupted a solemn moment at the grave of slain Israeli prime minister Yitzhak Rabin and displayed for the international media the latest of Hillary's choices. She was punishing her husband by proving to him how little she needed him. But would she let him hang himself?

When impeachment by the full House began to look inevitable in mid-December, Clinton was described by a political ally as being in "a state of disbelief." Only on the eve of the first impeachment vote on the House floor in 130 years did the President's partner break her months of silence to offer a tepid public appeal "to end divisiveness" in keeping with the holiday season. With the President's associates openly describing him as "devastated" and House Democrats buzzing about the possibility of his resignation, Hillary again rose like a lioness aroused. She could not let her husband's demons bring her down with him and cast the name Clinton into the annals of shamed presidents alongside that of Richard Nixon's.

Early on that fateful Saturday, December 19, she sped in a presidential limousine up to the Hill to breathe fire into dispirited House Democrats.

Defiant as ever, the First Lady—far more popular now than her husband with Democrats in Congress—charged Republicans with engaging in the politics of personal destruction. She was rewarded with a half-dozen standing ovations and hugs from members. Earlier, lawmakers had been invited to come to the White House immediately after the vote, but it looked as if few, if any, planned to show. Hillary had determined to "remind" them with the help of Charlie Rangel. "When it looked like the meeting was about to be adjourned," says Rangel, "I raised the idea that we all go up to express our support for the President and tell him he *couldn't consider* resigning."[25]

"Great!" chimed Hillary, as if the idea were newborn. "John Podesta, you make sure you do what you have to do," she directed the President's chief of staff.

But that afternoon, in a House chamber one member called "full of hate," no one, not even Hillary Clinton, could save her husband from the terrible shame of entering history as the only elected President of the United States to be impeached.[26] Not even the partisan "pep rally" later staged by Hillary and two busloads of House Democrats in the Rose Garden seemed to penetrate the gloom. Clinton emerged looking forlorn and friendless and, never mentioning the word "impeachment," flatly declared he would serve "until the last hour of the last day of my term." Turning to thread his way back through the smattering of party members, Bill Clinton clutched his wife's hand and didn't let go. The silent but eloquent evidence of his need for support from the woman who had provided it so many times in the past was, for many, the most memorable of the day's unforgettable images. She was his only sanctuary.

Most women rallied around her. In a group interview with activist middle-class Democratic women following a nationwide teleconference on women and Social Security chaired by Hillary, a divorced woman said, "I have asked myself, If I had gone through what she has been going through, could I have had not only the courage but the emotional stamina to be as poised and productive as she is?"

Congressman Dennis Kucinich told the media, "Everybody understands she is one of the leaders of the nation right now, as much as the President." It was a cold triumph for Hillary Rodham Clinton. She was at the peak of her power, but she couldn't use it. Still, she had to wait.

When Queen Hillary appeared on the cover of *Vogue,* the image caused more talk than just about anything she had done since coming to the White House. Her poll numbers spiked dramatically. She had been gaining popularity all through the fall election period, but she hit her all-time high, a 67 percent favorability rating, on December 28, 1998. Bill Clinton's favorability ratings had tailed off to the low 50s. In the hearts of the public, the couple had traded places.[27]

The more her husband's weaknesses were graphically catalogued and he was viewed by the public as a moral lowlife, the more she was elevated—almost beatified. But there was a falsity to this beatification of which she was painfully aware. The "pity press" made Hillary Rodham squirm beyond almost anything else. Hillary as victim? Her whole mission worldwide has been to empower women to shuck off the victim role and stand up for themselves.

By Christmas, encountering the Clintons was like noticing the negative space in a painting, the space in between; it's not the focal point, but by force of contrast it makes everything clearer. Even when they occupied the same table or podium, they seemed separate. They brought tension into ballrooms and left supporters feeling depressed, the dreams once shared with this golden couple dashed.

At a New Year's Eve party, Hillary came dressed in a mannish plaid jacket with tuxedo lapels. This year, she was making no effort to look sexy for Bill. After much debate, the Clintons had decided at the last minute to take some questions from the gathering of hundreds of their peers. But instructions for sanitizing the questions had gone out before the party: there was to be no mention of scandal or impeachment.

Taking their places in rocking chairs on a riser, the Clintons looked suddenly aged. They sat far apart. The President began the dreary festivities by saying, "This may surprise you, but I thought a lot of good things happened in 1998." In a froggy voice empty of life or energy, he ran down a laundry list of his impressive accomplishments, beginning with the first balanced budget since 1969. Hillary sat bent over like Rodin's *The Thinker.* It looked as if the wind had been knocked out of both of them. They spoke in the past tense about "what we were trying to do." After nearly an hour of this tortured performance, a question was addressed to Hillary: What will be your legacy?

"Oh, I don't need a legacy—I was on the cover of *Vogue.*"

It was a good line, delivered like Scarlett. But Hillary stepped on the laughter, sounding bitter and sardonic to some in the audience. "Nothing could equal that legacy," she said. "Health care is but a distant memory. So the epitaph should read, 'She was on the cover of *Vogue.*' "

She had used as synonymous with "legacy" the word "epitaph."

"You Guys Were Wrong"

In 1999, for the first time, Hillary's suspended dream of a political platform of her own took realistic form. Congressman Rangel proudly announced in January that the New York Democratic Party had "pulled together an offer that the First Lady can't refuse," including a guarantee that the nomination for senator of New York would be hers for the asking, without a primary.[28] Her almost certain opponent would be Rudolph Giuliani, New York's combative Republican mayor, who had Washington ambitions of his own.

On February 12—the day the Senate met to vote on the impeachment charges—Hillary waited in a separate corner of the residence from her husband, entertaining a man who had floated between the His and Hers sides of the White House for two years: Harold Ickes. The abrasive political strategist had a great deal in common with Hillary. They shared a passion for liberal causes, and he, too, felt betrayed by Bill Clinton, having learned the President fired him as an adviser by reading it in *The Wall Street Journal.* Ickes was one of the craftiest New York political operators Hillary knew and the first person she had consulted when she had begun to consider a Senate race in a state where she had never lived.

Clinton wandered by and looked in to greet his wife's guest. He was not invited into their huddle.

At 9:30 A.M. on Capitol Hill, shiny red voting folders were passed out to the senators. When they broke the gold seal, they found a score sheet inside. It had been 387 days since the Monica story had broken, and it had been covered in the news, play by play, every day since then. As the roll was called, one by one the mostly middle-aged and elderly men of the Senate stood up, buttoned their coats, and solemnly delivered their "Guilty" or "Not guilty" votes with a feel for the theatrical moment. The vote on the first article, which charged Clinton with lying under oath, went the President's way. It was the vote on the second article—charging him with preventing, obstructing, and impeding justice—that left him condemned by one half of the highest elected political representatives of the American people. It was not sufficient to remove him from office, but it laid bare the terrible fissure his misconduct had created.

Chief Justice William Rehnquist read out the final decision: "Two-thirds of the Senators present, not having found him guilty of the charges contained therein, it is therefore ordered and adjudged that the said William

Jefferson Clinton be, and he hereby is, acquitted of the charges in the said articles."

Hillary waited for maybe ten minutes after Rehnquist's gavel came down before continuing her marathon meeting with Ickes over lunch. Her first question was "Do I really want to run for United States senator with all that that entails?"

"It involves not only running and hopefully winning, but serving at least twelve years," Ickes told her, "because I think you need that to make a real impact." Then he ran down the nitty-gritty of what it's like to be a junior senator from New York. It's not about spending the weekend in glitzy Manhattan, he said, it's about doing "pothole work" in the Bronx, Brooklyn and Queens, Suffolk and Nassau counties, Rockland and Westchester Counties, and taking little planes to Plattsburgh or Elmira, and vacationing in the Catskills or on the Finger Lakes. The work is not well paid and not glamorous.[29]

Notwithstanding, he realized that Hillary was clearly very interested: "She's not a person who toys with things." And there were many layers of frustration behind the urgency she felt to speak with her own voice. "Go back to when [Bill] first started running for President," Ickes recounts. "You had the two-for-one thing—you know, how she said, 'Elect him, you get me, too.' Then there was the co-presidency thing. Then came the health care fiasco, which was mostly laid at her doorstep. Then she went underground a bit. Then she had the commodities-trading thing, and the questions about billing at the Rose law firm. Then came the pillorying of Hillary, and the constant effort to drive the President and Hillary out of office. For her to run and win a very, very prestigious seat would permit her supporters to say there was a lot more here than anybody thought: 'You guys were wrong!' "[30]

After four hours of discussion, Ickes found out the bottom line for Hillary: "This is a race for redemption. It's really that simple—redemption."[31]

In the Rose Garden, the wounded, pride-stripped President tried to express his remorse to the nation. He said the right words—he was profoundly sorry—but without noticeable humility. Then he turned, threw his head back, and thrust out his chin. A male figure opened the door to the Oval Office for him. There was no Hillary there.

OUT OF THE GATE

Necks had to crane from behind pillars in the Plaza Hotel's overflowing Grand Ballroom on March 3, when Hillary Rodham Clinton made her triumphal appearance at a New York fund-raiser luncheon on the same day the famous intern was set to do her Full Monica TV interview with Barbara Walters.

"It's a done deal," whispered one $10,000-ticket holder to another.

In the back of the ballroom, where an army of video cameramen was stacked up on three risers, the comments were typical of New Yorkers' cynicism:

"She's probably coming to New York to get therapy."

"Nah, she'd rather run for Senate than look inside. Besides, running for Senate is cheaper than therapy."

That night the skies of Manhattan were shattered by lightning and the streets screamed with fire engine sirens as Hillary sat down to an East Side dinner party while the Monica interview simultaneously reached 70 million Americans. The atmosphere inside the town house of Jurate Kasickes and Roger Altman was surreal and artificially serene. No one mentioned the interview. The hostess wouldn't even videotape it. "I couldn't, anyway," says Kasickes with a laugh. "The Secret Service was upstairs in the library watching a basketball game on the TV."

The guests were people Kasickes and Altman thought Hillary should know if she moved to New York: TV and movie mogul Barry Diller; *60 Minutes*'s Lesley Stahl; publisher and developer Mort Zuckerman; Pete Peterson of the Blackstone Group and his wife, Joan Ganz Cooney, founder of Children's Television Workshop, among others. Everybody was very aware of what was going on but extremely respectful. Nobody at the dinner table asked Hillary about the Senate race. And *nobody* mentioned Monica.

Instead, Kasickes said sweetly, "Tell us about your day." Hillary talked about the arts program in the school she had visited that morning. She looked tired and subdued.

"At her lunch appearance she'd been on such a high," empathized her hostess. "Then to know the world was watching Monica's debut as the femme fatale who swept her husband away, it had to have been the worst day of her life."[32]

Not even Chelsea could provide the glue in this splintered marriage anymore. And at this stage in her own individuation, she needed to extricate herself from the role of caretaker for her volatile parents. Three thousand miles away, Chelsea Clinton was able to lose herself in the sprawling, palm-shaded campus of Stanford University. When she returned to campus after tense visits to the White House, she could relax and take on the demeanor of just another student—the jeans and North Face jacket, the L.L. Bean backpack, the glow of innocent curiosity—and get on her bike and just ride, free at last. Her friends would draw around her and take her off to the Stanford CoHo for a caffe latte or to listen to hip-hop at a nighttime "groove." And on Monday morning she would be back in her class on The Human Organism, scribbling complicated formulae and graphs, totally engrossed in her own world. As a premed student, Chelsea had chosen to be a Human Biology major because of the breadth of its premise: that solving many of the major problems facing humanity today—from environmental degradation to AIDS, cancer, and the cost of health care—requires an understanding of both biology and the social sciences.

Chelsea looked slender but healthy and well rested in class last March, despite the tabloid rumors that she was not eating. Friends confirmed that she had been through rough patches and did suffer from a sense of betrayal by her father.[33] She identifies with her mother, who is the most important person in the world to her and to whom she looks for solace. Like her mother, she didn't speak of the scandal even to her closest friends, and nobody asked. But unlike her mother, Chelsea does read newspapers. One report depicted Chelsea as waking up before her seven Stanford housemates and sitting alone in the kitchen, reading up on the scandal in *USA Today*.[34] There could be no complete escape.

Front and center in the Stanford Bookstore: *Monica's Story*. Far more disturbing than the book was the state of her parents' marriage. Her mother had scarcely spoken to her father since that wicked August seven months before. On their family ski holiday in Utah, meant to celebrate Chelsea's nineteenth birthday, the fighting had been intolerable. Her mother's back had gone out. Her parents had fled from each other by returning a day early to Washington and their separate schedules. Hillary had also skipped the weekend in Hot Springs when a dreary little crowd had turned up in a drenching rain for the dedication of Bill Clinton's childhood home as a museum (for which funding had been embarrassingly defeated 41–8 by the Arkansas state legislature).

Clinton was still imploding. From one of the closest current advisers to both Bill and Hillary I learned why: "Hillary is moving on with her life and not helping him, not participating in his presidency any further," he prophesied inaccurately. "That means it won't add up to anything, it won't be a strong finish. He's never known how to make it happen. She is the one who has always, one way or another, made it happen, or energized those who had to make it happen."

"Just keep on keeping on" was Hillary's constant admonition to Chelsea.

HILLARY'S HIDDEN HAND IN KOSOVO

And that is exactly what Hillary and Chelsea did, together. During Chelsea's spring break, they took a grand tour through Egypt, Morocco, and Tunisia, following their tradition of combining adventure with soft foreign policy. Hillary wanted to help dispel the distrust by Arab states left over from the Persian Gulf War. This was the sixty-second time she had made a trip abroad since her husband had become President, and twenty of those journeys had been without him. Already, she had exceeded the number of countries visited by Eleanor Roosevelt over her lifetime. In a mild understatement, Hillary told reporters, "I always like getting away from Washington."[35]

On this trip she had a major foreign policy crisis on her mind: Kosovo. Serbian president Slobodan Milošević had intensified his ethnic cleansing campaign. The Saturday Hillary left for Africa, Clinton was meeting with his senior military advisers to discuss options for military action against Milošević. Both Defense Secretary William Cohen and Army general Hugh Shelton, chairman of the Joint Chiefs of Staff, were blunt in giving their negative assessments of an airborne bombing campaign: "You can't control a territory with airplanes."[36]

On March 21, Hillary Clinton was on the phone from North Africa forcefully expressing a very different view to the President. "I urged him to bomb," she told Lucinda Franks, a reporter on the trip. The Clintons argued the issue in lengthy phone calls over the next few days. Clinton's mind was crammed with what-ifs: What if bombing promoted more executions? What if it took apart the NATO alliance? Hillary shot back, "You cannot let this go on at the end of a century that has seen the major holocaust of our time. What do we have NATO for if not to defend our way of life?"

Hillary had been unhappy with Clinton's long hesitancy about using force in Bosnia. She was the first American official to go to Bosnia after the Dayton Peace Accords. Earlier, she had talked to U.S. generals there and at home about the need for military action, at one point urging Clinton to consider bombing without NATO support. Now she was saying, "We've got to do better in Kosovo." On her second night in Egypt she waited to hear the outcome of the eleventh-hour meeting between Milošević and Clinton's special diplomatic envoy, Richard Holbrooke. It failed. This time when the President called, according to Franks, Hillary told him, "You've got to bite the bullet."[37]

The next day Clinton declared that force was necessary. NATO ordered air strikes. Bombs began falling on Serbia on March 25. Within the week, the President's decision was being challenged from all sides. The bombing did indeed provide cover for an acceleration of Serb atrocities. Clinton is a nail-biter, Hillary remarked. So, on the thirty-first she spoke from Morocco, bolstering her husband's war policy with a staunchness rarely heard from a First Lady: "They could not permit this to go on with impunity until most of the Albanian population was either dead or displaced. . . . My husband and our NATO allies are determined to persevere until Milošević has embraced peace or NATO has significantly limited his ability to make war."[38]

Despite Clinton's lack of military experience and the steady barrage of criticism from all sides, after eleven weeks of relentless air strikes, Slobodan Milošević blinked. Clinton came out of the operation with a clear and decisive victory. Doubting hawks like William Safire had to pull in their talons. Months later, during testimony before Congress, a senior diplomat acknowledged, "For the average Kosovar, life today is better and the future more promising than at any time since Belgrade stripped Kosovo's autonomy away a decade ago."[39]

THE COUPLE CROSSOVER

Hillary was engrossed in thinking through her choices. "I want independence," she declared emphatically in the spring of 1999, as she was getting psyched up to plunge into electoral politics. "I want to be judged on my own merits." Although it sounded strange coming from a woman the world saw as iron-willed, Hillary confessed, "Now for the first time I am making my own decisions. I can feel the difference. It's a great relief."[40]

She also intended to set boundaries her husband could not cross without her permission. Bill Clinton had run on one track all his life. Now about to be forceably retired at nearly the top of his game, flashes of his despond came through even in campaign speeches for his wife. "I'm not running for anything," he told a hip, young audience in East Hampton, "and *I hate it*. I wish I were."[41] Next best, he was eager to handicap his wife's race and make her a winner. "He's already said he wants to run my constituency," Hillary said coolly. She made it clear she wanted him kept behind the scenes, at least for a while: "He has a great many interests." She made a vague reference to only one—"his library."

But in this ruptured political partnership Hillary was also a loser. Although she is a prescient political strategist who several times has spotted golden opportunities for Bill, she is not a natural retail politician. Hillary doesn't need the adulation of the crowds. Rather, she puts up with it. Good politicians are like actors: they want the theater, they crave the applause, they have to have it. Hillary wants to be a prime mover but not to have to press the flesh until the chairs are being upturned on the banquet tables.

In one of her first high-profile events in New York, Hillary "dissed" a room full of important people. It was a book party at the restaurant Le Cirque organized by Matilda Cuomo, the wife of New York's former governor, to highlight mentoring. But the real draw was the First Lady. Hillary's advance people issued instructions that a "press pen" should be set up at the far end of the salon with a velvet rope across.

"The New York press is not used to standing behind ropes," they were warned by Peggy Siegal, a New York publicist with a Rolodex that matches her social radar. The White House people did not listen. When *New York Post* gossip matriarch Cindy Adams was told to stand behind a rope, she thought she was hearing a foreign language. "The First Lady and I are very friendly," she insisted. It was futile. Neil Travis, another *Post* columnist, dashed into the party folding a silk handkerchief for his pocket. Given the rope treatment, he said, "I'm leaving."

Guests had made special efforts to leave their offices an hour early to comply with Secret Service regulations and waded through a cloudburst with expectations of an intimate cocktail party where they would shake Hillary's hand. After keeping them waiting for an hour, Hillary slipped into the main salon and delivered a sober seventeen-minute speech about mentoring. One sponsor was so bored that she concentrated on Hillary's body: "She doesn't have that fat ass or the piano legs anymore. I don't know if it's lipo, but she looks a lot better."

Then Hillary turned around and walked out. Everybody was stunned.

"It's not like these were street people," sniped Siegal, referring to guests such as Manhattan's district attorney, top developers, and Wall Street moguls.[42] Please God, Siegal prayed, don't let Maureen Dowd get wind of this—which of course she did. The sulfurously funny *New York Times* columnist trashed the First Lady and not for the first or last time.

Hearing about the Cuomo event, Lanny Davis remarked, "I expect that Hillary is going to need a lot of educating about dealing with the press."[43] Bill Clinton would have pumped every hand in that room or apologized so "sincerely" for being late that people would have left feeling as if he were their best friend. Harold Ickes was asked if he would be in charge of Hillary's "attitude reform." He chuckled but offered his view that the Clintons' poor experiences with the press had been to a large extent their own fault. "It's not an inconsequential factor" in Hillary's race, he said, "it's *the* key factor."[44]

None of Hillary's friends was encouraging her to plunge into the snake pit of New York politics. Not Linda Bloodworth-Thomason, not Harry Thomason, not Diane Blair, not her old Park Ridge pal Betsey Ebeling. Susan Thomases was dead set against her running. Even Harold Ickes was not pushing her to say yes. Congresswoman Nita Lowey, who had been planning to run for the Senate seat until Hillary popped up, was gracious to the point of obsequiousness, repeating all spring, "If she runs, I'll support her."

By June, it seemed obvious to Lowey that Hillary was going to run for the Senate. Lowey had to make her move. She called up Hillary. "I didn't ask," says the deft ten-year congressional veteran, and Hillary didn't say no. "She wasn't going to say anything to me in private that she wasn't prepared to say publicly." Lowey told the First Lady that if she moved to Westchester, Lowey's home district, maybe she could come over for a barbecue.

Hillary said, "I'd love to." And with that unarticulated set of clear messages, Lowey backed out.[45]

From the beginning, the biggest promoter of an independent Hillary Clinton candidacy was Bill Clinton. "Listen, he knows that she has given so much for so many years for his political career and it is coming to an end in the form that it has always taken," said Betsey Wright. "He will support her in whatever she wants to do, and right now he is even more sensitive about whatever Hillary wants to do."[46]

The Clintons were also entering a new and natural developmental stage in the lives of couples—what I call the "Couple Crossover" at middle life. As women age, they become more independent, aggressive, and political. It is natural for couples to experience a switch of polarities.[47] For years, Hillary had been boosting Bill's star; now he had reached a plateau. It was his turn to boost her star, and he had a strong self-interest in doing so: to get himself out of the doghouse. In the Clintons' case, the crossover was greatly intensified. Steve Pigeon, an upstate New York Democratic Party chairman, acknowledged, "In the White House, every time she spoke up on serious issues the public would flinch. 'Who is *she*? Who elected *her*?' She had to be careful because she didn't want to hurt the presidency." After meeting with her and Clinton to discuss Hillary's Senate hopes, Pigeon made a prescient observation: "There is a role reversal now. He is more strategy and behind the scenes, thinking like a campaign manager. Now she is the person in the arena. Just like she used to guide him, he can now guide her."[48]

The President gamely spent his 1999 summer vacation escorting his wife to fund-raisers for her New York Senate campaign. In Martha's Vineyard he confessed to an audience that he had felt ambivalent when Hillary chose, back in 1973, to move with him to Arkansas. "I was so afraid that I was taking her away from her life . . . the most gifted person I had ever known up to that time," he said. "And so all she is really doing today is what I thought, for the benefit of the country . . . maybe she should have been able to do in 1973. I'm very glad she didn't do it then, and very glad she is doing it today."[49]

Now Hillary was the surveyor of their future, and she was prepared to gamble it all on a move to New York State—a full year before the senatorial election that would secure her own mark on history or possibly reject her.

QUEEN HILLARY HITS THE STREETS

Hillary launched her exploratory committee after the Fourth of July weekend. Her strategy to counteract the carpetbagger charges was to spend the summer on a "listening and learning tour" of New York. It was really more like a nodding tour—a series of controlled and scripted tableaux that shut out the public. Only invited guests were allowed, with the media outnumbering locals two or three to one.

Even Senator Schumer was worried that Hillary was so guarded, she might not come down from her perch as First Lady to connect with real people. "I told her to go upstate and get her hands dirty," Schumer said in June. "She needs to sit in kitchens and living rooms and just listen."[50] But Hillary was busy successfully nurturing the state Democratic network, making the right calls, saying the right things. After she schmoozed with sixty-four Suffolk County party officials at a closed luncheon, the county chairman, Dominic Baranello, said, "I'm in love. I told Hillary she's made me young again."[51] George Guldi, the minority leader of the Suffolk legislature, made an astute prediction: "Hillary is a high-achieving woman, and high-achieving women overcompensate so heavily that she probably already knows more about New York than the sixty-four officials who were at the lunch."[52]

When Hillary did drop her guard for the one—and only—intimate interview in the harsh afterlight of the Monica scandal, she talked about her husband's "weakness" for chronic philandering and implied she now knew he was a sex addict. Hillary's choice of a public confessional, Tina Brown's jazzy new celebrity magazine, *Talk*, swept her up in a publicity spectacle that once more made the Clinton marriage the highest-rated national soap opera. She was ridiculed for blaming the fifty-two-year-old President's behavior on trauma he had suffered as a four-year-old when his mother and grandmother fought over him. What was most intriguing about the interview was what Mrs. Clinton didn't say. She didn't talk about her own role over twenty-five years in rationalizing, denying, forgiving, and enabling Bill Clinton's sexual addiction. It punctured the myth of her martyrdom.

As for how she was now dealing with her husband's "weakness," the message was contradictory. She said she had to be "vigilant" but later said, "He has to be responsible for his own behavior, whether I'm there or one hundred miles away." In a rare burst of candor she admitted, "He's a hard dog to keep on the porch."[53] The nearly-candidate sounded like she was inoculating herself against any future presidential sex scandals. The White House refused to say whether or not the President was in psychological therapy, apart from his meetings with the three religious counselors, but some on Hillary's own staff suspected that he hadn't really repented. There was talk about his promising to go into deep therapy once he left office.

During the summer of 1999 Hillary surveyed almost every inch of Westchester County before spying a nineteenth-century Dutch Colonial in the sleepy suburb of Chappaqua, forty minutes from Manhattan. The house was a larger version of her own childhood home—the solarium reminiscent of the one in Park Ridge where she would play in the sunlight and "pretend there were heavenly movie cameras watching my every move."[54] The Chappaqua house was on the market for only three days before Hillary marshaled her family to fly up from Camp David on a Sunday morning in late August to inspect the 5,200-square-foot home seated on a single green acre and shaded by fir and maple trees. She showed Bill and Chelsea the swimming pool. Like her father before her, Hillary had found her dream house. The community, too, had echoes of Park Ridge in the Fifties, being blandly upper-middle-class and almost exclusively white, with no downtown, no disorder.

It wasn't a very welcoming environment, especially for an ex-president. The prospect of surrendering his seat in the Oval Office to sit in a suburban den, waiting for Senator Clinton to come home from her week in Washington to drag him off to a rubber chicken dinner in Ronkonkama, was as drastic a life change for Bill Clinton to contemplate as Hillary's 1974 decision to abort her takeoff into Washington's power circles and move to Arkansas to support him. About all he could look forward to was playing a lot of golf. Except that certain members of the better golf clubs of Westchester shrank in horror at the prospect of their games being held up by this ex-president. Protest committees formed. Eight months before Bill Clinton's exit from the White House, he had not yet been accepted by a golf club in his wife's new domicile.

This time, the Clintons called upon a newer FOB to put up the cash—$1.35 million—to secure their mortgage on the $1.7 million house. Suddenly the gummy smile of Terry McAuliffe was plastered across newspapers, proud to say he was helping "the Big Guy" once again, having already earned the description by Vice President Al Gore as "the greatest fund-raiser in the history of the universe" for soliciting millions of dollars for the Clintons' legal defense fund, the Clinton library, and Mrs. Clinton's exploratory campaign.[55] Like so many of the Clintons' transactions, this deal had an odor about it. And like so many of the Clintons' defenses, their technical arguments missed the point and aroused more disgust. Under questioning by the press, Hillary was icy, but later decided to forgo the loan and seek a commercial mortgage like everyone else.

Hours after the Clintons submitted their bid on the house, they swooped down on East Hampton for their second summer of power-vacationing. But at a fund-raiser on the lawn of an oceanfront home belonging to the First Lady's lobbyist friend, Liz Robbins, Hillary did not lavishly introduce "my husband." She made a bread-and-butter speech about her own agenda, and then, as if he were someone she barely knew, she said curtly, "As a citizen, it is my pleasure to introduce you to the President of the United States."

Clinton's face was a rubber mask, allover pink, with eyes pinched as if behind peepholes. Only when a young pretty blonde pushed up front on the rope line and squeezed his hand suggestively and asked, "Can I get a kiss?" did Clinton come alive, lean in for the kiss, and breathe, "Thank you."

But he could still woo a crowd like no one else. "There is no more argument about what we did—it's worked!" he said, passionately defending his own legacy issue by issue. "When I met Hillary in 1971, we started a conversation about this stuff that has gone on until one-thirty this morning." Clinton then gave a revealing glimpse of the tenuous thread that still tied them to each other. "I said to her this morning, 'Are you still interested?' She said, 'You may be a lot of things, Bill Clinton, but you're not boring.' "

As her poll numbers kept slipping, her formal announcement as a candidate for U.S. Senate was postponed again and again. Hostile columnists, such as her former adviser Dick Morris, who now wrote for the anti-Clinton paper, the *New York Post*, kept trying to scare off potential supporters by predicting that Hillary was certain to pull out. But she never came close to folding. She desperately needed to prove her detractors wrong. "Tell me why you're doing this," the First Lady was asked by one of her friends, Shahara Llewellyn, who was highly dubious. "I have spent my life working on issues that are extremely important to me," Hillary explained. "Once you leave the White House, the opportunities for a legitimate platform to continue speaking out on the issues I care about will be greatly reduced. If I'm going to continue to make a difference, I feel I *should* run." Her explanation turned this core fundraiser around, but most of Hillary's closest friends and political advisors pleaded with her to reconsider.

She stuck to her decision. To run in the most exciting race in the country and compete for the most powerful political platform available was, from Hillary's point of view, an obvious choice.

But to many others, this choice of Hillary's initially inspired disbelief. Some were appalled at the arrogance of her assumption that Queen Hillary could simply pick a state and descend from her throne expecting her party to carry her, on a palanquin of union and teachers' votes, into the United States Senate. But many others were rather excited by the boldness of the idea. Here was a woman who wouldn't be humiliated into silence but who had the guts to rise up, again, reinvent herself, and find another way to make a difference. She was past fifty and finally ready to cut loose. Watch out, world, here comes the real, true Hillary.

CHAPTER EIGHTEEN

Hillary's Race for Redemption

It promised to be a Senate race unlike any in history—a grand opera, both comic and tragic, with subplots, scheming secondary characters, and what lead players! A First Lady who had been demonized by Republicans as the evil-doing embodiment of left-wing *feministas* playing opposite New York City mayor Rudolph Giuliani, a pugnacious politician whose flair for the dramatic often made him look more menacing than the Phantom of the Opera. Each brought to the battle a combative mix of arrogance and inse-curities, further fueled by the elemental hatreds both inspired. From the start they began running psyche to psyche.

For Hillary's opponent, Giuliani, "the whole thing started out as a joke,"[1] acknowledged Zenia Mucha, the senior adviser to New York's Republican governor George Pataki. Giuliani had never shown interest in running for the Senate; he wanted the governor's job. It was already occupied by an-other Republican, but no thanks to Giuliani. In the 1994 gubernatorial contest he had endorsed the Democrat, then-governor Mario Cuomo, against the unknown GOP challenger, George who? Pataki partisans had not forgiven that act of party betrayal. Some saw it as characteristically Machiavellian of Giuliani, a failed plot to keep another Italian Catholic from ascending to the leadership of their state party. Now that a U.S. Senate seat had opened up, Governor Pataki was ready to return the favor to Rudy. Ignoring the obvious choice, the governor had tried to field as his desig-nated candidate against Hillary another little-known Italian Catholic, a young Long Island congressman by the name of Rick Lazio.

"You don't run someone with high negatives, like Rudy, against an opponent with high negatives," Mucha kept arguing with insiders on behalf of the governor. "What you have with Rudy against Hillary is a polarization."[2] But other party strategists shook at the thought of running a virtual no-name against someone with the star power of the First Lady. And by midsummer of '99, Pataki asked Lazio to step aside; not to give up entirely, but, prophetically, to "postpone" his candidacy.

What started as a joke turned into a dare for Giuliani. When party stalwarts went to the mayor, according to Mucha, "It was not, 'Are you interested in running for United States Senate?' but more, 'Do you think you can beat her?'" It was not in Giuliani's nature to duck a fight. Besides, said a City Hall insider, "He's a performer, like every politician. And this is the biggest show of the year—bigger than the presidency."[3]

The new millennium began with Rudolph Giuliani on top, orchestrating his New Year's Eve extravaganza before a Times Square throng of two million revelers who danced in the streets without a single serious incident. He was the giant killer who had taken a debauched New York City known as ungovernable and scared it into civility. He could boast of a Central Park that a visitor could cross without being approached to buy drugs and where emptying one's bladder behind a tree might produce a "quality of life summons." Only his hero, Mayor Fiorello La Guardia, had stamped as strong an imprint on the city's seething surface.

So confident was this mayor of his godlike (or Godzilla-like) powers, he allowed himself to appear before the millions watching around the world with a woman near his side who was not his wife. It was not the first time reporters had noticed the dark-haired divorcée, usually swathed in silk and pearls, standing or sitting a few feet away from the mayor, on whom her eyes fell adoringly. But reporters had felt the lash of humiliation or worse—loss of access—whenever they questioned this mayor about anything remotely connected to his personal life. After six years of Giuliani rule, the famously vicious dogs of the New York press corps had been declawed. That night Giuliani's spouse of sixteen years, Donna Hanover, watched the sky light up at midnight from another location in Times Square.

Nothing seemed beyond this mayor's control—until Hillary Rodham Clinton showed up. Suddenly he faced another powerful force, a celebrity with worldwide wattage, threatening to cast a shadow on his sphere of influence. Being a man with more than a tendency toward paranoia, he took this invasion personally. And almost from the minute the First Lady expressed interest in a Senate seat from his state, Rudy Giuliani tried his best to keep her out of his city.

The head-butting had begun back in April 1999. Mrs. Clinton was invited by Rudy Crew, then the mayor's schools chancellor, to serve as "principal for a day" in a Queens school. Mayor Giuliani tried to block it. "He said her visit was just politics and not motivated by concern for children," Dr. Crew recalled. Mrs. Clinton attended anyway, and stayed on at Dr. Crew's suggestion through a long town hall meeting. When her picture appeared next to Dr. Crew's in *The New York Times*, their relationship became a constant source of irritation between the chancellor and his boss.

The next fall, Dr. Crew again asked Mrs. Clinton to appear in New York City, this time to highlight the need for state and federal dollars to help repair the city's deteriorated schools. A big press conference had been arranged where the First Lady and Congressmen Rangel would speak. Dr. Crew got word that the mayor was angry. He was supposed to figure out a way to cancel the event. He called the mayor's deputy, Tony Coles, and said, "That will never happen. You don't tell the First Lady of your nation that she can't come to your school and do this when you've gone to Washington and asked for her help." Crew believes this was the crowning insult which caused the mayor to oust him. "He didn't want my relationship with Hillary to be put into operation as they ran against each other."[4]

In June 1999, after hearing that *Talk* magazine wanted to throw a party to launch its first issue, with Hillary on the cover, Giuliani banned the whole bunch from his Brooklyn Navy Yard.

But Hillary kept coming back. And from the moment these two were lured into challenging each other, both were vilified at dinner tables, straw votes were taken, husbands and wives bickered, friends hung up on one another, and the professional political class felt its blood run hot again. They polarized by race, gender, ethnicity, you name it. By January 2000, fully 51 percent of registered voters in a Marist poll said they'd like to see someone else.[5]

At that point the Senate contest was not one where either candidate had to worry about name recognition or voter base or selling people on anything. It was all about hate. Nor was this merely a statewide race; it was a national sport. Giuliani's fund-raising operation set a 20-million-dollar goal. By bombarding Republican mailboxes across the country with anti-Hillary pitches, painting her as "a champion of every left-wing cause that you can imagine," the Giuliani campaign seemed set to smash the ceiling on contributions for a Senate candidate. Using the national database of prominent conservative fund-raiser Richard Viguerie, Friends of Giuliani met their goal of 20 million dollars in March—seven months before the election! Most out-of-state residents knew little about the mayor whose name had too many vowels to pronounce, beyond Giuliani's solid reputation for turning New York around. However, the 75 percent of total contributions to him that poured in from every state outside New York were not all for the love of Rudy. Hillary's candidacy was an outlet for those whose hatred of the Clintons defines their politics.

But for the first five months of the election year, Giuliani's operatic personality was the best thing Hillary had going for her.

BEHIND THE HATE OF HILLARY

During her first year of testing the waters before an official declaration of her candidacy, Hillary had displayed vividly many of the most striking qualities of her nature. She was diligent, unflappable, relentless, and fiercely focused on her long-term goal. Nothing distracted her from listening and learning how to be a retail politician. But to what end? voters wanted to know. Did she have a cause or a passion that related to the needs of the state she had selected as her launching pad? Or was this all about Hillary?

By January 2000 Hillary trailed nine points behind Rudy. Among male voters, one-quarter found *nothing* to like about her. But the real wake-up call was her 50-point downswing over the year among upstate women voters under forty-five (Hillary dropped from a 28-point lead to a 22-point deficit).[6]

An almost incoherent rage was frequently heard expressed by progressive Democratic white women who should have been her core supporters. "I don't trust her—who is she?" or "I'm sick of Bill Clinton, and she's cut from the same cloth." Scratching beneath the carpetbagger issue, one would often find a deeper sense of gender violation: "She's defended that lying lowlife all these years—I'm ashamed to be a member of the same gender," fumed a liberal Democratic publisher. "I never lived my life through a man," scoffed a doctor who pulled herself up from a barefoot rural Southern background to an M.D. The envy factor loomed large. To women who fought hard to move up in their careers, the spectacle of Hillary announcing her very first political candidacy from the balcony of the East Wing was just too Evita. She was starting at the top. Why? Because she was married to the top guy.

A secret poll was commissioned by one of Hillary's consultants to find out why so many women hated her. "Bottom line," the pollster confided to me, "she thinks she's better than they are. It's as if she's entitled."[7] Suburban moms who had also been to Wellesley and Yale compared themselves to Hillary and wondered, *Why not me?* Hillary had never held a high corporate position or been responsible for a bottom line; she had not been a distinguished jurist; she hadn't litigated a complex class-action suit. So how was it she made partner at the Rose Law Firm in three years?

Even Harriet Woods, a founder of the National Women's Political Caucus and former lieutenant governor of Missouri, worried that Hillary was stuck in her own life transition. "This is a woman who is really qualified to be a U.S. Senator—and I want her to be—good Lord, we only have nine women! But although I admire Hillary very much, I don't *care* about her an awful lot."[8]

In fairness, Hillary was handicapped as a woman by the perception that she was simply looking for a way to build a new life and she had chosen elective office as her means. It is acceptable for men to be that raw about wanting to build a career. When women enter this traditionally male arena, people want to be convinced they have gone into politics to make a difference, solve a problem, or champion a cause that no one else is addressing— and most women do. Harriet Woods, author of the book *Stepping Up to Power: The Political Journey of American Women,* would have advised Hillary "to show that she has a real passion for achieving something that will inspire people to want to support her."[9] But even women as politically experienced as Woods were shut out of Hillary's tightly controlled circle.

At a breakfast of older New York professional women who were supporting Bill Bradley's bid for the Presidency, the founder of NCBW (National Coalition of 100 Black Women, Inc.), Jewell Jackson McCabe, let the cork out of the bottle:

"New York stands as tall as any other state in terms of women who are courageous and capable and well educated. When you look at Constance Baker Motley, who argued ten Supreme Court cases, and Shirley Chisholm and Bella Abzug and Gloria Steinem and Nita Lowey—we've got qualified women. Why go outside the state?"

A spontaneous, even thunderous, burst of applause greeted her remarks.[10]

When January came and went and Hillary's polls continued to tank, she finally acquiesced to a formal announcement event. Her media advisers wanted to make a short film to "reintroduce" her, but they didn't know how. This complex, contradictory Tammy Wynette–feminist still had not clearly defined herself. And none of her operatives dared do it for her. The risky task fell to her old pal Hollywood producer Linda Bloodworth-Thomason. She and her husband, Harry, had argued strenuously against Hillary's running, as had most of her friends and advisers—except Bill Clinton.

The problem was her life story. "It's a minefield," groaned an adviser. And this election year, with an ebullient economy, voters were mostly intrigued with the Politics of Personal Biography. Could they cherry pick Hillary's bittersweet story?

Another problem was her remoteness. Hillary was still operating with a White House mentality, hiding behind her cordon sanitaire of Secret Service protectors in a way even the President doesn't do. "If she's going to go BIG PICTURE, she'll lose," said one of the savviest political consultants in New York, George Artz, press secretary for former mayor Ed Koch. "She has to go out in the streets—people want to be touched and touch the candidate and feel she's real. She's acting like the queen."[11]

The late New York governor Nelson Rockefeller, who was a stiff WASP on the campaign trail, needed his genial attorney general, Louis Lefkowitz, to take him around New York's fervently ethnic neighborhoods and warn him not to drink *milchik* with his *flayshig* (milk with his hot dog). Hillary needed a Nita Lowey to take her into the crowds to show she's a *haimisheh* gal—warm and approachable. But Hillary had jumped the line over Lowey, who had toiled for twelve years as a popular congresswoman from Westchester. Wherever this smart, safely attractive grandmother appeared, New Yorkers would swarm around her expressing regrets that her own candidacy had been usurped. In fact, it was the party scouts—Senators Schumer, Torricelli, and Moynihan, together with Congressman Rangel—who decided that Lowey, as effective as she is, didn't have a high-enough profile to outshine the presumptive challenger, and who had wooed and cajoled and pleaded with Hillary to bring her stature and intelligence and star power to New York.

Yet when the dean of New York City television journalists, Gabe Pressman, finally got his interview with Mrs. Clinton, she sounded mostly like a woman working out a life change.

> PRESSMAN: You explained why you want to be a senator, but a key question is why from New York?
> MRS. CLINTON: And, you know, it's a wonderful, fair question . . . I've always wanted to live in New York. Who doesn't want to live in New York?[12]

One seasoned New York observer wisecracked, "So, is a Senate seat from New York like a Fresh Air Fund vacation for disadvantaged Washington wives?"

Even a *New York Times* reporter admitted in private, "You get drawn into her psychological makeup—it's like getting sucked into your parents' problems; I want her to work it out. But what does that have to do with electing a senator?"

HILLARY AS NEXT-DOOR NEIGHBOR

Finally, on February 6, Hillary was ready to declare her candidacy. The promise of the day was that, at last, the Real Hillary would stand up and speak with her own voice.

The gymnasium on the SUNY-Purchase college campus in Westchester was packed with supporters, invited elected officials, bigfoot journalists— even Lucianne Goldberg, the self-proclaimed architect of Monicagate, was there. Banners, buttons, posters, everything in sight, "reintroduced" the candidate as HILLARY!—shorn of the stigma of Clinton and even of the heretofore obligatory Rodham. The slick video tribute for which she paid a quarter-million dollars featured what looked like a single mom who worked tirelessly for children's rights and told us she also makes "a mean tossed salad and a great omelet." Unsuccessfully coaxed in the past to reveal some vulnerability in order to soften her image, Hillary had told the former Clinton strategist Dick Morris, "I can't think of any." In the film, though, her friends told us that she couldn't sing. The most Hillaryesque touch was the plaintive opening ditty, rendered in the voice of a small child: "No one can stop me from being me."

The marching orders of the day were set by Hillary. She ascended like a queen, flanked by the two New York senators and followed by an inconspicuous president. It must have been the first time that a president of the United States shared the stage with another politician who never bothered to introduce him, even to acknowledge him, except to refer twice to "Bill," as in the *Showboat* lyric, "Just My Bill." Clinton sat, grinning, and looking like he wished he had someone to talk to. "It was felt that if he said anything, he'd upstage her," explained one of Hillary's operatives. Chelsea sat onstage next to her grandmother, who stared off into space.

"You know," Hillary began, "the first time I spoke to a group this large was at my college commencement in 1969. I'm a little older now . . . [laughter] . . . a little blonder . . . [laughter] . . . a lot humbler. I've gone to work, I've raised a child, and I've spent thirty years trying to better the lives of children and families. But I often return to one thing I said way back then—that politics is the art of making possible what appears to be impossible."

In the many times I have seen Hillary speak, she never fails to dazzle audiences by speaking in paragraphs without notes. That day, she was fully scripted. It was a sober policy speech, delivered with scarcely a smile or attempt at emotional connection with the residents of her adopted state, except when she acknowledged in a bad imitation of a Brooklyn cabbie that the campaign would be a fight: "But, hey, this is Noo Yawk!"

She reminded the audience that "families are the bedrock of our society." When it came time to take pictures, however, Hillary was being photographed only solo or with the senators. Nita Lowey had to go over and remind the candidate to stand together as a family with Bill and Chelsea.

The Speaker of the State Assembly was nonetheless pleased. Democrat Sheldon Silver, one of the three most powerful men in New York State government and a chief adviser of Hillary, saw her video as very positive. "This is who Hillary is: She is daughter, she is mother, she is a worker, she gets where she wants to go with hard work. That was the message she wanted to create."[13]

In that effort she had minimized a good deal of who she was. She wasn't prominently shown in her roles as a First Lady, she wasn't a wife, she wasn't the Rose Law Firm lawyer, she wasn't filmed as a family with her husband. It almost looked like outtakes from the syrupy Clinton promo film *The Man from Hope* shown at the '92 Democratic Convention, which depicted her as the political wife.

The slow-speaking assembly boss restated the campaign mantra: "The idea was to show that she was someone who is compassionate and caring. Not political and calculating." He said it was meant to dispel the impression people had taken from reading about Hillary and looking at her always as the lawyer and the President's wife. When people meet her in person, he said, "the impression is this is not some unusual person—this is the neighbor next door."[14]

A NIGHT TO REMEMBER

The night of Saturday, March 11, 2000, was yet another rite of passage for Hillary Clinton. Being a woman of grand ambition whose original choice was to channel her political aspirations through her naturally gifted husband, it had been chastening to stumble through the learning stages of elective candidacy. Now, suddenly, the show was on at the annual Inner Circle dinner, where the New York press corps roasts the city's mayor.

No more out-of-town tryouts. Hillary was opening in New York.

Although she and the New York mayor had been circling each other for a year with the wary menace of prizefighters, they still had not been in the same room. The Inner Circle spectacle at the Hilton in midtown Manhattan drew an unusually large crowd, thirteen hundred, including political pooh-bahs representing every fissure in New York's unstable political ground. They all packed into the grand ballroom hoping to witness the combatants touch gloves for the first time.

When the New York press corps had first asked Hillary to their show, her spokesman, Howard Wolfson, misunderstood and insisted that she per-form. He was told no, this was the mayor's show. Then she was invited by Mortimer Zuckerman, a personal friend and copublisher of New York's *Daily News,* and it became a command appearance for Hillary.

Most often the whispers in her wake these days were *beautiful.* In the chrysalis of transformation from political wife to independent woman, the jawline had been chiseled, the dominatrix eyebrows weeded, the weight dropped, and the result was a woman who was obviously enjoying, for the first time, being called beautiful. Three old birds, Democratic regulars who referred to themselves as jaded, admitted after seeing Hillary speak in a suburb of New York, "We weren't prepared to be impressed, and we are im-pressed." Said one woman, "First, the physical package. The polish. I would kill to get a hold of her hairdresser and makeup person. *Kill.*"[15]

Enter the First Lady looking like Cleopatra in full regalia, gowned to the floor in a pyramidal coatdress of black satin. Her neck was girdled in a col-lar of jewels. Her golden hair, swept high, shimmered. Swanning across the ballroom floor with Zuckerman, she stopped behind the back of Mayor Giu-liani's chair. And then, just as boldly as she had thirty years before when she walked the length of the Yale Law School library to dazzle Bill Clinton with a forthright introduction, the woman who is today the most famous in the world tapped the 107th mayor of New York on the shoulder. He scram-bled to his feet. She politely introduced herself. First round, Hillary.

For the early half of the interminable evening she watched the press show, *Livin' La Rudy Loca,* where the mayor was called Mr. Mean but the gags about her were meaner. The Hillary character jumped on a subway to Shea Stadium, "Where I can watch my favorite team, the New York Yan-kees!" When an annoyed straphanger educated her that the Yankees play in Yankee Stadium, the Hillary character trilled, "We live in Chappaqua now, you know. That's Indian for 'The Land of Separate Bedrooms.' " Necks swiveled in unison toward Table 28. She's laughing! Then she was hit with the lyrics, *If she could handle Monica, would Rudy cause her pain?* Heads whirled toward Table 28. "How does she look?" "Wan." In a skit where the Hillary character was jailed by the Mayor Giuliani character, she found herself sharing a cell with Sean (Puffy) Combs and his girlfriend, Jennifer Lopez. Bill Clinton showed up with "soft bail money" but instead of spring-ing his wife, he felt Jennifer's pain and strolled off arm in arm with the half-naked songstress.[16]

Intermission. Hillary rose, laughing ostentatiously, and announced, "I'm still standing." Before round three began, one of the mayor's men ap-proached Hillary's young spokesman, Wolfson, and asked to take the First Lady backstage. "Why should she go backstage?" snarled the handler, a stain of fear spreading across his shirt.

"Trad-*dish*-shun!" sang the mayor's man. Backstage, Hillary again ap-proached the unsuspecting mayor from behind and delicately laid a hand on his shoulder. He turned around. She faced him down with flattery. "Well, I hear you're the real star."

Giuliani stuttered a reply: "We're gonna see, we're gonna see. I like doing it."

"I can't wait to see it."

Her charm offensive seemed to rattle him. When Rudy's smile is forced, the lips turn down and his deathly white face goes flat as the Phantom's mask. (He later admitted he thought Hillary seemed "like a nice lady.") Re-gaining his edge after she left backstage, he got off a few sarcastic remarks to reporters: "I'm very, very encouraged at the fact we're drawing lots of out-of-towners to this performance of mine."

Of *mine.*

But it was Hillary's star power that radiated to every corner of the ballroom. New York bigwigs, such as financial media impresario Michael Bloomberg, attorney and labor mediator Theodore Kheel, and District At-torney Robert Morgenthau craned to see her. An informal receiving line formed three deep around her table. A big blonde at the next table, pinned in her seat by the throng around Hillary, appealed to garrulous ex-mayor Ed Koch to introduce her to Hillary. This was not just any big blonde; this was Zenia Mucha, the enforcer and political scorekeeper for New York's mild-mannered governor. Since the intrafamily rivalry between her Repub-lican boss and the Republican mayor approached that between Tony So-prano and his uncle Junior, one might have expected this to be merely a courtesy call. But like everyone else, Zenia could not wait to meet the famous Democrat. Koch introduced her to Hillary as "one strong woman to another."

Hillary did her fly-open eyes in recognition of an important personage. She asked that her greetings be conveyed to the First Lady of New York, Libby Pataki, "especially because she is so gracious." Zenia melted. "This woman looks classy. The show is particularly tough on her. And she's handling herself very well."[17] How could a mere mayor compete?

The man who had been telling the public he was too busy with his "day job" to waste his time campaigning against some lady from Arkansas, had, in fact, been sneaking out of City Hall early every day for a week to rehearse his acting and dancing with the cast of the Broadway musical *Saturday Night Fever*. Now all suited up in a white satin tux and black shirt, the usually dour former prosecutor was itching to gyrate, Travolta style, and show everyone what a fun guy he really is. Offstage voices set the theme of his show: *What's wrong with Rudy? What's wrong with Rudy?*

Some advisers had shuddered as Elliot Cuker, a flamboyant failed actor who boasts of being Rudy's closest friend, easily talked the mayor into parodying himself as a mean, angry, paranoid man with a dangerous multiple personality. "Bizarre, but we couldn't stop it."[18]

Under Cuker's direction, the mayor's reaction to his anger problem was to "act out" as one menacing character after another. Playing his psychiatrist, Cuker asked where the rage was coming from. Rudy said he thought it was coming from some primitive part of himself.

"You mean, like, Jekyll and Hyde?"

The show was getting uncomfortably real. That very day I had interviewed Giuliani's first police commissioner, William Bratton, who told me the mayor could be very charming, very warm, very gracious. "But there is a Dr. Jekyll/Mr. Hyde type of side to him."[19] So volatile had his mood swings become that one person close to the Giuliani administration described the mayor as "a nightmare of a man. One day he could be as sweet and charming as you'd ever want, then all of a sudden—it is bizarre, like watching a robin turn into a hawk."

Another hidden aspect of the mayor's complex personality was on display that evening. At his table was seated the same dark-haired "mystery woman" who accompanied him on New Year's Eve. Cuker was the beard when the mayor dined with the lady at his friend's midtown cigar bar, but a beard was scarcely necessary. Again, the media ignored her.

In the climactic *Saturday Night Fever* sequence, Giuliani was learning how to dance. His coach executed frontal hip thrusts. When Rudy still didn't get it, the dancer said, "Think Presidential." The audience groaned. Another person associated with the show said, "It's agonizing. It's degrading to the mayor. I gotta leave."

Through it all Hillary never flinched. She smiled her opaque Cleopatra smile and chuckled as consistently as if she were programmed with a laugh track. She was showing herself to this crowd of jovial jackals to be one classy lady. The photo of her the next morning in *The New York Times*, beaming and beautiful as she shook her opponent's hand, was worth a million words. A consultant to City Hall had to admit it.

"She was royalty. And she showed up the king."

QUEEN HILLARY DESCENDS TO TRUCK STOPS

A friend of Hillary's had warned her back in the fall of '99, "You know, Giuliani is such a rhinoceros, he's going to be taking a bite out of you every day." Gameface firmly in place, Hillary had revealed her fight strategy: "If there's one thing I've learned over the last seven years, it's how to hold my tongue."

She proved it when Rudy blasted her for "desecrating religion," based on her careful defense of the right of the Brooklyn Museum of Art to hang its "Sensation" show featuring a dung-encrusted painting of a Madonna. Although Hillary may have a checkered past, one thing she has always been is a stalwart do-good Methodist. When the Mayor's attack was read to her, Hillary started her day quaking with rage. But later, when she spoke to reporters, the rhetoric was disciplined, unemotional: "As a person of faith, I am appalled that he would make false statements about me and my respect for religion in order to raise money for his campaign."

Next, the First Lady had the audacity to say she wanted to march in his St. Patrick's Day Parade, with *his* cops and *his* firemen and *his* Emerald Societies. The mayor danced ahead of all the other dignitaries, darting from side to side up Fifth Avenue, grabbing for hands, flashing his jack-o'-lantern grin through a snow storm, and dissing Hillary. Asked where she was by a TV reporter, he shrugged, "I dunno. She got lost along the way." Seeking out another camera he said, "I think New Yorkers will elect a real New Yorker; she ought to go back to Arkansas." Once again, the mayor's affectionate shadow walked a few paces behind him. As one journalist later commented, he might as well have been snuggling with her in Macy's window. But once again, his lady friend went unnoticed by the public and unremarked by the press.

Hillary's young supporters ran alongside the barricades trying to stir up cheers but were drowned out by the shouts of "Hillary, go home!" Cops all along the way, when asked, "Has Hillary passed yet?" answered, "Hillary who?" The Illinois native marched dutifully through the sleet, surrounded by children, like a schoolmarm. She was booed. Not even the popular ex-mayor Ed Koch could shield her. Undaunted, Hillary smiled bravely and never flinched—another rite of passage.

The First Lady didn't immediately come down from her pedestal, but after being attacked by her own Westchester district congresswoman, Republican Sue Kelly, for being "a carpetbagger who does not know New York,"[20] Hillary forced herself to play her new role as a retail politician. In March 2000, while the media was enthralled with McCain mania, Hillary launched a nine-day Chappaqua charm offensive. Concentrating on women and children, she hopped from house party to supermarket, to temple, to school, to the local library where she read to toddlers—adopting the role of the community's Mother Goose.

The day after a Michigan school shooting took the life of a six-year-old girl, Hillary appealed to 150 fifth-graders at an elementary school in Rockland County. She spoke to the children as if they were her own. "And I want you to promise that you will never ever pick up a gun, ever, with any idea of using it against any person," she said. "Will you promise me that?" In unison, students hummed "Yes," or "I promise." The few adult onlookers were impressed with her sincerity and warmth. "I saw her more as a mother, and I never looked at it that way before," said Dr. Maryanne Evangelist, assistant superintendent in the Nyack School District. "Maybe in this kind of an environment she has less of a reason to be in a role, because the majority of the audience is children. The way she treats her daughter is probably the person she really is."[21]

Indeed, the one role in which Hillary seems utterly genuine is as a mother. Chelsea never fails to impress people with her beautiful manners, her *joie de vivre*, and her seriousness as a Stanford premed student. To Chelsea her mother is the most important person in the world. They had talked long and hard over the previous summer about Hillary's feeling she should make this race, and Chelsea had finally given her approval. Hillary continued to be vigilant about protecting her daughter, although Chelsea was now twenty-one. Even when pressured by an adviser to trumpet her maternal love for the benefit of soccer moms by campaigning with Chelsea in a mall, Hillary firmly refused. The adviser was told, "She will never exploit Chelsea."

The effectiveness of Hillary's charm was noticeable at a women's meeting in a reform synagogue in Chappaqua. She came early rather than late and took a back seat to other female panelists. When it was her turn to share, she spoke of closet space in the White House, scrambled eggs and applesauce (her homemade specialties), and the importance of having the blessings of those around us.

In the past, Hillary would speak at an event and exit almost immediately. But that night, she stayed to join in a Q&A and then to shake hands. No imperious press flak pushed people back. Hillary let ordinary people break the rope line and engage in lengthy conversations with her, not as the queen or the star, but, according to one woman in the audience, "as someone not that much different from myself."[22] Hillary was pleasantly surprised at the result: "When I say, 'Gosh, what is the best moisturizer you use?' people say, 'Gosh, she cares about the same things I do.' "[23]

Meanwhile, Giuliani brushed off pleas to campaign outside the city, leaving the outfield undefended. No sooner had the mayor's worried advisers promised he would hold a series of political events upstate to shore up his status with women, than Giuliani, a rabid Yankees fan, snubbed four hundred Rochester women expecting to dine with him so he could attend the rescheduled opener at Yankee Stadium. As usual, he made no apologies.

Hillary played the bush leagues day after day. She seldom hit any home runs notable enough to rate statewide coverage, but she was learning the game and feeling more confident about being on the mound instead of in the dugout with Bill pitching all the time. Picking the state apart precinct by precinct, Finger Lake by Finger Lake, she worked diners and senior centers and union halls—even truck stops—determined to hit all sixty-two counties before summer. And so she did. "Her one-on-ones give great word of mouth," said Steve Pigeon, the Democratic Party chairman of Erie County, which has the largest enclave of Democratic voters outside New York City. "We consistently hear, 'She's not at all what we expected. It's not the tough image.' They find her warm and friendly."[24]

Even Rudy's Republican cronies saw Hillary as a serious threat. Staten Island borough president Guy Molinari said of Hillary from day one, "She is a formidable candidate. It will be a very tough race. Never before in the history of this country have we seen one quite like this one." Former senator Al D'Amato claimed to have no animosity for Hillary, just total disdain. But he had to admit, "She is very, very, very smart, and calculated." Congressman Rangel's assessment was: "Giuliani's a street fighter, and I think he's insecure. And she is intimidating. HRC is *intimidating*."[25]

The lowest blow was inadvertently made by one of Giuliani's new best friends, Senator John McCain. Speaking to students at Columbia University in April, McCain predicted that if Hillary won, "she would be a star of the quality that has not been seen since Bobby Kennedy was elected senator from the State of New York." The remark also underscored an irony that went unmentioned whenever Giuliani attacked Hillary as a carpetbagger. Of the two candidates, the one who worked for the election of Bobby Kennedy in 1964 was not Hillary. She was then a Goldwater Republican. No, it was Giuliani, then a liberal Democrat, who passed out flyers to elect the last Democratic carpetbagger to run for a New York Senate seat.

MINE EYES HAVE SEEN . . .

If Hillary was working at being the good Mother Goose, Rudolph Giuliani was sticking with the only role he knew: the old-fashioned Italian father, the authoritarian padrone who says, "My way or no way," and whose unruly children fear and respect him for it.

It seemed to me from the start of the race that Rudy was divided against himself. He did not really want to be a senator. One of his champions, the state senate majority leader Joe Bruno, acknowledged that Giuliani was not keen on being just one of one hundred U.S. senators. "Giuliani would like to be governor."[26] The more seriously everyone began taking his contest with Hillary, the more bizarre and un-candidate-like his behavior had become. One highly placed Republican after another scratched his or her head and made a repetitive observation to me: *Rudy is out of control. Psychologically unstable. What's wrong with Rudy?*

Rudy's dark side was revealed to everyone in March when Patrick Dorismond, a twenty-six-year-old security officer of Haitian origin, was accidentally shot dead by an undercover cop. Dorismond became the third defenseless black man killed by a New York police officer in thirteen months, but rather than expressing sympathy to the family and two children of the slain man, Giuliani authorized opening sealed police records on Dorismond and began pumping out an incriminating picture of the victim.

Giuliani described the dead man as having a "propensity for violence," when in fact, he had only two convictions, both for disorderly conduct, and had paid small fines. When a former high official in the Giuliani police department saw the mayor on TV several days after the city had been shaken by the killing, he almost choked on his coffee. "I couldn't believe what he was saying. Why would he intentionally escalate it? I think he's losing it. Trust me, this is more than defending the police. I hear he's looking for a reason to get out of the Senate race. He can't stand the possibility of being beaten by a Clinton."[27]

Hillary Clinton once told me, "I don't do spontaneity." Cautious and guarded, she is not quick to respond to the unexpected, and, at worst—as when she remained silent for twelve hours after Suha Arafat's charge that Israeli forces used poison gas on Palestinians—Hillary freezes. But the mayor's efforts to criminalize a dead man and, by association, the incrimination of a whole minority community, inflamed her sense of injustice.

On the fifth night after the Dorismond killing they were waiting for Hillary in Harlem. Nine hundred people sat as still as gravestones in the Bethel AME Church, some cooling themselves with paper fans, while waiting an hour for the First Lady to come and speak to their pain. As she walked down the aisle, a choir burst into "The Battle Hymn of the Republic" and Hillary Clinton was heralded with

Mine eyes have seen the glory of the coming of the Lord . . .

In a trembly rasp, Congressman Charles Rangel said, "I feel in this church tonight the spirit of the Sixties and the civil rights movement." He cloaked Hillary in the mantle of Rosa Parks, whose refusal to move to the back of the bus, he said, was an unexpected inspiration. "Nor did we in New York expect it would be Hillary Clinton who would come to our city to help us regain our dignity as a great metropolis." As Hillary stepped forward, nine hundred people got to their feet and clapped their hands and everyone swayed. She didn't let them down.

"New York has a real problem, and we all know it—all of us, it seems, except the mayor of this city." Cheers of relief. She slammed Giuliani for rushing to judgment instead of waiting for the facts. "At just the moment when a real leader would reach out and heal the wounds, he has chosen divisiveness." But she was careful to withhold condemnation for the police.

In fact, that inspired evening wasn't anything like the Sixties. People were reflective, resolute, and empowered by what they heard. Most of them were already registered to vote, and they took home forms to register friends and family members. Ed Koch made a prediction to me: "Blacks and Hispanics are going to come out in this election like they've never come out before, because they hate [Giuliani] with a passion."[28]

Curiously, Giuliani went straight for Hillary's psyche in his counterattack. "There's a process called projection in psychology," the mayor explained at a news briefing. "It means accusing someone of what you're doing. That is precisely what Mrs. Clinton is doing." When he threw around other psychoanalytic terms such as "blocking" and "the unconscious," his press secretary explained that the mayor reads a lot of Freud.

By the beginning of April, Hillary had pulled ahead of Rudy in polls for the first time in months—by up to 10 points. Rudy had lost among all his core groups: fellow Catholics, city residents, suburbanites, even white men. His striking loss of support was summed up by analysts in one word: Dorismond. But to those who knew him best, it may not have been the racial crisis that provoked Giuliani's eccentric behavior. Rather, it was Giuliani's eccentric behavior that provoked the crisis.

One of the brightest of all mayors in the history of New York appeared to be bent on self-destruction.

By contrast, Hillary seemed to be energized by the construction of her brand new identity. She needed less sleep. She almost always looked fresh. She never seemed to be without a radiant smile, at least for the cameras. What a contrast with the sour, tired, silently suffering wife of the Monica year. But Hillary still had her own hidden insecurities. Her legendary guardedness was still in effect. She admitted to CBS-TV news reporter, Marcia Kramer, "I am a very well-known unknown person." When Hillary first started to run, a New Yorker who has helped her said, " 'Look, you have one major obstacle, either you learn to deal with the press or you'll be savaged.' I offered to set up dinners, I mean I know you all, Peter and Tom and the rest, and for her not to sit down with Peter [Jennings] or Tom [Brokaw], even at a private dinner in the Hamptons . . ."

But why did Hillary still refuse?

The supporter sighed. "Look, she is a woman of enormous talent who loves policy, she knows how to move things politically, but is she secure? This is the most important thing to write about Hillary—that she is not a woman of inner self-confidence, as she likes to portray herself. Underneath that arrogance is a very delicate defensive ego."

CHAPTER NINETEEN

Extra! Extra! The Hillary and Ricky Show!

April is the cruelest month, wrote T. S. Eliot. So it was for Hillary's opponent. Having laid a minefield in his own path over the previous year, by April 2000 the public began to witness the self-destruction of the Rudolph Giuliani Senate candidacy.

CANCER CLOUDS RUDY RUN

It appeared to begin with this stunning announcement by the mayor on the morning of April 27: During a routine physical he had been diagnosed with prostate cancer. For once the newshounds packed into the Blue Room were stunned into silence. When one dared ask what this meant for his Senate race, the mayor replied, "I have no idea. I hope I'll be able to run."

The plot twist rattled the city and Republicans nationwide and elicited an equally startling response from a City Hall insider: "This was the best news he's had in months. It humanizes him."[1] If the mayor declared that he would stay in the race despite this devastating news, his poll numbers would probably get a sympathy boost. Alternatively, the reluctant candidate now had an easy way out. Cancer offered him an exit strategy without the appearance that he was backing away from a fight.

There was, of course, no public gloating on the part of Hillary's campaign. The First Lady made only the most cursory of condolence calls to her chief critic, wishing the mayor a speedy recovery in a phone conversation that lasted one minute. Then she went back to beavering away in the

Finger Lakes area with her all-county strategy: *See, I don't bite.* But over the next two weeks, she would not complain while the media mostly ignored her and honed in on the spectacle of a political tyrant swept up in a psychological maelstrom largely of his own making.

Purely political calculations by the pundits glossed over the tempest brewing inside Rudy Giuliani. He was a tormented man. For the first time, he was faced with a foe that he couldn't fire or intimidate or put in jail: prostate cancer—the same disease that had taken his father's life. That confrontation alone, especially for a man who had always masked his insecurities by playing the bulletproof tough guy, would be enough to throw a candidate off balance. But on top of that Giuliani was in a midlife crisis meltdown.

For the past year the mayor had been leading a double life. The not-so-mysterious "gal pal" he had been showing off in public for months without a word in the press was finally outed by the mayor himself.

Judy Nathan, a divorcée in her mid-forties, happened to be a trained nurse. Faced with the shock of a sexually threatening malady, this was the woman he wanted by his side regardless of the personal and political repercussions. When the mayor paraded his date to a Saturday brunch on Madison Avenue, Nathan had smiled smugly for a *New York Post* photographer. From her expression in the published picture, it looked for all the world like the Other Woman had forced the married man to choose.[2]

The next day the mayor was all smiles when he acknowledged at a City Hall news conference that "she's a good friend, a very good friend." Everyone in the mayor's inner circle had known for months about his relationship with Judy Nathan. But none dared discuss it with him. And as Giuliani unraveled his life before them and the world, all by himself, none was more baffled than his most loyal aides.[3]

Rudy played the next act to the hilt. He had always loved opera; like ballgames, it was a place where he could release his tempestuous emotions without words. Prophetically, his favorite opera was Verdi's *Otello*, the tragedy of a powerful governor known as the Lion of Venice. The story is about trust, betrayal, and self-destruction. Things do not end well for the paranoid Otello. After realizing he has been tricked by his evil aide, Iago, into murdering his faithful wife and a loyal deputy, he collapses in a psychotic rage.

To those who knew of the mayor's youthful conflict over whether or not to become a priest, there was considerable significance in the death of Cardinal O'Connor at this same time. The two men were very close. But Giu-

liani had not been attending mass for some time. Now the father of all
father confessors in Giuliani's realm had passed away, and perhaps with
him went some of the guilt Rudy might have suffered over the revelation of
his adulterous behavior. Donna Hanover, his wife of sixteen years, had
never bad-mouthed the mayor. She was the picture of the stoically suffering professional mom whose life was circumscribed by a serious career
and the commitment to double-parenting her children. But the limits of
her dignity were breeched when Rudy refused to take her with him to Cardinal O'Connor's funeral.[4] She retaliated by choosing the steps of St.
Patrick's Cathedral to utter her first public statement since being shattered
by her husband's acknowledgement of "a very good friend," reminding the
world that this was a Catholic marriage and reiterating that she would rally
behind "this marriage and this man [which] have been very precious
to me."

Thus began the Giuliani Wars. In dueling press conferences over the following days the coldly compartmentalized Rudy and the weepy Donna
forced the public to focus on the personal over the political. At the Cardinal's funeral, the image of Hillary and Bill Clinton sitting shoulder to shoulder in the front row further emphasized the isolation of her opponent, who
sat one row behind the couple, alone.

Both candidates had appeared to have marriages held together only by
the delicate threads of political expediency. Hillary don't-call-me-Clinton
was essentially living a separate existence from her husband. Donna don't-
call-me-Giuliani Hanover, an actress and TV personality, had refused to attend her husband's last inaugural. But now, the candidate who had set
himself up as a moral pillar was about to pull down the temple around himself and rip open the curtains on his own miserable marital mess.

Barely two weeks after his cancer revelation, Mayor Giuliani held another astonishing press conference. His face waxen, gripping the wood
podium like a cross he had to bear, he stumbled through an interior monologue that carried him to the point of declaring, unilaterally, that he would
seek a separation from his wife. Mrs. Giuliani had not been informed.

His voice wavered. Was it fear of death? The terror of emotional exposure? Guilt? Perhaps some of all three. He had already avoided divorce once,
by having his first marriage annulled after fourteen years with the dubious
claim of ignorance that their families were distantly related. Now he was
revealing that he had been cheating on his second wife and mother of his
children for the past year, even as she was desperately trying to patch
things up. He had also lapsed as a churchgoer. Then what happened? He

was struck by a sexually threatening disease. God's punishment? Whatever was actually going through his mind, Rudy Giuliani began that day sound-ing like a penitent using his mayoral platform as a confessional.

Up to this point, even conservatives in the mayor's party had held their tongues over flagrant misbehavior that would have stoked hellfires of moral condemnation if the protagonists had been the Clintons. Not only had the mayor flabbergasted his party and the public, he had now devastated his wife and embarrassed his children in the most public forum. And hell hath no fury like a woman scorned—a second time.

Four hours later a deeply shaken Donna Hanover called her own press conference and shot the mayor between the eyes. With a few well-chosen lines Hanover painted the outlines of her husband's betrayal, not once but twice. Only a year before, in May of '99, Donna had finally been successful in ejecting her rival, the mayor's formidable communications director, Cristyne Lategano. The twenty-eight-year-old political amateur had attached herself to the mayor's side shortly after her hire in 1995. She had shaped his image as a fearless tyrant, all the while fueling his paranoia and forcing the ouster of his most faithful aides, including his own wife.[5] She was the Iago to his Otello.

The whispers inside City Hall were that Donna had discovered her husband and his communications director "communicating" intimately in the private lounge beneath his office. "We were told by Christyne Lategano never to call Donna again," described a former mayoral aide.[6] Having been cut out of Giuliani's political life as well as replaced in his affections, the mayor's wife abruptly instructed the news media to shorten her name from Hanover-Giuliani to just Hanover. A deep freeze had descended over the first couple's formerly storybook relationship.

But in May of '99, Giuliani had suddenly packed off Lategano on an extended "leave of absence," and he and his wife resumed their intimate relationship, according to Hanover. But that summer, Giuliani started the romance with Judy Nathan and used his police escort as cover while he spent weekends with the divorcée and her fifteen-year-old daughter in a condo in Southampton. He invited Nathan to his town meetings, to ride with his staff, even into his family's home for a Christmas party. Donna Hanover's friends said that she did not know her husband had been seeing another woman and was deeply distressed. As for his Iago, Cristyne Lategano was rewarded with another highly paid city job, as the head of the Bureau of Tourism, a field in which she had no past experience.

The Clintons' attack dog, James Carville, sounded off about the double standard: "The Washington commentariat constitutes the greatest concentration of hypocrites in the history of the world. All this is bad if a Democrat does it. If a Republican leaves his family, it's one of life's little tragedies."[7]

Of course, the President's lies under oath and the mayor's falsity to his family were not morally equivalent. But Hillary nonetheless reaped an unexpected benefit. Giuliani had managed the unthinkable—his antics made the Clintons look like cozy, long-married do-gooders dedicated to helping each other change the world.

AN UNEXPECTED UNITY

Eighteen months after the first what-if conversations between Hillary and state party stalwarts, her new identity as a serious seeker of electoral office was quite solidly established. The Clintonization of Hillary was having an increasingly tonic effect. A year before, she had been apprehensive. After all the years of watching the political master perform, it had been a shock to realize that she could no more duplicate her husband's moves than she could learn to shoot perfect baskets from watching Michael Jordan. As she told Joan Hamburg in a WOR radio interview in May, "It has been a real role reversal for my husband. I used to be the one, for years and years, [saying] 'You should have done it this way,' or 'Maybe you should have said it like this.' When we were preparing for my announcement speech, I just couldn't stop laughing because there *he* was going through *my* speech, for a change, telling me to say things better and making me read it over and over. . . . I wanted to take back all the times I said, 'You should have done this better.' "[8] But as she began to loosen up and shed some of the alien edge that had offended New Yorkers, she found to her surprise that this campaigning business was actually fun!

It was also a personal challenge: "If we don't have women who are willing to run, then we lose," she told Hamburg. "We have a style of politics that is very confrontational and in your face—I don't think we have to keep that style—more women should run and be warm and serious and funny and yet effective. We should be celebrating our differences."[9]

On the morning of May 16, the President reversed his plans and flew to Albany to be part of the throng of twelve thousand Democrats who officially anointed Hillary as their unanimous choice for New York State senator. "I just decided I ought to be there," Clinton told reporters. "It's a big deal for her . . . I just want to be there to support her." It wasn't just talk. Before leaving Washington, he made one of the more painful sacrifices for a politician. He vowed to give up his registration in Arkansas to become a voter in his wife's adopted state. "It's hard, you know, on a personal basis," he said. "But this is a commitment that we made together."[10]

In Albany the couple huddled backstage, and following the habits of her husband, Hillary scribbled revisions to her acceptance speech up to moments before her cue. The audience, pumped up and impatient after two hours of speeches, began chanting for Hillary and erupted into pandemonium when she emerged in the spotlight with her surprise guest. The President stepped aside. But once his wife had accepted her official nomination with some humility, she acknowledged publicly for the first time her debt to her mentor.

"I would not be standing here tonight were it not for Bill," she said.[11]

His face wreathed in smiles, Clinton acknowledged the rapturous applause with a wave and a thumbs-up. Hillary's words and her partner's obvious pride made it plain that she is Clinton's living legacy. That night she reminded supporters that she stands for "a new Democratic Party," using the mantra that she and her husband had devised together back in the Eighties when they redefined their party as one "dedicated to the values of community, opportunity, responsibility." Clearly, the Clintons both looked upon the First Lady's race as a referendum on their two terms in the White House.

Campaigning for herself, Hillary defends her husband's record as interchangeable with her own priorities. Having reversed the Reaganomics that tripled the national debt and drove the stock market into Black Monday, the Clinton administration husbanded the longest peacetime economic expansion in the history of the country. Hillary could boast that her husband's fiscal restraint had been good for business but without ignoring minorities, the working poor, or the victims of AIDS as did the Reagan administration.

She herself had helped to bolster working families by pushing for family medical leave and expanded health insurance and immunization for children. Both Clintons had worked tirelessly to move the peace process in Northern Ireland past one obstacle after another, and the IRA had finally agreed to put their weapons under inspection, pointing the way toward real power-sharing between Catholics and Protestants. An historic peace agreement between the Israelis and Palestinians was more elusive. Frustrated that the clock was running out on completing the promises of the Oslo and Wye River accords by the two sides' self-imposed deadline of September 13, Clinton nonetheless promised an agreement was "within view now." From the passage of NAFTA months into his Presidency, to the passage of the China trade bill in the closing months of his administration, the outlines of a post Cold-war Clinton Doctrine had emerged: economic engagement to foster political change. It was a record of achievements in which Hillary believed she shared.

Buoyed by the apparent unity of their party, the Clintons were a veritable picture of togetherness that night in Albany. He has always been very solicitous of Hillary, say friends, with the glaring exception of his dalliance with Monica and his tortured attempts at wriggling out of admitting the truth even to his wife. But in the last year, several mutual friends who have been close to the President at White House events were impressed by the gusto with which he prattles on about his wife's campaign.

"He really has pride of ownership, in that he's her partner and over the years he's had a lot of input in her ability to rise to this point," says Shahara Llewellyn, who is a partner with her husband Bruce in the family-owned Philadelphia Coca Cola Bottling Company. "I think the President is actually holding back the level of enthusiasm he feels for what she's doing, so as not to appear cocky or self-serving," Llewellyn continued. "It's a great source of pride when he sees his partner say words that he knows are his."[12] Later that night at a reception hosted by New York Democratic Chairwoman Judith Hope, Bill Clinton did allow himself to crow: "Did Hillary give a great speech tonight, or what?" He also assured the faithful, "She will be one of the great senators this country has ever produced."[13]

The Clintons were noticeably affectionate with each other, as they had been on numerous occasions both on- and offstage in recent months. Despite the fact that Hillary was spending most of her weeks and many weekends on the campaign trail in New York, Bill Clinton had produced none of the expected rumors of womanizing. On the contrary, his exhausted speechwriters said he was ever more the Energizer Bunny in his last year, mounting an average of three speeches a day and flying around the country to make executive orders protecting the nation's wilderness areas and coastal waters from polluters. A man who cannot sit still, Clinton had smashed the record for foreign trips by a sitting President, traveling to seventy-two countries by the middle of his last year in office, as compared to Ronald Reagan who visited twenty-four nations in his two terms.[14]

Weekend guests at the White House found Hillary to be charming and ebullient. "She and Bill hold hands and touch each other in a very loving way," says Shahara Llewellyn. "Better than me and Bruce," she chuckles. "My husband stopped holding my hand twenty years ago!"[15]

RUDY'S REVELATION

The contrast was stark. Giuliani's party was all dressed up and ready for their own prom at the end of May, but they didn't have a date. Giuliani hung on to his candidacy, agonizing over his personal decision in tragic arias that kept the public entertained but made his party leaders increasingly frantic. He changed his mind several times a day. Rudy's whole decision-making tree had collapsed. He discovered that when it comes to cancer, there are no certain answers. Doctors disagree; scientific studies contradict; treatment options present a dizzying array of possible side effects. He was terrified of the "complications" that often attend surgery to remove the prostate—incontinence and impotence. Although he insisted his marital woes would have no part in the final decision about his candidacy, the truth is that decisions forced by a cancer diagnosis are not divisible from the messy details of emotional relationships. The world suddenly saw the shadow self behind the invincible mayor, who was, after all, just a man—scared, needy, conflicted—a homewrecker who was also madly in love, a politician who had always lived to win but who wasn't willing to die for it.

"Rudy was adrift in life," his friend and self-appointed psychological counselor Eliott Cuker told *The New York Post*. "After he got the cancer, he began thinking, 'What does running really mean for me?' "[16] Following a high-adrenaline appearance at the 92nd Street Y, once the cheers of "Run, Rudy, run" died away, he passed a mostly sleepless night and arrived at last at the Aha! Moment. The next morning, May 19, he told his staff he had made the decision. Get Governor Pataki on the phone. Call a press conference. He was pulling out.

The news leapt around town like heat lightning. A cable TV producer alerted Hillary to the decisive moment. She and a small circle of aides gathered breathlessly in front of a TV set in a Manhattan union hall to watch the mayor's climactic aria. What they witnessed was an apparently transformed Rudolph Giuliani—the man who had taken it upon himself to restore morality to rotten Gotham, the champion of posting the Ten Commandments in every city schoolroom, the combatant whose fund-raising letters had accused Mrs. Clinton of "hostility toward America's religious traditions"—now acknowledging, so very publicly, his own human frailty.

He was able to admit, "You know, I think that I'm finding out more about what I think is important in life. And politics is important, but it is by far not the most important thing in life. Your life is more important, your health is more important, the people you love, your family, people that are close to you and really care about you."[17] In a voice faltering with sudden humility, he repeatedly said he was thinking about how to grow from this crisis and become a better person and a better mayor. He invoked the name of God several times and promised to do better by those New Yorkers he had left out—an olive branch to minority communities. Even to hard-hearted opponents, Rudy Giuliani sounded like a man facing crisis with the courage to see it as an open door.

Hillary was genuinely moved by her opponent's swan song. "I've got to call him," she said.

THE OPERA ISN'T OVER TILL THE NEW KID SINGS!

The show should have been a walk for Hillary from then on. But this opera had a surprise fourth act. The understudy for the male lead, Congressman Rick Lazio, a young gladiator who had been waiting in the wings for two years to jump into this role, was ready with a boffo entrance speech. He made it clear that he intended to paint Hillary as liberal, liberal, liberal, even, as he put it, "far left." Her ambition, he promised, would also be an issue (unlike his). He smiled disarmingly and showed off a classic Republican profile for a statewide New York candidate: the clean-cut ethnic with a solidly suburban Catholic family, a mostly moderate voting record which appealed to independents, plus past altar boy service to Newt Gingrich, which endeared him to conservatives, and enough boyish charm to get women to tune in to his message just to relive memories of their first prom date.

Lazio immediately went on the attack. Laughably, Hillary's camp, inventors of the War Room, slapped the wrist of the new kid for being "insulting." The native Long Islander made much of being a native son. He also came to the race with a record, which the Clinton camp immediately picked apart to exaggerate those votes that could paint him as a right-wing extremist. But the greater problem Hillary would have in challenging Lazio's record was the evident fact that she didn't have one. Or rather, she lacked the sort of record a typical male politician would have built for himself. Thirty years of performing public service with nonprofit organizations and backing up a husband's political life doesn't count for much in a high-stakes electoral battle, not even against a forty-two-year-old with fewer than eight years in the U.S. House of Representatives. And with the exit of Rudy, Hillary had lost the greatest asset in their battle—the bully was gone.

The Rudy-haters were suddenly bereft. From impassioned blacks who would have fallen over themselves to get to the polls and stomp their neme-sis, to Manhattanites who know a Machiavellian mayor drunk on power when they see one, to upstate Republicans who felt snubbed by a city-bound candidate whom they never trusted anyway, the hardened political ground was suddenly fluid, roiling with aftershocks, with all the cards on the table thrown up in the air to come down in an unpredictable disorder. From a contest where only a tiny slice of voters had described themselves in polls as undecided, now just about every voting bloc—blacks, Hispanics, women, Jews, gays, suburbanites, the elderly—was up for grabs.

Within the first week of this puppyish newcomer's bounding on stage, before half the population even knew who he was, Lazio drew dead even with the hardworking Hillary. Now it would be a fight for the middle. A regular Democrat vs. Republican race. So eager was this boychik to catch up with Hillary, who was ten years his senior, the day before his unanimous nomination at an upbeat convention of New York State Republicans he fell on his face—literally. Marching in a Memorial Day parade, he tripped and split his lip, requiring eight stitches. It was another reminder that Rudy's exit had not eased the competitive pressure on Hillary. Rick Lazio was every bit as ambitious as she, and much hungrier for the job than Rudy.

"It's definitely not a cakewalk for her," was the sober assessment of New York's former Democratic governor Mario Cuomo.[18] "I think Rick Lazio is going to be Hillary Clinton's worst nightmare," predicted Fred Brown, president of the New York State Black Republicans Council. Unlike the divi-sive Giuliani, he said, Mr. Lazio would "destroy the myth" that blacks and Hispanics would automatically favor Mrs. Clinton.[19]

"She's as confident as I've ever seen her," insisted a friend and supporter after schmoozing with Hillary at two events in late May. The First Lady said she pretty much really understood the lay of the land by that time, not just on an intellectual level but on a hands-on level. She professed to find Lazio an easier candidate for her to define. It was much clearer in her mind, she said, how to run against a true Republican rather than "a quasi-Republican like Giuliani." In fact, Lazio's positions, like Giuliani's, were not that different from hers. They were both broadly pro-choice, although Lazio championed more restrictions on a woman's right to choose. They both supported further gun restrictions, but Hillary made a strong case for licensing and registering gun owners just like car owners. Still exceedingly

cautious, she intended to stick with the more conventional issues of education, health care, and abortion rights, on which her positions were favored
in the polls. No matter what she said or did, however, in eighteen months
she had never garnered more in the polls than 45 percent of the vote.

The promise of summer and fall of 2000 was greater support from the
Democratic Party. As their official nominee, the DNC and state party organization would start pumping huge amounts of soft money into the pro-
motion of Hillary, and Judith Hope promised to double the magnitude of
their phone bank on the First Lady's behalf. Mrs. Clinton would also be confident enough in her own voice by then to roll out the biggest cannon of all:
President Bill Clinton, who, judging by his job approval ratings (which had
peaked at 73 percent during his impeachment and held almost steady at 60
percent ever since) and his shamelessly stupendous fund-raising abilities,
the man could run for president in New York tomorrow and save for the
Constitution be reelected by a landslide.

As his last years became divisible into last months, Bill Clinton spoke
often and wistfully about how much he would miss working in the Oval
Office and relaxing at Camp David and hearing the flourishes of the Marine
Band, and how he would love to run for the presidency forever. One of the
youngest of the nation's chief executives to be forcibly retired, at the age of
fifty-four, Clinton continued to deflect questions of what he intended to do
with the rest of his life. He phlegmatically mentioned he would write a book
but said he didn't know how he would otherwise earn a living. Although he
had the gall to represent his impeachment as good for the country, describing it as "one of the major chapters in my defeat of the revolution Mr. Gingrich led,"[20] it could end up restricting his earning power. Eight months
before his exit from national office, the Arkansas Supreme Court's discipli-
nary committee recommended that he be disbarred. His defenders blamed
the same old right-wing conspiracy. The Southeastern Legal Foundation,
which brought one of the complaints, was indeed partly funded by Clinton's eternal pursuer, Richard Mellon Scaife. But Susan Webber Wright,
the judge who found him in contempt of court and fined him $90,686, had
filed an earlier complaint.[21] And having cut off Arkansas by registering to
vote in his wife's adopted state, he wasn't going to see a Clinton library built
any time soon.

What options was he considering? I continually asked people close to
the Clintons. "I would venture he's given it almost no thought," said one of
his former press secretaries. "That's way too scary. He'll drive off that
bridge when he comes to it."

With a blank slate before him after January 20, 2001, Clinton will be more dependent than ever on the kindness of Hillary. His former press secretary Mike McCurry was asked by a student audience at Northwestern University what President Clinton will be doing in twenty years. McCurry barked out the obvious answer:

"Whatever Hillary wants him to do!"[22]

THE ROAD NOT YET TRAVELED

Thirty years before, Hillary ruminated that she might spend her life solving other people's problems while completely defaulting on solving her own. As a young woman she wrote, "I wonder who is me. I wonder if I'll ever meet her. If I did, I think we'd get along famously."[23]

In her early adulthood, Hillary's choice was to set her life course by following the man she loved. She married a politician and chose to go down his road. Now she knows where that road ends—draped in the tattered cloak of Bill Clinton's legacy and wandering off into middle-aged oblivion. But the other road, the one less traveled by—the Hillary Rodham road—is still open to her. She certainly has the energy and the pluck. The passion for public service still smolders inside her. And now it is sparked by the need for redemption, even revenge. Having thrashed her way through the dark wood of our contemporary political jungle and survived a thousand cuts, she has perhaps developed the rhinoceros skin that her patron saint, Eleanor Roosevelt, said was necessary for women in politics. Hillary has always tried to follow Eleanor Roosevelt's ruthless intention to have an impact on her century. And what was it her friend Sara Ehrman had told her years before, when she had announced her headstrong choice to marry Bill Clinton?

"Yes, but remember, Hillary. Eleanor Roosevelt only became powerful when she stopped caring about her marriage."[24]

No matter what happens in the future, she is already a different person. Hillary has come through the little death of midlife and stood up against scorn. As she tries on her own political form, she is dreaming not only of a different life but of a different world. Her ambitions are broader than a change in personal identity.

Standing in the ruins of Al-Badi Palace in Morocco in March 1999, swathed in a coppery sunset, Hillary gave a long, heartfelt address on human rights: "We can alter the direction of the planet when we follow leaders who speak of peace and work against war, who serve their people by healing divisions, not creating them." She wound up exhorting her audience of royals, ministers, and ambassadors—and herself—to "alter the direction of this planet by dreaming of a different direction that we can all take in our own lives."[25]

Traveling this road, Hillary Rodham may at last meet herself. And perhaps they will get along famously.

Notes

TITLE PAGE

1. Interview with Hillary Rodham Clinton, CNN, May 14, 1999.

CHAPTER 1:   INTO THE FLAMES

1. Author's interviews with Melanne Verveer, 1998.
2. *Today*, NBC Television, January 27, 1998.
3. Author's interviews with Dee Dee Myers, 1998.
4. Author's interviews with Dick Morris, 1998.
5. Author's interview with a former White House counsel, 1998.
6. Author's interview with a high-ranking government official, 1998.
7. Author's interview with Matt Lauer, 1999.
8. Gail Sheehy, "Hillary's Choice," *Vanity Fair*, January 1999.
9. Author's interview with Mary Steenburgen, 1992.
10. Author's interviews with Linda Bloodworth-Thomason, 1992.
11. Author's interviews with Bernard Nussbaum, 1998.
12. *Today*, January 27, 1998.
13. Interview with Hillary Rodham Clinton, CBS Radio, January 19, 1998.
14. Author's interviews with Hillary and Bill Clinton, January to March 1992.
15. Gail Sheehy, "What Hillary Wants," *Vanity Fair*, May 1992.
16. Author's interviews with Hillary and Bill Clinton, 1992.
17. Sheehy, "What Hillary Wants."
18. Author's interview with Christopher Hitchens, 1998.
19. From grand jury testimony of Sidney Blumenthal, June 4, 1998.
20. Ibid.
21. Author's interviews with Betsey Wright, 1998.
22. Author's interviews with Dorothy Rodham, 1998.
23. Author's interviews with Mandy Grunwald, 1998.
24. *Meet the Press*, NBC Television, January 25, 1998.
25. Author's interviews with Ed Matthews, 1998.
26. Author's interview with Jim Hoge, 1998.

CHAPTER 2:   SLEEPING THROUGH THE REVOLUTION

1. Author's interviews with Dorothy Rodham, 1992.
2. Hillary Rodham Clinton, "Talking It Over," *Chattanooga Free Press*, March 8, 1998.
3. As described by Hillary Rodham in a letter to John Peavoy, November 1, 1966.

4.   Author's interview with Paul Carlson, 1999.

5.   Martha Sherrill, "The Education of Hillary Clinton," *The Washington Post*, January 11, 1993.

6.   Hillary Rodham Clinton, *It Takes a Village* (New York: Simon & Schuster, 1996), p. 22.

7.   *Daily Mail* (London), March 30, 1994.

8.   Author's interview with Islan Thomas, 1999.

9.   Clinton, *It Takes a Village*, p. 20.

10. Sherrill, "The Education of Hillary Clinton."

11. Author's interviews with Dorothy Rodham, 1992.

12. Clinton, *It Takes a Village*, p. 33.

13. Ibid., p. 40.

14. Miriam Horn, *Rebels in White Gloves* (New York: Random House, 1999).

15. Ibid.

16. Author's interviews with John Peavoy, 1999.

17. Author's interviews with Dorothy Rodham, 1992.

18. Author's interviews with David Rupert, 1999.

19. Author's interview with Rick Ricketts, 1999.

20. Ibid.

21. Author's interviews with Hillary Rodham Clinton, 1992.

22. Author's interview with Hugh Rodham, Jr., 1992.

23. George Eliot, *Middlemarch* (New York: Modern Library, 1994).

24. Author's interviews with Arthur Curtis, 1999.

25. Author's interviews with Don Jones, 1999.

26. "I'm smarter . . . you should Laurie": author's interviews with Arthur Curtis, 1999.

27. Sherrill, "The Education of Hillary Clinton."

28. Clinton, *It Takes a Village*, p. 22.

29. Author's interviews with John Peavoy, 1999.

30. Author's interview with Paul Cavaco, 1999.

31. Sherrill, "The Education of Hillary Clinton."

32. Author's interview with Jeff Phillips, 1999.

33. Author's interviews with Dorothy Rodham, 1992.

34. Author's interviews with Don Jones, 1999.

35. Author's interviews with Arthur Curtis, 1999.

36. Author's interviews with Don Jones, 1999.

37. "In 1960 . . . a hawk": author's interview with Paul Carlson, 1999.

38. David Halberstam, *The Children* (New York: Ballantine, 1998), p. 315.

39. Author's interview with Patsy Henderson Bowles, 1999.

40. "A Hard Rain's A-Gonna Fall," Bob Dylan.

41. Author's interviews with Don Jones, 1998–99.

42. Ibid.

43. Author's interviews with Paul Carlson, 1999.

44. Author's interviews with Don Jones, 1999.

45. Letter from Hillary Rodham to John Peavoy, November 14, 1965.

46. Author's interview with Paul Carlson, 1999.

47. Author's interviews with Don Jones, 1999.

48. Gail Sheehy, "What Hillary Wants, *Vanity Fair,* May 1992."

49. "Paul . . . Martin Luther King, Jr.": author's interviews with Don Jones, 1999.

50. Author's interviews with Dorothy Rodham, 1992.

51. Author's interviews with Patsy Henderson Bowles, 1999.

52. Rodham letter to Peavoy, February 23, 1968.

53. Author's interviews with Don Jones, 1999.

54. Author's interviews with Arthur Curtis, 1999.

55. Ibid.

56. Rodham letter to Peavoy, November 14, 1965.

CHAPTER 3: "I WONDER WHO IS ME?"

1. "Hillary's Class," *Frontline*, PBS Television, November 25, 1998.

2. Author's interviews with Hillary Rodham Clinton, 1992.

3. Donnie Radcliffe, *Hillary Rodham Clinton, A First Lady for Our Time* (New York: Warner Books, 1993), p. 52.

4. Author's interview with Janet Altman Spragens, 1999.

5. Letter from Hillary Rodham to John Peavoy, October 8, 1965.

6. Ibid.

7. Rodham letter to Peavoy, September 22, 1965.

8. Rodham letter to Peavoy, September 30, 1965.

9. Rodham letter to Peavoy, October 8, 1965.

10. Rodham letter to Peavoy, February 24, 1967.

11. Rodham letter to Peavoy, October 19, 1965.

12. Rodham letter to Peavoy, October 31, 1965.

13. Rodham letter to Peavoy, September 30, 1965.

14. Ibid.

15. Rodham letters to Peavoy, October 8 and 19, 1965.

16. Rodham letter to Peavoy, October 8, 1965.

17. Gail Sheehy, *Passages* (New York: Dutton, 1976).

18. Rodham letter to Peavoy, July 11, 1967.

19. Ibid.

20. Rodham letter to Peavoy, February 9, 1966.

21. *The Boston Globe*, January 12, 1993.

22. Ibid.

23. Author's interview with Geoffrey Shields, 1992.

24. Gail Sheehy, "What Hillary Wants," *Vanity Fair*, May 1992.

25. Rodham letter to Peavoy, March 1966.

26. Rodham letter to Peavoy, January 11, 1967.

27. Rodham letter to Peavoy, February 9, 1966.

28. Rodham letter to Peavoy, February 24, 1967.

29. Rodham letter to Peavoy, April 13, 1967.

30. Author's interview with Jan Piercey, 1992.

31. Author's interviews with Don Jones, 1999.

32. *The Boston Globe*, January 12, 1993.

33. Ibid.

34. Author's interviews with Don Jones, 1999.

35. Rodham letter to Peavoy, July 11, 1967; author's interview with Anthony D'Amato, 1999.

36. Walter J. Ong, *In the Human Grain: Further Explorations of Contemporary Culture* (New York: Macmillan, 1967).

37. Heinz Eulau, *The Behavioral Persuasion in Politics* (New York: Random House, 1963).

38. Rodham letter to Peavoy, June 6, 1967.

39. Rodham letter to Peavoy, February 24, 1967.

40. Rodham letter to Peavoy, March 1, 1968.

41. Author's interview with Geoffrey Shields, 1999.

42. Author's interview with Alan Schecter, 1999.

43. Author's interview with Ann Sherwood Sentilles, 1999.

44. Rodham letter to Peavoy, April 21, 1966.

45. *The Boston Globe*, January 12, 1993.

46. Rodham letter to Peavoy, April 13, 1967.

47. Author's interviews with Don Jones, 1999.

48. J. D. Salinger, *Catcher in the Rye* (London: Hamish Hamilton, 1987), pp. 205–206.

49. Author's interviews with Don Jones, 1999.

50. Rodham letter to Peavoy, April 13, 1967.

51. Author's interviews with John Peavoy, 1999.

52. Rodham letter to Peavoy, April 13, 1967.

53. Rodham letter to Peavoy, November 15, 1967.

54. Rodham letter to Peavoy, February 24, 1967.

55. Rodham letter to Peavoy, November 14, 1965.

56. Rodham letter to Peavoy, February 23, 1968.

57. Rodham letter to Peavoy, November 15, 1967.

58. Rodham letter to Peavoy, February 23, 1968.

59. Rodham letter to Peavoy, August 23, 1967.

60. Rodham letter to Peavoy, February 19, 1966.

61. Rodham letter to Peavoy, March 25, 1969.

62. Rodham letter to Peavoy, February 23, 1968.

63. Rodham letter to Peavoy, October 31, 1965.

64. Author's interviews with John Peavoy, 1999.

65. Rodham letter to Peavoy, April 13, 1967.

66. Clinton Rossiter, Introduction to *The Federalist* (Middletown, Conn.: Wesleyan University Press, 1961).

67. "He spotted . . . that happened": author's interview with Alan Schecter, 1999.

68. *The Boston Globe*, January 12, 1993.

69. Gail Sheehy, *New Passages* (New York: Random House, 1995).

70. *The Boston Globe*, January 12, 1993.

71. Author's interview with Alan Schecter, 1999.

72. *The Boston Globe*, January 12, 1993.

73. Ibid.

74. Ibid.

75. Ibid.

76. Author's interview with Eleanor Dean Acheson, 1999.

77. Ibid.
78. Hillary Rodham, commencement address, Wellesley College, May 31, 1969.
79. Author's interview with Eleanor Dean Acheson, 1999.
80. Rodham letter to Peavoy, September 22, 1966.
81. Author's interviews with Nancy Pietrefesa, 1999.
82. Rodham letter to Peavoy, March 1, 1968.

CHAPTER 4:   FIRST LOVE

1.   Author's interviews with David Rupert, 1999.
2.   Author's interviews with Nancy Pietrefesa, 1999, and John Danner, 1999.
3.   Author's interview with Leslie Friedman, 1999.
4.   "There's a lot . . . we laughed": author's interviews with David Rupert, 1999.
5.   Author's interviews with Nancy Pietrefesa, 1999.
6.   Author's interview with Melvin Laird, 1999.
7.   Congressional Record—House, June 11, 1968, p. 16,690.
8.   Jack Anderson and Michael Binstein, "First Lady an Understudy to Laird," *Bench-Marks: A Publication of Marshfield Medical Research Foundation,* September 12, 1998.
9.   *The Washington Post,* January 12, 1993.
10. David Brock, *The Seduction of Hillary Rodham* (New York: Free Press, 1996), p. 17.
11. Author's interview with Alan Schecter, 1999.
12. Ibid.
13. Author's interviews with Nancy Pietrefesa, 1999.
14. Brock, *The Seduction of Hillary Rodham.*
15. *The Chicago Daily News,* June 1969.
16. *Arkansas Democrat-Gazette,* July 22, 1990.
17. "Some of us . . . probably true": author's interviews with David Rupert, 1999.
18. Author's interviews with Lanny Davis, 1999.
19. Lani Guinier, *Becoming Gentlemen* (Boston: Beacon Press, 1997).
20. Author's interview with Drucilla Ramey, 1999.
21. *Connecticut Law Tribune,* October 12, 1992.
22. Author's interview with Ken Kaufman, 1999.
23. Author's interviews, Yale Law School, Class of 1973.
24. Author's interview with John Danner, 1999.
25. Author's interviews with David Rupert, 1999.
26. Letter from Hillary Rodham to John Peavoy, November 15, 1967.
27. "I am a . . . in a partner": author's interviews with David Rupert, 1999.

CHAPTER 5:   PRUDE MEETS PASSION

1.   Author's interview with Bill Clinton, 1992.
2.   Ibid.
3.   Author's interviews with Hillary Rodham Clinton, 1992.
4.   Author's interview with Bill Clinton, 1992.
5.   Author's interviews with Hillary Rodham Clinton and Bill Clinton, 1992.
6.   Author's interview with Burke Marshall, 1992.

7. Gail Sheehy, "Hillary's Choice," *Vanity Fair*, February 1999.

8. Author's interview with Nancy Bekavac Singer, 1992.

9. David Maraniss, *First in His Class* (New York: Simon & Schuster, 1995), p. 240.

10. Author's interview with William Coleman, 1992.

11. Gail Sheehy, *Panthermania: The Clash of Black Against Black in One American City* (New York: Harper & Row, 1971).

12. Carole Bass, "Rights of Passage," *The Connecticut Law Tribune*, October 12, 1992.

13. Author's interviews with Robert Treuhaft, 1999, and Drucilla Ramey, 1999.

14. Author's interviews with Malcolm Burnstein, 1999.

15. Sheehy, *Panthermania*.

16. *Los Angeles Times*, August 1989.

17. Ibid.

18. Author's interviews with Malcolm Burnstein, 1999.

19. Ibid.

20. Ibid.

21. Letter from Hillary Rodham to Don Jones, 1967.

22. "The plot thickens . . . a great life": author's interviews with David Rupert, 1999.

23. Author's interview with Bill Clinton, 1992.

24. Gail Sheehy, *Character: America's Search for Leadership* (New York: William Morrow, 1988).

25. Ibid.

26. "But about political . . . like Hillary before": author's interview with Betsey Wright, 1992.

27. Author's interview with Bill Clinton, 1992.

28. Bass, "Rights of Passage."

29. Author's interview with Albert Solnit, 1999.

30. Bass, "Rights of Passage."

31. David Brock, *The Seduction of Hillary Rodham* (New York: Free Press, 1996), p. 118.

32. Garry Wills, *The New York Review of Books*, 1992.

33. Author's interviews with Paul Fray, 1999.

34. Author's interviews with Paul and Mary Lee Fray, 1999.

35. Author's interviews with Carolyn Yeldell Staley, 1992, and Joe Purvis, 1999.

36. Author's interview with Virginia Kelley, 1992.

37. Author's interviews with Paul Fray, 1999.

38. Author's interview with John Doar, 1992.

39. Maraniss, *First in His Class*, p. 297.

40. Brock, *The Seduction of Hillary Rodham*, p. 52.

41. *Arkansas Democrat-Gazette*, July 22, 1990.

42. *The National Journal*, February 28, 1998.

43. Brock, *The Seduction of Hillary Rodham*.

44. Author's interviews with Paul Fray, 1999.

45. Author's interview with Rose Crane, 1999.

46. Author's interviews with Paul Fray, 1999.

47. "I'm driving . . . slammed the door": author's interviews with Bernard Nussbaum, 1999.

CHAPTER 6: THE HOT SPRINGS KID

1. Gail Sheehy, "Hillary's Choice," *Vanity Fair*, February 1999.
2. The widowed Virginia Cassidy Blythe later married Roger Clinton, divorced him, remarried him, and after his death married Jeff Dwire, who died of a heart ailment; she then married Dick Kelley.
3. Author's interviews with Joe Purvis, 1999.
4. Virginia Kelley, *Leading with My Heart* (New York: Simon & Schuster, 1994), p. 69.
5. "Bill Clinton's Hidden Life," *U.S. News & World Report*, July 20, 1992 (edited text of Clinton's own words in a series of interviews with editors Donald Baer, Matthew Cooper, and David Gergen).
6. *The Washington Post*, March 13, 1999.
7. Baer, Cooper, and Gergen, "Bill Clinton's Hidden Life." (Clinton first revealed this tortured part of his biography halfway through his 1992 campaign, once he realized he had lost control during the Democratic primaries over how the public viewed him. He acknowledged to the editors that he might have underestimated the importance of biography in a presidential campaign.)
8. Author's interview with Bill Clinton, 1992.
9. David Maraniss, *First in His Class* (New York: Simon & Schuster, 1995).
10. Ibid., p. 28.
11. Author's interview with James Morgan, 1998.
12. Author's interview with Wilma Booker, 1998.
13. Bill Clinton press conference, Little Rock, July 14, 1987.
14. Author's interviews with Paul Fray, 1999.
15. Author's interviews with Joe Purvis, 1999.
16. Author's interviews with Paul Fray, 1999, and James Morgan, 1998. See also Maraniss, *First in His Class.*
17. Author's interviews with Joe Purvis, 1999.
18. Author's interviews with Mack McLarty, 1999.
19. Baer, Cooper, and Gergen, "Bill Clinton's Hidden Life."
20. Author's interviews with Joe Purvis, 1999.
21. Author's interviews with Paul Fray, 1999.
22. Author's interviews with Carolyn Yeldell Staley, 1999.
23. "The Choice '96," *Frontline*, WGBH Television (David Fanning, executive producer), November 5, 1996.
24. Kelley, *Leading with My Heart*, p. 121.
25. Author's interviews with Paul Fray, 1999.
26. Kelley, *Leading with My Heart*, p. 81.
27. Author's interview with Q. Byrum Hurst, 1999.
28. David Maraniss, *The Clinton Enigma* (New York: Simon & Schuster, 1998).
29. Kelley, *Leading with My Heart*, p. 81.
30. Author's interviews with Ed Matthews, 1999.
31. Author's interviews with Carolyn Yeldell Staley, 1992.
32. Lucinda Franks, "The Intimate Hillary," *Talk*, August 1999.
33. *New York Post*, April 20, 1999.

34. Author's interviews with Carolyn Yeldell Staley, 1992.

35. Author's interview with Larry Gleghorn, 1999.

36. Author's interviews with Carolyn Yedell Staley, 1992.

37. Walsh and Brownstein, "Just Applying Old Principles to a 'New World out there,' " *U.S. News & World Report,* January 26, 1998.

38. Kelley, *Leading with My Heart,* p.14.

39. Author's interview with Hillary Rodham Clinton, 1992.

40. Author's interview with Rose Crane, 1998.

41. Nancy Collins, "A Legacy of Strength and Love: President Clinton Talks About His Mother, Virginia Kelley," *Good Housekeeping,* November 1995.

42. Walsh and Brownstein, "Just Applying Old Principles to a 'New World out there.' "

43. Author's interviews with Carolyn Yeldell Staley, 1992.

44. Walsh and Brownstein, "Just Applying Old Principles to a 'New World out there.' "

45. *The Boston Globe,* December 11, 1994.

46. *20/20,* ABC Television, March 3, 1999.

47. Andrew Morton, *Monica's Story* (New York: St. Martin's Press, 1999).

48. Author's interview with Bill Clinton, 1992.

49. Gail Sheehy, "What Hillary Wants," *Vanity Fair,* May 1992.

50. Author's interview with Bill Clinton, 1992.

51. Kelley, *Leading with My Heart,* p. 149.

52. Author's interview with Judith Hope, 1998.

53. Donald Baer, "Man-Child in Politics Land," *U.S. News & World Report,* October 14, 1991.

54. Author's interviews with Carolyn Yeldell Staley, 1992.

55. Garry Wills, "Beginning of the Road," *Time,* July 20, 1992.

56. Baer, "Man-Child in Politics Land."

57. Author's interviews with Don Baer, 1998.

58. Maraniss, *First in His Class,* p. 60.

59. Wills, "Beginning of the Road."

60. Author's interview with Ron Addington, 1999.

61. Author's interviews with Paul Fray, 1999.

62. David Brock, *The Seduction of Hillary Rodham* (New York: Free Press, 1996), p. 60.

63. Liza Mundy, "Hillary Clinton and the Limits of Choice," *The Washington Post Magazine,* March 21, 1999.

64. Author's interviews with Paul Fray, 1999.

65. Author's interviews with Nancy Pietrefesa, 1999.

66. "Everything was hunky-dory . . . it was horrible": author's interviews with Paul Fray, 1999.

67. Author's interviews with Paul and Mary Lee Fray, 1999.

68. Maraniss, *First in His Class.*

69. Author's interviews with Mary Lee Fray, 1999.

70. Author's interviews with Nancy Pietrefesa, 1999.

71. Author's interviews with Carolyn Yeldell Staley, 1992.

72. Author's interviews with Betsey Wright, 1992.

73. Author's interviews with Max Brantley, 1999, and Paul Fray, 1999.

74. Author's interviews with Paul Fray, 1999.

75. Author's interviews with Mary Lee Fray, 1999.

76. Author's interview with Neal McDonald, 1999.
77. "We knew three . . . so be it": author's interviews with Paul and Mary Lee Fray, 1999, and Neal McDonald, 1999.

CHAPTER 7: ARKANSAS DIAMONDS AND DENIM

1. Author's interview with Jerry Bookout, 1999.
2. Author's interview with Bobby Roberts, 1999.
3. *Arkansas Democrat-Gazette*, January 11, 1979.
4. Author's interviews with Nancy Pietrefesa, 1999.
5. Author's interviews with Carolyn Yeldell Staley, 1999.
6. Virginia Kelley, *Leading with My Heart* (New York: Simon & Schuster, 1994), p. 199.
7. Author's interviews with Susan McDougal, 1999.
8. David Maraniss, *First in His Class* (New York: Simon & Schuster, 1995).
9. Author's interviews with Hillary Rodham Clinton, 1992.
10. Hillary Rodham Clinton, "Good Marriages Are More Than a Piece of Paper," syndicated column, October 8, 1995.
11. Author's interviews with Susan McDougal, 1999.
12. Author's interviews with Don Jones, 1999.
13. Gail Sheehy, *Passages* (New York: Dutton, 1976).
14. Author's interviews with Arthur Curtis, 1999.
15. Author's interviews with Betsey Wright, 1992.
16. Author's interviews with Mack McLarty, 1999.
17. Diana McLellan, "The State of Their Union," *Ladies' Home Journal*, September 1994.
18. Joseph Lash, *Eleanor and Franklin* (New York: Konecky & Konecky, 1999).
19. Letter from Hillary Rodham to John Peavoy, November 14, 1965.
20. Author's interviews with John Peavoy, 1999.
21. Author's interviews with Susan McDougal, 1999.
22. Author's interview with Jerry Bookout, 1999.
23. Author's interview with Bobby Roberts, 1999.
24. "Uneasy Rider," Charlie Daniels, 1973.
25. Maraniss, *First In His Class*.
26. Author's interview with Bobby Roberts, 1999.
27. Author's interview with Carolyn Yeldell Staley, 1992.
28. Author's interviews with Susan McDougal, 1999.
29. John Brummett, *Nightline*, ABC Television, February 9, 1994.
30. Author's interviews with Claudia Riley, 1999.
31. Brummett, *Nightline*.
32. *Money*, April 1994.
33. Wallace Tripp, *A Great Big Ugly Man Came Up and Tied his Horse to Me* (Boston: Little, Brown, 1973).
34. Author's interviews with Jane Sherburne, 1999.
35. Brummett, *Nightline*.
36. Author's interviews with Susan McDougal, 1999.
37. Author's interviews with Nancy Pietrefesa, 1999.
38. Ibid.
39. Author's interview with Webster Hubbell, 1992.

40. Author's interview with Skip Rutherford, 1999.
41. Author's interviews with Nancy Pietrefesa, 1999.
42. Author's interview with Larry Gleghorn, 1999.
43. A term then used to describe any woman whose first birth is at an age over twenty-five.
44. Author's interview with Betty Lowe, 1999.
45. Author's interviews with Carolyn Huber, 1992.
46. Author's interviews with Diane Blair, 1992.
47. Author's interviews with Nancy Pietrefesa, 1999.
48. Author's interviews with Carolyn Yeldell Staley, 1992.
49. Ibid.
50. Maraniss, *First in His Class*, p. 363.
51. George Fisher, *The Best of Fisher* (Fayetteville: University of Arkansas Press, 1993). p. 142.
52. Author's interview with Bobby Roberts, 1999.
53. Author's interviews with Gene Lyons, 1999.
54. Author's interviews with Susan McDougal, 1999.
55. Author's interviews with Dick Morris, 1998.
56. Author's interviews with Susan McDougal, 1999.
57. Author's interviews with Max Brantley, 1999.
58. Author's interviews with Susan McDougal, 1999.
59. Author's interviews with Nancy Pietrefesa, 1999.
60. Author's interview with Bobby Roberts, 1999.
61. Author's interviews with Dick Morris, 1998.
62. Author's interview with Bobby Roberts, 1999.
63. *Arkansas Democrat*, November 6, 1980.

CHAPTER 8: THE RODHAM REGENCY IN ARKANSAS

1. Author's interview with Carolyn Huber, 1992.
2. Author's interviews with Max Brantley, 1999.
3. Gail Sheehy, *Passages* (New York: Dutton, 1976).
4. *Arkansas Gazette*, November 21, 1980.
5. Author's interview with Bill Clinton, 1992.
6. Author's interview with Jan Piercey, 1992.
7. Author's interview with Bobby Roberts, 1999.
8. Author's interviews with Carolyn Yeldell Staley, 1999.
9. "You know . . . can't do this": author's interviews with Dick Morris, 1998.
10. United Press International, May 14, 1982.
11. Author's interview with Herb Rule, 1992.
12. Author's interviews with Betsey Wright, 1992.
13. Author's interview with Bill Clinton, 1992.
14. Author's interviews with Hillary Rodham Clinton, 1992.
15. Author's interviews with Diane Blair, 1992.
16. Gail Sheehy, "What Hillary Wants," *Vanity Fair*, May 1992. (Fisher cartoon.)
17. Author's interview with Bobby Roberts, 1999.
18. Author's interviews with Dick Morris, 1998.
19. Doug Smith, "Analysis by Governor White," *Arkansas Gazette*, February 22, 1981.

20. Author's interviews with John Brummett, 1999, and Max Brantley, 1999.

21. Bill and Hillary Clinton's financial statement, released July 23, 1999.

22. Author's interviews with Claudia Riley, 1999.

23. Author's interview with Bobby Roberts, 1999.

24. *Arkansas Gazette*, February 28, 1982.

25. Author's interview with John Brummett, 1999.

26. Miriam Horn, *Rebels in White Gloves* (New York: Random House, 1999), pp. 151–152.

27. Author's interviews with Nancy Pietrefesa, 1999.

28. Author's interview with John Brummett, 1999.

29. Author's interviews with Dick Morris, 1998.

30. Author's interviews with Nancy Pietrefesa, 1999.

31. Author's interview with Frank White, 1999.

32. Ibid.

33. Author's interviews with Paul Fray, 1999.

34. Author's interview with John Brummett, 1992.

35. Author's interview with Bobby Roberts, 1999.

36. Author's interview with John Brummett, 1999.

37. Ibid.

38. Author's interviews with Betsey Wright, 1992.

39. Author's interviews with Nancy Pietrefesa, 1999.

40. David Maraniss, *First in His Class* (New York: Simon & Schuster, 1995), p. 394.

41. "Bill Clinton's Hidden Life," *U.S. News & World Report*, July 20, 1992 (edited text of Clinton's own words in a series of interviews with editors Donald Baer, Matthew Cooper, and David Gergen).

42. Author's interviews with Betsey Wright, 1992.

43. Author's interviews with Eileen McGann, 1999.

44. Author's interviews with Carolyn Huber, 1992.

45. Author's interviews with Betsey Wright, 1992.

46. Author's interview with Jan Piercey, 1992.

47. Author's interviews with Dick Morris, 1998.

48. Author's interviews with Don Jones, 1999.

49. Study by Alexander Kern, University of Florida, 1978.

50. *Arkansas Gazette*, July 29, 1983.

51. Author's interviews with Dick Morris, 1998.

52. Norman King, *Hillary: Her True Story* (New York: Birch Lane Press, 1993), p. 99.

53. "You could never . . . stroke of genius": author's interview with Jerry Bookout, 1999.

54. Author's interview with Larry Gleghorn, 1999.

55. Ibid.

56. Author's interview with Skip Rutherford, 1999.

57. Author's interview with Carolyn Huber, 1992.

58. Author's interviews with Betsey Wright, 1999.

59. Author's interview with Skip Rutherford, 1992.

60. Author's interview with Rob Walton, 1992.

61. Author's interviews with Hillary Rodham Clinton, 1992.

62. Author's interview with Larry Gleghorn, 1999.

63. Author's interviews with Paul Fray, 1999.

64. Author's interviews with Don Jones, 1999.

65. Author's interview with Larry Gleghorn, 1999.

66. Author's interviews with Betsey Wright, 1992.

67. Author's interview with Bill Clinton, 1992.

68. Author's interviews with Betsey Wright, 1999.

69. Karen Tumulty and Nancy Gibbs, "The Better Half," *Time*, December 1998.

CHAPTER 9: MONEY BUSINESS

1. Author's interviews with Don Jones, 1999.

2. At the time, Entergy was called Middle South Utilities.

3. "You'll get killed . . . we've always had": author's interviews with Dick Morris, 1999.

4. David Brock, *The Seduction of Hillary Rodham* (New York: Free Press, 1996).

5. Author's interview with Bobby Roberts, 1999.

6. *The Washington Times*, May 19, 1995.

7. Hillary Clinton, press conference, Washington, D.C., April 22, 1994.

8. David Maraniss, *First in His Class* (New York: Simon & Schuster, 1995), p. 428.

9. Author's interview with Max Brantley, 1999.

10. *American Lawyer*, July 1992.

11. Author's interview with Thomas Mars, 1999.

12. David Brock, "Living with the Clintons," *The American Spectator*, January 1994.

13. Gene Lyons, *The New York Review of Books*, August 8, 1996.

14. David Brock, "The Fire This Time," *Esquire*, April 1998.

15. Daniel Wattenberg, "Love and Hate in Arkansas: L. D. Brown's Story," *The American Spectator*, April 1994.

16. Author's interviews with Betsey Wright, 1999.

17. James D. Retter, *Anatomy of a Scandal* (Los Angeles: General Publishing Group, 1998).

18. *The Washington Post*, June 2, 1996.

19. Brock, *The Seduction of Hillary Rodham*, p. 201.

20. *The Washington Post*, June 2, 1996.

21. Author's interviews with Jane Sherburne, 1999.

22. Ibid.

23. *Whitewater, From the Editorial Pages of the Wall Street Journal* (New York: Dow-Jones & Co., 1994).

24. *Arkansas Democrat-Gazette*, January 31, 1996.

25. Hillary Rodham Clinton, *It Takes a Village* (New York: Simon & Schuster, 1996), p. 150.

26. *The Washington Post*, March 10, 1992.

27. On average, the bond counsel earns from $1 to $1.75 on each $1,000 of bonds issued, according to the Arkansas Development Finance Authority.

28. Clinton, *It Takes a Village*, p. 150.

29. Ibid., p. 151.

30. Author's interview with Hugh Rodham, Jr., 1992.

31. Author's interview with Carolyn Huber, 1992.
32. Author's interviews with Dick Morris, 1998.
33. *The Commercial Appeal*, April 20, 1992.
34. Author's interview with Herb Rule, 1992.
35. Author's interview with Jan Piercey, 1992.
36. *American Lawyer*, July 1992.
37. Author's interview with Joe Giroir, 1999.
38. Author's interviews with Dick Morris, 1999.
39. Author's interview with John Brummett, 1999.
40. Author's interviews with Dick Morris, 1998.
41. *Money*, July 1992.
42. Author's interviews with Eileen McGann, 1999.
43. *Money*, July 1992.
44. Author's interviews with Don Jones, 1999.
45. Lecture notes from Don Jones.
46. Author's interviews with Don Jones, 1999.
47. Gail Sheehy, "The Road to Bimini," *Vanity Fair*, September 1987.
48. Author's interview with Max Brantley, 1999.
49. Author's interviews with Bernard Nussbaum, 1998.
50. Author's interviews with Betsey Wright, 1999.
51. Maraniss, *First in His Class*, p. 441.
52. Ibid.
53. Author's interview with John Brummett, 1999.
54. Author's interviews with Betsey Wright, 1999.
55. Author's interview with Max Brantley, 1999.
56. Author's interviews with Betsey Wright, 1999.
57. Author's interviews with Bernard Nussbaum, 1998.
58. Author's interviews with Dick Morris, 1998.
59. Author's interviews with Betsey Wright, 1999.

CHAPTER 10: DIVORCE OR REDEDICATION?

1. Author's interviews with Dorothy Rodham, 1992.
2. Larry Van Dyn, "How do you feel about that, Mr. President?," *The Washingtonian*, June 1994.
3. *The Washington Post*, April 1, 1998.
4. *Newsday*, March 22, 1998.
5. Gannett News Service, January 2, 1999.
6. *Arkansas Democrat-Gazette*, March 14, 1998.
7. Associated Press, February 3, 1992.
8. David Brock, *The American Spectator*, January 1994; *The Times* (London), December 21, 1993; *The Sunday Times* (London), May 1, 1994.
9. *The Washington Times*, December 21, 1993.
10. Author's interviews with Betsey Wright 1999.
11. Lucinda Franks, commenting on her interview with Hillary Rodham for *Talk* magazine on *Larry King Live*, August 2, 1999.

12. Author's interviews with Betsey Wright, 1999.

13. "Wal-Mart Helps Wealthiest Arkansans Salvage Good Year," *Arkansas Business*, July 12, 1999. The Bland family was reported to be worth $64 million.

14. *Arkansas Democrat-Gazette*, February 21, 1988; *Arkansas Democrat Gazette*, March 30, 1997.

15. Author's interviews with James Jenkins, 1999.

16. Author's interview with Danny Ferguson, 1999.

17. *Arkansas Democrat-Gazette*, August 2, 1997.

18. Author's interviews with James Jenkins, 1999.

19. *Arkansas Business*, July 12, 1999.

20. Western New England College records.

21. Chancery Court of Pulaski County, Arkansas, 1984.

22. Author's interviews with James Jenkins, 1999.

23. Entergy Arkansas was then called Arkansas Power and Light.

24. *Daily Mail* (London), December 29, 1993.

25. Author's interviews with James Jenkins, 1999.

26. *Daily Mail* (London), December 27, 1993.

27. Danny Ferguson's deposition in the Jones case; *Daily Mail*, December 30, 1993.

28. Author's interviews with Dick Morris, 1999.

29. Author's interview with Dorothy Stuck, 1992.

30. Author's interview with Carolyn Huber, 1992.

31. Author's interviews with Dick Morris, 1999.

32. Ibid.

33. Author's interviews with Betsey Wright, 1999.

34. David Maraniss, *First in His Class* (New York: Simon & Schuster, 1995), p. 422.

35. Author's interviews with Nancy Pietrefesa, 1999.

36. Author's interview with a former Clinton White House aide.

37. Author's interviews with Eileen McGann, 1999

38. Gail Sheehy, "What Hillary Wants," *Vanity Fair*, May 1992

39. Author's interviews with Betsey Wright, 1999.

40. *The New Straits Times*, September 19, 1999.

41. Author's interviews with Betsey Wright, 1999.

42. Author's interviews with Bob Boorstin, 1999.

43. Ibid.

44. Author's interviews with Betsey Wright, 1999.

45. Author's interviews with Dick Morris, 1998.

46. Author's interviews with Betsey Wright, 1999.

47. Author's interviews with Ed Matthews, 1999.

48. Author's interviews with Betsey Wright, 1999.

49. Author's interviews with Ed Matthews, 1999.

50. Lucinda Franks, "The Intimate Hillary," *Talk*, September 1999.

51. Author's interview with Max Brantley, 1999.

52. George Stephanopoulos, *All Too Human* (Boston: Little, Brown, 1999), p. 372.

53. Sheehy, "What Hillary Wants."

54. *Arkansas Democrat-Gazette*, May 30, 1990.

55. Brock, *The Seduction of Hillary Rodham*.

56. *The New York Times*, February 23, 1997.
57. *Chicago Tribune*, January 30, 1992.
58. "As tensions mounted . . . people he loves": author's interviews with Dick Morris, 1999.
59. Marannis, *First in His Class*, p. 456.
60. *The Seattle Times*, April 13, 1991.
61. "I sure don't think . . . I don't know": author's interview with Skip Rutherford, 1999.
62. Author's interview with Al From, 1999.
63. Ibid.
64. Author's interview with Max Brantley, 1999.
65. Author's interview with Skip Rutherford, 1999.
66. Author's interviews with Bernard Nussbaum, 1998.
67. Author's interview with Hugh Rodham, Jr., 1992.
68. Sheehy, "What Hillary Wants."

CHAPTER 11:   TWO FOR THE PRICE OF ONE

1. Author's interview with Bill Clinton, 1992.
2. George Stephanopoulos, *All Too Human* (Boston: Little, Brown, 1999).
3. Author's interview with Steve Kroft, 1992.
4. Stephanopoulos, *All Too Human.*
5. Author's interview with Steve Kroft, 1992.
6. Author's interview with Susan Thomases, 1992.
7. Author's interview with Steve Kroft, 1992.
8. "Hillary Rodham Clinton," *Biography,* A&E, 1995.
9. Ibid.
10. Author's interview with Clinton campaign aide, 1992.
11. Author's interview with Jan Piercey, 1992.
12. Seth Rosenfeld, "Watching the Detective," *San Francisco Examiner,* January 31, 1999.
13. *The Washington Post*, July 26, 1992.
14. As per Dick Morris in *San Francisco Examiner,* January 31, 1999, op cit.
15. *The Washington Post*, July 26, 1992. Palladino was originally hired through Jim Lyons, a Denver attorney whose firm performed legal work for the Clinton campaign. About $28,000 in payments to Lyons's law firm, included on Clinton's May report to the Federal Elections Commission, were actually payments to Palladino. Thereafter, fees and expenses for the private investigator were simply reported to the FEC as "legal fees."
16. Gannett News Service, August 13, 1992.
17. Author's interviews with Dorothy Stuck, 1992.
18. "Yes. I have . . . you can grow beyond": author's interviews with Hillary Rodham Clinton, 1992.
19. Author's interviews with Linda Bloodworth-Thomason, 1992.
20. Stephanopoulos, *All Too Human,* p. 71.
21. "A crisis meeting . . . a draft I never dodged": ibid., p. 77.
22. Author's interviews with Hillary Rodham Clinton, 1992.
23. Author's interview with Anne Cox Chambers, March 1992.

24. Author's interviews with Hillary Rodham Clinton, 1992.

25. Author's interviews with Lanny Davis, 1999.

26. Author's interviews with Jane Sherburne, 1999.

27. Author's interviews with Don Jones, 1999.

28. Author's interviews with Lanny Davis, 1999.

29. Author's interviews with Jane Sherburne, 1999.

30. Jeff Gerth, "The 1992 Campaign: Personal Finances," *The New York Times*, March 7, 9, and 25, 1992.

31. Michael Isikoff and Mark Miller, "Road to a Subpoena," *Newsweek*, February 5, 1996.

32. Ibid.

33. *Nightline*, ABC Television, March 11, 1993.

34. Survey by Yankelovich Clancy Shulman, March 1992.

35. Author's interview with Tom Brokaw, 1992.

36. Author's interview with Hugh Rodham, Jr., 1992.

37. Hillary Clinton speech, March 1992.

38. Author's interviews with Hillary Rodham Clinton, 1992.

39. Author's interview with Sherry Lansing, 1999.

40. Author's interviews with Hillary Rodham Clinton, 1992.

41. Author's interview with Cynthia Schneider, 1999.

42. Author's interviews with Hillary Rodham Clinton, 1992.

43. "Hillary's protectiveness . . . leave the room": Gail Sheehy, "What Hillary Wants," *Vanity Fair*, May 1992.

44. Author's interview with Bill Clinton, 1992.

45. Author's interviews with Hillary Rodham Clinton, 1992.

46. "A letter arrived . . . that were bogus": author's interviews with Betsey Wright, 1999.

47. *The New York Times*, July 17, 1992.

48. "He's a warm . . . their men are": author's interviews with Albert Gore, Sr., and Pauline Gore, 1992.

49. Associated Press, November 4, 1992.

50. *The Washington Post*, November 4, 1992.

CHAPTER 12: THINGS FALL APART

1. Author's interview with Danny Ferguson, 1999.

2. *Daily Mail* (London), December 30, 1993.

3. Author's interview with Danny Ferguson, 1999; Ferguson's testimony in the Jones case, 1997.

4. *Daily Mail* (London), December 27 and 29, 1993.

5. *The Washington Post*, March 13, 1998.

6. Inaugural Committee video footage.

7. United Press International, March 21, 1993.

8. Paul F. Boller, Jr., *Presidential Wives* (New York: Oxford University Press, 1988).

9. Author's interviews with two knowledgeable sources who were present.

10. Author's interviews with knowledgeable sources.

11. Author's interviews with Bernard Nussbaum, 1998.

12. Gail Sheehy, "Hillary's Choice," *Vanity Fair*, February 1999.

13. Author's interviews with Bill Curry, 1992.

14. Author's interview with John Robert Starr, 1999.

15. *The New York Times,* January 26, 1993.

16. *Chicago Tribune,* August 8, 1992.

17. George Stephanopoulos, *All Too Human* (Boston: Little, Brown, 1999).

18. Author's interview with Helen Thomas, 1999.

19. Author's interviews with knowledgeable sources.

20. Author's interview with a former White House adviser.

21. Author's interviews with Melanne Verveer, 1998.

22. Author's interviews with Bernard Nussbaum, 1998.

23. *Newsday,* April 23, 1994.

24. Brobdingnag: The region in Jonathan Swift's *Gulliver's Travelers* where everything was of enormous size.

25. Arkansas spending: *Arkansas Democrat Gazette,* September 27, 1989. U.S. spending for the year 1990: *The Boston Globe,* February 10, 1989. Fairfax County, Virginia: see *The Washington Post,* March 1, 1989.

26. Author's interviews with Dee Dee Myers, 1998.

27. Author's interviews with Bob Boorstin, 1999.

28. Author's interviews with Dick Morris, 1999.

29. Kerry Boyer, "Clinton Helped Lincoln-Based Business Take Off," *Greater Cincinnati Business Record,* December 14, 1992.

30. David Brock, *The Seduction of Hillary Rodham* (New York: Free Press, 1996), p. 370–71.

31. Author's interviews with Jane Sherburne, 1999.

32. Ibid.

33. Author's interview with Max Brantley, 1999.

34. Peter Boyer, "Life After Vince," *The New Yorker,* September 11, 1995.

35. Author's interview with a former White House counsel.

36. Author's interview with a former senior White House aide.

37. Martha Sherrill, "Two Weeks Out of Time," *The Washington Post,* April 3, 1993.

38. Author's interviews with Ed Matthews, 1999.

39. *USA Today,* March 30, 1993.

40. Author's interviews with Dee Dee Myers, 1998.

41. *The New York Times,* April 7, 1993; *St. Petersburg Times,* April 7, 1993.

42. Author's interview with Alan Schecter, 1999.

43. Author's interviews with Ed Matthews, 1999.

44. Author's interviews with Eileen McGann, 1999.

45. David Broder, *The System* (Boston: Little, Brown, 1997), p. 143.

46. Ibid.

47. *The New York Times,* February 28, 1993; *The New York Times,* February 6, 1994.

48. *USA Today,* February 2, 1993.

49. Author's interviews with Dee Dee Myers, 1998.

50. Author's interviews with Jane Sherburne, 1999.

51. Brock, *The Seduction of Hillary Rodham,* p. 386.

52. Author's interview with Jim Hamilton, 1999.

53. Author's interviews with Betsey Wright, 1999.

54. Boyer, "Life After Vince."

55. Author's interview with Betty Lowe, 1999.

56. Author's interview with Phil Carroll, 1999.

57. Author's interviews with Betsey Wright, 1999.

CHAPTER 13: DOWN HILL

1. *The Boston Globe*, December 11, 1994.

2. *The New York Times*, February 6, 1994.

3. CNN News, October 27, 1993.

4. *Houston Chronicle*, October 28, 1993.

5. Author's interview with Charles Rangel, 1999.

6. Associated Press, August 17, 1994.

7. *Dayton Daily News*, August 5, 1994.

8. Stephanopoulos, *All Too Human* (Boston: Little, Brown, 1999).

9. Ibid.

10. Author's interviews with Bernard Nussbaum.

11. Ibid.

12. "You've done nothing . . . and maybe beyond": author's interview with Bernard Nussbaum and another participant, 1999.

13. James D. Retter, *Anatomy of a Scandal* (Los Angeles: General Publishing Group, 1998).

14. *The Washington Post*, December 21, 1993.

15. Johnson, Smick International Report, March 9, 1994.

16. Bob Woodward, *Shadow* (New York: Simon & Schuster, 1999), p. 250.

17. Ibid, p. 279.

18. Author's interviews with Jane Sherburne, 1999.

19. "You know . . . to do that": author's interviews with Susan McDougal, 1999.

20. Author's interviews with Jane Sherburne, 1999.

21. Author's interview with David Gergen, 1999.

22. Author's interviews with James Jenkins, 1999.

23. *Investor's Business Daily*, July 9, 1997.

24. "I used to . . . myself that way": author's interviews with Dick Morris, 1999.

25. Author's interviews with Bob Boorstin, 1999.

26. Gail Sheehy, "Inner Quest of Newt Gingrich," *Vanity Fair*, 1995.

27. "You know, Dick . . . what to do": author's interviews with Dick Morris, 1998.

CHAPTER 14: TUNING IN TO ELEANOR

1. Author's conversation with Hillary Rodham Clinton, January 1995.

2. Author's interviews with Don Jones, 1999.

3. Author's interview with Manuel Castells, 1999.

4. Manuel Castells, *The New Global Economy in the Information Age* (Philadelphia: Penn State University Press, 1993).

5. Author's interviews with Bill Curry, 1998.

6. "He ducked . . . I swear": author's interviews with Dick Morris, 1999.

7. Bob Woodward, *The Choice* (New York: Simon & Schuster, 1996), p. 56.

8. Author's interviews with Neel Lattimore, 1998.

9. Author's interviews with Bill Curry, 1998.

10. Author's interview with Jeff Phillips, 1999.

11. "A few weeks after . . . the dish is empty": author's interviews with Dick Morris, 1999.

12. "Eleanor Roosevelt . . . our past mistakes": Keynote address by First Lady Hillary Rodham Clinton at the dedication of Eleanor Roosevelt College, San Diego, California, January 26, 1995.

13. Woodward, *The Choice.*

14. *Los Angeles Times,* June 25, 1996.

15. Kenneth T. Walsh, "Being there for Bill," *U.S. News & World Report,* February 27, 1995.

16. Author's interviews with Neel Lattimore, 1998.

17. *Newsday,* October 10, 1996.

18. "At a meeting . . . room for collaboration": Author's interview with Jane Sherburne, 1999.

19. *The New York Times,* March 30, 1995.

20. Author's interview with Martha Teichner, 1999.

21. Author's interviews with Bill Curry, 1998.

22. Wallace Tripp, *A Great Big Ugly Man Came Up and Tied His Horse to Me* (Boston: Little, Brown, 1973).

23. This differs from the account in Bob Woodward's book, *Shadow* (New York: Simon & Schuster, 1999), but was confirmed by Sherburne.

24. "An eight-foot table . . . and ushered him out": author's interviews with Jane Sherburne, 1999.

25. Hillary Rodham Clinton, "Talking It Over" (syndicated column), July 23, 1995.

26. "With the brio . . . another point of view": author's interviews with Jane Sherburne, 1999.

27. Joe Klein, "The Body Count," *Newsweek,* August 7, 1995.

28. "When she called . . . emotionally as well": author's interviews with Jane Sherburne, 1999.

29. Andrew Morton, *Monica's Story* (New York: St. Martin's Press, 1999), p. 58.

30. Ibid.

31. "If we had known . . . sense of humor": author's interview with Rebecca Salatan, 1996.

32. Author's interviews with Dick Morris, 1998.

33. Author's interview with Rebecca Salatan, 1996.

34. Bill Clinton, press conference, Washington D.C., April 18, 1995.

35. George Hager and Eric Pianin, "Shutdown," *Washingtonian,* April 1997.

36. Author's interviews with Dick Morris, 1998.

37. Monica Lewinsky's testimony, Starr Report.

38. White House Press office, "White House Briefing on Budget Compromise," *U.S. Newswire,* November 21, 1995.

39. Author's interviews with Dick Morris, 1998.

CHAPTER 15: FIRST WOMAN OF THE WORLD

1. Author's interviews with Melanne Verveer, 1999.
2. "If she goes . . . talk to anyone": author's interviews with Neel Lattimore, 1998.
3. *The New York Times*, September 5, 1995.
4. "Women comprise . . . once and for all": Hillary Rodham Clinton speech, UN Fourth World Conference on Women, September 5, 1995.
5. Author's interviews with Melanne Verveer, 1999.
6. Author's interviews with Jane Sherburne, 1999.
7. David Watkins's memo, released January 5, 1996.
8. *The Washington Post*, June 2, 1996.
9. Bob Woodward, *Shadow* (New York: Simon & Schuster, 1999).
10. *The Washington Post*, June 2, 1996.
11. *Whitewater; from the Editorial Pages of The Wall Street Journal* (New York: Dow-Jones & Co., Inc, 1994).
12. *20/20*, March 3, 1999.
13. *The Washington Post*, June 2, 1996.
14. Ibid.
15. Author's interviews with Jane Sherburne, 1999.
16. *The Washington Post*, January 8, 1996.
17. *The Washington Post*, June 2, 1999.
18. "She stammered . . . what they were": Woodward, *Shadow*.
19. "You would die . . . I think you ought to see": author's interview with Jane Sherburne, 1999.
20. *The Washington Post*, January 8, 1996.
21. "That afternoon . . . attracted to": Andrew Morton, *Monica's Story* (New York: St. Martin's Press, 1999), p. 69.
22. "I called Susan. . . . How can I?": author's interview with Jane Sherburne, 1999.
23. "One big mistake . . . interest in the notes": author's interview with Jane Sherburne, 1999.
24. Author's interviews with Christopher Dodd, 1999.
25. Hillary Rodham Clinton, *It Takes a Village* (New York: Simon & Schuster, 1996), from book jacket note.
26. Hillary Rodham Clinton speech at Glide Church, San Francisco, 1996.
27. Author's interviews with Dorothy Rodham, 1992.
28. Associated Press, February 27, 1997.
29. Author's interviews with Dick Morris, 1999.
30. Walter Isaacson, "Q&A," *Time*, June 3, 1996.
31. "A lot of psychobabble . . . Arkansas ever was": author's interviews with Dick Morris, 1998.
32. Helen Thomas, *Front Row at the White House* (New York: Scribner, 1999), p. 294.
33. Author's interview with Martha Teichner, 1999.
34. "The First Lady . . . have any problems": author's interview with Martha Teichner, 1999.
35. *The New York Times*, August 19, 1996.
36. "He's even better . . . that it's sexual": author's interview with Peter Duchin, 1999.

37. Isaacson, "Q&A."

38. Gail Sheehy, "Hillary's Choice," *Vanity Fair*, February 1999.

39. Author's interview with Al From, 1999.

40. Ibid.

41. Author's interviews with friends of Oscar de la Renta, 1998–99.

CHAPTER 16: EVERYTHING THERE IS TO KNOW

1. Author's interviews with Betsey Wright, 1998.

2. Author's interviews with Betsey Wright, 1999.

3. Author's interview with Danny Ferguson, 1999; transcript, Danny Ferguson deposition, *Jones v. Clinton*, November 9, 1997.

4. Bob Woodward, *Shadow* (New York: Simon & Schuster, 1999), p. 374.

5. *The Washington Post*, March 13, 1998.

6. Woodward, *Shadow*.

7. Ibid.

8. *The Washington Post*, February 9, 1998.

9. Margaret Carlson, "The Shadow of Her Smile," *Time*, September 21, 1998.

10. Author's interviews with Eileen McGann, 1999.

11. Author's interviews with Dick Morris, 1998; Morris's testimony under oath for Kenneth Starr.

12. Author's interview with Dick Morris, 1999.

13. Jerome D. Levin, Ph.D., director of the Alcoholism and Substance Abuse Counselor Training Program at the New School for Social Research and author of *The Clinton Syndrome: The President and the Self-Destructive Nature of Sexual Addiction*.

14. Author's interviews with Ed Matthews, 1999.

15. Author's interviews with Bill Curry, 1998.

16. Ibid.

17. Julia Malone, "Campaign Finance: Clinton's friend's memos are grist for his critics," *The Atlanta Journal & Constitution*, March 12, 1997.

18. Author's interview with a former Clinton press secretary.

19. *The Washington Times*, March 6, 1997.

20. White House Personnel Office, August 1999.

21. Jeffery Rosen, "Starr Crossed," *The New Republic*, December 14, 1998.

22. Ibid.

23. *The Union Leader*, October 16, 1998, and *The Washington Post*, February 3, 1999.

24. Lucinda Franks, "The Intimate Hillary," *Talk*, September 1999.

25. Woodward, *Shadow*, p. 385.

26. Author's interviews with Neel Lattimore, 1998.

27. Author's interviews with Dick Morris, 1998.

28. Ibid.

29. Author's interviews with Don Baer, 1999.

30. Author's interviews with Gene Lyons, 1999.

31. *Newsweek*, May 11, 1998.

32. Author's conversation with Lorene Jobs, 1998.

33. Lanny Davis, *Truth to Tell* (New York: Free Press, 1999), p. 262.

34. Ibid, p. 265.
35. Author's interview with Francie Pepper, 1999.
36. Ibid.
37. Author's interview with Tom Twomey, 1999.
38. "Clinton was talking . . . relationship with Monica": author's interviews with a knowledgeable source.
39. Gail Sheehy, "Hillary's Choice," *Vanity Fair*, February 1999.
40. Author's interview with Jesse Jackson, 1999.
41. Ibid.
42. Hillary Rodham Clinton, *It Takes a Village* (New York: Simon & Schuster, 1996), p. 15.
43. Andrew Morton, *Monica's Story* (New York: St. Martin's Press, 1999), p. 122.
44. Author's interview with Richard Friedman, 1999.
45. Author's interviews with Rose Styron, 1999.
46. "This year . . . after dark": Gail Sheehy, "Hillary's Choice," *Vanity Fair*, February 1999; interviews with guests.
47. "The big man . . . Hillary's husband": author's interviews with guests.
48. Author's interview with Robert Kiley, 1999.
49. Author's interview with Alan Dershowitz, 1999.
50. *Baltimore Jewish Times*, September 25, 1998.
51. Author's interview with Joe Lieberman, 1999.
52. Ibid.
53. Author's interviews with Lanny Davis, 1999.
54. The Gallup Organization.
55. *The Washington Post*, March 21, 1999.
56. Woodward, *Shadow*, p. 448.
57. "No . . . I never did, either": author's interview with Dorothy Rodham, 1998.
58. "Is she talking . . . that she collects": author's interviews with Ed Matthews, 1999.
59. Author's interviews with Mandy Grunwald, 1998.
60. Author's interviews with Gene Lyons, 1999.
61. Author's interview with Joe Lieberman, 1999.
62. Author's interview with a former White House official.
63. Author's interviews with Betsey Wright, 1998.
64. "I have been . . . conquered me": Bill Clinton, speech at prayer breakfast, September 11, 1998.
65. "She had tear-filled . . . I'm getting there": author's interviews with Ed Matthews, 1999.
66. "In the Methodist . . . probably a lifetime": author's interviews with Phillip Wogaman, 1999.
67. Author's interviews with Betsey Wright, 1999.
68. *The New York Times*, September 15, 1998.
69. Author's interview with James Dunn, 1999.
70. Woodward, *Shadow*.
71. Author's interviews with Ed Matthews, 1999.
72. Author's interviews with Don Jones, 1999.
73. Author's interviews with Ed Matthews, 1999.

CHAPTER 17:   THE REBIRTH OF HILLARY RODHAM

1. Author's interviews with David Rupert, 1999.
2. Author's interviews with Dick Morris, 1998.
3. Author's interview with Congressman Jim McDermott, 1998.
4. *The New York Times,* September 21, 1998.
5. *Daily Mail* (London), September 23, 1998.
6. Letter from Hillary Rodham to John Peavoy, February 9, 1966.
7. Author's interview with Tony Podesta, 1999.
8. Author's interviews with Charles Rangel, 1999.
9. Ibid.
10. Author's conversation with Isabel Goetz, 1999.
11. Author's interviews with Neel Lattimore, 1998.
12. Author's interviews with Ann Lewis, 1999.
13. *Vogue,* December 1998.
14. "Regal was the look . . . I left": author's interview with Paul Cavaco, 1999.
15. Author's interviews with Neel Lattimore, 1998.
16. Author's interviews with Judith Hope, 1998.
17. Author's interview with Tom Twomey, 1999.
18. Author's interviews with Judith Hope, 1998.
19. Author's interview with Lizabeth Newman, 1999.
20. Letters from Hillary Rodham to John Peavoy: October 31, 1965; November 14, 1965; November 1, 1966; December 12, 1966; December 1967.
21. *Larry King Live,* August 21, 1999.
22. Author's interviews with Judith Hope, 1998.
23. "That had been . . . a beautiful butterfly": author's interviews with Ed Matthews, 1999.
24. Author's interviews with Bill Curry, 1999.
25. Author's interviews with Charles Rangel, 1999.
26. The only other U.S. President to be impeached, Andrew Johnson, assumed the presidency only after Abraham Lincoln was assassinated. Richard Nixon resigned before impeachment.
27. The Gallup Organization.
28. *The New York Times,* January 17, 1999.
29. "Hillary waited . . . not glamorous": author's interview with Harold Ickes, 1999.
30. James Bennet, *The New York Times Magazine,* May 30, 1999.
31. Author's interview with Harold Ickes, 1999.
32. Author's interview with Jurate Kasickes, 1999.
33. Ibid.
34. Author's interviews with classmates of Chelsea Clinton, 1999.
35. Susan Schindehette, "The Tie that Binds," *People,* February 15, 1999.
36. *The Boston Globe,* March 13, 1999.
37. *Chattanooga Free Press,* April 1, 1999.
38. *Newsday,* March 24, 1999.
39. Capitol Hill Hearing Testimony of Ivo Daalter, September 30, 1999.
40. Lucinda Franks, "The Intimate Hillary," *Talk,* August 1999.

41. Democratic National Committee, "Evening Under the Stars," East Hampton, August 28, 1999.
42. Author's interview with Peggy Siegal, 1999.
43. Author's interviews with Lanny Davis, 1999.
44. Author's interview with Harold Ickes, 1999.
45. Author's interviews with Nita Lowey, 1999.
46. Author's interviews with Betsey Wright, 1999.
47. Gail Sheehy, *New Passages* (New York: Random House, 1995).
48. Author's interview with Steven Pigeon, 1999.
49. Associated Press, August 21, 1999.
50. Author's interview with Charles Schumer, 1999.
51. Author's interview with Dominic Baranello, 1999.
52. Author's interview with George Guldi, 1999.
53. Lucinda Franks, "The Intimate Hillary."
54. Rodham letter to Peavoy, November 1, 1966.
55. *The New York Times*, September 4, 1999.

CHAPTER 18: HILLARY'S RACE FOR REDEMPTION

1. Author's interview with Zenia Mucha, March 2000.
2. Ibid.
3. Author's interview with a knowledgeable source, March 2000.
4. "Mrs. Clinton was invited . . . against each other": author's interview with Dr. Rudy Crew, March 2000.
5. Marist Poll, January 2000.
6. Ibid.
7. Author's interview with a knowledgeable source, March 2000.
8. Author's interview with Harriet Woods, March 2000.
9. Harriet Woods, *Stepping Up to Power: The Political Journey of American Women* (Colorado: Westview Press, 2000).
10. Author's interview with Jewell Jackson McCabe, March 2000.
11. Author's interview with George Artz, February 2000.
12. WNBC-TV, "The Gabe Pressman Show," February 13, 2000.
13. Author's interview with Speaker of the New York State Assembly Sheldon Silver, March 2000.
14. Ibid.
15. Author's interview with Marion Maher, March 2000.
16. Livin' La Rudy Loca, writing chairman Jim Ryan, Larry Sutton.
17. Author's interview with Zenia Mucha, April 2000.
18. Author's interview with several City Hall insiders, March 2000.
19. Author's interview with Bill Bratton, March 2000.
20. Gannett News Service, February 9, 2000.
21. Author's interview with Dr. Maryanne Evangelist, March 2000.
22. Author's interviews, Temple Beth-El, Chappaqua, New York, March 2000.
23. Hillary Rodham Clinton's interview with Marsha Kramer, March 2000.
24. Author's interview with Steve Pigeon, March 2000.

25. Author's interview with Charles Rangel, February 2000.

26. Author's interview with Joe Bruno, March 2000.

27. Author's interview with a knowledgeable source, March 2000.

28. Author's interview with Ed Koch, February 2000.

CHAPTER 19:   EXTRA! EXTRA! THE HILLARY AND RICKY SHOW!

1. Author's interview with a knowledgeable source, April 2000.

2. *New York Post*, May 5, 2000.

3. *Daily News*, May 11, 2000.

4. Ibid.

5. *New York Times*, August 1, 1999.

6. Author's interview with a former mayoral aide, March 2000.

7. *Washington Post*, May 12, 2000.

8. "The Joan Hamburg Show," May 11, 2000.

9. Ibid.

10. *The Daily News*, May 17, 2000.

11. Ibid.

12. Author's interview with Shahara Llewellyn, May 2000.

13. *USA Today*, May 17, 2000.

14. *USA Today*, May 26, 2000.

15. Author's interview with Shahara Llewellyn, May 2000.

16. *New York Post*, May 21, 2000.

17. Mayor's press conference, May 26, 2000.

18. *USA Today*, May 17, 2000.

19. *New York Times*, May 31, 2000.

20. *New York Times*, April 25, 2000.

21. *Arkansas Democrat Gazette*, May 24, 2000.

22. Gail Sheehy, "Hillary's Choice," *Vanity Fair*, February 1999.

23. Hillary Rodham letter to John Peavoy, March 1, 1968.

24. *New York Post*, February 2, 1998.

Index

Millions of readers defined their lives through GAIL SHEEHY's landmark work, *Passages,* and have followed her continuing examination of the stages of adult life in her bestsellers, *The Silent Passage, New Passages,* and *Understanding Men's Passages.* As a political journalist and contributing editor to *Vanity Fair,* Ms. Sheehy has written character studies of national and world figures including Bill and Hillary Clinton, Bob and Elizabeth Dole, George Bush, Mikhail Gorbachev, Margaret Thatcher, Saddam Hussein, Newt Gingrich, and Gary Hart. The mother of two daughters, she divides her time between New York and California, where she lives with her husband, editor and educator Clay Felker.

Visit Gail's Web site at www.gailsheehy.com for the most current information on her books and appearances.

A B O U T   T H E   T Y P E

This book was set in Photina, a typeface designed by
José Mendoza in 1971. It is a very elegant design with
high legibility, and its close character fit has made it a
popular choice for use in quality magazines and art
gallery publications.